LAOS

T0295652

BUSINESS SUCCESS GUIDE
FOR EVERYONE GUIDE
BASIC PRACTICAL INFORMATION AND CONTACTS

International Business Publications, USA
Washington DC, USA - Laos

LAOS
BUSINESS SUCCESS FOR EVERYONE GUIDE
BASIC PRACTICAL INFORMATION AND CONTACTS

UPDATED ANNUALLY

We express our sincere appreciation to all government agencies and international organizations which provided information and other materials for this guide

Cover Design: International Business Publications, USA

2017 Edition Updated Reprint International Business Publications, USA
ISBN 978-1-5145-0344-7

For additional analytical, business and investment opportunities information,
please contact Global Investment & Business Center, USA
at (703) 370-8082. Fax: (703) 370-8083. E-mail: ibpusa3@gmail.com
Global Business and Investment Info Databank - www.ibpus.com

Printed in the USA

For additional analytical, business and investment opportunities information,
please contact Global Investment & Business Center, USA
at (703) 370-8082. Fax: (703) 370-8083. E-mail: ibpusa3@gmail.com
Global Business and Investment Info Databank - www.ibpus.com

LAOS
BUSINESS SUCCESS FOR EVERYONE GUIDE
BASIC PRACTICAL INFORMATION AND CONTACTS

TABLE OF CONTENTS

For additional analytical, business and investment opportunities information,
please contact Global Investment & Business Center, USA
at (703) 370-8082. Fax: (703) 370-8083. E-mail: ibpusa3@gmail.com
Global Business and Investment Info Databank - www.ibpus.com

**For additional analytical, business and investment opportunities information,
please contact Global Investment & Business Center, USA
at (703) 370-8082. Fax: (703) 370-8083. E-mail: ibpusa3@gmail.com
Global Business and Investment Info Databank - www.ibpus.com**

**For additional analytical, business and investment opportunities information,
please contact Global Investment & Business Center, USA
at (703) 370-8082. Fax: (703) 370-8083. E-mail: ibpusa3@gmail.com
Global Business and Investment Info Databank - www.ibpus.com**

**For additional analytical, business and investment opportunities information,
please contact Global Investment & Business Center, USA
at (703) 370-8082. Fax: (703) 370-8083. E-mail: ibpusa3@gmail.com
Global Business and Investment Info Databank - www.ibpus.com**

For additional analytical, business and investment opportunities information,
please contact Global Investment & Business Center, USA
at (703) 370-8082. Fax: (703) 370-8083. E-mail: ibpusa3@gmail.com
Global Business and Investment Info Databank - www.ibpus.com

**For additional analytical, business and investment opportunities information,
please contact Global Investment & Business Center, USA
at (703) 370-8082. Fax: (703) 370-8083. E-mail: ibpusa3@gmail.com
Global Business and Investment Info Databank - www.ibpus.com**

**For additional analytical, business and investment opportunities information,
please contact Global Investment & Business Center, USA
at (703) 370-8082. Fax: (703) 370-8083. E-mail: ibpusa3@gmail.com
Global Business and Investment Info Databank - www.ibpus.com**

LAOS STRATEGIC AND DEVELOPMENT PROFILES

STRATEGIC PROFILE

Capital and largest city	Vientiane 17°58′N 102°36′E
Official languages	Lao
Spoken languages	Lao Hmong Khmu
Ethnic groups (2005[1])	55% Lao 11% Khmu 8% Hmong 26% other[a]
Religion	Buddhism
Demonym	Laotian Lao
Government	Marxist–Leninistone-party socialist state
• **General Secretary and President**	Bounnhang Vorachith
• **Prime Minister**	Thongloun Sisoulith
• **Vice President**	Phankham Viphavanh
Legislature	National Assembly
Formation	
• **Kingdom of Lan Xang**	1354–1707
• **Luang Phrabang, Vientiane and Champasak**	1707–1778
• **Vassal of Thonburi and Siam**	1778–1893
• **War of Succession**	1826–8
• **French Indochina**	1893–1949
• **Independence from France**	19 July 1949
• **Declared Independence**	22 October 1953
• **Laotian civil war**	9 November 1953 – 2 December 1975
• **Lao Monarchy abolished**	2 December 1975
• **Current constitution**	14 August 1991
Area	
• **Total**	237,955 km^2 (84th) 91,428.991 sq mi
• **Water (%)**	2
Population	

- **2014 (Jul) estimate**   6,803,699[2](104th)
- **2015 census**   6,492,228[3]
- **Density**   26.7/km^2 (177th)
  69.2/sq mi

GDP (PPP)   2014 estimate
- **Total**   US$34.400 billion[4]
- **Per capita**   US$4,986[4]

GDP (nominal)   2014 estimate
- **Total**   US$11.676 billion[4]
- **Per capita**   US$1,692[4]

Gini (2008)   36.7[5]
medium

HDI (2014)   0.575[6]
medium · 141st

Currency   Kip (LAK)

Time zone   ICT

Date format   dd/mm/yyyy

Drives on the   right

Calling code   +856

ISO 3166 code   LA

Internet TLD   .la

Laos, officially the **Lao People's Democratic Republic**, is a landlocked socialist republic communist state in southeast Asia, bordered by Myanmar (Burma) and the People's Republic of China to the northwest, Vietnam to the east, Cambodia to the south, and Thailand to the west. Laos traces its history to the Kingdom of Lan Xang or *Land of a Million Elephants*, which existed from the 14th to the 18th century. After a period as a French colony, it gained independence in 1949. A long civil war ended when the communist Pathet Lao came to power in 1975.

Private enterprise has increased since the mid-1980s, but development has been hampered by poor communications in the heavily forested and mountainous landscape. 80%[1] of those employed practice subsistence agriculture; this is coupled with widespread starvation due to the many failures of communism and the state's command economy. The country's ethnic make-up is extremely diverse, with only around 60% belonging to the largest ethnic group, the Lao.

In 1975 the communist Pathet Lao took control of the government, ending a six-century-old monarchy. Initial closer ties to Vietnam and socialization were replaced with a gradual return to private enterprise, an easing of foreign investment laws, and the admission into ASEAN in 1997.

GEOGRAPHY

Location: Southeastern Asia, northeast of Thailand, west of Vietnam

Geographic coordinates: 18 00 N, 105 00 E

Map references: Southeast Asia

Area:
total: 236,800 sq km
land: 230,800 sq km
water: 6,000 sq km

Area - comparative: slightly larger than Utah

Land boundaries:
total: 5,083 km
border countries: Burma 235 km, Cambodia 541 km, China 423 km, Thailand 1,754 km, Vietnam 2,130 km

Coastline: 0 km (landlocked)
Maritime claims: none (landlocked)
Climate: tropical monsoon; rainy season (May to November); dry season (December to April)
Terrain: mostly rugged mountains; some plains and plateaus

Elevation extremes:
lowest point: Mekong River 70 m
highest point: Phou Bia 2,817 m

Natural resources: timber, hydropower, gypsum, tin, gold, gemstones

Land use:
arable land: 3%
permanent crops: 0%
permanent pastures: 3%
forests and woodland: 54%
other: 40%

Irrigated land: 1,250 sq km
note: rainy season irrigation - 2,169 sq km; dry season irrigation - 750 sq km (1998 est.)
Natural hazards: floods, droughts, and blight
Environment - current issues: unexploded ordnance; deforestation; soil erosion; a majority of the population does not have access to potable water

Environment - international agreements:
party to: Biodiversity, Climate Change, Desertification, Environmental Modification, Law of the Sea, Nuclear Test Ban, Ozone Layer Protection
signed, but not ratified: none of the selected agreements

Geography - note: landlocked

PEOPLE

Population: 5,497,459

Age structure:
0-14 years: 43% (male 1,191,608; female 1,173,144)
15-64 years: 54% (male 1,447,788; female 1,500,016)
65 years and over: 3% (male 85,028; female 99,875)

For additional analytical, business and investment opportunities information,
please contact Global Investment & Business Center, USA
at (703) 370-8082. Fax: (703) 370-8083. E-mail: ibpusa3@gmail.com
Global Business and Investment Info Databank - www.ibpus.com

Population growth rate: 2.5%
Birth rate: 38.29 births/1,000 population
Death rate: 13.35 deaths/1,000 population
Net migration rate: 0 migrant(s)/1,000 population

Sex ratio:
at birth: 1.05 male(s)/female
under 15 years: 1.02 male(s)/female
15-64 years: 0.97 male(s)/female
65 years and over: 0.85 male(s)/female
total population: 0.98 male(s)/female

Infant mortality rate: 94.8 deaths/1,000 live births

Life expectancy at birth:
total population: 53.09 years
male: 51.22 years
female: 55.02 years

Total fertility rate: 5.21 children born/woman

Nationality:
noun: Lao(s) or Laotian(s)
adjective: Lao or Laotian

Ethnic groups: Lao Loum (lowland) 68%, Lao Theung (upland) 22%, Lao Soung (highland) including the Hmong ("Meo") and the Yao (Mien) 9%, ethnic Vietnamese/Chinese 1%
Religions: Buddhist 60% (in October 1999, the regime proposed a constitutional amendment making Buddhism the state religion; the National Assembly is expected to vote on the amendment sometime in 2000), animist and other 40%
Languages: Lao (official), French, English, and various ethnic languages

Literacy:
definition: age 15 and over can read and write
total population: 57%
male: 70%
female: 44%

GOVERNMENT

Country name:
conventional long form: Lao People's Democratic Republic
conventional short form: Laos
local long form: Sathalanalat Paxathipatai Paxaxon Lao
local short form: none

Data code: LA
Government type: Communist state
Capital: Vientiane

For additional analytical, business and investment opportunities information,
please contact Global Investment & Business Center, USA
at (703) 370-8082. Fax: (703) 370-8083. E-mail: ibpusa3@gmail.com
Global Business and Investment Info Databank - www.ibpus.com

Administrative divisions: 16 provinces (khoueng, singular and plural), 1 municipality* (kampheng nakhon, singular and plural), and 1 special zone** (khetphiset, singular and plural); Attapu, Bokeo, Bolikhamxai, Champasak, Houaphan, Khammouan, Louangnamtha, Louangphabang, Oudomxai, Phongsali, Salavan, Savannakhet, Viangchan*, Viangchan, Xaignabouli, Xaisomboun**, Xekong, Xiangkhoang

Independence: 19 July 1949 (from France)
National holiday: National Day, 2 December (1975) (proclamation of the Lao People's Democratic Republic)
Constitution: promulgated 14 August 1991

Legal system: based on traditional customs, French legal norms and procedures, and Socialist practice

Suffrage: 18 years of age; universal

Executive branch:

chief of state: President BOUNNYANG Vorachit (since 20 April 2016); Vice President PHANKHAM Viphavan (since 20 April 2016)

head of government: Prime Minister THONGLOUN Sisoulit (since 20 April 2016); Deputy Prime Ministers BOUNTHONG Chitmani, SONXAI Siphandon, SOMDI Douangdi (since 20 April 2016)

cabinet: Council of Ministers appointed by the president, approved by the National Assembly

elections/appointments: president and vice president indirectly elected by the National Assembly for a 5-year term (no term limits); election last held on 20 April 2016 (next to be held in 2021); prime minister nominated by the president, elected by the National Assembly for 5-year term

election results: BOUNNYANG Vorachit (LPRP) elected president; PHANKHAM Viphavan (LPRP) elected vice president; percent of National Assembly vote - NA; THONGLOUN Sisoulit (LPRP) elected prime minister; percent of National Assembly vote - NA

Legislative branch:

description: unicameral National Assembly or Sapha Heng Xat (132 seats; members directly elected in multi-seat constituencies by simple majority vote from candidate lists provided by the Lao People's Revolutionary Party; members serve 5-year terms)

elections: last held on 20 April 2016 (next to be held in 2021)

election results: percent of vote by party - NA; seats by party - LPRP 128, independent 4

Judicial branch:

highest court(s): People's Supreme Court (consists of the court president and organized into criminal, civil, administrative, commercial, family, and juvenile chambers, each with a vice president and several judges)

judge selection and term of office: president of People's Supreme Court appointed by National Assembly on recommendation of the president of the republic for a 5-year term; vice presidents of People's Supreme Court appointed by the president of the republic on recommendation of the National Assembly; appointment of chamber judges NA; tenure of court vice-presidents and chamber judges NA

subordinate courts: appellate courts; provincial, municipal, district, and military courts

Political parties and leaders: Lao People's Revolutionary Party or LPRP [KHAMTAI Siphandon, party president]; other parties proscribed

Political pressure groups and leaders: noncommunist political groups proscribed; most opposition leaders fled the country in 1975

International organization participation: ACCT, AsDB, ASEAN, CP, ESCAP, FAO, G-77, IBRD, ICAO, ICRM, IDA, IFAD, IFC, IFRCS, ILO, IMF, Intelsat (nonsignatory user), Interpol, IOC, ITU, NAM, OPCW, PCA, UN, UNCTAD, UNESCO, UNIDO, UPU, WFTU, WHO, WIPO, WMO, WToO, WTrO (observer)

Diplomatic representation in the US:
chief of mission: Ambassador VANG Rattanavong
chancery: 2222 S Street NW, Washington, DC 20008
telephone: [1] (202) 332-6416
FAX: [1] (202) 332-4923

Diplomatic representation from the US:
chief of mission: Ambassador Wendy Jean CHAMBERLIN
embassy: Rue Bartholonie, B. P. 114, Vientiane
mailing address: American Embassy, Box V, APO AP 96546
telephone: [856] (21) 212581, 212582, 212585
FAX: [856] (21) 212584

Flag description: three horizontal bands of red (top), blue (double width), and red with a large white disk centered in the blue band

ECONOMY

The government of Laos, one of the few remaining one-party communist states, began decentralizing control and encouraging private enterprise in 1986. The results, starting from an extremely low base, were striking - growth averaged 6% per year from 1988-2008 except during the short-lived drop caused by the Asian financial crisis that began in 1997. Laos' growth exceeded 7% per year during 2008-13. Despite this high growth rate, Laos remains a country with an underdeveloped infrastructure, particularly in rural areas. It has a basic, but improving, road system, and limited external and internal land-line telecommunications. Electricity is available in 83 % of the country.

Laos' economy is heavily dependent on capital-intensive natural resource exports. The labor force, however, still relies on agriculture, dominated by rice cultivation in lowland

For additional analytical, business and investment opportunities information,
please contact Global Investment & Business Center, USA
at (703) 370-8082. Fax: (703) 370-8083. E-mail: ibpusa3@gmail.com
Global Business and Investment Info Databank - www.ibpus.com

areas, which accounts for about 25% of GDP and 73% of total employment. Economic growth has reduced official poverty rates from 46% in 1992 to 26% in 2010. The economy also has benefited from high-profile foreign direct investment in hydropower, copper and gold mining, logging, and construction though some projects in these industries have drawn criticism for their environmental impacts. Laos gained Normal Trade Relations status with the US in 2004 and applied for Generalized System of Preferences trade benefits in 2013 after being admitted to the World Trade Organization earlier in the year. Laos is in the process of implementing a value-added tax system. Simplified investment procedures and expanded bank credits for small farmers and small entrepreneurs will improve Laos' economic prospects. The government appears committed to raising the country's profile among investors, but suffered through a fiscal crisis in 2013 brought about by public sector wage increases, fiscal mismanagement, and revenue shortfalls. The World Bank has declared that Laos' goal of graduating from the UN Development Program's list of least-developed countries by 2020 is achievable, and the country is preparing to enter the ASEAN Economic Community in 2015.

GDP (purchasing power parity):
$20.78 billion (2013 est.)
country comparison to the world: 132
$19.18 billion (2014 est.)
$17.78 billion (2011 est.)
note:data are in 2013 US dollars

GDP (official exchange rate):
$10.1 billion (2013 est.)

GDP - real growth rate:
8.3% (2013 est.)
country comparison to the world: 9
7.9% (2014 est.)
8% (2011 est.)

GDP - per capita (PPP):
$3,100 (2013 est.)
country comparison to the world: 176
$2,900 (2014 est.)
$2,700 (2011 est.)
note:data are in 2013 US dollars

Gross national saving:
27.4% of GDP (2013 est.)
country comparison to the world: 38
26.2% of GDP (2014 est.)
25.2% of GDP (2011 est.)

GDP - composition, by end use:
household consumption:
66.9%
government consumption:
9.8%
investment in fixed capital:

31.7%
investment in inventories:
-1.3%
exports of goods and services:
40%
imports of goods and services:
-48.4%
(2013 est.)

GDP - composition, by sector of origin:
agriculture:
24.8%
industry:
32%
services:
37.5% (2013 est.)

Agriculture - products:
sweet potatoes, vegetables, corn, coffee, sugarcane, tobacco, cotton, tea, peanuts, rice; cassava (manioc, tapioca), water buffalo, pigs, cattle, poultry

Industries:
mining (copper, tin, gold, gypsum); timber, electric power, agricultural processing, rubber, construction, garments, cement, tourism

Industrial production growth rate:
11% (2013 est.)
country comparison to the world: 12

Labor force:
3.373 million (2013 est.)
country comparison to the world: 100

Labor force - by occupation:
agriculture:
73.1%
industry:
6.1%
services:
20.6% (2014 est.)

Unemployment rate:
1.9% (2010 est.)
country comparison to the world: 11
2.5% (2009 est.)

Population below poverty line:
22% (2013 est.)

Household income or consumption by percentage share:

For additional analytical, business and investment opportunities information,
please contact Global Investment & Business Center, USA
at (703) 370-8082. Fax: (703) 370-8083. E-mail: ibpusa3@gmail.com
Global Business and Investment Info Databank - www.ibpus.com

lowest 10%:
3.3%
highest 10%:
30.3%

Distribution of family income - Gini index:
36.7
country comparison to the world: 83
34.6 (2002)

Budget:
revenues:
$2.481 billion
expenditures:
$2.642 billion (2013 est.)

Taxes and other revenues:
24.6% of GDP (2013 est.)
country comparison to the world: 135

Budget surplus (+) or deficit (-):
-1.6% of GDP (2013 est.)
country comparison to the world: 77

Public debt:
46.3% of GDP (2013 est.)
country comparison to the world: 77
49.1% of GDP (2014 est.)

Fiscal year:
1 October - 30 September

Inflation rate (consumer prices):
6.5% (2013 est.)
country comparison to the world: 183
4.3% (2014 est.)

Central bank discount rate:
4.3% (31 December 2010)
country comparison to the world: 94
4% (31 December 2009)

Commercial bank prime lending rate:
23.2% (31 December 2013 est.)
country comparison to the world: 14
22.3% (31 December 2014 est.)

Stock of narrow money:
$1.389 billion (31 December 2013 est.)

For additional analytical, business and investment opportunities information,
please contact Global Investment & Business Center, USA
at (703) 370-8082. Fax: (703) 370-8083. E-mail: ibpusa3@gmail.com
Global Business and Investment Info Databank - www.ibpus.com

country comparison to the world: 141
$1.154 billion (31 December 2014 est.)

Stock of broad money:
$4.071 billion (31 December 2013 est.)
country comparison to the world: 136
$3.673 billion (31 December 2014 est.)

Stock of domestic credit:
$4.716 billion (31 December 2013 est.)
country comparison to the world: 114
$4.034 billion (31 December 2014 est.)

Market value of publicly traded shares:
$1.012 billion (2014 est.)
$NA

Current account balance:
-$484.3 million (2013 est.)
country comparison to the world: 98
-$315.5 million (2014 est.)

Exports:
$2.313 billion (2013 est.)
country comparison to the world: 141
$1.984 billion (2014 est.)

Exports - commodities:
wood products, coffee, electricity, tin, copper, gold, cassava

Exports - partners:
Thailand 34%, China 21.5%, Vietnam 12.2%

Imports:
$3.238 billion (2013 est.)
country comparison to the world: 145
$2.744 billion (2014 est.)

Imports - commodities:
machinery and equipment, vehicles, fuel, consumer goods

Imports - partners:
Thailand 62.1%, China 16.2%, Vietnam 7.3%

Reserves of foreign exchange and gold:
$845.4 million (31 December 2013 est.)
country comparison to the world: 141
$796.9 million (31 December 2014 est.)

For additional analytical, business and investment opportunities information,
please contact Global Investment & Business Center, USA
at (703) 370-8082. Fax: (703) 370-8083. E-mail: ibpusa3@gmail.com
Global Business and Investment Info Databank - www.ibpus.com

Debt - external:
$6.69 billion (31 December 2013 est.)
country comparison to the world: 110
$6.288 billion (31 December 2014 est.)

Stock of direct foreign investment - at home:
$15.14 billion (31 December 2014 est.)
country comparison to the world: 81
$12.44 billion (31 December 2011 est.)

Exchange rates:
kips (LAK) per US dollar -
7,875.9 (2013 est.)
8,007.3 (2014 est.)
8,258.8 (2010 est.)
8,516.04
8,760.69

ENERGY

Electricity - production:
3.629 billion kWh
country comparison to the world: 127

Electricity - consumption:
2.4 billion kWh
country comparison to the world: 136

Electricity - exports:
2.537 billion kWh
country comparison to the world: 41

Electricity - imports:
1 billion kWh
country comparison to the world: 65

Electricity - installed generating capacity:
3.217 million kW
country comparison to the world: 87

Electricity - from fossil fuels:
2.6% of total installed capacity
country comparison to the world: 201

Electricity - from nuclear fuels:
0% of total installed capacity
country comparison to the world: 122

Electricity - from hydroelectric plants:
97.4% of total installed capacity
country comparison to the world: 9

Electricity - from other renewable sources:
0% of total installed capacity
country comparison to the world: 191

Crude oil - production:
0 bbl/day
country comparison to the world: 186

Crude oil - exports:
0 bbl/day
country comparison to the world: 140

Crude oil - imports:
0 bbl/day
country comparison to the world: 206

Crude oil - proved reserves:
0 bbl
country comparison to the world: 152

Refined petroleum products - production:
0 bbl/day
country comparison to the world: 161

Refined petroleum products - consumption:
3,391 bbl/day
country comparison to the world: 177

Refined petroleum products - exports:
0 bbl/day
country comparison to the world: 191

Refined petroleum products - imports:
3,160 bbl/day
country comparison to the world: 170

Natural gas - production:
0 cu m
country comparison to the world: 151

For additional analytical, business and investment opportunities information,
please contact Global Investment & Business Center, USA
at (703) 370-8082. Fax: (703) 370-8083. E-mail: ibpusa3@gmail.com
Global Business and Investment Info Databank - www.ibpus.com

Natural gas - consumption:
0 cu m
country comparison to the world: 163

Natural gas - exports:
0 cu m
country comparison to the world: 132

Natural gas - imports:
0 cu m
country comparison to the world: 86

Natural gas - proved reserves:
0 cu m
country comparison to the world: 156

COMMUNICATIONS

Telephones - main lines in use:
112,000
country comparison to the world: 143

Telephones - mobile cellular:
6.492 million
country comparison to the world: 99

Telephone system:
general assessment:
service to general public is improving; the government relies on a radiotelephone network to communicate with remote areas
domestic:
4 service providers with mobile cellular usage growing very rapidly
international:
country code - 856; satellite earth station - 1 Intersputnik (Indian Ocean region) and a second to be developed by China

Broadcast media:
6 TV stations operating out of Vientiane - 3 government-operated and the others commercial; 17 provincial stations operating with nearly all programming relayed via satellite from the government-operated stations in Vientiane; Chinese and Vietnamese programming relayed via satellite from Lao National TV; broadcasts available from stations in Thailand and Vietnam in border areas; multi-channel satellite and cable TV systems provide access to a wide range of foreign stations; state-controlled radio with state-operated Lao National Radio (LNR) broadcasting on 5 frequencies - 1 AM, 1 SW, and 3 FM; LNR's AM and FM programs are relayed via satellite constituting a large part of the programming schedules of the provincial radio stations; Thai radio broadcasts available in border areas and transmissions of multiple international broadcasters are also accessible

Internet country code:

.la

Internet hosts:
1,532
country comparison to the world: 166

Internet users:
300,000
country comparison to the world: 130

TRANSPORTATION

Airports:
41
country comparison to the world: 103

Airports - with paved runways:
total: 8
2,438 to 3,047 m: 3
1,524 to 2,437 m: 4
914 to 1,523 m: 1 (2013)

Airports - with unpaved runways:
total: 33
1,524 to 2,437 m: 2
914 to 1,523 m: 9
under 914 m:
22

Pipelines:
refined products 540 km (2013)

Roadways:
total: 39,568 km
country comparison to the world: 89
paved: 530 km
unpaved: 39,038 km

Waterways:
4,600 km (primarily on the Mekong River and its tributaries; 2,900 additional km are intermittently navigable by craft drawing less than 0.5 m)
country comparison to the world: 24

MILITARY

Military branches:
Lao People's Armed Forces (LPAF): Lao People's Army (LPA; includes Riverine Force),

For additional analytical, business and investment opportunities information,
please contact Global Investment & Business Center, USA
at (703) 370-8082. Fax: (703) 370-8083. E-mail: ibpusa3@gmail.com
Global Business and Investment Info Databank - www.ibpus.com

Air Force

Military service age and obligation:
18 years of age for compulsory or voluntary military service; conscript service obligation - minimum 18-months

Manpower available for military service:
males age 16-49: 1,574,362
females age 16-49: 1,607,856 (2010 est.)

Manpower fit for military service:
males age 16-49: 1,111,629
females age 16-49: 1,190,035 (2010 est.)

Manpower reaching militarily significant age annually:
male: 71,400
female: 73,038 (2010 est.)

Military expenditures:
NA%
0.23% of GDP
NA%

Military - note:
serving one of the world's least developed countries, the Lao People's Armed Forces (LPAF) is small, poorly funded, and ineffectively resourced; its mission focus is border and internal security, primarily in countering ethnic Hmong insurgent groups; together with the Lao People's Revolutionary Party and the government, the Lao People's Army (LPA) is the third pillar of state machinery, and as such is expected to suppress political and civil unrest and similar national emergencies, but the LPA also has upgraded skills to respond to avian influenza outbreaks; there is no perceived external threat to the state and the LPA maintains strong ties with the neighboring Vietnamese military

TRANSNATIONAL ISSUES

Disputes - international:
southeast Asian states have enhanced border surveillance to check the spread of avian flu; talks continue on completion of demarcation with Thailand but disputes remain over islands in the Mekong River; concern among Mekong River Commission members that China's construction of dams on the Mekong River and its tributaries will affect water levels; Cambodia and Vietnam are concerned about Laos' extensive upstream dam construction

Illicit drugs:
estimated opium poppy cultivation in 2008 was 1,900 hectares, about a 73% increase from 2007; estimated potential opium production in 2008 more than tripled to 17 metric tons; unsubstantiated reports of domestic methamphetamine production; growing domestic methamphetamine problem

IMPORTANT INFORMATION FOR UNDERSTANDING LAOS[1]

Official Name: Lao People's Democratic Republic

PROFILE

GEOGRAPHY

Area: 236,800 sq. km. (91,430 sq. mi.); area comparable to Oregon.
Capital--Vientiane (est. 569,000). *Other principal towns*--Savannakhet, Luang Prabang, Pakse, Thakhek.
Terrain: rugged mountains, plateaus, alluvial plains.
Climate: tropical monsoon; rainy season (May to November); dry season (November to April).

PEOPLE

Nationality: *Noun and adjective*--Lao (sing. and pl.).
Population : 5.4 million.
Annual growth rate: 2.7%.
Ethnic groups: Lao Loum 53%; other lowland Lao 13% (Thai Dam, Phouane); Lao Theung (midslope) 23%; Lao Sung (highland), including Hmong, Akha, and the Yao (Mien) 10%; ethnic Vietnamese/Chinese 1%.
Religions: Principally Buddhism, with animism among highland groups.
Languages: Lao (official), French, various highland ethnic, English.
Education: *Literacy*--60%.
Health : *Infant mortality rate*--89.32/1,000. *Life expectancy*--55.87 years for women, 52.63 years for men.
Work force (2.6 million, 1999): *Agriculture*--85%; *industry and services*--15%.

GOVERNMENT

Branches: *Executive*--president (head of state); Chairman, Council of Ministers (prime minister and head of government); nine-member Politburo; 49-member Central Committee. *Legislative*--99-seat National Assembly. *Judicial*--district, provincial, and a national Supreme Court.
Political parties: Lao People's Revolutionary Party (LPRP)--only legal party.
Administrative subdivisions: 16 provinces, one special region, and Vientiane prefecture.
Flag: A red band at the top and bottom with a larger blue band between them; a large white circle is centered.

ECONOMY

Natural resources: Hydroelectric power, timber, minerals.
Agriculture (51% of GDP): *Primary products*--glutinous rice, coffee, corn, sugarcane, vegetables, tobacco, ginger, water buffalo, pigs, cattle, and poultry.
Industry (22% of GDP, 1999): *Primary types*--garment manufacturing, electricity production, gypsum and tin mining, wood and wood processing, cement manufacturing, agricultural processing.
Industrial growth rate --7.5%.
Services --27% of GDP.

---

[1] **U.S. Department of State,** *Bureau of East Asian and Pacific Affairs*

Trade: *Exports* --$370 million: garments, electricity, wood and wood products, coffee, rattan. Major markets--France, U.K., Germany, Holland, Thailand, Belgium, U.S., Italy, Japan, Vietnam. *Imports* --$570 million. *Major imports*--fuel, food, consumer, goods, machinery and equipment, vehicles and spare parts. *Major suppliers*--Thailand, Singapore, Japan, Vietnam, China.

GEOGRAPHY, TOPOGRAPHY AND CLIMATE

The Lao People's Democratic Republic (Lao PDR) has a land area of 236,800 square kilometers, stretching more than 1,700 km from the north to south and between 100 km and 400 km from the east to west. The Lao PDR has an eastern border of 1,957 km with the Socialist Republic of Vietnam, a western border of 1,730 km with the, Kingdom of Thailand, a southern border of 492 kin with t he Kingdom of Combodia, and northern borders of 416 kin with the People's Republic of China and 230 km with the Union of Myamar.

Although the Lao PDR has no direct access to the sea, it has an abundance of rivers, including a 1,865 km stretch of the Mekong (Nam Kong), defining its border with Myanmar and a major part of the border with Thailand. Ma'or stretches of the Mekong and its tributaries are navigable and provide alluvial deposits for some. of the fertile plains. About two thirds of the country is mountainous, with ranges from 200 to the 2,820 meters high. The mountains pose difficulties for transportation and communication and complicate development, but together with the rivers they produce vast potential for hydro power.

The Lao PDR is a tropical country, whose climate is affected by monsoon rains from May to September. In Vientiane, the average temperatures range from a minimum of C 16.4 degrees in January to a maximum of C 13 degrees in April.

WATER RESOURCES

Its abundant water resources is probably the most important natural resource endowment of the country. There are only three hydroelectric plants in operation so far, of which Nam Ngum I is the biggest. These three plants with a combined capacity of 200 MW, reportedly realizes only less than five percent of the country's hydroelectric potential. About 90% of hydroelectric power production is exported to Thailand, constituting one of the leading exports of the Lao PDR. Plans are underway to construct a number of new hydroelectric power facilities, which are described in greater detail in Section B.

FOREST RESOURCES

Forests cover about 47% of the country, comprising a wide variety of commercial tree species suitable for production of saw timber, plywood, parquet, furniture, etc.... The most important high value species are hardwoods belonging to the Diterocarpaceae family and rosewoods belonging to the Genera Pterocarpus, Dalbergia and Afzelia. Pines and other coniferous species are also available but in comparatively small quantities. Eighty percent of domestic energy consumption is based on fuel wood, and an estimated 300,000 hectares of forest are lost annually largely due to shifting cultivation and logging activities. In the effort to protect forest resources from unsustainable felling of trees, the total annual allowable cut (AC) has been set by the Tropical Forest Action Plan (1991) to 280,000 cubic meters per annum, exportation of logs was temporarily restricted to restructure forest management, and protective measures have been implemented to prevent depletion of forests due to shifting fanning practices.

MINERAL RESOURCES

Sizeable deposits of gemstones such as sapphire, zircon, amethyst, gold, iron are and tin are know to exist in the country. Gemstones, gold, coal and tin are estimated to have a high economic value. More geologic surveys are needed to identify location of mineral deposits that would allow their exploitation in commercial quantities. Meanwhile, exploration of potential petroleum deposits are underway. Economic exploitation of mineral resources will depend on development of the required physical infrastructures.

ADMINISTRATIVE STRUCTURE OF LAOS

ATTAPEU PROVINCE

Attapeu Province is best known for the Bolaven Plateau, which also extends into Champassak, Salavan and Sekong provinces. The Bolaven Plateau is covered in the Champassak section - The plateau is best accessed from Pakse, in Champassak province.

Attapeu province is rugged,wild and very scenic, but transportation is very difficult, especially by land in the rainy season.

The town of Samakhi Xai (Attapeu) is situated in a large picturesque valley. The population of the province is more Lao Loum than the neighbouring provinces.

Parts of the Ho Chi Minh Trail can be explored from Attapeu, although using a local guide is essential.

BOKEO PROVINCE

Bokeo province is the smallest province in the country and borders Thailand and Myanmar.   This is the Lao side of the 'Golden Triangle'. The province has 34 ethnic groups, the second most ethnically diverse province in Laos. The photo shows a group of Akha (Ikaw or Kaw) people from the Golden Triangle area taken in 1900.

Huay Xai is the border town with Thailand, the city is busy and prosperous.

Located in the center of Huay Xay is Chomkao Manilat temple. The view from the the temple hill over Houy Xay city,the Mekong river and surrounding mountains is a definite reward for making it up the many steps.

BOLIKHAMSAI PROVINCE

Bolikhamsai province contains part of the wilderness area known as the Nakai - Nam Theun National Biodiversity Conservation Area the largest conservation area in the country at 3700 sq km. The area is home to over a dozen threatened species including Asiatic black bear, clouded leopard, elephant, giant muntjac, guar, Malayan sun bear, and tiger.

The saola (spindlehorn) or Vu Quang Ox - *Pseudoryx nghetinhensis* was discovered in neighbouring Vietnam in 1992 and sighted since then in Laos in the conservation area. Only two other land mammals have been classified with their own genus this century. The first live saola was captured in neighbouring Khammouane province in 1996.

The capital of Bolikhamsai is Paxxan, which can be reached from Vietntiane by bus in about three hours.

For additional analytical, business and investment opportunities information, please contact Global Investment & Business Center, USA at (703) 370-8082. Fax: (703) 370-8083. E-mail: ibpusa3@gmail.com Global Business and Investment Info Databank - www.ibpus.com

CHAMPASSAK PROVINCE - PAKSE

The province of Champassak is home to one of Asia's great, but least visited temples, Wat Phu. Pakse, the capital is situated at the confluence of the Se river and the Mekong (Pakse means 'mouth of the Se') and is a busy trading town. The province also houses much of the Bolaven Plateau, an area that is home to a number of ethnic minorities. To the south is Si Pan Don (four thousand islands), where the Mekong reaches up to 14km wide during the rainy season and the Khone Phapeng Falls.

Pakse has a number of comfortable places to stay and is a good base from which to explore the surrounding area. The town has one of the largest markets in the region. Within Pakse is the Champassak Museum where trader can see relics from Wat Phu as well as from the Bolaven Plateau.

HOUA PHAN

Houa Phan province is situated in the northeast of Laos and was the base of the Lao People's Revolutionary Army activities. There are over 100 caves in the Vieng Xai district of Houa Phanh many of which were used as hideouts and bunkers during the Indochina war.

Lao Aviation flies daily to the capital Xam Neua from Vientiane - The most famous caves in the area are:

Tham Than Souphanouvong: formerly known as Tham Phapount. In 1964, Prince Souphanouvong set up his residence in this cave. Tham Than Kaysone: formerly known as Tham Yonesong, was established for the residence of Mr. Kaysone Phomvihane. Tham Than Khamtay: was the residence of Mr. Khamtay Siphandone, consisting of many area, such as a meeting room, reception room and research room.

Other attractions include Keo Nong Vay Temple located in Xam Neua district.

Hot springs in Xam Tay district are located about 154 km away from Xam Neua the waters reach a temperature of around 40 degrees Celcius. Xam Tay waterfall is located Xam Tay district.

Saleu and Nasala villages, well known for their weaving activities, located in Xieng Kor district on the road No: 6 to Xieng Khouang province 125 km away from Xam Neua.

KHAMMOUANE PROVINCE

Khammouane province contains two vast wilderness areas known as the Khammuane Limestone National Biodiversity Conservation Area and the Nakai - Nam Theun National Biodiversity Conservation Area.

The Kahmmuane Limestone is a maze of limestone karst peaks forming a stone forest of caves, rivers and pristine jungle. For most of the wet season, the area is not accessible by road - most 'roads' being tracks with log bridges across deeps streams. These tracks are often routes across rice paddies near the river banks - during the rainy season, the only way to get around is by boat.

The National Tourism Authority of Lao PDR is currently investigating ecotourism projects in this beautiful region. The capital of Khammouane province is Tha Kek, situated across the Mekong from Nakorn Phanom in Thailand.

LUANG PRABANG

Luang Prabang is the jewel of Indochina, and a UNESCO World Heritage Site since 1995. The ancient royal city is surrounded by mountains at the junction of the Mekong and its tributary, the Khan river. In the centre of the city is Mount Phousi with stunning views of the surrounding temples and hills. Luang Prabang is a city where time seems to stand still. As part of the UNESCO plan, new buildings have been limited and development must be in keeping with this magical place.

Minority village in Luang Namtha

Luang Prabang is small, and just about everywhere can be reached by foot. Walking and travelling by bicycle is the best way to see this tiny city.

LUANG NAMTHA PROVINCE

Located in the northern part of Laos, Luang Namtha shares its northwestern border with Myanmar and its northeastern border with China. The province is mountainous, home to large numbers of minorities. The Nam Ha National Biodiversity Conservation Area is located in the southwest of Luang Namtha - a pristine habitat of dense tropical rainforest covering almost all of the protected area.

UNESCO are funding a ecotourism project in Luang Namtha that will be capable of sustaining sustainable development in the province. The concept of the project is to provide education, conservation, management and sustainable economic benefits for the local population. The province is home to a 39 minorities the largest number in the country.

OUDOMXAI

Located in the northern part of Laos. This mountainous province has 23 ethnic groups each with it own distinct culture, religion, language and colorful style of dress. The provincial capital , Muang Xay lies between two strings of Hmong villages.

Lao Aviation flies to Oudomxai from Vientiane

Oudomxai can be reached overland from Luang Prabang. Oudomxay is also accessible from Bokeo and Luang Namtha Provinces. Oudomxay is an ideal base for excursions and trekking to varied sights and attractions as well as destination in its own right. Muang Xai, has one of the best produce markets in the area.

Near Muang Xai, there is a waterfall, Lak Sip – Et (located at km No 11) and hot springs near Muang La.

PHONGSALI PROVINCE

Phongsali province the most remote in northern Laos is surrounded on three sides by China and Vietnam. The Phu Den Din National Biodiversity Conservation Area along the Vietnamese border with mountains as high as 1950m with over 70% forest cover is home to the asiatic black bear, bantang, clouded leopard, elephant, guar and tiger.

For additional analytical, business and investment opportunities information,
please contact Global Investment & Business Center, USA
at (703) 370-8082. Fax: (703) 370-8083. E-mail: ibpusa3@gmail.com
Global Business and Investment Info Databank - www.ibpus.com

The capital Phongsali, can be reached from Muang Xai with buses leaving once a day. Phongsali has a year round cool climate with temperatures as low as 5 degrees Celcius at night. Rain can be heavy - bring a jacket and warm clothes.

Muang Khoa is a small town situated on the junction of Route 4 and the Nam Ou river. The journey to Muang Khoa along route 4 from Udomxai takes about four hours. It is possible to travel up river to Phongsali from here, or down to Luang Prabang.

SALAVAN PROVINCE

Salavan Province is best known for the Bolaven Plateau, which also extends into Attapeu, Champassak and Sekong provinces. The Bolaven Plateau is covered in the Champassak section.. The plateau is best accessed from Pakse, in Champassak province.

Salavan province is home to the Phu Xieng Thong National Biodiversity Conservation Area, covering nearly 1,000 sq km in the western part of the province next to the Mekong river. It is thought that asiatic black bear, banteng, clouded leopard, Douc langur, elephant, gibbon, guar, Siamese crocodile and tiger and inhabit this area.

SEKONG PROVINCE

Sekong Province is best known for the Bolaven Plateau, which also extends into Attapeu, Champassak and Salavan and provinces. The Bolaven Plateau is covered in the Champassak section. The plateau is best accessed from Pakse, in Champassak province. Sekong province is rugged,wild and very scenic, but transportation is very difficult, especially by land in the rainy season.

SAYABOURI PROVINCE

Sayabouri province is quite close to Vientiane, but being quite mountainous is quite remote.   The province shares its borders with six Thai provinces. The capital of the province, Sayabouri is on the banks of the Nam Hung, a tributary of the Mekong.

The province houses the Nam Phoun National Biodiversity Conservation Area which is 1150 sq km of forested hills that contain Asiatic black bear, dhole, elephant, guar, gibbon, Malayan sun bear and Sumatran rhino.

The southern part of the province has many scenic waterfalls, but getting around this part of the province is very difficult.

SAVANNAKHET

Savannakhet town is situated on the banks of the   Mekong river opposite Mukdahan in Thailand. The province bridges the country between Thailand and Vietnam and the town is a very active junction for trade between the two countries. The town itself can be easily explored by foot and has a number of interesting temples, including Vietnamese temple and school and a large Catholic church. Much of the town's architecture is French Colonial.

VIENTIANE

Vientiane, capital of Laos is Asia's biggest village. Busy and hectic in comparison to the rest of the country, it is quiet compared with any other city in Asia. Vientiane, as all of Lao's major cities, is situated on the Mekong river which forms the lifeline of the country. Vientiane is the hub for all travel in the country. The city has a population of 450,000, about 10% of the country.

Vientiane is a city full of surprises. Here trader can find fields of rice and vegetables, agriculture hidden behind tree lined avenues. French Colonial architecture sits next to gilded temples. Freshly baked French bread is served next to shops selling noodle soup.

There is little modern in Vientiane. Old French colonial houses are being restored as offices and as restaurants and hotels. There are only a handful of modern buildings which sometimes look remarkably out of place in this quiet capital.

XIENG KHOUANG PROVINCE

Xieng Khouang province is situated in the north of Laos, a province of green montains and karst limestone. Much of the province was heavily bombed during the Vietnam war and old war scrap is used in building houses throughout the province. The capital of Xieng Khouang is Phonsavan. Situated at an altitude of 1,200m is an excellent climate. Decmber and January can be chilly so bring a light jacket or fleece for cool evenings and mornings.

PEOPLE

Laos' population was estimated at about 5.4 million in 1999, dispersed unevenly across the country. Most people live in valleys of the Mekong River and its tributaries. Vientiane prefecture, the capital and largest city, had about 569,000 residents in 1999. The country's population density is 23.4/sq. km.

About half the country's people are ethnic Lao, the principal lowland inhabitants and politically and culturally dominant group. The Lao are descended from the Tai people who began migrating southward from China in the first millennium A.D. Mountain tribes of Miao-Yao, Austro-Asiatic, Tibeto-Burman--Hmong, Yao, Akha, and Lahu--and Tai ethnolinguistic heritage are found in northern Laos. Collectively, they are known as Lao Sung or highland Lao. In the central and southern mountains, Mon-Khmer tribes, known as Lao Theung or midslope Lao, predominate. Some Vietnamese and Chinese minorities remain, particularly in the towns, but many left in two waves--after independence in the late 1940s and again after 1975.

The predominant religion is Theravada Buddhism. Animism is common among the mountain tribes. Buddhism and spirit worship coexist easily. There also is a small number of Christians and Muslims.

The official and dominant language is Lao, a tonal language of the Tai linguistic group. Midslope and highland Lao speak an assortment of tribal languages. French, once common in government and commerce, has declined in usage, while knowledge of English--the language of the Association of Southeast Asian Nations (ASEAN)--has increased in recent years.

HISTORY

Laos traces its first recorded history and its origins as a unified state to the emergence of the Kingdom of Lan Xang (literally, "million elephants") in 1353. Under the rule of King Fa Ngum, the wealthy and mighty kingdom covered much of what today is Thailand and Laos. His successors, especially King Setthathirat in the 16th century, helped establish Buddhism as the predominant religion of the country.

By the 17th century, the kingdom of Lan Xang entered a period of decline marked by dynastic struggle and conflicts with its neighbors. In the late 18th century, the Siamese (Thai) established hegemony over much of what is now Laos. The region was divided into principalities centered on Luang Prabang in the north, Vientiane in the center, and Champassak in the south. Following its colonization of Vietnam, the French supplanted the Siamese and began to integrate all of Laos into the French empire. The Franco-Siamese treaty of 1907 defined the present Lao boundary with Thailand.

During World War II, the Japanese occupied French Indochina, including Laos. King Sisavang Vong of Luang Prabang was induced to declare independence from France in 1945, just prior to Japan's surrender. During this period, nationalist sentiment grew. In September 1945, Vientiane and Champassak united with Luang Prabang to form an independent government under the Free Laos (Lao Issara) banner. The movement, however, was shortlived. By early 1946, French troops reoccupied the country and conferred limited autonomy on Laos following elections for a constituent assembly.

Amidst the first Indochina war between France and the communist movement in Vietnam, Prince Souphanouvong formed the Pathet Lao (Land of Laos) resistance organization committed to the communist struggle against colonialism. Laos was not granted full sovereignty until the French defeat by the Vietnamese and the subsequent Geneva peace conference in 1954. Elections were held in 1955, and the first coalition government, led by Prince Souvanna Phouma, was formed in 1957. The coalition government collapsed in 1958, amidst increased polarization of the political process. Rightist forces took over the government.

In 1960, Kong Le, a paratroop captain, seized Vientiane in a coup and demanded formation of a neutralist government to end the fighting. The neutralist government, once again led by Souvanna Phouma, was not successful in holding power. Rightist forces under Gen. Phoumi Nosavan drove out the neutralist government from power later that same year. Subsequently, the neutralists allied themselves with the communist insurgents and began to receive support from the Soviet Union. Phoumi Nosavan's rightist regime received support from the U.S.

A second Geneva conference, held in 1961-62, provided for the independence and neutrality of Laos. Soon after accord was reached, the signatories accused each other of violating the terms of the agreement, and with superpower support on both sides, the civil war soon resumed. Although the country was to be neutral, a growing American and North Vietnamese military presence in the country increasingly drew Laos into the second Indochina war (1954-75). For nearly a decade, Laos was subjected to the heaviest bombing in the history of warfare, as the U.S. sought to destroy the Ho Chi Minh Trail that passed through eastern Laos.

In 1972, the communist People's Party renamed itself the Lao People's Revolutionary Party (LPRP). It joined a new coalition government in Laos soon after the Vientiane cease-fire agreement in 1973. Nonetheless, the political struggle between communists, neutralists, and rightists continued. The fall of Saigon and Phnom Penh to communist forces in April 1975 hastened the decline of the coalition in Laos. Months after these communist victories, the Pathet Lao entered Vientiane. On December 2, 1975, the king abdicated his throne in the constitutional monarchy, and the communist Lao People's Democratic Republic (LPDR) was established.

For additional analytical, business and investment opportunities information, please contact Global Investment & Business Center, USA at (703) 370-8082. Fax: (703) 370-8083. E-mail: ibpusa3@gmail.com Global Business and Investment Info Databank - www.ibpus.com

The new communist government imposed centralized economic decisionmaking and broad security measures, including control of the media and the arrest and incarceration of many members of the previous government and military in "re-education camps". These draconian policies and deteriorating economic conditions, along with government efforts to enforce political control, prompted an exodus of lowland Lao and ethnic Hmong from Laos. About 10% of the Lao population sought refugee status after 1975. Many have since been resettled in third countries, including more than 250,000 who have come to the United States.

The situation of Lao refugees is nearing its final chapter. Over time, the Lao Government closed the re-education camps and released most political prisoners. From 1975 to 1996, the U.S. resettled some 250,000 Lao refugees from Thailand, including 130,000 Hmong. By the end of 1999, more than 28,900 Hmong and lowland Lao had repatriated to Laos--3,500 from China, the rest from Thailand. Through the Office of the United Nations High Commissioner for Refugees (UNHCR), the International Organization for Migration (IOM), and non-governmental organizations, the U.S. has supported a variety of reintegration assistance programs throughout Laos. UNHCR monitors returnees and reports no evidence of systemic persecution or discrimination to date. As of December 1999, about 115 Hmong and lowland Lao remained in Ban Napho camp in Thailand awaiting third-country resettlement by the UNHCR.

GOVERNMENT AND POLITICAL CONDITIONS

The only legal political party is the Lao People's Revolutionary Party (LPRP). The head of state is President Khamtay Siphandone. The head of government is Prime Minister Sisavath Keobounphanh, who also is Chairman of the LPRP. Government policies are determined by the party through the all-powerful nine-member Politburo and the 49-member Central Committee. Important government decisions are vetted by the Council of Ministers.

Laos adopted a constitution in 1991. The following year, elections were held for a new 85-seat National Assembly with members elected by secret ballot to 5-year terms. This National Assembly, expanded in 1997 elections to 99 members, approves all new laws, although the executive branch retains authority to issue binding decrees. The most recent elections took place in December 1997. The FY 2000 central government budget plan calls for revenue of $180 million and expenditures of $289 million, including capital expenditures of $202 million.

PRINCIPAL GOVERNMENT OFFICIALS NEW CABINET MEMBERS APPROVED

The National Assembly, the country's top legislature on 15 June approved the appointment of Mr. Thongsing Thammavong as Prime Minister and four deputy prime ministers and cabinet members.

The First Plenary Session of the 7 th NA approved the proposed list of four deputy prime ministers are Mr. Asang Laoly, Dr. Thongloun Sisoulith, Mr. Duangchay Phichit and Mr. Somsavat Lengsavad. Four of them are members of Politburo under the Lao People's Revolutionary Party Central Committee.

Under the approval, Dr. Thongloun Sisoulith is responsible for Ministry of Foreign Affairs and Mr. Duangchay Phitchit takes the post the Minister of National Defence.

The NA also approved the appointment of government members accordingly,

Mr. Bounthong Chitmany serves as President of State Inspection Committee and Head of Anti-Corruption Agency;

Mr. Phankham Viphavanh, Minister of Education and Sports;

Mr. Thongbanh Seng-aphone, Minister Public Security; Mrs Onchanh Thammavong, Minister of Labour and Social-Welfare;

Mr. Chaleune Yiabaoher, Minister of Justice;

Mr. Soulivong Daravong, Minister of Energy and Mining;

Mrs Bounpheng Mouphosay, Minister for Government's Office;

Mr. Vilayvanh Phomkhe, Minister of Agriculture and Forestry;

Mr. Sinlavong Khouphaythoune, Minister and Head of Government's Office;

Mr. Nam Viyaket, Minister of Industry and Commerce;

Mr. Sommad Pholsena, Minister of Public Works and Transport;

Mr. Somdy Duangdy, Minister of Planning and Investment;

Mr. Phouphet Khamphounvong, Minister of Finance;

Prof Dr. Bosengkham Vongdara, Minister of Information, Culture and Tourism;

Prof Dr. Eksavang Vongvichit, Minister of Public Health;

Mr. Bounheuang Duangphachanh, Minister for Government's Office;

Mr. Khampane Philavong, Minister of Interior;

Prof Dr. Bountiem Phitsamay, Minister for Government's Office;

Dr. Douangsavad Souphanouvong, Minister for Government's Office;

Mrs Khempheng Pholsena, Minister for Government's Office;

Prof Dr. Boviengkham Vongdara, Minister of Science and Technology;

Mr. Noulin Sinbandith, Minister of Natural Resources and Environment;

Mr. Hiem Phommachanh, Minister of Post, Telecommunication and Communication;

Mr. Sompao Phaysith, Governor of the State Bank of Laos;

Mr. Khamphanh Sitthidampha, President of People's Supreme Court and

Mr. Khamsan Souvong, Head of General Prosecutor's Office.

Laos maintains an embassy in the United States at 2222 S Street NW, Washington, D.C. 20009 (tel: 202-332-6416).

ECONOMY

Currency	Lao Kip
Fiscal year	1 October - 30 September
Trade organisations	ASEAN, WTO
Statistics	
GDP	$17.66 billion (PPP; est.)
GDP growth	8.3% (2014 est.)
GDP per capita	$2,700 (PPP; est.)
GDP by sector	services (42.6%), industry (20.2%), agriculture (37.4%) (est.)
Inflation (CPI)	7.6% (est.)
Population below poverty line	26% (est.)
Labour force	3.69 million (est.)
Labour force by occupation	agriculture (75.1%), industry (n/a), services (n/a) (est.)
Unemployment	2.5% (est.)
Main industries	copper, tin, gold, and gypsum mining; timber, electric power, agricultural processing, construction, garments, cement, tourism
Ease of doing business rank	165th
External	
Exports	$2.131 billion (est.)
Export goods	wood products, garments, electricity, coffee, tin, copper, gold
Main export partners	Thailand 32.8% China 20.7% Vietnam 14.0% (est.)
Imports	2.336 billion (est.)
Import goods	machinery and equipment, vehicles, fuel, consumer goods
Main import partners	Thailand 63.2% China 16.5% Vietnam 5.6% (est.)
Gross external debt	$5.953 billion (31 December 2011 est)
Public finances	
Public debt	$3.179 billion
Revenues	$1.76 billion
Expenses	$1.957 billion (est.)
Economic aid	$345 million (est.)
Foreign reserves	$773.5 (31 December est.)

The **economy of the Lao Peoples' Democratic Republic** is rapidly growing, as the government began to decentralise control and encourage private enterprise in 1986. Currently, the economy grows at 8% a year, and the government is pursuing poverty reduction and education for all children as key goals. The country opened a stock exchange, the Lao Securities Exchange in 2011, and has become a rising regional player in its role as a hydroelectric power supplier to neighbors such as China, Vietnam and Thailand. Laos remains one of the poorest countries in

Southeast Asia, but may transition from being a low middle-income country to an upper-middle income one by 2020. A landlocked country, it has inadequate infrastructure and a largely unskilled work force. The country's per capita income in 2009 was estimated to be $2,700 on a purchasing power parity-basis.

The Lao economy depends heavily on investment and trade with its neighbours, Thailand, Vietnam, and, especially in the north, China. Pakxe has also experienced growth based on cross-border trade with Thailand and Vietnam. In 2009, despite the fact that the government is still officially communist, the Obama administration in the US declared Laos was no longer a marxist-lenninist state and lifted bans on Laotian companies receiving financing from the U.S. Export Import Bank. In 2011, the Lao Securities Exchange began trading. In 2014, the government initiated the creation of the Laos Trade Portal, a website incorporating all information traders need to import and export goods into the country.

Subsistence agriculture still accounts for half of the GDP and provides 80% of employment. Only 4.01% of the country is arable land, and a mere 0.34% used as permanent crop land, the lowest percentage in the Greater Mekong Subregion. Rice dominates agriculture, with about 80% of the arable land area used for growing rice. Approximately 77% of Lao farm households are self-sufficient in rice.

Through the development, release and widespread adoption of improved rice varieties, and through economic reforms, production has increased by an annual rate of 5% between 1990 and 2005, and Lao PDR achieved a net balance of rice imports and exports for the first time in 1999. Lao PDR may have the greatest number of rice varieties in the Greater Mekong Subregion. Since 1995 the Lao government has been working with the International Rice Research Institute of the Philippines to collect seed samples of each of the thousands of rice varieties found in Laos.

The economy receives development aid from the IMF, ADB, and other international sources; and also foreign direct investment for development of the society, industry, hydropower and mining (most notably of copper and gold). Tourism is the fastest-growing industry in the country. Economic development in Laos has been hampered by brain drain, with a skilled emigration rate of 37.4% in 2000.

Laos is rich in mineral resources and imports petroleum and gas. Metallurgy is an important industry, and the government hopes to attract foreign investment to develop the substantial deposits of coal, gold, bauxite, tin, copper, and other valuable metals. In addition, the country's plentiful water resources and mountainous terrain enable it to produce and export large quantities of hydroelectric energy. Of the potential capacity of approximately 18,000 megawatts, around 8,000 megawatts have been committed for exporting to Thailand and Vietnam.

The country's most widely recognised product may well be Beerlao which is exported to a number of countries including neighbours Cambodia and Vietnam. It is produced by the Lao Brewery Company.

FOREIGN RELATIONS

The new government that assumed power in December 1975 aligned itself with the Soviet bloc and adopted a hostile posture toward the West. In ensuing decades, Laos maintained close ties with the former Soviet Union and its eastern bloc allies and depended heavily on the Soviets for most of its foreign assistance. Laos also maintained a "special relationship" with Vietnam and formalized a 1977 treaty of friendship and cooperation that created tensions with China.

With the collapse of the Soviet Union and with Vietnam's decreased ability to provide assistance, Laos has sought to improve relations with its regional neighbors. The Lao Government has focused its efforts on Thailand, Laos' principal means of access to the sea and its primary trading partner. Within a year of serious border clashes in 1987, Lao and Thai leaders signed a communiquŽ, signaling their intention to improve relations. Since then, they have made slow but steady progress, notably the construction and opening of the Friendship Bridge between the two countries.

Relations with China have improved over the years. Although the two were allies during the Vietnam War, the China-Vietnam conflict in 1979 led to a sharp deterioration in Sino-Lao relations. These relations began to improve in the late 1980s. In 1989 Sino-Lao relations were normalized.

Laos' emergence from international isolation has been marked through improved and expanded relations with other nations such as Australia, France, Japan, Sweden, and India. Laos was admitted into the Association of Southeast Asian Nations (ASEAN) in July 1997 and applied to join WTO in 1998.

Laos is a member of the following international organizations: Agency for Cultural and Technical Cooperation (ACCT), Association of Southeast Asian Nations (ASEAN), ASEAN Free Trade Area (AFTA), ASEAN Regional Forum, Asian Development Bank, Colombo Plan, Economic and Social Commission for Asia and Pacific (ESCAP), Food and Agriculture Organization (FAO), G-77, International Bank for Reconstruction and Development (World Bank), International Civil Aviation Organization (ICAO), International Development Association (IDA), International Fund for Agricultural Development (IFAD), International Finance Corporation (IFC), International Federation of Red Cross and Red Crescent Societies, International Labor Organization (ILO), International Monetary Fund (IMF), Intelsat (nonsignatory user), Interpol, International Olympic Commission (IOC), International Telecommunications Union (ITU), Mekong Group, Non-Aligned Movement (NAM), Permanent Court of Arbitration (PCA), UN, United Nations Convention on Trade and Development (UNCTAD), United Nations Educational, Social and Cultural Organization (UNESCO), United Nations Industrial Development Organization (UNIDO), Universal Postal Union (UPU), World Federation of Trade Unions, World Health Organization (WHO), World Intellectual Property Organization (WIPO), World Meteorological Organization (WMO), World Tourism Organization, World Trade Organization (observer).

U.S.-LAO RELATIONS

The United States opened a legation in Laos in 1950. Although diplomatic relations were never severed, U.S.-Lao relations deteriorated badly in the post-Indochina War period. The relationship remained cool until 1982 when efforts at improvement began. For the United States, progress in accounting for Americans missing in Laos from the Vietnam War is a principal measure of improving relations. Counternarcotics activities also have become an important part of the bilateral relationship as the Lao Government has stepped up its efforts to combat cultivation; production; and transshipment of opium, heroin, and marijuana.

Since the late 1980s, progress in these areas has steadily increased. Joint U.S. and Lao teams have conducted a series of joint excavations and investigations of sites related to cases of Americans missing in Laos. In counternarcotics activities, the U.S. and Laos are involved in a multimillion-dollar crop substitution/integrated rural development program. Laos also has formed its own national committee on narcotics, developed a long-range strategy for counternarcotics activities, participated in U.S.-sponsored narcotics training programs, and strengthened law enforcement measures to combat the narcotics problem.

For additional analytical, business and investment opportunities information, please contact Global Investment & Business Center, USA at (703) 370-8082. Fax: (703) 370-8083. E-mail: ibpusa3@gmail.com Global Business and Investment Info Databank - www.ibpus.com

U.S. Government foreign assistance to Laos covers a broad range of efforts. Such aid includes support for Laos' efforts to suppress opium production; training and equipment for a program to clear and dispose of unexploded ordnance; school and hospital construction; public education about the dangers of unexploded ordnance and about HIV/AIDS; support for medical research on hepatitis. Economic relations also are expanding. In August 1997, Laos and the United States initialed a Bilateral Trade Agreement and a Bilateral Investment Treaty.

Principal U.S. Embassy Officials

Ambassador-- Rena Bitter

Ambassador Rena Bitter is a career Senior Foreign Service Officer with more than 20 years of experience in Washington and overseas. Most recently, Ambassador Bitter served as Consul General at the U.S. Consulate General in Ho Chi Minh City, Vietnam. Prior to that, she served as the Director of the State Department Operations Center, the Department's 24/7 Briefing and Crisis Management Center. In Washington, she served on the Secretary of State's Executive Staff and as a Special Assistant to Secretary Colin Powell. Her overseas tours include Amman, London, Mexico City and Bogota. Ambassador Bitter grew up in Dallas.

Deputy Chief of Mission--Susan M. Sutton

The American Embassy in Laos is on Rue Bartholonie, B.P. 114, Vientiane, tel: 212-581/582/585; fax: 212-584: country code: (856): city code (21).

Information on the embassy, its work in Laos, and U.S.-Lao relations is available on the Internet at http://www.usembassy.state.gov/laos.

TRAVEL AND BUSINESS INFORMATION

The U.S. Department of State's Consular Information Program provides Consular Information Sheets, Travel Warnings, and Public Announcements. **Consular Information Sheets** exist for all countries and include information on entry requirements, currency regulations, health conditions, areas of instability, crime and security, political disturbances, and the addresses of the U.S. posts in the country. **Travel Warnings** are issued when the State Department recommends that Americans avoid travel to a certain country. **Public Announcements** are issued as a means to disseminate information quickly about terrorist threats and other relatively short-term conditions overseas which pose significant risks to the security of American travelers. Free copies of this information are available by calling the Bureau of Consular Affairs at 202-647-5225 or via the fax-on-demand system: 202-647-3000.

Consular Information Sheets and Travel Warnings also are available on the Consular Affairs Internet home page: http://travel.state.gov. Consular Affairs Tips for Travelers publication series, which contain information on obtaining passports and planning a safe trip abroad are on the internet and hard copies can be purchased from the Superintendent of Documents, U.S. Government Printing Office, telephone: 202-512-1800; fax 202-512-2250.

Emergency information concerning Americans traveling abroad may be obtained from the Office of Overseas Citizens Services at (202) 647-5225. For after-hours emergencies, Sundays and holidays, call 202-647-4000.

For additional analytical, business and investment opportunities information,
please contact Global Investment & Business Center, USA
at (703) 370-8082. Fax: (703) 370-8083. E-mail: ibpusa3@gmail.com
Global Business and Investment Info Databank - www.ibpus.com

Passport information can be obtained by calling the National Passport Information Center's automated system ($.35 per minute) or live operators 8 a.m. to 8 p.m. (EST) Monday-Friday ($1.05 per minute). The number is 1-900-225-5674 (TDD: 1-900-225-7778). Major credit card users (for a flat rate of $4.95) may call 1-888-362-8668 (TDD: 1-888-498-3648). It also is available on the internet.

Travelers can check the latest health information with the U.S. Centers for Disease Control and Prevention in Atlanta, Georgia. A hotline at 877-FYI-TRIP (877-394-8747) and a web site at http://www.cdc.gov/travel/index.htm give the most recent health advisories, immunization recommendations or requirements, and advice on food and drinking water safety for regions and countries. A booklet entitled Health Information for International Travel (HHS publication number CDC-95-8280) is available from the U.S. Government Printing Office, Washington, DC 20402, tel. (202) 512-1800.

Information on travel conditions, visa requirements, currency and customs regulations, legal holidays, and other items of interest to travelers also may be obtained before your departure from a country's embassy and/or consulates in the U.S. (for this country, see "Principal Government Officials" listing in this publication).

U.S. citizens who are long-term visitors or traveling in dangerous areas are encouraged to register at the U.S. embassy upon arrival in a country (see "Principal U.S. Embassy Officials" listing in this publication). This may help family members contact you in case of an emergency.

For additional analytical, business and investment opportunities information, please contact Global Investment & Business Center, USA at (703) 370-8082. Fax: (703) 370-8083. E-mail: ibpusa3@gmail.com Global Business and Investment Info Databank - www.ibpus.com

STRATEGIC INFORMATION FOR CONDUCTING BUSINESS

FREE TRADE AREAS (FTAS)

Preferences that Laos benefits from free trade agreements which is most important to Laos is the ASEAN Trade in Goods Agreement (ATIGA). Laos has also signed free trade agreements with ASEAN dialogue countries: Closer Economic Relations (Australia and New Zealand), China, India, Japan and Korea. In addition, Laos is a party to other FTAs: Lao-Vietnam Trade Agreement and the Asia-Pacific Trade Agreement (APTA).

Laos is exporting and benefiting from preferential treatment to ASEAN markets mainly to Thailand with the exports totaled US$623 million in 2012, followed by Vietnam and Singapore, amounting to US$69 million and US$44 million, respectively. The preferential exports to Malaysia and Indonesia were each less than US$2 million. Laos also exports to ASEAN dialogue partners including China, Japan and Korea with such exporting items as agriculture, garments, handicrafts and non-timber forestry products. Other dialogue partner markets include Australia India and New Zealand.

ATIGA

Laos benefits from trade preference in the form of tariff exemption or reduction under the ATIGA from 9 other ASEAN members: Brunei, Cambodia, Indonesia, Malaysia, Myanmar, the Philippines, Singapore, Thailand and Vietnam. Exports from Laos destined to these markets are subject 0% tariff rates for most agricultural and industrial products since 2010, except for those under the General Exception List (GEL) as well as under the Sensitive List (SL) exporting to newer ASEAN members (Cambodia, Myanmar and Vietnam) which will be cut to 0% rate by 2018. The document required for preference under this regime is the certificate of origin Form D.

ASEAN-Australia and New Zealand Free Trade Agreement (AANZFTA)

Laos can export with reduced or exempted tariff rates under the AANZ free trade area from 11 countries: Australia, Brunei, Cambodia, Indonesia, Malaysia, Myanmar, New Zealand, the Philippines, Singapore, Thailand and Vietnam. The document required is the certificate of origin Form AANZ.

ASEAN-China Free Trade Agreement (ACFTA)

The trade preference in terms of tariff exemption or reduction under the ACFTA covers 10 countries (9 other ASEAN members and China). The document required for preferential treatment is the certificate of origin Form E.

ASEAN-India Free Trade Agreement (AIFTA)

The trade preference in terms of tariff exemption or reduction under the AIFTA covers 10 countries (9 other ASEAN members and India). The document required is the certificate of origin Form AI.

ASEAN-Japan Free Trade Agreement (AJFTA)

The trade preference (tariff exemption or reduction) under the AJFTA covers 10 countries (9 other ASEAN members and Japan). The document required for preferential treatment is the certificate of origin Form AJ.

ASEAN-Korea Free Trade Agreement (AKFTA)

Laos is subject to exempted or reduced tariffs under the AKFTA from 10 countries which includes 9 other ASEAM members and Korea. The document required for preferential treatment is the certificate of origin Form AK.

Asia Pacific Trade Agreement (APTA)

Laos benefits from trade preference in terms of tariff exemption or reduction under the APTA from countries: Bangladesh, China, India, Korea and Sri Lanka. The document required for preferential treatment is the certificate of origin Form APTA.

Laos-Vietnam Trade Agreement

Apart from ASEAN, Laos also benefits from reciprocal access under the trade agreement between Laos and Vietnam for 32 tariff lines with 50% of the AFTA/CEPT rate, while all other products are 0% rate, except for 155 tariff lines which fall under the GEL of Vietnam.

ECONOMY AND ECONOMIC DEVELOPMENT

The physical and Socio-economic characteristics of the Lao PDR set out in the previous paragraphs have given rise to the following development potentials and constraints :

- abundance of water resource giving vast scope for the development of hydroelectric power facilities.

- large irrigation potential which, once developed, could increase food production capacity and allow for further crop diversification.

- potential for sustained development of high-value timber, provided forest resource management and reforestation programs are improved.

- significant export potential for non-wood forest products (such as cardamom, benzoin, sticklac and other resins).

- considerable scope for increasing the quantity of minerals already being exported, and for both mining and exporting minerals which are only now being identified.

- proximity to large external markets which implies a potentially strategic position for entrep6t trade, although until now most economic activity tends to be concentrated along the Mekong River and the border with Thailand.

- economic and social fragmentation since many parts of the country are physically isolated and since the population consists of a wide variety of ethnic groups.

- prevalence of subsistence farming and barter exchange among the vast majority of the population.

- insufficient physical infrastructure (such as transportation networks and communications systems).

- insufficient information on the country's key physical social, economic and climatic variables, and inadequate access to information on markets, technologies and investment opportunities available abroad.

- limited domestic financial resources, necessitating dependence on external assistance to finance a large part of the Government's investment program and the balance of payment deficit

- lack of skilled manpower and insufficient institutional capacities required to support a flexible, growing economy.

- high transportation costs, particularly for import-exports.

ECONOMIC DEVELOPMENT AND OPPORTUNITIES

ECONOMIC GROWTH

On average, the Gross Domestic Product (GDP) during a whole period was 219,853 billion kip, on average about 43,970 billion kip per annum and grew at about 7.9% annually, which is higher than the Sixth Five-year Plan target (plan target was 7.5%) and it was 1.08 times higher than the Fifth Five-year Plan implementation (average 6.24% per annum). Within this, the agriculture sector grew at 4%, industry 12.6% and services 8.4% (The structure and growth in the GDP can be seen in Table 1). The reason behind this satisfactory growth was, the overall economic direction guided by the Party; peaceful an secured political, social and economic stability; global and regional economic integration; and the legal system. Of particular reference is the law on promotion of private domestic and foreign investment, which has permitted attracting international capital and boost competition. When compared to other countries in the region, Lao PDR's economic growth has been considerably higher.

Table 1: Comparison between actual and targeted GDP growth rate in the Sixth Plan (2006-2010)

Sector	Target (2006-2010)	Target (average % per annum)	Actual (average % per annum)
Agriculture & Forestry	3~3.4%	3.2%	4.0%
Industry	13~14.0%	13.7%	12.6%
Services	7.5~8.0%	7.3%	8.4%
Total	7.5~8.0%	7.6%	7.9%

Sources: National Socio-Economic Development Plan 2006-2010 and Annual Statistics Yearbooks, 20052008.

For additional analytical, business and investment opportunities information, please contact Global Investment & Business Center, USA at (703) 370-8082. Fax: (703) 370-8083. E-mail: ibpusa3@gmail.com Global Business and Investment Info Databank - www.ibpus.com

GDP per capita in either Kip or US Dollar has increased considerably, exceeding the target of the Five-year Plan (2006-2010). In the year 2007-2008, GDP per capita reached US$ 818, and in 2008-2009, it was estimated at US$ 906. In 2009-2010, the GDP per capita reached US$ 1069, which was an increase of about 18% when compared to 2008-2009. These figures suggest that there has been an increase in the Household Consumption Index per month, from 1.1 million Kip in 2002-03 to 2.2 million Kip in 2007-08 (i.e. doubled): consumption in urban areas increased from 1.7 to 2.9 million Kip, and in rural areas increased from 900 thousand to 1.8 million Kip. In summary, household consumption per month at an average has been rising at 14.8% per year.

Table 2: GDP per capita (plan vs. actual)

Period	Plan (US$ per capita per annum)	Actual (US$ per capita per annum)	Actual Vs. Plan (%)
2005/2006	556	573	3.1
2006/2007	619	687	11.0
2007/2008	682	818	19.9
2008/2009	752	906	20.5
2009/2010	823	1069	29.8

Source: Department of Statistics, Ministry of Planning and Investment (*) Based on preliminary data

ECONOMIC STRUCTURAL CHANGES

The economic structure changes as an economy transforms from a subsistence agriculture and raw material-based economy to a processing and market-oriented economy. This also has a positive impact on the domestic natural resources.

Economic structure and value added in each of each sector has exhibited an increase, which is in accordance with set direction. In 2008-2009, the agriculture and forestry sector accounted for 30.4% of the GDP and had value added at 14.36 billion Kip; Industry sector covered 24.9% and had value added at 11.74 billion Kip; Services sector was equivalent to 38.4% and had value added at 18.14 billion Kip. In 2009-2010, it is projected that agriculture and forestry sector covers about 39.2%, industry sector covers 26% and services sector covers 39% of the GDP. Details on the sector growth will be provided in Section 3, Part 1 of this Report].

In summary, in the past five years, the sectoral composition of the GDP suggests that agriculture and forestry sector accounted for 30.4%, industry 26.1%, and services 37.2%.

FINANCIAL SECTOR GROWTH

[1] Financial Status of the Banking system

During the past five years, the banking sector has contributed to financial stability, and foreign exchange is flowing steadily: This is reflected in the money supply growth at 23% per year which was accounted 19.6% of GDP. Foreign exchange inflow was around 35% of GDP in 2009-2010. The reason of increasing money supply or M2 was that the ever-increasing numbers of foreign investors. Money supply in a narrow sense (i.e., finances outside the banking system and daily savings in Kip) accounts for about 30% of the total money, while other money supply accounts for 70% of which An estimated 80% of the total savings were in foreign currency during period 2006-2008 (increased 3% compared to year 2005). Both domestic and foreign net assets have increased. Foreign currency reserves have increased, and its present stock is enough to pay for importing goods and services for about six months. In short, the financial status of the banking system is stable.

[2] Banking Sector Development

Banking sector is one of the sectors that grew rapidly and distinctly in this Five-year Plan. This is because of the government putting much effort in creating better conditions and ease to do business. Especially, the law and regulation have been improved to facilitate the sector to compete better internationally and be able to support the economic sector to boost rapid development and growth. In a very short time, a number of new banks have been established leading to the benefit of the society; particularly, businesses have more alternatives to access and make use of world-class services and modern technologies at a lower service charge. Besides, effort is being made to launch the first-ever stock market with a great deal of effort by the government, and will be launched in 2011. Banks loans to the business sector increased by about 85% at the end of 2008 compared to March 2008; they further reached 82.3% in March 2009. These achievements suggest that the society is more confident on banking sector. At the same time, Non-Performing Loans or NPL have decreased drastically, from 10.52% in 2006 to 3.84% in July 2009. This is lower than the plan projections of about 5% of the total credit. However, the rural poor still have limited access to institutional loans. In sum, the quality of services and access to loans, have both improved and the banking system has become more modernised.

[3] Inflation

In the recent past, inflation has been effectively managed; inflation rate decreased from 8% in 2005-2006 to 4.1% in 2006-2007, increased to 7.9% in 2007-2008, and decreased to 0.74% in the last six months of 2008-2009 (inflation has been persistently low in the recent past, lowest since 1990, when data collection began). In 2010, inflation is likely to increase about 4.71%. However, the overall consumer prices are still stable and on average inflation rate in 5 years was 5.09% which remains at one-digit per year, and lower than the economic growth rate.

[4] Foreign Exchange rate

Kip currency is gradually getting appreciated. In 2005-2006 the exchange rate (average) was equal to 10,411.0 Kip/US$, which improved to 9,679 Kip/US$ in 2006-07; 8,980 Kip/US$ in 2007-2008; and 8,532 Kip/US$ in 2008-09. In 2009-2010, the exchange rate was equal to 8,372 Kip/US$. The difference between the bank rate and market rate was about 0.25% in December 2005, which reduced to 0.01% in November 2009. In terms of Baht, the figures were 0.14% and 0.15% respectively, in the same period. The appreciation of the Kip is in line with the depreciation of the US$ and the influx of the foreign investment in country. Kip's appreciation is affecting the country's exports only little, because exports to an extent still depend on natural resources, the costs and prices of which are denominated in foreign exchange. On the other hand, comparing Kip with other currencies, especially Kip to Baht, the Kip is still lower. This lower rate is partly because of the extensive trading between Lao PDR and Thailand in favour of the latter.

WORKFORCE AND EMPLOYMENT

The workforce structure in the economic sectors has changed corresponding to the economic structure, and the industrialisation and modernisation strategy. Capacity building of the workforce, improving the curriculum at the vocational level, the coordination mechanism, and occupational opportunities inside and outside the country, has progressively improved.

Labour intensive sectors have collaborated with both public and private training centres with a view to provide training to un-skilled workers. This is especially for those workers who have just finished lower and upper secondary school levels to be suitable with the real work. Persons having received vocational training and skills have increased from 5,070 in 2006 to 5,374 persons in 2007, further increased to 16,158 persons in 2008 and to 29,766 persons in 2009. Overall, in the last four years training has been provided to 56,368 persons compared to the plan target, the achievement is 81.33%. If taken into account the target number for 2010 (currently being implemented), the total number of trainees will reach to 74,069 persons, which will have exceeded the target of the Sixth Five-year Plan by 6.88% (target in the Five-year Plan was 69,300 persons). Seen sector-wise, persons trained in the agriculture-forest sector are expected at 16,152 persons, industry and construction at 27,856 persons and services at 30,061persons.

Job has been created through improving coordination mechanism to in accordance with the current market demand. Besides, there is also collaboration between relevant parties (in both public and private sectors), and forgetting information on the demand and supply, participatory approaches have been used. Job placement agencies are gradually and systematically expanding: agent companies and their affiliates have expanded from three in 2005 to nine in 2009-2010. In 2006, they arranged jobs for 6.404 workers; in 2007 for about 21,099 workers; in 2008 for about 74,992 persons; and in 2009 the number increased to about 241,949 workers.

In all, about 317,444 workers got into jobs during the plan, which is equivalent to 58.35% of the target (the target is about 544 thousand workers, which averages 108,800 workers, annually). New jobs expected in 2010 are 325,440 workers. This will result in the numbers employed is 642,884 workers, exceeding the five-year target by 18.2%. Domestic job opportunities can accommodate 626,691workers: labour force in agricultural and forestry will be 584,589 workers, in the industrial and construction sector will be 38,435 workers, and in the service sector will be 3,667 workers. Job opportunities outside the country will be able to provide for 16,193 workers: in agricultural and forestry sector is 1,042 workers, in the industrial and construction sector is 13,396 workers, and in the services sector is 1.755 workers. Attempt was also made to collect data on registering people who need jobs. This number was 298,775 workers, of which, 192,904 workers wanted to be in agricultural and forestry sector, 74,194 workers in the industrial and construction sector, and 29,677 workers in the services sector.

Compared to the 5-year plan, which has a target of 390,000 persons registering for jobs, actual job creation through this channel was 76.6%. With cooperation from labour management organisations of different countries, it is found that there is an estimated demand for 10,434 positions in Thailand (152 for women), 300 positions per year in Japan and 1,000 positions a year in Malaysia. Cooperation was sought with the Ministry of Labour, Republic of Korea, in order to prepare for the export of Lao labour for working in Korea.

The labour structure by economic sectors has slowly changed, the changes having taken place in the same direction as the economic structure– industrialisation and modernisation. The share of labour in the agriculture and forestry sector has slightly declined, from 78.5% in 2005 to 75.1% in 2010, and correspondingly the shares increased in industry and construction from 4.8% to 5.5%, and in services from 16.7% in 2005 to 19.5% in 2010 (see Table 3). The proportion of labour shift from the agricultural sector to non-agricultural sectors is 0.7% annually. In that, the services sector accommodated larger numbers compared to the industrial sector.

For additional analytical, business and investment opportunities information,
please contact Global Investment & Business Center, USA
at (703) 370-8082. Fax: (703) 370-8083. E-mail: ibpusa3@gmail.com
Global Business and Investment Info Databank - www.ibpus.com

Share of labour by sectors

No.	Sector	Year		Estimate
		2005	2010	2006-2010
1	Agriculture-forestry	78.5%	75.1%	73.9%
2	Industry	4.8%	5.5%	9.3%
3	Service	16.7%	19.5%	16.9%

Source: Calculations based on Population Censuses 2005 and NSEDP VI (2006-2010)

SOURCES FOR DEVELOPMENT

[1]. Public investment

An account of Public Investment Programmes (PIP) during the last five years suggests that fund allocation for PIPs in each sector and locality has been effectively made in the government's priority 11 programmes 111 projects. The investments made were 24,747 billion Kip. Of the total investments, 3,982 billion Kip were from domestic sources which were accounted for 98.7% of 5-year approval (2,150 billion kip invested in economics area and 956 billion kip in social area and 876 billion kip in other areas) and 20,765 billion Kip from foreign sources.

[2]. Attracting Official Development Assistance

During the last five years, given the difficult economic circumstances around the world, Official Development Assistance (ODA) globally and in some regions has shown a falling trend. However, development partners and some friendly countries, which have promised to assist Lao PDR, have continuously provided assistance to support socio-economic development policies of the Party and the Government. During these five years, funds from ODA expended on 2,251 projects in total, as reported in the annual foreign aid report of ODA implementation amounted to US$2,443 million, or on an average US$ 488 million per year. Apart from this, there was a *National contribution fund (public fund)* of US$ 88.66 million (an average of US$ 17.73 million per year). The implementation of grant projects is strongly contributed to the socio-economic development of the country. In general, the ODA funds have been effectively used.

[3]. Attracting Foreign Direct Investments (FDI)

The economy attracted a total private (domestic and foreign) investment of 1,022 projects during the last five years. The approved projects during the plan period were valued at US$ 10.01 billion, out of which domestic investors made investments worth US$ 2.2 billion. The largest proportion of approved funds was in the electricity sector at US$ 3.44 billion (shared 31.24 %), followed by mining US$2.88 billion (shared 25.82%), services US$1.48 billion (shared 13.44%) and then other sectors US$3.21billion (shared 29.15%). During 2008-2009 alone, approved projects amounted to US$4.3 billion. The largest investment inflows are from China, Thailand and Vietnam.

Table 4: Private domestic and foreign investment from 2006-2010 (US$ billion)

Fiscal year	Total investment	Local investment

Total	11.01	2.2
2005-2006	2.7	0.4
2006-2007	1.4	0.2
2007-2008	1.22	0.3
2008-2009	4.31	0.9
2009-2010	1.64	0.3

Source: Investment Promotion Department, Ministry of Planning and Investment (June 2010)

Foreign investment has significantly contributed to economic development supported economic growth and reforms, merchandise production, and in the economic structure. This has raised the spectrum of products manufactured, job creation, and local development. Moreover, support has been made to strengthen private sector.

Overall, the achievements have come about due to proper government measures and policies put in place for attracting funds; e.g. the Investment Law has been improved, improvements in the investment approval process through "one door" approach, increased local authorisation in approving and managing foreign investments – bases on type of projects and values of investment. The government sets up meetings with local and foreign investors and entrepreneurs once a year in order to be up-to-date about the difficulties that they face and find solutions. Besides, investment-promoting activities have taken place for attracting more foreign investors.

STATE BUDGET

The Sixth Five-year Plan targeted state revenue at 14-16% of the GDP and public expenditure at around 20-22% of the GDP. Budget deficit was to be limited at about 6-8% of the GDP.

Through the implementation of the plan, the status of the public budget has gradually improved. The revenue collection has been above the target for three years in sequence. The increase in revenue has largely been from taxes and customs, which accounted for average about 70% of the total revenue. During 2006-2010, the estimated total revenue was 38.5 trillion Kip, which accounted for 17.31% of GDP and equivalent to 105% of the plan. In this, the domestic revenue was 32.3 trillion Kip.

The total budget expenditure was 49 trillion Kip, accounted for 22.29% of GDP, equivalent to 103% of the plan target. This has resulted in a budget deficit of 10.95 trillion Kip (after including the grants). The average budget deficit was 4.98% of the GDP, achieved 63.05% of the plan (plan target was 6.1% of GDP). Overall, The main expenditure item was public sector salary, which is the first priority of government. The salary index rose through three subsequent years at an annual average of 18.66%.

In the beginning of 2007, the amended version of State Budget Law was put into effect. The main purpose of modifying this law was to improve the budget management mechanism, by centralising and putting forth three sectors, namely treasury, customs and tax, in the central budget. In mid-2007, the Audit Law was enforced. The State Audit Organisation can now directly report to the National Assembly. In general, the government's financial status has gradually improved.

TRADE BALANCE

The Sixth Five-year Plan has had the aim to benefit from trade: to stimulate economic growth through competition and effective use the country's absolute advantage, international economic commitments[under ASEAN Free Trade Area (AFTA)], and bilateral and multilateral trade agreements, including accession to WTO. Expansion in international trade has provided boost to domestic trade, by opening up trade between cities and rural areas. In addition, the government has put effort to improve exports, promote cross-border-trade, and promote production for both domestic consumption and exports. Expansion in trade has improved human development. The living conditions of the ethnic people have improved in many ways, through employment creation, labour migration, crossborder-trade, and rural electrification, and others.

The general priorities of the Sixth Five-year Plan were to contribute more towards exports by increasing the share of export goods that create high value addition which can contribute to economic growth, moreover, try to integrate export into each sector in order to increase employment opportunities, generate higher income to people as well as to country.

During the five years 2006-2010, the export value of Lao PDR's goods was US$ 5.69 billion and shared 23.4% of GDP, which has exhibited an increasing trend every year, especially the export value in 2009, which expected to reach US$ 1,005.3 million. It was a slight drop compared to the value in 2008. It is anticipated that exports will reach US$ 1,789 million in 2010 as compared to the first year of the plan, it increased for two times. Majority of the export commodities are mining products (silver, gold and copper), garments, agricultural products (coffee, corn, tea, peanut, rice , livestock...), electricity, and wood and wood products.

In 2009, the largest proportion of export earnings came from mining—45% of total export— of which copper had the largest share(33% of total exports), while the share of gold and silver combined was 9.28%. The second largest share was of garments, accounting for 12.7%, which was a decline by 10-11% when compared to exports of this item in 2008. Export of electricity was 9.97%, which was a slight increase compared to the 2008 figures. Apart from this, wood products constituted 4.9%, and coffee 2.25%. Details are shown in Table 5 below:

Table 5: Export structure of Lao PDR by commodities 2005-2009 (%)

Commodities	2005	2006	2007	2008	2009
Wood product	14.13	11.09	9.71	6.02	4.90
Coffee	1.35	1.11	3.13	1.69	2.25
Agricultural products/NTFP	3.65	2.52	1.80	4.82	9.06
Others	3.74	2.72	2.52	2.60	15.43

Garment	20.04	14.45	13.69	23.45	12.70
Electricity	17.81	11.47	9.13	9.89	9.97
Mining	39.16	56.55	59.94	51.44	45.26
Gold and silver	15.69	12.47	10.06	7.38	9.28
Copper	20.40	41.99	47.89	40.85	33.51
Other	3.07	2.08	1.99	3.21	2.47
Fuel	0.13	0.09	0.09	0.09	0.44

Total export FOB:	100.00	100.00	100.00	100.00	100.00

Source: Bank of Lao PDR.

Imports to Lao PDR during the five years (2006-2010) had a value of US$6.61 billion, which covered 27.3% of GDP and it also shows an increasing trend. In 2009, imports were valued at approximately US$ 1,413.5 million, which was a slight increase compared to the imports in 2008.Itis estimated that imports will further increase to US$ 1,670.97 million by 2010.

The imported products were largely for investment: machinery and equipment, for activities ranging from production to construction and electricity generation (e.g. in 2008, these items of import had a share of 40%, which increased to 69.61%in 2009). Next, imports for consumption, such as food, medicines and clothings (e.g. in 2009 those imports constituted 21.87% of the total imports, which was decrease by half compared to that in 2008). Third, the share of raw materials and equipment for the garment sector was 4.72% of the total imports (their share fell three times compared to that in 2008). Details are shown in the table below:

Export and Imports from 2005-2009

Trade deficit: The foreign trade balance of Lao PDR is continuously in deficit. During the five years 2006-2010, the trade deficit amounted to US$ 0.92 billion (average deficit: US$184 million per year), equivalent to 16.17% of the total exports. However, the trade sector has shown a better performance; e.g., the trade deficit as a proportion of the GDP declined from 10.79% during 2001-2005, to 3.8% during 2006-2010 (the target for 20062010 is 5.8% of GDP).

Import structure of Lao PDR by commodities 2005-2009 (%)

Commodities	2005	2006	2007	2008	2009
Import for investment	44.14	46.75	55.69	40.45	69.61

Machineries and production equipment	14.35	13.44	16.62	22.46	47.23
Vehicles (50% of total)	5.33	5.65	10.91	3.92	11.10

Fuel (50% of total)	9.75	9.16	16.31	10.65	6.28
Construction/electronic equipment	14.71	18.50	11.85	3.42	5.00
Import for consumption	45.20	41.52	33.93	43.57	21.87
Materials and garment machines	7.92	9.31	7.55	12.48	4.72
Luxury products	1.14	0.99	0.95	1.44	1.20
Electricity	1.38	1.23	1.66	1.92	2.45
Fuel	0.23	0.21	0.22	0.13	0.14
Total import (CIF)	100.00	100.00	100.00	100.00	100.00

Source: Bank of Lao PDR.

SUB-REGIONAL, REGIONAL AND MAIN SECTORAL DEVELOPMENT

SECTORAL DEVELOPMENT

AGRICULTURE AND FORESTRY

The Agriculture and Forestry Sector in the recent years grew at 4% and accounted for 30.4% of the total GDP in 2009. In that, crop and livestock production grew at 4.07%, which accounted for 88.6% of value added in the sector. Fisheries production also grew at 4.03%, and accounted for 11.4% of the value added in the sector. Overall, agriculture and forestry production has improved and is able to supply sufficient production for basic domestic needs.

The main areas for plantation and agricultural production, especially the rice crop, are located in the central part of the country, accounting for 55% of sown area, and 57% of the sectoral production. The southern part accounts for 23% both area and production and northern part, for 22% of total area and 20% of production. Savannakhet Province has the largest area under crops (mainly rice) accounting for 22% area under rice in the country, followed by Champassack Province (12%), Vientiane Capital (9%), Saravane (9%) and Vientiane Province (8%). The agricultural land per household is approximately 1.6 hectares in the country. Below is a map showing the differences in agricultural land per household in different provinces.

Promoting Crop and Vegetable Production: The production of some of the main food and vegetable items has been promoted, namely of rice, corn, sugarcane, coffee, tea, tobacco, peanut, soybean, green bean, cassava and cotton, in addition to livestock. Since 2006, locally grown rice was sufficient for self-consumption and also set aside some for sale. On average annual rice production has reached 2.9 million tones in 2009 (increased from 2.56 million tones in 2005). This is 88% of the target set in the Sixth Five-year Plan (3.3 million tones), which increased by 26.4% compared to the figure in 2005-2006. Paddy rice production per person as per latest available estimates is 470 kg/person/year. This is sufficient to meet the basic needs of the society. However, the price of rice has been fluctuating seasonally from time to time, due to issues relating to distribution.

Land yield rate increased from 3.49 tones per hectare in 2005, to 3.54 tones per hectare in 2008. Rice production is estimated to have reached 3.14 million tones in the planting season of 2009, of which wet seasonal rice is expected to account for 78%, irrigated rice 14.4% and upland rice 7%.

Between 2006 and 2010, the wet seasonal rice crop was sown in an estimated 631,000 hectares, yielding 2.3 million tones of rice each year; and irrigated rice was sown in an estimated 89,000 hectares, yielding 423,000 tones. Irrigated rice production, however, has not met its target both due to internal and external factors: natural disasters, environment, oil price fluctuation, production costs, and market imperfections, being some of them. Area under upland rice has reached an estimated 110,000 hectares/year, yielding 205,000 tones. Apart from rice, production of other crops has also risen significantly compared to the recent years, and is able to meet the basic consumption needs of the society. Buying and selling is normal (i.e. there is no panic buying or selling), production is sufficient, and price steady. Self production of vegetables, tacos, cassava and such crops has steadily risen to replace importing.

Along with producing food for domestic consumption, the plan has also encouraged agricultural produce to be processed in factories to add value; e.g. in corn (for making animal feed) for domestic markets and exports. Corn plantation area increased 32.7% between 2005 and 2010: from 113.8 thousand ha to 151 thousand ha. The production of this crop increased 88.% from 403.5 thousand tones in 2005 to 760 thousand tones in 2010. It is grown mainly in the Northern provinces: Xayaboury, Bokeo, Huaphanh, Oudomxay, Luang Prabang and Xiengkhuang. Furthermore, cassava production increased three times between 2005 and 2010: from 51 thousand tones to 161 thousand tones. It is being exported for processing to flour factories. Sugarcane production has risen by3 times also, from 218 thousand tones in 2005 to 703 thousand tones in 2010. In addition, coffee vegetables and organic vegetables (cabbage, chayote, coriander and other vegetables) are grown in Pakxong and the Bolevan Plateau, again mainly for export.

Livestock and Fisheries Production: In order to supply larger quantities of food for consumption, there has been a shift in the production system, from the traditional (natural) methods (of open grazing or feeding) towards livestock husbandry in captivity, so that the animals are better reared. Some additional steps being undertaken are: encouraging community/collective growing, controlling animal migration, supplying vaccines, and expanding veterinary services to villages (coverage of cattle vaccination is 36%, pig vaccination 26%, and poultry vaccination 24%). Bird flu is well under control. The livestock and fisheries sector has modernised to an extent, and contemporary livestock farms in locales close to big cities, and in mountainous areas, have begun to emerge. In addition to meeting the urban demand, this trend has encouraged cross-border trade in livestock (cattle, pigs and poultry) and fish. The total domestic supply value of livestock and fisheries is US$ 102.4 million dollars (the main production is of cattle and buffaloes: 40,000 cattle and 45,000 buffaloes, respectively). In addition, production of fish seedlings has been expanded in 32 governmental stations for supplying these to farmers and the community as a whole. The supply is able to meet 46% of the country's demand, or approximately 300 million numbers of fish seedlings.

Forest Production : This sector is able to supply products domestically, worth US$ 31.4 million, and for exportsworthUS$74.4 million. Reforestation and tree plantation are encouraged among all communities and government agencies, the private sector, other organisations and citizens. They are planting commercial trees: eucalyptus, teak, agar wood, and rubber. Foreign investment from

Vietnam, Thailand and China has also steadily increased in the tree plantation sector. They are mainly investing in rubber plantations in the northern, southern and central provinces, and eucalyptus plantations in the central provinces. Although tree plantation has increased (with cooperation from all stakeholders), the up-keep of plants is still wanting due to lack of funds for supporting technical staff to local areas.

Wood and Non-Timber Forest Products: There are policies, rules, laws and recommendations to guide implementation. Deforestation and illegal-logging steadily have decreased each year, which has encouraged the private sector and businesses to concentrate on wood-processing to add value for export, as well as reforestation, in order to increase the quantity of wood for production in the times to come. Trees could be cut only when there is need to construct important government infrastructure(s) at the place where the tree(s) are. Additionally, cutting trees is permitted in pre-surveyed sustainable forests.

Non-timber forest produce is collected regularly. Some main products are, rattan (8.1 million lines), bamboo (5.1 million lumps), fence (38 thousand bars), dried bark (for lighting firewood, 178 thousand *lah*, a traditional volume measure), Agar wood 180 tones, and other NTFP (wood oil, skin, bark, flowers, root, tuber, etc.) 64,667 tones. Nowadays, reforesting and forest development has spread to all communities. Saplings planted increased by 219%, from 36 million to 113 million saplings between 2005 and 2008, used for reforesting 40,000 hectares. In 2005 were planted in 14,000 hectares – this is an increase by 191%. Degraded forested areas were regenerated in 127,000 hectares in 2008, compared to 57,000 hectares in 2005, recording a 124% increase.

INDUSTRIAL SECTOR

During the past years, the industrial sector grew at about 12.6% per annum. The average (2006-2010) share of mineral exploration in the value added in industry is 35.4%, of value-added (processing) activities it is 34.3%, and electricity and water sub-sectors form the rest. Take a look at figure 5 below for more detail:

Average share of value added in the industrial sector 2006-2010

Source: Statistic Department, Ministry of Planning and Investment

[1]. Energy and Mining Sector

1. Electricity Sector During 2006-2010, electricity production average increased 22.12% (current price) and increased 9.3% (fixed price) which covered 3.1% of GDP and reached 97% of the plan target. Since 2005, five dams have been completed namely, Nam Mang 3 (40 MW), Nam Theun 2 (1,088MW), SeSet 2 (76MW), Nam Lik 1/2 (100MW) and Nam Ngeum 2 (615MW) together having a capacity of 1,919 Megawatts, which can supply energy of 8,022 GWH per annum increased about 3 times compared to 2005. In this, three dams are private investment. Presently, there are 14 dams that have minimum energy 1 MW, if including small dams, there are 27 dams across the country, which have capacity of 2,583.72MW and can produce energy of 11,514 GWH. Additionally, there are six hydroelectric dams to be constructed during the sixth 5-year plan which estimate to have a capacity of 662.2 MW.

Of these, the dam construction that aimed to be complete in 2011 consists of SeKaman 3, Nam Ngeum 5, Nam Yon and ThatSalan; to be complete in 2012 include Theun Hinboun extension phase and Nam SeXong dams. Furthermore, there is Hongsa Thermal Power Plant (1,878MW), which are currently under the process of resettling the people and completing the environment concerned requirements. The plant is expected to be officially opened in 2011.

There are eight dams under construction, namely, Sekaman3, NamNgeum2, NamLik1/2, Nam Yon, NamNgeum5, and expansion of Theun HinBoon, TadSaland and Nam Song.

They are expected to be complete between 2010 and 2012. These dams together have a potential capacity of 1,377 Megawatts, and can produce electricity equivalent to 5,950 million KWH a year. It is expected that 317 Megawatt power will be consumed domestically and 1,060 Megawatts would be exported. The total income is expected to be US$303 million per year, of which the government's share would be US$90 million per annum.

The length of electricity transmission lines in the country is 29,601 Km, of which 138 Km are very high pressure lines of 500 KV; 406 Km are of 230 KV (mostly for export); 2,060.9 Km are high pressure lines of 115 KV; 14,577.2 Km are medium pressure lines of 22KV, 34KV, 35KV; and 12,419 Km are low pressure lines of 0.4 KV. Until August 2010, 98% of all districts, 60.48% of all villages and 72% of all households had electricity had access to a power connection.

Some power transmission lines are under construction: the NARPD Project in the north, of length 1,627 Km, is 98% complete; REP1 Project in the south of 2,472 Km is 93% complete; GMS Project in Pakxong-Jiangxai-Bangyor area is64% complete; and PaksanThakek-Savannakhet line of 285 Km is 18% complete. Additionally, 115KV transmission lines in NamNgeum5 of 142 Km, 230KV transmission lines in NamLik-HinHurb-ThaLard-Vientiane Capital, and 500 KV lines from the NaBong-Thai border are under construction. Moreover, there are also medium-low lines in Sukuma District, Mounlapamok District and Pin District-TadHai area, which are being constructed.

The total private investment in the electricity sector between 2006 and 2009 was of US$2,995.5 million, which is an increase of 88.5% compared that in the last plan period (2001-2005). In all, electricity production increased 9.3% per year. Electricity sector has shared 15% of total industrial production and accounted of 3% of GDP.

2. Mining Industry

The total mining production value amounted to 16,772.47 billion kip, with an average annual increase of 19.91% during 2006-2010 (at current price), which has increased by about 5 times of the figure in the previous five years (2001-2005). The sector accounts for 9.5% of GDP. Exploration and production of gold bars during the four years between 2006 and 2009 reached

33.13 tones (in 2006 produced 12.65 tones, in 2007 produced 9.2 tones, in 2008 produced 5.81 tones, and 2009 produced 5.47 tones) while the plan of 2010 aims to reach 5 tones (the figure showed the decline in production of gold because there has been changes each year in the amount of gold extracted from the gold ore). Within these four years, the production of copper plates was 321,487 tones and copper dust 585,607 tones; where the total sale of copper reached US$ 3,274 million. As a part of the agreement between the companies and government, the government received its share worth US$ 445 million from Lane Xang Mineral at Sepone gold mining during 2006 and 2009. In 2010, the company is expected to share US$ 148 million with the government. the local level received US$ 500,000 annually for rural development. Additionally, Phubia Mining shared US$ 18 million to the government in 2010 and US$ 200,000 annually to local level, earmarked for spending on rural development.

The total investment value in the mining sector in 5 years has been US$ 2,545.3 million, which is a five-fold increase compared to the last five years (2001-2005). Currently, there are 154 domestic and foreign companies operating mining sector, operating 269 projects, 49 of which are at the exploration stage and 220 projects are under survey process. Some processing factories have also been established, e.g. the Kali Salt Factory established in Thongmung Village, Saythany District, Vientiane Capital. The factory has a capacity of 50,000 tones per annum and will be extended to 1 million tones per annum in the future. A similar factory is under construction in Thakek District, Khammouane Province. Besides, a steel factory is being set up in Vientiane Province.

Geology: The most important activity in this sector is to create geo-mining and mineral maps, since minerals can be identified best with larger and detailed maps. Mining and mineral maps with a ratio of 1:1,000,000 have now been drawn up for every province. Next, maps with a ratio 1:200,000 have been completed for 54.86% of Laos' total geographic area, and maps having a larger ratio of 1:50,000 have been completed for Sepon, Sanakharm, and along the Mekong River Bank in the Northern provinces and target areas for exploration.

3. Manufacturing

The manufacturing sector experienced a growth of 9.4% per year during 2006-2010. Manufacturing is a relatively low investment sector, having a high job opportunity when compared to other industrial sectors. Some of the main sectors in manufacturing have had a steady growth, such as garments and textiles, wood processing and food processing. The total number of manufacturing enterprises is 24,331, accounted for 19.2% of total number of enterprises (source: Economic Census, 2006).

Textile and Garment:

This is one of the sectors, which has experienced positive growth rate, thereby generating employment opportunities and incomes for the communities. Currently, there are 463 garment factories in the country. Of which, 39 are big factories, 18 are medium sized factories and 406 are small sized factories. Besides, there are some related factories including five laundry factories, 12 sew logos factories, 10 print logos factories, and three produce cartons factories. The total investment of the private sector in textiles and garments during 2006-2009 was US$ 15.715 million, an increase of 84.9% compared to the previous five years (2001-2005). There are a number of pressing issues in the textiles and garments sector, needing address: lack of sufficient funds, lack of connection in production, discontinuous production, high transportation costs, and production tax. Handicraft sector: In the previous years, handicraft product has been gradually developed in the sense of a decorative design and skills. Because of the product design the handicraft market is expanded both in the domestic and the global. In addition, this product has been received the award from the handicraft competition in the region. Currently, there is an establishment of handicraft business unit both in an individual and join together, especially the rural and remote areas. The important role of this sector is to create jobs and generate income to people as well as contributing for poverty reduction which is the party and government's policies. Additionally, the handicraft group was established due to the government promotion policy.

Presently, the domestic and foreign investment in the handicraft sector is around 40 units, and able to increase sell around 7-8% per year. In addition, there are 18 promoted handicraft businesses that have found.

Construction Materials:

This sector has experienced rapid growth resulting from market demand. Cement production can now supply 80% of the country's demand. The production is of international standards and is widely recognised and acceptable in domestic market. Investments in this sector trends to increase. Presently, there are six cement factories (there were only two in the last five-year plan period, namely, the two factories at Vang Vieng). The largest factory now is in Khammuane Province. Cement production has reached 1.2 million tonnes per year. The planed target was to produce 1.3 million tonnes by 2010 which increased 44% per year). Besides, there are factories that can supply construction materials to meet domestic demand to an extent. The factories including 24 steel factories which produce still bar and processing steel, 10 title factories and 308 concrete factories.

Food Processing and Beverage:

Production of beer, other alcoholic beverages, soft drinks and cigarettes has experienced a steady growth; it now fully meets the domestic demand as well as exports a part of the produce. During 2006-2009, beer production achieved 5,180,179 hectolitres, an average annual increase of 14%. A second beer factory in Champassack Province, a Tiger Beer factory, and Savannaket beer were constructed, and are in operation. The Economic Census of 2006 suggests that the food processing sector had 15,804 business units in that year, of which 28 units were large factories, employing more than 100 workers. Another 171 units employed 10-99 workers (classified as medium-sized units). The rest 15,625 units were small, employing less than 10 workers per unit.

This sector has the potential to grow, since Lao PDR has plenty of good quality soil to support many crops and livestock. However, food processing is still nascent, as most farmers are not oriented towards producing for the market. In addition, there are difficulties related to non-availability of raw materials in some seasons, as the transport system is not adequately equipped to transport raw material over long distances. There are also market-oriented issues: many farmers find it profitable to sell their products along the border, as the price is higher there compared to what the local food-processing industry pays. Therefore, in order to compete in the international export market, this sector must improve both product quality and standards.

In sum, the manufacturing sector has the potential to grow and supply adequate quantities of cement, steel bar/processed steel, natural fertilizer, processed food, beverages, etc. to the society. Small and medium size enterprises (SMEs) have contributed appreciably to the manufacturing sector because of an increase in business activities in manufacturing: 24,331 business units accounting for 19.2% of all businesses.

SERVICES SECTOR

The services sector has grown at a rate slower than the industry sector; its annual growth rate is estimated at 8.4% during 2006-2010. Services, is one important sector for socioeconomic development. During this period (average for 2006-2010), the contribution of the services sector was 37.2% to the GDP. Its major components are wholesale and retail trade and repairing business, constituting 51%; public service 17.3%; and transport, warehousing, post and telecommunication 12.5%.The rest its constituents are financial services, rental services and public services, including social and private services, hotels and restaurants, and others.

1). Internal trade

During 2006-2010, the trade sector substantially focused on local markets development, and a number of measures have been taken up to promote the movement of the goods across the country to ensure their supply to all in the society, in both urban and rural areas to help building the foundations of a market economy. Infrastructure for trade facilities such as a market system, (including cross-border markets), cross-border trade, shopping malls, supply systems (wholesale and retail), shops, warehousing system, vehicle parking, and boat landing spots have all improved. The quality of services too has continuously been improved; e.g. the enterprise registration process has been simplified, by shortening miscellaneous processes to facilitate businesspersons. In order to enhance participation and to be more active of the private sector for strengthening the services, trade and product circulation have been improved within the country. Trade exhibitions are arranged, and agricultural product distribution systems in the rural areas have been established.

Structure of service sector 2006-2010
Source: Department of Statistics, Ministry of Planning and Investment.

In all, domestic market has been widely opened and developed step by step. Product circulation has been gradually increased. From 2006-2010, the total value of product circulation was 29,395 billion Kip, which has annually increased 11%. Trade infrastructure has been widely expanded. Up to the present, there are 628 markets ranging from urban to rural. Of which 73 are big sized markets, 156 are medium sized markets and 429 are small sized markets. Besides, there are establishments of shopping malls, supermarkets, and night-markets in four major provinces include Vientiane Capital, Luangprabang, Savannakhet and Champasack. The construction of markets and shopping malls mostly funded by the private (both domestic and foreign) investors and managed in different forms such as concession under a certain period assigned by the government and the provincial authorities according to the regulations. In short, the markets in urban are largely extended which result in the ability to distribute products into rural and remote areas. Besides, currently there are 17 international checkpoints, 43 domestic checkpoints, and 63 border-trade are between the people who live in different parts of the country. At the end of 2009, the number of enterprises, business units, and entrepreneurs are totally 122,182 who are registered and received approval to regularly operate their business activities. This increase has also raised the value added in trade; as a result, the average annual growth in trade is estimated at 7.6% between 2006 and 2010, contributing about 51% to the value added in services.

2). Communication, transport, post and telecommunication:

a. Communication and transport During 2006-2010, public works and transport focused on implementing 25 projects to support for the priority 11 programmes and 111 projects, especially meant for the Eighth Master Plan on Communication and Transport. There are two focal projects: (1) Construct/improve communication, transport and networking between sub-regions and regions; and (2) Construct/improve communication, transport and networking within the country. Currently, the transportation system consists of four types:

(1) Mechanised road transport with the length of 33,768km, handling 80% of the total transport volume during 2006-2008 – goods transport increased by 5-8%, and passenger transport by 8-10% annually. This mode of transport has enabled supplying goods and passenger transport to all districts throughout the country.

(2) Water transport with the length of more than 300 km, accounting for18% of the total transport volume.

(3) In the air transport sector, there are 11 airports that handle 2% of the total transport volume.

(4) Transport by train.

The road-bridge construction sector shows a better performance than others. The road network has increased by 17% during the five years (2006-2009), from 33,803 Km to 39,568 Km. On average, it increased 4.6% annually or about 1,824 Km each year. Paved roads increased from 4,582 Km to 4,882 Km, or about 7% annually. Bridge across Mekong River (Savannakhet – Moukdahan), road no.1 in Vientiane Capital, road no. R3 (Bortan-Houisay), improvement of road no. 9 (Sevannakhet-Seno), road no. 12 (Thakack-Gnommalard) have been completed. Bridge across Mekong River (Thakack-Nakonpranom) was 40% completed, road no. 2E (Meungkoua-Taijang) was 31% compelted, road no. 14A was under construction. Moreover, rail way station (Dongphousy-Thanalang) with length of 3 km has been completed. ADB project for small city development has been completed for 12 cities, and water supply project in northern and central parts has been completed for 69%.

Despite the vast improvement and construction in the road systems, the demand for road development is yet very high since only a small proportion of the roads are paved. Most roads are constructed from natural rocks and earth, especially the provincial, district and rural roads. These roads are risky for travel in the rainy season. Also, some roads connecting provinces and districts too are not operational throughout the year. The technical standards of a majority of the national roads that fall within sub-regions and remote regions are low compared to the quality of the national roads in neighbouring countries. This impairs benefits to accrue to the country, which could otherwise be reaped by providing transit transport services. Basic techniques, material, equipment, and even transport vehicles are not yet competitive here compared to those in the neighbouring countries. As a result, coordination between domestic transportation system and international systems is weak. In sum, the basic infrastructure for communication and transport, as well as relevant services, are still insufficient in both quantity and quality.

The transport service in 2006-2009 has accomplished moving 111.9 million tonnes of cargo, 1% below the plan target. Passenger transport was 210 million persons, lagging behind the target by two percent.

b). Posts and telecommunication The post and telecommunication network has grown rapidly, and improved. The postal and telecommunication service has been growing, and is now able to provide services within the country and overseas, such as domestic and international money order, EMS/Fedex service within the country and overseas, domestic and overseas mailing, and collection of domestic and overseas stamps. Public post boxes are gradually reaching rural areas.

There are 119 post offices throughout the country. There are108 smaller post offices, mainly in the districts. One office has been added during the plan period. In 2009-2010, it is estimated that there will be 3 additional offices set up in the districts, adding up to 117 offices in the districts. Optical-fibre cables have been laid across 11,500 Km. There are 99 telecommunication centres at present, 38 government enterprises, 58 Lao corporations, two centres of Star-Telecom, and one centre of Milicom Lao.

All the telecommunication centres combined can provide 3.6 million connections. Of these,

149.3 thousand are for landlines (99.4 thousand have already been subscribed, a 2.7% increase over the previous year); 3.39 million are for mobile phones (2.59 million have already been subscribed, a 53% increase); and 50 thousand Vin-phone (wireless landlines) (29.57 thousand are subscribed, a 5% increase). The 2009-2010Plan entails encouraging firms to expand more telecommunication services to rural areas, providing high quality services, and expand service from cities to villages to cover 80%.

In 2009-2010, additional optical-fibre cables will be installed to cover a total length of 13.2 thousand Km, a 15% increase over the previous year. Thus, 90% of the provinces and 80% of districts can be reached via telephones. The establishment of the new Base Transceiver Station (BTS) has enabled 2,000 receiving stations. By end-2009-2010, it is forecasted that three million connections will be subscribed, an increase of 10% over the previous year. This is achieving 48 telephone connections/100 persons. According to the projection for 2009-2010, revenue income from postal service will amount to 40.11 billion Kip, an increase by 2% over the previous year. This will contribute 4.4 billion Kip to the budget, an increase by 2% over the previous year, and will contribute to the total revenue from the post and telecommunication sector at 2,127 billion Kip, exceeding the planned target by 32%. The sector will be able to contribute 600 billion Kip to the state budget, an increase of 7% over the previous year.

Service infrastructure has expanded and improved regularly. Roads, electricity network, irrigation systems, airports and others, directly and indirectly support production, transport, trade and investment, improving people's life, national stability, and peace. Land and air transportation have expanded and synchronised within the region for supporting tourism and the telecommunication network.

In conclusion, communication and transport, warehousing, and post and telecommunication play an important role and generating revenues and critically support other sectors to grow. On average, the sector's value added has increased by 7.8% per year. Its contribution to the GDP is about 4.6%.

3). Tourism

Tourism is an important sector, which creates multiple benefits and generates income for the ethnic people as well, in both cities and rural areas. It has a direct and indirect association with other economic sectors. Of recent, tourism in Lao PDR has had a rapid growth as the tourist arrival data suggest. In 2009, tourist arrivals were 2,008,363; an increase by 15.55% compared to 2008.It is estimated that this will further increase to 2,216,986 in 2010 (i.e. an approximate increase of 10.39%). Through the period 2006-2010 (combined), the number of tourists coming to Lao PDR was 8.79 million, or 1.76 million per year. The average annual increase was 15.8%. This generated US$ 258.04 million in revenue (equivalent to 5.19% of the GDP, which is a 16.8% annual increase in revenue). In the Sixth Five-year Plan period compared to that in the Fifth tourist arrival in Lao PDR increased 44.5% and revenue generated from the tourism sector was doubled.

Tourist arrivals to regions and provinces: During 2006-2008, the largest number of tourists came to the central region, i.e. 62.4% of the total tourist arrivals. This region experienced an annual increase of 22.7%. The northern region received the next largest tourist arrival, having a share of 28.2%. This region experienced an annual increase of 37.5%. In the southern region, the total tourist arrival was the least, having a share of only 9.4%. This region also experienced an annual increase of 31.9% in tourist arrivals during 20062008.The province receiving the largest number of tourists is Vientiane Capital, 28.7% of total tourists in the country, which is 46.1% of all tourists to the central region. This is because Vientiane Capital is where tourists first arrive—it being the centre for transport and communication—before travelling to other provinces. The second largest proportion of tourist arrivals is in Savannakhet province (15.5% of all tourists, and 24.9% of tourists to the central region). Tourists can now travel to Savannakhet with relative ease, as the second Friendship Bridge has been built between Savannakhet and Moukdahan (in Thailand). The third largest proportion of tourists goes to Luang Prabang Province; about 11.3% of all tourists, and 40% of tourists to the northern region (data pertain to 2008).This is because Luang Prabang is a famous world heritage city, and is also an important eco- and cultural tourism attraction. In term of revenue generation from tourism, the largest amounts emerged from the central region: 62.39% of the total revenue generation in the tourism sector, equivalent to US$ 160,653,188. The increase in revenues from tourism in this region was about 15% through 2006-2010.The northern region generated about 28.2% of the total revenue from tourism, equivalent to about US$ 72,609,457.

The annual increase in revenues from tourism in this region was about 22.5% through 2006-2010.The south generated about 9.42% of the total revenue from tourism, equivalent to US$ 24,523,113 million. The annual increase in revenues from tourism in this region was about 19.75% through 2006-2010. Seen provincial-wise, Vientiane Capital generated the largest revenue, contributing about 28.7% of the total and rising annually by about 8%. Next was Savannakhet, contributing about 15.53% of the total and rising annually by about 27%. Third was Luang Prabang, contributing about 11.26% of the total and rising annually by 24.15%.

The total number of hotels and guesthouses was 1,385 in 2008. This was an increase of about 4.1% over 2007. In this, the number of hotels was 265, increasing 25.6% over the previous year. The number of guesthouses was 1,120, staying unchanged over 2007. In 2009, the number of hotels and guesthouses was 1,484, an increase of7.2% over 2008. In this, hotels were 357, an increase of 34.7% over 2008. Guesthouses were 1,127, an increase of 0.6% over 2008. In 2010, the number of hotels was 383, the number of guesthouses and resorts was 1,379, and the number of restaurants was 1389. On average through 2006-2010, the number of hotel increased by 21% annually, and guesthouses by 5%.

Hotels were largely concentrated in Vientiane Capital; they being 43% of the total. Next are Champassack, with 13.2% of the hotels, and then Luang Prabang with 11.7% of the hotels in 2008. Guesthouse and resorts were also the most in the capital; at 16.5% of the total. They were 16% in Vientiane Province and 14.4% in Luang Prabang in 2008.

There were a total of 742 restaurants in 2008, which increased to 1,148 in 2009, an increase by55%. They were mainly located in the northern region (45.3%), followed by the central region (44.5%), and then the southern region (10.2%). Vientiane Province had the largest number of restaurants at 16.4%, followed by Borikhamxay province at 13.5%, and Oudomxay 11.6%. Vientiane Capital had only 9.3% of total number of restaurants.

There were 164 entertainment centres in 2008, which was an increase by 20% over 2005, and 7.2% over 2007. The central region has the highest number of entertainment centres: they being 70% of the total. The northern region comes next (17.1%), and then the southern region (12.8%). Vientiane Capital had the highest number of the entertainment centres at56% of the total, Champassack at 9.1%, and Huaphanh at 4.9%.

The number of tourist companies has increased double: they were 64 in 2005, 93 in 2006, 113 in 2007, 143 in 2008, and 169 in 2010. From 2005 to 2010, the number of tourists companies increased by 105 companies or double compared to 2005. Their branches have also risen: in 2005 there were 36 branches, in 2006 44 branches, in 2007 49 branches, and in 2008 65 branches. Between 2005 and 2008, the number of tourist companies' branches increased by 29, or 81%.

Currently there are 1,493 tourist attractions in the country, of which 849 are eco-tourism attractions, 435 cultural tourist attractions, and 209 historical tourist attractions. Of these, 626 tourist attractions have been fully developed and are opened for visitors. There are 141 places wherein surveys have been completed but the sites are yet not developed. Tourist attractions that are currently being surveyed are 230, and those not yet in any process, 496. These tourist attractions have been put on a high priority, for developing them according to the local conditions and the tourist needs. Collaboration between the National Tourist Authority (NTA) and provincial authorities is essential for achieving this goal.

The above achievements are a result of the high priority attached to implementing an open door and promotion policy on tourism. This is discussed below:

There are facilities established relating to the arrival and departure from the country; e.g. the new open international checkpoint at Muengmom Village, Tonpeung District in Bokeo Province. There are currently 22 international checkpoints, of which 18 checkpoints issue tourist visas at arrival having 30-day validity. In addition, visa holders can apply for an extension in every province. This facility was earlier available only in Vientiane Capital.

Visa is waived for citizens of the ASEAN, and Japan, Russia and Mongolia. Additionally, it is now possible to obtain a three-month valid visa, if a person obtains it at a Lao Embassy abroad, with a proviso to extend it for another three months. At international checkpoints, a two-month valid visa can be granted with a proviso to extend it for another two months.

The government has initiated market advocacy and promotion campaigns, which include establishing and improving information centres related to tourism at the NTA and in all provinces. It has also created tourism websites, and additionally participated in international tourism expos regularly, e.g. ITB in Berlin, Germany, TTM in Bangkok, Thailand, CITM in Shanghai, China, Trade and Tourism Expo in Nanjing, China, ASEAN Tourism Festival in Singapore, JATA in Japan, and ITE in Ho Chi Minh City, Vietnam. Lao PDR was a host country for the World Ecotourism Conference in Vientiane Capital in 2008-2009.

The government has coordinated and collaborated with culture-related sectors and local authorities to organise events and traditional festivals for promoting tourism in the country. This includes international stages, such as the Wat Phu festival in Champassack; Kottabong Stupa Festival in Khammuane; Elephant Festival in Xayaboury; Ing Hang Stupa Festival in Savannakhet; Tai Dam Ethnic Group Festival in Luangnamtha; Tuang Ethnic Group Festival in Oudomxay; and Cotton Flower Festival in Bokeo.

The business sector is also an important component in the development of tourism, e.g. improvement in the quality of services. This helps attract high-income tourists, and prolong the length of tourist stay in the country. The top 10 countries sending high-spending tourists to Lao PDR are Thailand, Vietnam, China, the United States of America, France, Britain, Japan, Australia, Germany and Canada.

REGIONAL AND INTERNATIONAL ECONOMIC INTEGRATION

Integration of the Lao economy at the regional and international levels, by implementing open-door economic policies on an independent and mutually beneficial basis, has progressively increased economic and trade co-operation and trade negotiations at the bilateral, regional, sub-regional and multilateral levels. Multilateral trade cooperation, economic cooperation with ASEAN and the Asia region, and cooperation with ASEAN's dialogue partners and APTA have been highly successful; some examples:

Multi-lateral trade cooperation: Despite that Lao PDR has yet to become a member of WTO (though it was expected in the 6th NSEDP), negotiations for entry into it have so far been successful, albeit gradually. 700 questions raised by the WTO have been answered, and meetings with operational units for 'WTO Entrance' have been organised on five occasions. Next, field trips were conducted to China and Vietnam to prepare for WTO entrance. Preparations for WTO entrance have also entranced the capacities in many sectors: e.g. improvements in laws and regulations–Law on Value Added Tax, Law on Enterprise, Law on Intellectual Property, Law on Standards, Law on Forestry, Decree on Implementation of Tax Law, Law on Livestock and Veterinary, Law on Plant Protection, Law on Investment Promotion, National Policy on Food Safety, Decree on Procedures of Import Approval, Law on Fisheries, Provision on Fisheries, Presidential Provision on Collection of Fees and Service Fees, and Decree on Safety of Food.

Economic cooperation with ASEAN and the region: Lao PDR has signed the ATIGA, and an agreement with ACIA is under the process, both being pre-conditions for joining AFTA. They will require to be ratified by the National Assembly some time soon. Agreement has been made with the ASEAN Service Trade Agreement under ASEAN Agreement on Services for seven categories of services, and the eighth is being negotiated.

Cooperation on the scope of ASEAN and its dialogue partners: For furthering free trade, ASEAN-China negotiation was recently completed; it came into force from Jan 1, 2010 (between ASEAN+6 and China). An Agreement of Economic Cooperation between ASEAN and Japan was made earlier, and its implementation began from December 1, 2008, wherein predefined import-

For additional analytical, business and investment opportunities information, please contact Global Investment & Business Center, USA at (703) 370-8082. Fax: (703) 370-8083. E-mail: ibpusa3@gmail.com Global Business and Investment Info Databank - www.ibpus.com

export proforma are being used. In 2009, an agreement on establishing free trade between the ASEAN, Australia and New Zealand was signed. Additionally, a 'Products of ASEAN and India' agreement was signed, an agreement on investment between ASEAN and the Republic of Korea was made, and a feasibility study was carried out on establishment of free trade area between ASEAN+3 (EAFTA) and ASEAN+6 (CEPEA). These agreements should form the basis for furthering economic cooperation with the ASEAN, and Asia in general.

Implementation of Asia-Pacific Trade Agreement (APTA): Lao PDR is a member of APTA and has continuously participated, performed and taken part in negotiations on trade agreements, tax reduction plans, trade and service facilitation, and so on, in the Asia-Pacific region.

Bilateral Trade cooperation: This has expanded, particularly with countries nearby; e.g. Lao-Vietnam trade relations, Lao-China trade relations, and Lao-Thailand trade relations. As of now, Lao PDR has signed bilateral agreements relating to trade and economy with 18 countries, namely, Bulgaria, Thailand, Myanmar, North Korea, China, Vietnam, Cambodia, Malaysia, India, Russia, Belarus, Argentina, USA, Turkey and Kuwait.

In short, efforts to negotiate with other countries for finding support for Lao PDR to join the WTO, and also expand openness in the economy, have made significant progress. In the last five years, cooperation within the ASEAN has been fairly successful. Economic cooperation with ASEAN has been successfully achieved, as suggested in the above-mentioned negotiations and agreements. In addition, Lao PDR has jointly signed an agreement on the ASEAN-Korea economic cooperation and signed seven agreements related to ASEAN and ASEAN-China Economic Cooperation. These agreements are to gradually enhance cooperation between the ASEAN and its negotiation partner countries, to achieve the goal of establishing ASEAN Economic Association, and thus have collective markets in the future. For implementing APTA, Lao PDR has reduced import tariff on 1,803 items (within the scope of APTA), and due to these, other countries have shown their support to expand free trade within the framework of APTA.

Opening for the international trade: Trade cooperation has enhanced, creating new markets and enhancing market access in different regions. Export and import volumes and values thereof, too have increased and the spectrum widened during 2006-2010 reached 83%, up from 65% in 2005. However, the trade proportion (export plus import as a ratio of GDP) in Lao PDR is still low compared to other ASEAN members, except Myanmar (see Table 7).

Inter-Country Comparison on Opened Trade or Integration 2006-2008

Countries	Opened Trade Rate (Export plus import as a ratio of GDP)
Lao PDR	83.2
Vietnam	159.1
Cambodia	105.6
Thailand	151.1
Philippines	85.1
Hong Kong	406.5
Malaysia	205.9
Singapore	443.2

Myanmar	52.8

Source: Department of Statistics, Ministry of Planning and Investment and WTO

Export markets and structure: In 2010, the total value of export was US$1,789 million and import was US$1,670 million. Of which exporting minerals covered 58% and exporting energy covered 16% of total export. In 2008, Lao PDR had traded with more than 90 countries. The (import plus export) volume was US$ 2,495 million, or equivalent to 47.28% of the GDP. Lao PDR exported products to over 50 countries within the region and outside, totalling US$1091.91 million, or equivalent to 20.69% of the GDP. The main export markets were, Thailand accounting for 59.60% of the total exports (or equivalent to US$650.78 million), Vietnam 13.37%, Australia 6.19%, and China 1.85% (for details, see Table 8 below).

Export Market Structure with Main Trade Partners, Year 2008

No.	Countries	Value	Percentage
		(Million US$)	(%)
1	Thailand	650.78	59.60
2	Vietnam	145.99	13.37
3	Australia	67.59	6.19
4	China	20.20	1.85
5	Switzerland	10.05	0.92
6	Poland	9.61	0.88
7	Republic of Korea	9.50	0.87
8	United States of America	4.04	0.37
9	Germany	5.13	0.47
10	Netherland	4.37	0.40
11	Others	164.66	15.08
Total		1,091.91	100.00

Source: Calculation of Department of Statistics based on data from Tax Department, Ministry of Finance and Bank of Lao PDR

In summary, the structure of export market in the last 5 years including Asia market accounted for 67.54%, EU accounted for 20.40%, Oceania (Australia) 10%, and South America 2.02%. In this, ASEAN (10 countries) covered 53.55%, ASEAN+ 3 covered 63.03%. In Asia market, 10 ASEAN countries shared 79.29% of Asia market. Of which, Thailand was 36.09%, Vietnam was 11.37%, Malaysia 5.97% compared with ASEAN+3, China held 6.03%, Japan 1.07%, and South Korea 9.93%. Inside EU market, England covered 5.34%, France 2.3%, and Germany 3.34%. For the structure of import market during the last 5 year was from Asia countries 96%, EU 2.3%, and the rest was from North America (Canada and America) and Oceania (New Zealand and Australia). For Asia market, Lao PDR imported from 10 ASEAN countries about 81.34%. In this, Thailand had highest proportion 76.26%, followed by Vietnam 12.25%, China 8.3%, Japan 2.6%, South

Korea 1.88% and Malaysia 0.6%. In EU market, Germany covered 1.04%, France 0.7%, and other countries.

INFRASTRUCTURE

During the implementation of the Sixth Five-year Plan (2006-2010), construction of infrastructure was brisk. Its average annual growth was 11.26%, contributing to 4.8% of the GDP, through direct and indirect effects, trade and others investments. The passenger and goods transport have increased, (agricultural) wood production raised, national security and stability demonstrated and seamless transportation round the year ensured. Land and air transportation network within the region is working better.

Mekong River bank erosion projects have been completed, such as the one in Tonpeung district, the one Hatsayfong district, and in some other areas. Water supply projects have been completed in Dongmakhai area. Currently, there are a number of on-going projects on small-scale urban development, Phase 1. Water supply and health services projects in the northern and central parts of Laos, as well as water supply improvement projects in Kaoliew and Chinaimo area have been taken up. Construction of Nam Mung 3 hydroelectric project (of 40 MW) was completed in 2005; and Nam Lik ½ hydroelectric project was also completed. Moreover, there are several Projects that are expected to be complete in 2011 are as follows: Nam Ngum 2, Sekamarn 3, Nam Ngum 5, and Tad Salan.

In 2012, several more projects will be complete, such as the expansion of Theun-HinBoon and Nam Song Dam. Electricity transmission line projects in the north, the central-south region transmission lines, medium electricity transmission lines to seven districts in Oudomxay Province were fully complete, and the one to Nalae District. Furthermore, some irrigation projects were completed, such as the project in Nam Tin, Xayaboury Province, and DongPhoSi, Vientiane Capital. In addition, irrigation improvement projects in the natural disaster-hit areas have been taken up, in addition to improving a few obsolete irrigation systems.

National investment in tourism facilities, especially those related to accommodation (hotels and guesthouses) has increased, and during 2006-2010, the investment (only FDI) in tourism was valued at US$ 166 million [approximately US$ 33 million was invested into only construction for accommodation (hotels and restaurants)]. In addition, investments into various tourism facilitating sectors, particularly telecommunication and transportation infrastructure, have been made, valued at US$ 34.45 million in 2008 and US$ 83.77 million in 2009 which was doubled of 2008.

The government's investment into tourism has mainly focussed on improving interprovincial roads, water transport and air transport, inducting a number of new and high-technology vehicles into the transportation system, increasing flights, and expanding bus services and similar services. Investment into these sectors during 2006-2010 has had a total value of 2,060 billion Kip, which is an increase of 7.3% comparing to 2001-2005.Of this, 272 billion Kip came from domestic funding (increased 12%), and 1,788 billion Kip from international funding (increased 20%).

Luangnamtha Airport has been renovated and improved. R3 Road has been constructed and this is the road-link to other countries in that region. Additionally, Road No 12 has also been constructed. Lao-Thai Friendship Bridge 2 (connecting Savannakhet to Moukdahan in Thailand) and other roads have also been officially opened. Further, infrastructure at tourist sites has been improved, such as at Konglor Cave and Tad Kuang Xi Waterfall. Work on facilities such as public toilets, lookout sites, parking lots, and the like has been initiated on many other sites. Electricity and water supply has also been improved.

The basic infrastructure development has created opportunities to ethnic people to be able to access production, education, health care services, and markets more and more. Industry and commerce sector, investment (private and public), construction of basic infrastructures and rural electricity have been developed. The increased number of (both domestic and foreign) tourists leading to repairing, transportation, warehouse, telecommunication, hotel, restaurant and other services have expanded.

REGIONAL DEVELOPMENT

For assessing regional development, changes in the structures of three main sectors have been viewed here: agriculture, industry and services, in addition to poverty. At the outset it needs statement that monitoring and evaluation mechanisms of programmes and projects are not yet in systematic. There is also lack of accurate statistics, Therefore, there are difficulties in evaluating, particularly with regards to each target; e.g. the budget, investment, and outcomes as well as effective of investment of priority projects under the 11 programmes and 111 projects in each region. However, the few assessments carried out the activities or projects implemented during 2006-2010.

[1]. Proportion to the national economy of the north, central and the south

In each region, the economy has grown in differentially. The level of development in the central region is higher than that in north and south, owing to enabling factors like better availability of natural and human resources, and superior infrastructure. The GDP of the central part constituted 70.7% of the country's GDP in the financial year 2006-2010, while that of the north constituted 15.3% and the south, only 14.1%. The north has a difficult geography: it has a lot of hills and sub-mountain terrain. It additionally lacks basic infrastructure. Here, agricultural production relies upon rainwater. However, the north also possesses some positive features: water resources to produce hydropower, mining and tourism potential.

[2]. The changes of economic structures in regions

The economic structural change in the north: Agriculture and forestry sector constitutes a high proportion of the economy but it trends to decline. While the proportion of industry and service sector have increased as compared to 2005. Despite that the northern region has the potential for economic development; industries there have not been developed. Presently there are a few dams, some small-scale mining, handicraft and family-food processing.

The economic structural change in the central part: In this region, the economic structural change in the same direction to the northern region. The share of the agricultural sector in the GDP has decreased, whereas that of industry and services sector have risen. The service sector has highest share in the GDP. However, the production in this part is still concentrated in the lowlands (along Mekong Rivers), and the services sector is mainly trade, transport and tourism (including border trade).

The economic structural change in the south: The southern part of Laos is located at an international economic triangle, and has a high development potential. The agricultural sector has the highest share in GDP (>50%), though it appears to be on the decrease.

In conclusion, the economic structures in the three parts are matched with the overall development trend to be the industrialization. It is also seen that small-scale/family production is much higher than large-scale production. However, the changes indicated that there are local

For additional analytical, business and investment opportunities information, please contact Global Investment & Business Center, USA at (703) 370-8082. Fax: (703) 370-8083. E-mail: ibpusa3@gmail.com Global Business and Investment Info Databank - www.ibpus.com

potentials. In terms of regional variation, GDP per capita in the central part for financial year 2009-2010 was about US$ 1,142, in the north was about US$771, and in the south it was about US$ 718. In 2009-2010, the average GDP per capita expected to increase compared to 2008-2009, GDP per capita in the central part will be about US$ 1,400; in the north will be about US$500; and in the south it was about US$ 783.

Table 9: Estimation of Economic Structure and GDP per Capita in Each Part from 2006-2010

	GDP Growth (%)	Economic Structure			GDP per Capita (USD)
		Agri. (%)	Industry (%)	Services (%)	
North:	8.45	55.63	21.20	23.07	771
Phongsay	6.72	53.44	25.77	20.78	720
Luangnamtha	7.81	69.74	14.52	15.73	668
Borkeo	7.65	49.04	19.07	31.92	1,004
Oudomxay	10.86	58.34	20.54	21.10	651
Luangpabang	9.36	47.00	18.00	35.00	821
Xayabouly	8.41	48.83	25.1	25.36	1,057
Houaphanh	8.97	65.6	14.14	20.24	397
Xiengkouang	7.78	53.08	32.46	14.43	852
Central:	9.94	40.67	34.03	22.81	1,142
Vientiane P.	8.69	48.55	39.54	11.91	751
Vientiane C.	11.85	19.64	44.67	35.55	2148
Borikhamxay	7.8	38.03	27.27	34.19	1,029
Khammouane	10.84	44.81	36.28	17.14	887
Savannakhet	10.5	52.33	22.4	25.27	897
South:	10.65	46.87	24.04	29.09	718
Champasack	9.76	45	26.3	28.7	1,097
Salavanh	10.14	56.86	18.41	24.73	710
Attapeu	12.28	36.01	36.36	27.6	654
Xekong	10.43	49.6	15.08	35.31	412

Source: Socio-economic plan 2006-2010, Department of Statistic, Ministry of Planning and Investment

[3]. The successful implementation of projects and activities

1. The north:

* In this region, the development has focused agriculture and rural development, urban development relates on building industrial and services bases, and social development, all aimed towards reducing poverty and economic differences between provinces and regions. More specifically, the focus has been on building infrastructure, as stated below:

* Build and maintain irrigation systems, roads, schools, hospitals etc., e.g. the irrigation system on Nam Seng, Nam Mao-Nam Naen.

* Completed construction of Road no. R3 (Boten-Huayxay); completed building and upgrading Nam Tha-Na Lae Highway; currently constructing Road no.2W (Ngeun District-Pakbang District), Road no.2E (Khwa District-Taichang District), Road no.1D (strategic road for national defence and security between Xiangkhuang-Bolikhamxay); and completed Mekong River bank erosion protection in Thonpeung District.

* Completed installing the electricity transmission line connecting Ngoi district-Vieng Kham district in Luang Prabang Province; Completed installing medium pressure transmission line for 7 districts (Xay, Nga, Hu, Pakbeng, Namor, La districts) in Oudomxay Province; and Namtha district-Namlea district in Luangnamtha Province. Completed construction of power stations in Xay District and Namor District; completed connecting the electricity high pressure transmission line of 115 KV from China to Namor District, Oudomxay Province. Completed restoration and maintenance of the infrastructure destroyed from flooding in 2008.

* Constructed and repaired irrigation system such as the irrigation system on Nam Seng, Nam Mao-Nam Naen, and others.

* Promoted dry season crops for commercial purposes, especially production of maize in Xayaboury increased from 9,500 tons in 2005 to 328,196 tons in 2010. The maize is also grown in Oudomxay, Bokeo, Huaphanh and Xiengkhuang provinces, aimed for export to Thailand, China and Vietnam. Moreover, private and foreign investors were promoted to plant industrial crops/trees especially, rubber trees.

* Promoted and develop natural, cultural tourism sites, for example take up community tourism projects, and organise festivals and events to attract tourists in well known places like Luang Prabang, Vang Vieng, Sing district and Xiengkhuang. Moreover, improved tourism infrastructure, up-grade tourism, services, and border trade.

* Improved education, and provide educational and other materials and equipment to Kumbans. romoted higher education: Fully complete establishing Soupanouvong University at Luang Prabang.

* Established a community health security fund for enabling people to access to health services.

*In addition to the development of infrastructure and urban development, the government has achieved some outstanding production in the north such as rice and vegetable commercial production, especially in Sayabury and Bokeo. Cattles feeding reached an outstanding achievement in Sayabury while big raising has shown a success in Huaphanh. Besides, there are also some industrial tree plantation include rubber tree, tea tree, sugarcane, especially in Phonsaly, Luangnamtha and Oudomxay. Some border-trade areas have been developed such as Lao-China border trade area in Luangnamtha, Lao-Thai border trade area in Bokeo and

Sayabury, and Lao-Vietnam border trade area in Huaphanh. The development in the north has been tapped in various sectors such as handicraft, fabric, silk and wood weavings. There is also a gold mining in Long District, Luangnamtha Province. The poverty has been reduced in the north according to Section 3.3.1 and Appendix 2. Sayabury Province has the lowest poverty rate compared to the poverty rate in Huaphanh Province which remains high.

2. The central part:

* Central region has advantage location for production and has a favourable infrastructure to connect with neighbors at both local and international levels. A large number of flat areas in the region provides an enabling condition for rice production for commercial and export, especially in Savannakhet. Cement manufacturing has widely expanded in Vientiane Province and Savannakhet Province; while two Industrial Parks have been established in Vientiane Capital including Industry and Commerce Park (at KM21) with the area of 110 ha and Vientiane Industrial Park (VIP). Infrastructure has improved in Khanthabury District (Savannakhet), Vientiane Capital and Pakse District; and industrial development zone has been established in Savannakhet.

* Government focused on build Vientiane Capital which included main construction activities as follows:

* For the preparation for the celebration of the 450 years of Vientiane Capital, the government has repaired roads, Thatluang Park, and Saysetha Park in the capital

* Build the Dongdok-Dongposy Road (450 Years of Vientiane Capital); repaired Road no.9 (Savannakhet-Seno), Road no.12 (Thakek-Yommalath); constructed road connecting Kasi District-Nan District; operated Vientiane-Nongkai Railway; completed construction of Mekong River Bridge connecting Savannakhet-Moukdahan; organised the opening ceremony for the Mekong bridge constructed from Khammuane to Nakonphanom (in Thailand); completed construction of road no. 1 Vientiane Capital. Opened an airport in Savannakhet Province; and carried on a construction of river bank erosion protection in Vientiane Capital and Anouvong Part.

* Completed construction of Nam Lik ½ dam and Namtheun 2 dam, which Namtheun 2 is currently under testing phase. Carried out a construction of Theun Hinboun dam in an extension phase, opened a cement factory in Vangvieng and another factory in Khammoune; opened sugar factory, constructed copper processing factory, tin processing factory in Savannakhet; installed electricity transmission lines in eight villages in Vientiane Capital (Ban Maknowdong, Dong Bong, Phathana, Phosay, Thadeau, Judson, Hoisa kang and Dongmakmo) and 12 focus areas in Phintadhai district.

* Completed SEA GAMES stadia and successfully hosted 25th SEA GAMES

*Additionally, complete construction project in the memory of (former) President Soupanouvong (21 March Public Park) in Khammuane province; increase/improve animal husbandry: cows, buffalos, pigs (in farms), chicken (in farms), goats, and fish (culture in nets and ponds). In services, tourism, education, public health, skill development and international cooperation (which has already been improved by the provincial authorities). The province that has lowest poverty rate is Vientiane Capital while the highest is Savannakhet and Bolikhamxay. However, on average the poverty rate in the central region stays below the national poverty line (see Appendix 2).

3. The southern part:

*Beside basic infrastructure development that mentioned in point 3.1.5 above, there still have some specific projects that focused on development of the southern part which are follows:

* Build and maintain irrigation systems, and promote irrigated rice, and crops such as cabbages and cardamom;

* Expand animal husbandry, like cows, buffalos, pigs, chickens, goats, and fish-culture. Continue to develop according to the Master Plan on integration of the economic triangle: road projects from ThaTeag district-BanBeng (fund from development projects for economic triangle), 15A Road Project, and Nam Se Don Bridge. Completed construction of Road no.14A (Pakse-Cambodia border); completed construction of a road connecting Sekong-Vietnam border; upgraded and renovated Pakse Airport; constructed and repaired irrigation; promoted people to grow rice and other vegetables like cabbages, bok choy, cardamom, and promoted animal husbandry like cattle, buffalos, pigs, chickens and others.

* Continue installing electricity transmission lines to connect six Lao-Thai border villages, Sukhumma district, and start connecting with power (completed four villages), 26 villages on the Lao-Cambodia border (Mounlapamok district, Champassack Province).

* Cooperate with different sectors to improve services and trade at border checkpoints, develop tourist attractions, continue focussing on educational development, and provide materials and equipments.

* Monitor and control outbreak of Avian Influenza

* Complete national sport events in Champassack Province; aim to improve skills development and other tasks

*As a result, the southern provinces has been developed in various sectors such as agriculture and industry as well as service which results in a decline of the poverty rate in Champasack, which has the lowest poverty rate in the southern region and in the nation wide, followed by the poverty rate in Attapeu Province which is below the National Poverty Level (see Appendix 2). The outstanding products are mostly of agriculture including coffee, beans, potatoes, tobacco and vegetables. Champasack ranked as the top producer of these commodities. Rubber tree plantation spreads over the southern region. Apart from this, there are some important urban developments in Pakse, Saysetha, Lanam and Saravan Districts, especially the development of trade and transport infrastructures. Some important districts for communication between the central region, the producers and markets include Samakkeexay and Thathome in Attapeu; Kongsedon in Saravan; Thatheng in Sekong; Paksong and Pathoumphone in Champasack. Therefore, the government has paid attention to develop these districts in terms of construction and renovation of the infrastructure. Additionally, food processing showed a good potential in this region such as processing of coffee, tea and wood; border trade market has been clearly developed alongside the development and promotion of the tourism sector (see details in Section 3.1.3)

SOCIAL DEVELOPMENT

* In apparel with economic development, part and government also focuses on cultural-social development in order to improve living standard of Lao people; Moreover, the government has make high effort to lift up social index to be closer to neighboring countries and region. In each year, the proportion of public investment in social sector has been increased. It is shown below:

RURAL DEVELOPMENT - POVERTY ERADICATION AND DEVELOPMENT

1. Rural development and poverty eradication

Lao PDR has a larger proportion of poor people (poverty rate) compared to most other countries in East Asia and Pacific. According to poverty estimates made in 2008 based on LECS4 Survey pertaining to 2007-2008, the poverty rate was 27.6%. This rate is quite high when compared with the rates prevailing in neighbouring countries like Vietnam, Cambodia, and Thailand. Poverty is higher in rural and remote areas; for example, in priority areas in the north and south. Inequality between the rich and the poor also poses a problem for poverty reduction.

According to the principles and goals laid down by the Party and the government relating to poverty eradication by 2010 and to achieve Millennium Development Goals (MDGs) by 2015 and to move the nation out from its least-developed country status by 2020, poverty reduction has become the main mission, and a priority. So far, the government has attached high priority to poverty reduction through accelerating rural development, e.g. through Ban and Kumban development in the whole country. Both financial and human capital, have been invested towards this end. Focal areas have been defined and special policy has been put for remote areas and former revolution areas.

Through the real implementation, all activities were in progress and achieved at satisfactory level, especially, focusing on building capacities of 2,760 local officials for Kumban development, and completing Kumban development plans in 133 Kumbans in 69 poor districts totalling 1,620 projects; of these 491 projects have been approved and funded 124 billion kip by the government. Additionally, village development fund has been established in 54 districts, 528 villages with the fund members of totally 34,856 families, which covered 46 poorest districts and 4 poor districts which amounted to 42,53 billion Kip to date, of which, 6,78 billion kip is a saving of the people, totalling 1,664 projects. Besides, the Agriculture Promotion Bank provided loans worth 1,248 billion Kip to farmers to invest in agriculture, animal husbandry and small business to 130,000 families located in 4,152 villages, in 140 districts. Nayobai Bank released total loans worth 805,55 billion Kip to 65,431 households located in 1,171 villages, 46 districts. The Poverty Reduction Fund (PRF) of 203 billion kip has been distributed between 2006 and 2010 to implement 1,673 projects in five target provinces, which covered 21 poor districts, 161 kumbans and 1,900 villages. Furthermore, there are sources from also villager's development fund and saving group of the Women's Union, Lao Youth Union, Trade Union, Lao Front for National Construction, Spring Water Fund, Rice Bank, Animal Bank, Credits from Farmer's Group, saving money and other sources of fund established in a number of villages that are supported and directed by Lao Front for National Construction, mass organization, international organization and other financial institutions.

The progress made in poverty eradication has so far been satisfactory. Examples: poverty in terms of consumption has been decreased; food consumption has improved; property ownership rights have risen, etc. Seen from LECS Surveys between 1992-1993 and 20072008, poverty trends have shown a decline at all levels: provincial, regional and country. In 1992-1993, the poverty rate was 46%, which declined to 39.1% in 1997-1998, 33.5% in 2002-2003, 27.6% in 2007-2008, 26% in 2009-2010. From these figures, we observed that from FY 1992-1993 to FY 1997-1998 the poverty rate decline significantly during this 10- year period. The poverty rate in the priority areas (the poorest districts) has been decreased more than other areas. Furthermore, roads, electricity, water supply, schools and hospitals in villages and Kumbans in the 47 priority (poor) districts have been developed and improved[2].

Northern part: In urban areas, the poverty rate decreased from 30.6% in 2002-2003 to 14.6% in 2007-2008, while in rural areas, from 39.1% to 36.5% in the same period. The lowest poverty rate is in Xayaboury Province; here it decreased from 25% in 2002-2003 to 15.7% in 2007-2008. Next comes Luang Prabang; here it decreased from 39.5% in 20022003 to 27.2% in 2007-2008. In Huaphanh, however, the poverty rate is still high at 50.5 % (data: 2007-08).

Central part: In urban areas, the poverty rate decreased from 20.1% in 2002-2003 to 22.2% in 2007-2008, while in rural areas, from 39.0% to 33.5% in the same period. Borikhamxay has a lowest poverty rate; here it decreased from 28.7% in 2002-2003 to 21.5 in 200708.The highest poverty rate is in Xiengkhuang Province at 42% (data: 2007-08).

Southern part: In urban areas, the poverty rate decreased from 12.8% in 2002-2003 to 11.3% in 2007-2008, while in rural areas, from 35.5% to 25.5% in the same period. The province having the lowest poverty rate is Champassack; here it decreased from 18.4% in 2002-03 to 10% in 2007-08. In contrast, in Sekong province the poverty rate is still high: 51.8% in 2007-08

However, poverty rate of Lao PDR is still high compared to other countries in the region. Poverty is still a problem in the northern part in contrast to the central and southern parts.[3] To an extent, poverty reduction depends upon the geography; for example, at the border areas shared with Vietnam the poverty rate is high at 54.5%, with Myanmar 28.2%, and with Cambodia 23.1%. At the same time, locations close to the Mekong River (area: fertile and connected) have a lower poverty rate at 16.1%. Next, though the poverty rate has decreased by 3.8% per year, the inequality coefficient (Gini) has increased from 32.6% to 35.4%, or risen by 1.7% per year (see details in Appendix 2). Even though the inequality coefficient in Lao PDR is relatively small compared to that in other countries in the region, the absolute need for a better income distribution and greater job creation in order to address poverty requires underscoring. There is also the problem of seasonal un/underemployment in the agricultural sector, which contributes to poverty and needs address.

Percentage of Poverty indicators in Poorest Provinces

	Provinces	2002/2003 (LECs II)	2007/2008 (LECs IV)
I	Northern Provinces		

[3] Lao PDR poverty from 2002/03-2007/08, Department of Statistics, MPI

1	Huaphanh	51.5	50.5
2	Phongsaly	50.8	46.0
3	Xiengkhuang	41.6	42.0
4	Oudomxay	45.1	33.7
5	Borkeo	21.1	32.6
6	Luangnamtha	22.8	30.5
7	Luang Prabang	39.5	27.2
8	Xayabouly	25.0	15.7
II	Central Provinces		
1	Khammuane	33.7	31.4

2	Savannakhet	43.1	28.5
3	Vientiane Province	19.0	28.0
4	Borikhamxay	28.7	21.5
5	Vientiane Capital	16.7	15.2
III	Southern Provinces		
1	Sekong	41.8	51.8
2	Saravane	54.3	36.3
3	Attapeu	44.0	24.6
4	Champasack	18.4	10.0

Positive and favourable factors in poverty reduction in the recent years:

- Strong and continuous economic growth: With shift from a centralised economy to a market economy, the GDP and GDP per capita have risen at a fairly brisk rate. We can see from the increasing of industrial and agriculture products. The number of large and small factories and other establishments has increased in all non-farm sectors. Agricultural production has expanded, and crops in which there has been a significant increase in production are maize, sugarcane, yellow beans, tea, coffee and (industrial and other) plantation-crops, among others. Several new establishments have come up and livestock too has increased in localised areas.[4]
- Consumption growth per capita: The consumption per capita of Lao people has increased steadily since 1992-1993. The growth rate in households having consumption levels above the poverty line is higher compared to the growth rate in households having consumption levels lower than the poverty line. Steady economic growth has thus ensured higher incomes to people and has become an important factor in poverty reduction. The household consumption per month at an average increased 14.8% per year. Consumption in urban area increased about 12% and in rural area 16.4%. Xayabouly Province has highest household consumption which increased 22.5% per year (or 2.8 times in 2007-2008 compared to 2002-2003). It was higher than the average household consumption of whole country.

- Poverty reduction at local levels: The number of projects and also the budget related to rural development and poverty reduction at the provincial level, particularly in priority areas, has grown significantly. Technical divisions and local authorities have approved funds for rural development and poverty reduction through Ban and Kumban development plans. There is a separate budget earmarked for Kumban development of about 300-350 billion Kip each year. In FY 2008-2009, this budget was 296 billion Kip to cover 440 projects, including 164 specific government projects costing 36 billion Kip.[5] It is due to these allocations and expenditures that the poverty rate has steadily declined.
- Rural development: This is a very important activity and the main priority of socioeconomic development at the regional level. The government has supported small-scale industries for creating employment opportunities and improving living conditions of the rural people. For this, it has attempted to improve transportation and communication systems, helped create conditions to enhance production for household consumption as well as markets, provided loans and market access to farmers, and facilitated drawing-in people into the market sphere. In FY 2007-2008, 51% of the villages in the country had markets. Land policies and permanent land-use rights have been implemented to give land to people to grow forests and tree plantations. In FY 2007-2008, 95% of the rural or agriculture-dependent households owned land. Each of these steps has helped reduce poverty rate in rural areas from 37.6% in FY 2002-03 to 31.7% FY 2007-08. Access to

basic infrastructure has also gradually improved; for example, the number of villages having primary schools increased by 79% between1997-98 and 2002-03, and by 89% between 2002-03 and 2007-08. For rural villages these numbers were 80% and 91%, respectively for the two periods. This is reflected in the literacy rate, which increased from 85% in FY2002-03 to 87% in FY2007-08.

In addition to education, access to public health has also increased, especially in remote areas. Data for FY 2007-08 suggests that 66% of the villages have medicine bags (or kits), compared to only 36% having them in FY 2002-03. Moreover, access to other infrastructure, particularly electricity, has increased compared to that in FY 2002-03; this has exceeded the target by about 50%. In sanitation, 78% of all households now have access to clean water.

Due to implementation of plans relating to stopping slash and burn cultivation and correspondingly providing people other jobs, there are now only 76 thousand hectares of land under rotated-shifting cultivation and 3.8 thousand hectares under shifting cultivation inFY2008-2009. Compared to five years back, shifting cultivation has decreased by about 33%. Local governance reforms have also been implemented. A large number of civil servants have been trained, to be in-charge in different organisations of the Party and the government. This achievement confirms with the accurate and appropriate directions of the Party concerning rural development.

- Shifting from agricultural production to industrialisation: A change in the economic structure in the three sectors—agriculture, industry and services—has resulted in change in the product proportions. The Report on Poverty Assessment in Lao PDR in 2006 stated that the annual industrial growth since 2000 was 12%.[6]It is evident that industrial growth would help raise people's income and reduce poverty.
- Developments in education and public health for poverty reduction: Since 2001, education and public health sectors have significantly improved. In 2005, investment in education amounted to 1,025.64 billion Kip, whose impact should be seen in the Sixth Plan (2006-2010). The Statistical Report of 2008suggests that the number teachers and students in public and private schools (kindergartens, primary schools, secondary schools and colleges) have been increased continuously since 1990, helping raise the enrolment rate. The government has also attached high priority to public health. In FY 2001-2005 the government approved investments for 15 projects in public health amounting to 96 billion Kip. Twelve of these related to development of public health and living conditions. The other three related to sustainable financial system, organisational improvement, and preparing regulations and law on public health.[7]The Statistical Report of 2008 indicates that the number of hospitals, primary health centres, nurses and health workers have risen in numbers each year, in turn helping decrease the general mortality rates, maternal mortality rates, and infant mortality rates. The standards of living have improved due to these factors.

- Infrastructure development for poverty reduction: The government has invested towards developing essential infrastructure, to provide services to all in the rural society. Some examples are of roads, communication systems and electricity. In 2008, there were 4,923 villages having roads accessible in two-seasons. Next, in every district about 60% of villages had telephone connections. 49% of the villages had access to electricity.[8]The energy and mining sectors have also directly (positively) impacted people dwelling in concession areas or development project sites; they have been allocated jobs, stable housing, and other income earning options. Economic infrastructure and culture/social activities have expanded as well, in locales like NTPC 2, Num Ngurm 2, Lane Xang Minerals Limited (at Sepon), and other projects.

- Population growth and poverty: The size of the population and its growth are strongly related to development. A majority of the poor people's households are large and rate of economic dependence in these households is higher, compared to others. Data from population censuses and LECS surveys suggest that the number of large households have decreased gradually since 1985. In the 47 priority districts, between 1992-1993 and 19971998, poverty increased at the same rate as the increase of large-sized households. Between 1997-1998 and 2002-2003 the poverty rate reduced, together with a decrease in large-sized households.[9] This trend is also seen in 2007-2008.[10] Having smaller households (i.e. a slow population growth) thus is critical to poverty reduction.

DEVELOPMENT OF PRIORITY AREAS

The government has attempted improving people's livelihoods in 6 priority areas for central management including Phalavek District, Ao District, Oam District, Longchang District, Sanluang Area and Nam Sian Area. The first four priority areas are in Vientiane Province while the last two are in Xiangkhouang Province. Within these priority areas, the government has constructed infrastructure to serve purposes of politics; national defence and security; promotion of commercial production. Furthermore, there is an improvement in rural development infrastructure which resulted in an establishment of production group and saving group in Champassack, Attapeu, Sekong, Huaphanh and Vientiane provinces. An amount equivalent to 81 billion Kip have been allocated, meant for village and Kumban establishment, roads, agricultural infrastructure, education, public health and job-creation, all aimed to improving people's living conditions. Effort has also been made to increase production on the one hand, and improve the organisational structure at local levels on the other, thereby ensuring better livelihoods for the people.

EDUCATION AND HUMAN RESOURCE DEVELOPMENT

The educational network and formal education system has continuously expanded in remote areas, especially the poor districts. Teachers possessing low qualifications have received training, particularly those who work in remote areas. Next, in order to produce more teachers, pedagogy institutes have increased in numbers. They train teachers to work specially in local areas where teachers are not available in sufficient numbers. The ultimate purpose is to gradually ensure high quality education.

Kindergartens and nurseries have expanded from 969 in 2005, to 1,284 in 2009, an increase by 315. An enrolment rate of children aged between 3-4 years was 14.6% (on average increased 3% annually, while the target on education for all or EFA target was 10.4% in 2009-2010) and achieved 36.7% enrolment rate of children at the age of 5 years (the target on education for all or EFA target was 27.4% in 2009-2010). The number of primary schools increased from 8,573 in 2005 to 8,968 in 2009-2010, increased by 395. Next, the enrolment rate at the primary school level has been increased from 84.2% in 2005 to 93% in 2009-2010 (the target on education for all or EFA target was 88.8% in 2009-2010). These data suggest that the government is working hard to provide equal opportunities in education for Lao citizens, both male and female, in urban and rural/remote areas, especially effort has been put into implementing the National Education Reform Strategy by increasing year of school from 5+3+3 to 5+4+3. Currently, there are 58,404 teachers in the country, increased by 34% compared to the figure in 2005. Additionally, the number of vocational schools and universities also increased in some area such as Souphanouvong University in Luang Prabang, Savannakhet University, University of Medical Science and Champasak University. At present, there are 154 technical schools in the country that have enrolled totally 122,026 students. The government has increased investment in education; its expenditure on this sector has risen from 11.63% of the budget in 2005, to 13.21% in 2009.

PUBLIC HEALTH

The government has continued to improve people's health care according to the direction 'health protection is central, though treatment is important'. Public health network has been expanded together with increasing number of medical staff in every year. They have worked hard to help people access quality health care services. The life expectancy of Lao people is 64.7 years (female: 67.7, male: 62.7). Try to make hard effort to help people access quality health facilities for maintaining them in good physical and mental health. Public health networks have continued to improve and expand in rural areas and in the remote hinterland. Trainings were provided to medical staff at all levels; currently the number of medical staff is 9,861 which increased by 2,897. The number of primary health centres has now increased to 813. Besides, some infrastructure has been completed: laboratories, hospitals, and primary health care centres; efforts have been made to build model health villages based on the 8 contents of basic health in the framework of 'village and Kumban development'; health practitioners and nurses have been provided training in theory and exposed to practice, to serve public as well as follow the code of conduct regarding treatment; vaccination for mothers and children has reached 71% of the plan target; and attention has been paid to health education and nutrition after the flooding.

Next, clean water supply has reached 78% population; 52% of the population uses hygienic latrines; 48% schools have latrines in their campuses; 1.6 million impregnated mosquito nets have been distributed to people living in malaria-risk areas; and community health funds have been expanded. Attention was paid to HIV/AIDS treatment and protection among target group of people, especially ensured that 80% of sex workers have access to the service and protection; which resulting in the rate of infection stayed below 1%. Additionally, about 92% of TB infected people received treatments. Furthermore, about 1.8% of the population (i.e. 19,211 families with 111,600 members, or 3.7% of the target population of three million) in 934 villages in 20 districts of 9 provinces are under the health monitor. It is now possible to detect and control outbreaks of Avian Influenza and H1N1 for 2 times. The monitoring and warning systems of infectious diseases have significantly improved.

SCIENCE AND TECHNOLOGY

The law on intellectual property, law on standards of fuel registration, national standards on construction materials and six standards of foods and agriculture products have been adopted. Plant experiment on agar-wood has been successful. E-governance has been completed 40% of installation. Next, 11 Community E-information Centres have been set up and a standard Lao Font for IT systems has also been developed. 20 intellectual property disputes have been resolved and fake products have been destroyed. The research on using the used oil (agr-oil) in diesel engines has been successful. In addition, 16 Winmax poles have been completed installing in provinces, it is expected that E-governance project will be completed installing and will be used by June, 2009. A National Science Park has been built in Borikhamxay Province (with cooperation between the Lao and Italian governments).

RESOURCES AND ENVIRONMENT

Attention has been paid on building up human resources to be responsible for macro management in national resources and environment. In order to ensure sustainable rapid economic development is going along with utilizing and managing natural resource effectively and efficiently; Accumulating management on water resources has been done in the countries members to Mekong River Commission in 1995 on Mekong River sustainable development. Through the implementation of certain strategic programs of Mekong international committee and upper Mekong region countries in FY 2009-2010. The aims are to use and development Mekong basin sustainably for beneficiary of people under Mekong sub-region.

Through the implementation of programs in four country members, some achievements has been seen clearly by cooperating with Mekong International Committee are as follows:

In Basin Development Program (BDP), we have completed research on basin's areas of Mekong River brunch in Lao PDR and have also completed compiling projects that related to water source development and they were classified in 9 priority projects at regional level and 40 priority projects in Lao PDR which specifically about water resources accumulating management.

For environmental program, we have been completed the report on water quality in Mekong basin and collecting data and recording about soil in surround Mekong sub-regoin areas. Moreover, we have been completed strengthening water resource accumulating management in 4 countries.

Water resource management centre, flooding recovery, and flood disaster management study have been done in member countries. Compiling geographic and hydrograph information and hydrograph experiment have been done.

Completed surveying on water ways in risk areas from Luangpaban to Parkse and Houisay to Laungpabang. Moreover, completed install signs along water ways and improving strategic management plan on fishery in Mekong basin and other basins. In addition, Fishing areas also have been surveyed.

Moreover, there still have main programs on studying hydroelectric power potentials in Mekong basin and defining scope of evaluation on environmental impact and guideline on constructing dam in Mekong River. Agreement on office location of Mekong international committee, Lao PDR and Cambodia are the host together. Beside the cooperation mentioned above, there still have more achievement as shown bellows:

Continue drafting and improving legal documents to manage environment and water sources by making huge basic infrastructure development model such as NTPC 2, and Sepon Gold Mining to strongly ensure both social and environmental aspects. Lao PDR has participated with worldwide on fighting against climate change by making national strategy on climate change to define directions and measurements on adaptation and releasing from climate change impacts in main sectors of national economic including agriculture, forestry, water sources, and public health. Moreover, it also includes stopping slash and burn cultivation, planting trees to cover 70% by 2020 and constructing warning system such as earthquake warning station and atmosphere station to ensure that our lives and properties are protected.

Continue improving forecast and hydrograph network to fortune whether to be used for social-economic development to be base for making warning system.

Lao PDR was host on holding conference for leaders of in Mekong sub-region countries in 2008. The conference was about economic cooperation among sub-region countries. The Vientiane operation plan was adopted. Continue implementing 9 sector cooperation programmes, and working on transportation across country contract. Pay attention on implementing main programmes on environmental protection. Additionally, we are responsible for coordinating of the country to implement 6 international protocols on environment which are Climate Change

Protocol in 1995 and Tokyo Protocol 2003, Stockholm Protocol in 2006 and Mekong Protocol in 1995

LABOUR AND SOCIAL WELFARE

1. Labour Amendments in the Labour Law have been completed; a decree on minimum wages has been promulgated– the minimum monthly wage has increased from 290,000Kip to 348,000Kip; a decree on establishing labour recruitment agencies has been completed; and the Labour and Social Welfare Minister's decree on import and employment of migrant workers has been amended. In apparel with legal documents, labour sector paid attention on developing basic infrastructure of skill-development and vocational cetre in each part.

At present, there are 153 skill-development (training) and vocational centres which have trained 79,128 labours. It exceeded target 15.14% and have arranged jobs for 556,661 people which over target about 2.23%. Of which, 4 out of 153 are under the authority of the Ministry of Labour and Social Welfare, 57 are under other government agencies, and 92 are private. The government has attended to improve the quality of these centres in each region. There are improvements in the training curricula, reflected in the production of 7 textbooks in mechanics, computer engineering, electrical engineering, car mechanics, electronic engineering, carpentry, garment making, and cooking. The labour productivity has improved, resulting from skills imparted to both semi-skilled to fully skilled workers. Currently, the courses offered range from 2 weeks to 3 years. Supply teaching-learning materials, provided internship courses and aligned to the emerging demand.

The government has implemented labour agreements related to payroll, working hours and a social welfare system established in 1,606 work places, covering 98,342 workers. It has also resolved 141 disputes between employers and workers from among 254 dispute cases, bringing a benefit of 1,684 million Kip to the workers.

2. Social welfare The government established Decree No. 70/PM, as an elaboration of Decree No. 178/PM on Public Social Welfare. Next, in the same context it integrated decrees 71/PM, 194/PM, and 145/PM into Decree 343/PM. Issued temporary regulation on public social welfare fund management; completed implementing national program on against human trafficking and sexual abuse on children decree no. 160/PM on approving and implementing of the program. Compensation system for civil servants has been improved from 5 compensations in decree no.178/PM to 8 compensations in decree no. 70/PM. Improve the contribution budget rate into public social welfare fund up to 16.5% of which the contribution budget of civil servants (employees) increased from 5% to 8% and the contribution budget of government (employer) was 8.5% of salary treasury. Treatment system of social welfare member has been improve by playing first and refund later. Now a day, labours have been protected and prevented from social welfare system which covers around 11.7% of total population in Lao PDR.

IMPORTANT SECTORS FOR INVESTMENTS

AGRICULTURE

At least 5 million hectares of Laos's total land area of 23,680,000 hectares are suitable for cultivation; however, just 17 percent of the land area (between 850,000 and 900,000 hectares) is, in fact, cultivated, less than 4 percent of the total area. Rice accounted for about 80 percent of cultivated land during the 1989- 90 growing season, including 422,000 hectares of lowland wet rice and 223,000 hectares of upland rice, clearly demonstrating that although there is interplanting of upland crops and fish are found in fields, irrigated rice agriculture remains basically a monoculture system despite government efforts to encourage crop diversification. Cultivated land area had increased by about 6 percent from 1975-77 but in 1987 only provided citizens with less than one-fourth of a hectare each, given a population of approximately 3.72 million in 1986. In addition to land under cultivation, about 800,000 hectares are used for pastureland or contain ponds for raising fish. Pastureland is rotated, and its use is not fixed over a long period of time.

In the early 1990s, agriculture remains the foundation of the economy. Although a slight downward trend in the sector's contribution to gross domestic product (GDP--see Glossary) was evident throughout the 1980s and early 1990s--from about 65 percent of GDP in 1980 to about 61 percent in 1989 and further decreasing to between 53 and 57 percent in 1991--a similar decrease in the percentage of the labor force working in that sector was not readily apparent. Some sources identified such a downward trend-- from 79 percent in 1970 to about 71 percent in 1991-- but both the LPDR's State Planning Commission and the World Bank reported that 80 percent of the labor force was employed in agriculture in 1986. Available evidence thus suggests that the percentage of the labor force employed in agriculture in fact remained relatively steady at about 80 percent throughout the 1970s and 1980s.

Agricultural production grew at an average annual rate of between 3 and 4 percent between 1980 and 1989, almost double its growth rate in the preceding decade, despite two years of drought-- in 1987 and 1988--when production actually declined. Paddy rice production declined again in 1991 and 1992 also because of drought. By 1990 the World Bank estimated that production was growing at an increasingly faster rate of 6.2 percent. Increased production, long one of the government's goals, is a result in part of greater use of improved agricultural inputs during the 1970s and 1980s. The area of land under irrigation had been expanding at a rate of 12 percent per annum since 1965, so that by the late 1980s, irrigated land constituted between 7 and 13 percent of total agricultural land. Although still a small percentage, any increase helps to facilitate a continued rise in agricultural productivity. Smallscale village irrigation projects rather than large-scale systems predominate. Use of fertilizers increased as well, at an average annual rate of 7.2 percent; given that commercial fertilizer use had been virtually nonexistent in the late 1970s, this, too, is an important, if small, achievement in the government's pursuit of increased productivity. In addition, the number of tractors in use nearly doubled during the decade, from 460 tractors in 1980 to 860 in 1989.

CROPS AND FARMING SYSTEMS

Most farmers employ one of two cultivation systems: either the wet-field paddy system, practiced primarily in the plains and valleys, or the swidden cultivation system, practiced primarily in the hills. These systems are not mutually exclusive, especially among the Lao Loum (see Glossary) or lowland Lao in areas remote from major river valleys. Swidden cultivation was practiced by approximately 1 million farmers in 1990, who grew mostly rice on about 40 percent of the total land area planted to rice.

Swidden agriculture is highly destructive to the forest environment, because it entails shifting from old to new plots of land to allow exhausted soil to rejuvenate, a process that is estimated to require at least four to six years. The extent of destruction, however, depends on the techniques used by the farmers and the overall demographic and environmental circumstances that relate to the length of the fallow period between farming cycles. Further, traditional agricultural practices allowed for forest regeneration and not the stripping of forest cover, which is a current commercial logging practice. Swidden fields are typically cultivated only for a year, and then allowed to lie fallow, although Kammu (alternate spellings include Khamu and Khmu) anthropologist Tayanin Damrong reports that at least through the 1970s some fields were planted two years in a row. An increasing population, encroachment on traditional swidden farming areas by other villages or ethnic groups, and gradual deterioration of the soil as a result of these pressures have led to increasingly frequent shortfalls in the harvests of midland swidden farmers.

The swidden farming process begins with clearing the selected fields in January or February, allowing the cut brush and trees to dry for a month, and then burning them. Rice or other crops are seeded by dibble shortly before the rains begin in June, and the growing crops must be weeded two or three times before the harvest in October. Swidden farming households are seldom able to harvest a rice surplus; in fact, the harvest usually falls one to six months short of families' annual rice requirements.

Erosion from deforestation is a direct and serious result of swidden agriculture. By the 1960s, however, swidden agriculture was not a threat to the forest environment. Moreover, swidden cultivation is less productive than wet-field cultivation because it requires between ten and fifty times as much land per capita--if one includes the fallow fields in the calculation--yet produces just 20 percent of the national rice harvest. Mature fallows or young forests have other benefits such as wild food gathering, animal habitat, and watershed protection. Government policy following the introduction of the New Economic Mechanism discourages the practice of swidden cultivation because it works against the goals of increased agricultural productivity and an improved forest environment. Also, the government wishes to control the population in close clusters. However, farmers have resisted the change, largely because wet-field cultivation often is not feasible in their areas and because no alternative method of subsistence has presented itself, especially given the lack of markets and infrastructure necessary for cash-cropping to be an attractive, or even a possible, venture. Further, government traders' defaults on purchase contracts with farmers in the late 1980s made farmers with better physical access to markets skeptical about cash-crop production. In general, despite government efforts to increase export-oriented agricultural production, the "rice monoculture" persisted in Laos through the early 1990s.

RICE

Rice is the main crop grown during the rainy season, and under usual conditions, rainfall is adequate for rice production. However, if rain ceases to fall for several weeks to a month at a critical time in the rice growing cycle, yields will be significantly affected. Upland rice varieties, although adapted to a lower moisture requirement, are also affected by intermittent rains because farmers have no means of storing water in their fields.

Rice accounted for over 80 percent of agricultural land and between 73 percent and 84 percent of total agricultural output of major crops throughout the 1980s, except in 1988 and into the early 1990s (see table 4, Appendix). Rice paddies also yield fish in irrigation ditches in *na* (lowland rice fields). Production of rice more than doubled between 1974 and 1986, from fewer than 700,000 tons to 1.4 million tons; however, drought in 1987 and 1988 cut annual yields by nearly one-third, to about 1 million tons, forcing the government to rely on food aid for its domestic requirements. In 1988 and 1989, some 140,000 tons of rice were donated or sold to Laos. With improved weather and the gradual decollectivization of agriculture--an important measure under the New Economic Mechanism--rice production surged by 40 percent in 1989. The increase in production reflected the importance of the agricultural sector to the economy and was largely responsible for the economic recovery following the droughts. In 1990 production continued to increase, although at a much slower rate, and the point of self-sufficiency in rice was reached: a record 1.5 million tons. Sufficiency at a national level, however, masks considerable regional differences. The southern Mekong provinces of Khammouan, Savannakhét, and Champasak regularly produce surpluses, as do Vientiane and Oudômxai provinces, but an inadequate transportation system often makes it easier for provinces with shortages to purchase rice from Thailand or Vietnam than to purchase it from other provinces.

According to some sources, the percentage of the labor force engaged in rice production declined gradually, by over 30 percent between 1986 and 1991, a trend encouraged by the government because it tended to increase export-oriented production. However, some feared this trend would threaten sustained self-sufficiency in food, another key goal of the government. Sustained selfsufficiency however, more likely depends on a continued increase in the use of agricultural inputs such as fertilizers and improved strains of rice, and on the implementation of extension and research services rather than on the actual number of workers involved in planting.

The overall increase in rice production throughout the 1980s was the result of higher productivity per hectare, rather than of an increase in the land area planted in rice; in fact, the area planted in rice decreased during the 1980s, from 732,000 hectares in 1980 to 657,000 hectares in 1990. Because farmers make little use of fertilizers or irrigation, however, most land still yielded only one annual crop in the early 1990s, despite government efforts to foster the use of double-crop rice.

OTHER CROPS

Only about 150,000 hectares were planted with major crops other than rice in 1990, an increase from approximately 80,000 hectares in 1980. Principal nonrice crops include cardamom--sometimes considered a forestry product--coffee, corn, cotton, fruit, mung beans, peanuts, soybeans, sugarcane, sweet potatoes, tobacco, and vegetables. The only crop produced for export in substantial quantities is coffee. Although the total area planted to these crops is small relative to the area planted to rice, it increased from 10 percent of total cropped area in 1980 to about 18 percent in 1990. Although the increase in part reflects the drop in rice production during the drought years, it also demonstrates some success in the government's push to diversify crops. Yields for all the major crops except coffee, vegetables, and cardamom--for which some figures are only available from 1986--increased gradually between 1980 and 1990, most notably corn (by 70 percent), fruit (by 65 percent), peanuts (by 28 percent), and mung beans (by 25 percent). Despite increasing agricultural output, however, Laos is still an importer of food, heavily dependent on food aid.

Statistics for agricultural production do not reflect either the nature of the subsistence agricultural economy or the importance of opium to the hill economy. Opium, legal in Laos and once even accepted as a tax payment, is a lucrative cash crop for the Lao Sung (see Glossary)--including the Hmong (see Glossary)--who have resisted government efforts to replace opium production with the production of other goods, for which the market is much less profitable. Opium production provides the funds necessary to the household when there is a rice deficiency, common among swidden farmers. Crop substitution programs, however, have had some effect, and to some extent tougher laws against drug trafficking and government cooperation on training programs have also contributed to reduced output. In 1994 Laos remained the third largest producer of illicit opium for the world market, according to United States drug enforcement officials. These officials estimate the potential yield of opium declined 47 percent--from 380 tons in 1989 when a memorandum of understanding on narcotics cooperation between the United States and Laos was signed--to an estimated 180 tons in 1993. The 22 percent decline in opium production in 1993 from 1992, however, was largely attributed to adverse weather conditions.

LIVESTOCK

The government encourages animal husbandry through programs for cattle breeding, veterinary services, cultivation of pasture crops, and improvement of fish, poultry, and pig stocks. Between 1976-78 and 1986-88, the stock of all farm animals increased greatly: cattle by 69 percent to 588,000 head; goats by 128 percent to 73,000; pigs by 103 percent to 1.5 million; horses by 59 percent to 42,000; buffaloes by 55 percent to 1 million; and chickens by 101 percent to 8 million.

For additional analytical, business and investment opportunities information, please contact Global Investment & Business Center, USA at (703) 370-8082. Fax: (703) 370-8083. E-mail: ibpusa3@gmail.com Global Business and Investment Info Databank - www.ibpus.com

Increases, however, would, have been significantly greater without diseases and a persistent shortage of animal feed. Disease is a serious problem: there is a significant annual mortality of chickens and pigs in most villages, and buffaloes are also frequently subject to epidemics.

FISHING

For many Laotians, freshwater fish are the principal source of protein; per capita consumption averages 5.1 kilograms annually. Fishpond culture had begun in the mid-1960s, and production--mainly carp raised in small home lots--grew an average 30 percent annually . The Mekong districts in the south have especially high potential for greater increases in fish production. The average annual catch was 20,000 tons, all of which was consumed domestically.

FORESTRY

In the 1950s, forests covered 70 percent of the land area; yet, by 1992, according to government estimates, forest coverage had decreased by nearly one-third, to just 47 percent of total land area. Despite the dwindling expanse, timber--including ironwood, mahogany, pine, redwood, and teak--and other forestry products-- benzoin (resin), charcoal, and sticklac--constitute a valuable supply of potential export goods. The forest has also been an important source of wild foods, herbal medicines, and timber for house construction and even into the 1990s continues to be a valued reserve of natural products for noncommercial household consumption. Since the mid-1980s, however, widespread commercial harvesting of timber for the export market has disrupted the traditional gathering of forest products in a number of locations and contributed to extremely rapid deforestation throughout the country

Deforestation increased steadily throughout the 1980s, at an annual average rate of about 1.2 percent in the first half of the decade according to the United Nations (UN) and other monitoring agencies. This rate represents the destruction of about 150,000 to 160,000 hectares annually, as compared with annual reforestation of about 2,000 hectares. The government, however, reported a deforestation rate double this figure. Deforestation results from clearing forestland for shifting cultivation and removing logs for industrial uses and fuel. The volume of logs (roundwood) removed for industrial purposes increased by about 70 percent between 1975- 77 and 1985-87, to about 330,000 cubic meters; however, this volume was dwarfed by that removed for domestic (fuel) purposes. Between 1980 and 1989, the volume of logs removed for fuel increased by about 25 percent, to about 3.7 million cubic meters; only about 100,000 cubic meters were removed for industrial purposes. By 1991 these figures had increased to approximately 3.9 million cubic meters and 106,000 cubic meters, respectively.

Following the introduction of the New Economic Mechanism, decentralization of forest management to autonomous forest enterprises at the provincial level encouraged increased exploitation of forests. At the central and provincial levels, autonomous forest enterprises are responsible for forest management.

Timber resources have been commercially exploited on a small scale since the colonial period and are an important source of foreign exchange. In 1988 wood products accounted for more than one-half of all export earnings. In 1992 timber and wood products were almost one-third of the total principal exports.

The government needed to reconcile its opposing objectives of decentralized forestry management and environmental protection. In January 1989, the government imposed a ban on logging--initially announced in January 1988 as a ban on the export of unprocessed wood--

although exemptions are granted on a case-by-case basis. This measure was followed by the imposition of high export taxes on timber and other wood products, included in the June 1989 tax reforms. Toward the end of 1989, logging was again permitted, but only based on quotas extended to individual forestry enterprises. In response to the restrictions, production of unprocessed logs (roundwood or timber) decreased slightly in 1989, but, according to the Asian Development Bank , production more than recovered the following year. The effect of the restrictions is most clearly shown in the export statistics for 1989--exports of timber and wood products had decreased by 30 percent from the previous year. In 1991 a new decree banned all logging until further notice, in hopes of controlling widespread illegal logging and subsequent environmental destruction. However, there was little practical impact, and illegal logging remains widespread. The smuggling of logs to Thailand also is significant.

AGRICULTURAL POLICY

Agriculture, the most important sector of the economy, clearly benefited from the introduction of the New Economic Mechanism. The changes positively affected performance by establishing a consistent policy that induced increased agricultural production over a number of years--before the droughts in 1987 and 1988-- particularly in paddy production.

In June 1988, in line with the policies described by the New Economic Mechanism, the government passed a resolution to reform the agricultural sector. As announced at the Fourth Party Congress in 1986, the principal goal was to reorient the sector toward a market economy. The abolition of the much hated agricultural tax as well as the socialist restrictions on marketing helped to create necessary incentives for farmers.

The major change was in the pricing policy. The practice of setting low producer prices for a wide range of crops was ended, boosting incomes in rural areas. (In 1987 the procurement price of rice was only 30 percent of the market price).

Other changes were implemented. Restrictions on internal trade of agricultural products were removed allowing free markets to operate, at least for important crops such as rice. Laws also were enacted to guarantee farmers' rights to private ownership of land, including the right to use, transfer commercially, and bequeath. Tax exemptions for specified periods also were decreed.

The reforms emphasize the government's belief that further increasing and diversifying agricultural production requires the participation encouragement of the private sector. Food security, as always, remains a key objective, but the focus of the new agricultural policy is on the production of cash crops that can be processed--to increase their value--and then exported. The means for reaching that goal include the popular 1989 measure of abandoning the poorly developed attempts at establishing the socialist infrastructure of agriculture--a cooperative farming system.

The primary objective of the cooperative farming system, based on the Vietnamese model, had been to help the nation achieve selfsufficiency in food. Reflecting the government's pursuit of this goal, the number of government-assisted cooperative farms nearly tripled between 1978, when the drive to reorganize agriculture began, and the introduction of the New Economic Mechanism in 1986. At that time, cooperative farms numbered about 4,000 and employed about 75 percent of the agricultural labor force although most were cooperatives only on paper, and there was no practical cooperative management. By 1988, however, employment in the cooperatives had decreased and included only 53 percent of all rural families and about half of all rice fields.

The distribution and sale of collectively managed land to families began in 1989. Most families in the old settled areas had their original land returned, which they still recognized. By mid1990 most state farms and agricultural cooperatives had been disbanded. This move, in conjunction with the removal of many restrictions on food prices and the distribution of agricultural goods, helped to precipitate a modest growth in agricultural output of about 7 percent in 1990.

At the Fifth Party Congress in March 1991, the government reiterated the basic objective of its agricultural policy: a shift from subsistence production to cash crop production through crop diversification and improved linkages to export markets. Although rural farmers have limited experience in marketing their farm produce and are cautious about participating actively in the market, they are beginning to produce and sell their specialized crops and livestock and buy manufactured goods on a regular basis. At the congress, the government also affirmed its support for the private ownership of land and its intent to protect farmers' rights to long-term use of land, to bequeath land to their children, and to transfer their land rights in exchange for compensation. These assurances, among other improvements in the economic atmosphere, are an attempt to make Laos more attractive to foreign investors.

ENVIRONMENTAL PROBLEMS AND POLICY

Laos suffers from a number of environmental problems, the most important of which are related to deforestation. Expanding commercial exploitation of the forests, plans for additional hydroelectric facilities, foreign demand for wild animals and nonwood forest products for food and traditional medicines, and a growing population put increasing pressure on the forests. Deforestation not only destroyed at least 150,000 to 160,000 hectares of valuable forest annually in the 1980s, but also caused erosion--leading to siltation of reservoirs, navigation channels, and irrigation systems downstream--and reduced groundwater levels. The practice of swidden cultivation not only contributes greatly to deforestation, but, in 1987, also made Laos one of eleven countries in the world that together were responsible for over 80 percent of net world carbon emissions amounting to a per capita emission of ten tons annually, compared with the world average of 1.17 tons per capita. Further, during the Second Indochina War (1954-75), Laos was heavily bombed and left with tons of unexploded ordnance and bomb craters that ultimately altered the local ecology.

The government's desire to preserve valuable hardwoods for commercial extraction and to protect the forest environment, as well as international concern about environmental degradation and the loss of many wildlife species unique to Laos, have motivated efforts to prohibit swidden cultivation throughout the country. This policy has a significant effect on the livelihoods of upland villagers dependent on swidden cultivation of rice. Traditional patterns of village livelihood relied on forest products as a food reserve during years of poor rice harvest and as a regular source of fruits and vegetables. By the 1990s, however, these gathering systems were breaking down in many areas. The government has restricted the clearing of forestland for swidden cropping since the late 1980s and is attempting to resettle upland swidden farming villages in lowland locations where paddy rice cultivation is possible. However, both the government's inability to ensure compliance with the measures and the attraction of Thai money for forest products inhibits implementation of the restrictions.

Although a lack of environmental planning, surveys, and legislation diminishes the likelihood of substantial improvement of the environment in the near future, a number of decrees were issued to encourage environmental protection. These decrees include general principles for protecting forestland; prohibitions on cutting certain tree species; regulations on hunting, fishing, and the use of fire during the dry season; and regulations on the management and protection of forestland, wildlife, and fish. The use of manure and compost encouraged to help rejuvenate soil. Burning also encourages many forms of forest growth.

The government's commitment to environmental protection is affirmed in the constitution and in its policy of finding new occupations for swidden cultivators. In 1991 the Ministry of Agriculture and Forestry established a land use program under the National Forest Resource Conservation and Development Strategy. The program reserves 17.0 million hectares, including 9.6 million hectares for forest protection, 2.4 million hectares for wildlife reserves and national parks, and 5.0 million hectares for production. However, the commitment is mainly on paper: the highest priority park--Nam Theun--will be flooded by a hydroelectric dam by 2000.

INDUSTRIAL OUTPUT AND EMPLOYMENT

Estimates of the industrial sector's contribution (including construction) to GDP vary, but most sources find it to be slowly increasing, from about 10 percent in 1984 to about 17 percent in 1993. The World Bank estimated the sector's contribution at 14 percent in 1989. Most sources also indicated an increase in the percentage of the labor force employed in the sector, from about 5 percent in 1970 to about 7 percent in 1980. However, World Bank figures available in mid-1993 indicated that the sector employed only just over 2 percent of the labor force in 1986. All sources agree that the growth of the industrial sector had increased throughout the 1980s; the World Bank estimated an average annual growth rate of 3.4 percent between 1980 and 1989, despite negative growth in the drought years of 1987 and 1988 during which exports of hydroelectricity were substantially lowered. By 1990 the growth rate had leveled off, from a surge of nearly 32.0 percent in 1989 to about 12.7 percent in 1992. The virtual end of the command economy fueled the 1989 industrial boom and supported steady growth for at least the medium term. Principal activities in the industrial sector include manufacturing, construction, mining, processing agricultural and forestry goods, and producing hydroelectricity.

MANUFACTURING

There is a paucity of any real industry in Laos outside of timber harvesting and electricity generation. Nonetheless, "manufacturing" represents about half of all industrial activity. Other manufacturing activities include the production of agricultural tools, animal feed, bricks, cigarettes, detergents, handicrafts, insecticides, matches, oxygen, plastics, rubber footwear, salt, soft drinks and beer, textiles and clothing, and veterinary products. Manufacturing employed only approximately 2 percent of the labor force in 1991. A few factories in the Vientiane area have been rehabilitated since the mid-1980s. As of 1994, the garment industry was "booming" with investment from China, France, Taiwan, and Thailand; there were more than forty garment factories in the Vientiane area.

The manufacturing subsector was composed of over 600 factories and plants, of which one-third were state-owned in 1991. Most manufacturing is for domestic consumption and is centered in the Vientiane area. As of mid-1994, there was little manufacturing in or near Laotian towns. In 1989 and 1990, there was a rapid increase in cottage industries such as cotton spinning and weaving, traditional village crafts, basket-weaving, and the production of alcoholic beverages. As part of the informal business sector, however, cottage industries are not covered by national statistics.

Between 1980 and 1990, over 80 percent of manufacturing was in the production of clothing, food and beverages, metal products, tobacco products, and wood products (see table 6, Appendix). Industrial roundwood production increased 71 percent between 1975- 77 and 1985-87 to an annual average of 330,000 cubic meters and then declined to 309,400 cubic meters in 1990.

For additional analytical, business and investment opportunities information, please contact Global Investment & Business Center, USA at (703) 370-8082. Fax: (703) 370-8083. E-mail: ibpusa3@gmail.com Global Business and Investment Info Databank - www.ibpus.com

Sources differ over the growth trend for lumber production; the UN reported a decrease in production of 61 percent between 1980 and 1988, and the Asian Development Bank showed an increase of nearly 400 percent in the same period. Cigarette production rose from 1.10 billion units per year from 1981-84; to 1.12 billion units in 1985 and an estimated 1.20 billion units per year for 1986-90. Statistics over a lengthy period of time for the production of other major goods are not readily available; however, the Asian Development Bank estimated that the value of metal products, food and beverages, and clothing (at 1991 prices) had increased greatly between 1980 and 1990, by 55 percent, 195 percent, and 196 percent, respectively (see table 7, Appendix). A general upward trend in the growth of production is borne out by official LPDR statistics from the first half of the decade. The World Bank reported that the manufacturing subsector grew by 35 percent in 1989, slowing to about 4 percent the following year.

ENERGY

Mountainous terrain and heavy annual rainfall give Laos considerable hydroelectric potential. The Mekong River and its tributaries in Laos have an estimated hydroelectric potential of between 18,000 and 22,000 megawatts, or roughly half that of the river as a whole. The remaining potential belongs to Cambodia and other riparian countries. Total installed capacity in 1991 was 212 megawatts, the majority of it hydroelectric, or only about 1 percent of the potential.

Production of hydroelectricity, the country's major export until 1987, expanded slowly throughout the 1980s, from 930 thousand megawatt-hours in 1980 to about 1.1 million megawatt-hours in 1989, an increase of about 17 percent. The majority of electricity produced--approximately 75 to 80 percent, as of 1992--is exported to Thailand, which has an agreement to purchase all surplus electricity. The remainder is supplied to power networks for domestic consumption. Through 1986 the sale of electricity to Thailand was the country's most important source of foreign exchange. Despite increased production, in 1987 hydroelectricity yielded its place as the principal export to wood products, because of the drought, which lowered water levels, and a reduction in the unit price of electricity to Thailand. By 1991 a new agreement between Laos and Thailand had raised the unit price of electric power.

The largest hydropower facility in Laos is the Nam Ngum dam, sited on the Nam Ngum River, north of Vientiane. The Nam Ngum plant began operation in 1971 with an installed generating capacity of thirty megawatts; by 1987 additional turbines had increased capacity to 150 megawatts. In the early 1970s, the Nam Ngum facility provided electricity to Vientiane; the supply was gradually extended to surrounding villages on the Vientiane plain. As of the early 1990s, approximately 80 percent of the power produced at Nam Ngum was exported to Thailand; some was diverted to the south for town and village electrification.

A second hydroelectric dam was completed at Xeset near Saravan (Salavan) in southern Laos in 1991. The Xeset plant has an installed capacity of twenty megawatts.

About twenty smaller hydropower facilities and diesel plants supply additional power. Since the mid-1980s, Thakhek and Savannakhét had access to a regular power supply through a repurchase agreement with Thailand whereby a cable under the Mekong diverts power from the Thai electrical grid; villages along Route 9 east of Savannakhét have been receiving electricity since the late 1980s. Louangphrabang has seasonal access to power from a hydroelectric dam supplemented by diesel generators. A power transmission line from Nam Ngum to Louangphrabang is scheduled for completion in the mid-1990s and will bring electrification to many villages near Route 13 that previously relied on kerosene lamps and battery-operated florescent lights.

For additional analytical, business and investment opportunities information, please contact Global Investment & Business Center, USA at (703) 370-8082. Fax: (703) 370-8083. E-mail: ibpusa3@gmail.com Global Business and Investment Info Databank - www.ibpus.com

Hydroelectric capacity will further increase as a result of agreements signed either for construction of new facilities or for conducting feasibility studies for additional sites. Thailand is the primary investor in the hydroelectric sector; Australia, Denmark, Finland, Japan, Norway, and Sweden also have companies with interests in various projects.

As of 1992, other provincial centers relied primarily on diesel generators, which are run for three to four hours nightly and serve only a fraction of the surrounding population. Most district centers do not have electricity other than small private generators that light the houses of a few dozen subscribers for several hours each evening. Automobile batteries and voltages inverters are used as a means of supplementing the limited hours of power. These devices enable Laotians to watch television and listen to stereo cassette players, even in remote locations.

Despite assistance from the International Development Association, the Asian Development Bank, the United Nations Development Programme (UNDP), and other donors to increase rural electrification services, national consumption of electricity increased slowly. The average annual increase between 1970 and 1980 was 14.5 percent--an overall increase of 287 percent- -to 325 million kilowatt-hours. After 1980 the growth of consumption slowed greatly, to an average annual rate of just 1.5 percent, reaching 365 million kilowatt-hours in 1988. Per capita consumption was just 93.6 kilowatt-hours, one of the lowest rates in the region.

According to the World Bank, energy consumption grew at an average annual rate of 4.2 percent between 1965 and 1980, slowing to 1.8 percent in the 1980-90 period. Fuelwood constitutes about 85 percent of total energy consumption. Per capita consumption of fuelwood is between one and three cubic meters annually, accounting for more that ten times the consumption of wood for commercial purposes. Total usage--including fuelwood and charcoal--was 3.9 million cubic meters in the 1985-87 period, a 21 percent increase over the 1975-77 period. In 1985 hydroelectric power accounted for approximately 5 percent of annual energy consumption. Most consumption was in Vientiane; domestic use accounted for about 89 percent in 1983 and industrial use, only about 10 percent. The transportation sector, especially civil aviation, which consumed imported petroleum products, accounted for the remaining 5 percent of energy consumption.

The cost of fuel imports--primarily from the Soviet Union until 1991--has placed a heavy burden on the economy, constituting nearly 19 percent of all imports in 1986. In 1989 approximately 124,000 tons of petroleum fuel were imported, an increase of nearly 40 percent over the preceding year

In 1987 an oil pipeline of 396 kilometers was laid from Vientiane to the border with Vietnam, close to the port of Vinh, facilitating the import of oil from the Soviet Union. The pipeline's capacity is 300,000 tons annually, considerably in excess of the annual national oil consumption rate of approximately 100,000 tons.

MINING

Assessments of mineral reserves are imprecise, because by 1991 most of the country had not been geologically surveyed in a detailed manner. According to 1991 estimates, deposits of gemstones, gold, gypsum, iron, lead, potash, silver, tin, and zinc have relatively high commercial development potential, but mining activity is on an extremely small scale. In addition, Laos has small deposits of aluminum, antimony, chromium, coal, and manganese, as well as potential for oil and natural gas. In 1989 exploration agreements for oil and gas were signed with British, French, and United States companies.

For additional analytical, business and investment opportunities information, please contact Global Investment & Business Center, USA at (703) 370-8082. Fax: (703) 370-8083. E-mail: ibpusa3@gmail.com Global Business and Investment Info Databank - www.ibpus.com

Mining operations are carried out by state mining enterprises, and supervised by the Department of Geology and Mines and small- scale miners. Production of tin--the principal mineral export-- decreased 50 percent between 1975 and 1988, to about 240 tons. Gypsum production increased 167 percent between 1980 and 1988, to about 80,000 tons. Salt production increased 233 percent between 1981 and 1988, to eleven tons. Coal production increased more than 600 percent between 1982 and 1988, to about 800 tons. In addition to commercial enterprises, some individual households pan for alluvial gold on the Mekong as well as on small streams during the dry season to supplement household incomes.

Further development of the mineral sector is contingent upon the willingness of private companies to invest. However, the lack of adequate data, a trained labor force, dependable and adequate infrastructure, and legislation (a mining code was being drafted as of 1991) inhibit private companies from major investments, although private investment was growing as of 1993.

INDUSTRIAL POLICY

The organization of the industrial sector prior to 1986 was centered on the state. Between 1979 and 1984, most state-owned enterprises incurred huge losses, and industrial sector output decreased by 10 percent. At the same time, gross industrial production began to shift slightly, to the private sector: private industrial output as a percentage of gross industrial output doubled to 8 percent between 1980 and 1983, whereas state output decreased slightly from 93 percent to 89 percent. In the early 1980s, a slow increase in the number of private enterprises began, reflecting both the government's newly relaxed policy on the private sector and the private sector's greater efficiency and profitability compared to that of the state sector.

Following the introduction of the New Economic Mechanism, the private sector's involvement in industry increased even more, as industrial management was decentralized and most prices-- except prices of basic utilities, air transport, postal service, and telecommunications--were freed from price controls. In 1988 Decree 19 granted state-owned enterprises expanded financial and managerial responsibilities.

As a result of these changes, some state-owned enterprises were forced to curtail production sharply or close down entirely, precipitating a short-run drop in manufacturing output. It was not until March 1990, however, that the government provided a legal basis for the actual privatization of state-owned enterprises, through the promulgation of Decree 17.

Under this decree, most state-owned enterprises were transformed into enterprises under other forms of ownership, through leasing, sale, joint ownership, or contracting with workers' collectives. Exceptions included enterprises deemed necessary to the nation's security or economic and social health, such as utilities and educational facilities. The extension of credit to unprofitable state-owned enterprises was discontinued, and state-owned enterprises were required to set prices and salaries at free market levels. By the end of the year, the private sector's contribution to net material product (see Glossary) had increased dramatically, to 65 percent.

The government reported at the Fifth Party Congress in 1991 that its "disengagement" policy was succeeding; two-thirds of the approximately 600 state-owned enterprises have been either partially privatized or leased to domestic or foreign parties. The remaining state-owned enterprises were granted greater autonomy in making investment decisions and setting input and output targets, in hopes of improving their productivity.

PROSPECTS FOR GROWTH

For additional analytical, business and investment opportunities information,
please contact Global Investment & Business Center, USA
at (703) 370-8082. Fax: (703) 370-8083. E-mail: ibpusa3@gmail.com
Global Business and Investment Info Databank - www.ibpus.com

By the start of the 1990s, Laos had obtained some impressive results from the implementation of economic reforms under the New Economic Mechanism. The experiment in cooperative farming had ended as an ideological failure, and although rice harvests had reached self-sufficiency levels, they still depend to a large degree on favorable weather conditions. New decrees guarantee farmers the right to long-term use and transfer of property. In response to the encouragement of the manufacturing and services sectors through privatization, investment promotion, and other means, these sectors have slowly begun to supplant agriculture's share of GDP. The private retail sector has blossomed. Removal of restrictions on interregional transit and improvement of foreign relations with Thailand have fueled growth in the transport subsector, simplified trade activities, and are likely to reduce the prices of many goods. The potential for tourism as a foreign exchange earner has brightened as foreign investors join with Laotian companies to provide improved aviation and tourism services.

The opening of the Friendship Bridge between Thailand and Laos symbolizes the new relationship with countries outside the former Soviet bloc: trade with and aid from both developed and neighboring countries have increased. Despite an inflationary surge in the late 1980s, the reduction of credit to money-losing state-owned enterprises and a tight monetary policy helped to bring inflation down to more manageable levels in the early 1990s. Tax reform has also worked to slow the increase in the fiscal deficit.

Despite these successes, however, many of the troubles that saddled Laos at the beginning of the 1990s remain. Perhaps the two most crucial constraints continue to be a poorly educated and trained labor force and a limited, poorly maintained transportation network with endemic problems. Many of Laos's most experienced and educated citizens had fled the country in the late 1970s, and the poorly run and underfunded educational system is inadequate to make up for this important loss of managerial and technical skill. Similarly, insufficient investment in operations and maintenance over the years has resulted in a road system poorly equipped to handle the increased traffic that liberalization precipitated. Without a better educated and trained labor force and an improved infrastructure, measures to increase foreign investment and encourage export-oriented production are not likely to yield sustainable economic progress.

Even the push to privatize stateowned enterprises and encourage efficient, profit-oriented production depend upon the availability of trained managers to direct production. Thus, the sustainability of reforms implemented by the start of the 1990s depends, at least in part, upon the ability of the government to turn its attention to the long-term infrastructure and human capital requirements of a market-based economy.

TRANSPORTATION AND TELECOMMUNICATIONS

Because of its mountainous topography and lack of development, Laos has few reliable transportation routes, and as of mid-1994, there were no railroads. This inaccessibility has historically limited the ability of the government to maintain a presence in areas distant from the national or provincial capitals and to some extent limits communication among villages and ethnic groups. The Mekong and Nam Ou are the only natural channels suitable for large draft boat transportation, and from December through April low water limits the size of the craft that may be used on many routes. Between 1985 and 1990, freight and passenger traffic increased at rates of 14 percent and 8 percent, respectively. This occurred largely as a result of the government's abolishment, in 1986, of restrictions on the interprovincial movement of goods, which had artificially isolated markets throughout the country. In 1991 approximately 91 percent of freight traffic--measured in ton-kilometers--was carried by road and 9 percent by river, whereas 95 percent of passenger traffic--measured in passenger-kilometers--was carried by road, 3 percent by river, and the remaining 2 percent by domestic air service.

For additional analytical, business and investment opportunities information, please contact Global Investment & Business Center, USA at (703) 370-8082. Fax: (703) 370-8083. E-mail: ibpusa3@gmail.com Global Business and Investment Info Databank - www.ibpus.com

As of 1991, freight transport services were provided by four state transport enterprises, a number of provincial transport enterprises, and the private sector. The state has a monopoly on freight transport between Laos and ports in Vietnam. Although no longer regulated by provincial government, the private sector's participation in road transport remains severely restricted by government regulations; in 1990 the private sector accounted for just 13 percent of freight transport and 43 percent of passenger transport. According to the Asian Development Bank, it is considered unlikely that the transportation subsector will eventually be a focus of the government's privatization efforts because poor road conditions, lack of spare parts, an aging vehicle fleet, and low transport tariffs--in some cases below operating costs--make such a move doubtful, at least for the short term. The Ministry of Communications, Transport, Posts, and Construction oversees transport and telecommunications.

ROADS

Laos had a minimal road network in the early 1990s. By 1991 the country's total road length was about 13,970 kilometers, an increase of just 22 percent over 1976. Of the total length, 24 percent, or 3,353 kilometers, is paved and 30 percent gravel; the remaining roads are trails unusable during the rainy season.

Route 13, a main north-south road, was built under French colonial rule. The highway parallels the Mekong and extends from the Cambodian border to Louangphrabang; the quality of the road varies over its length. Together with a few transmountain roads, Route 13 connects Laos with Vietnam and provides a rudimentary national road system. In addition, there are three east-west roads, Routes 7, 8, and 9, which are linked to Routes 7, 8, and 9 in Vietnam to facilitate access to Vietnamese seaports (see fig. 7).

In the late 1960s, China constructed a network of paved roads in northern Laos, linking most of the northern provincial capitals and for the first time facilitating motorized transportation across this region. These roads enabled government officials to reach some hitherto remote areas of the country, which helped begin the process of national integration that continues in the 1990s. These roads were maintained in reasonably good repair into the 1990s, providing an important new means of increased intervillage communication and movement of market goods, as well as a locale for additional settlements. However, as of 1993, the link between this network and Louangphrabang was, a 100-kilometer stretch of dirt track passable only during the dry season.

During the 1990s, all major routes in the center and south are being improved and/or surfaced, and a larger network of feeder roads is gradually being constructed by provincial governments. Development of these roads will facilitate a greater government presence at the village level and easier travel by villagers to district and provincial centers. Such improved transportation will also assist villagers seeking medical care and those sending children to school at district centers. Improved transportation may also be an additional stimulus to villagers looking for wage labor outside the village; tribal groups in northern Laos have engaged in seasonal labor in northern Thailand since at least the 1930s.

As roads improve and marketing networks expand, the government has encouraged commercial production for trade and export. As a result, the independence and relative isolation of lowland villages has been reduced. Travel, whether for visiting or marketing-- particularly the extensive market network developed as a result of the long-standing opium trade--or because of military conscription, broadens the outlook of villagers and makes then aware of the relationships between Laos and its neighbors, of national policy issues, and of the possibility of a different material standard of living. Lao in lowland villages travel by oxcart over level terrain, or on foot. The steep mountains and lack of roads have caused upland ethnic groups to rely entirely on pack baskets and pack horses for transportation. Wheeled vehicles traditionally have not been used. Travel in most areas is still difficult and expensive, and most villagers travel only limited distances if at all.

Despite the fact that the road network is the backbone of the transportation network, it had received very little maintenance work prior to 1985. The protracted war and period of government reorganization, limited financial resources, and lack of maintenance equipment have contributed to its deterioration, with serious consequences throughout the economy, including hindering domestic and foreign trade, discouraging foreign investors, and slowing domestic revenue collection.

In early 1990, an agreement was signed with Thailand and Australia for the construction of the 750-meter Friendship Bridge-- which opened in April 1994--across the Mekong River, linking Thailand and Laos by road for the first time. As a result, tourism is expected to increase dramatically and freight transport costs to decrease, facilitating regional trade.

MOTOR VEHICLES

In 1987 there were about 30,000 motor vehicles, divided equally between commercial and private vehicles; this number represents an increase of about 67 percent from 1979. Between 1977 and 1990, the number grew by an estimated 12.3 percent annually. Although government statistics estimated close to 1 million vehicles in 1990, this estimate included scrapped vehicles.

INLAND WATERWAYS

Inland waterways, including the Mekong River, constitute the second most important transport network in the country. There are about 4,600 kilometers of navigable waterways, including sections of the Mekong, the Ou, and nine other rivers. The Mekong accounts for about 1,330 kilometers of the total navigable length. Although the Mekong flows through Laos for approximately 2,030 kilometers, it is only navigable for about 70 percent of this length, mainly because of rapids and low water levels in the dry season. Between Vientiane and Savannakhét, the river can accommodate boats with between seventy and 140 deadweight tons; otherwise it can carry between fifteen and fifty deadweight tons, depending on the season. Residents of lowland villages located on the banks of smaller rivers have traditionally traveled in pirogues for fishing, trading, or visiting up and down the river for limited distances.

Both public and private trade associations handle river traffic, including the State River Transport Company, based in Vientiane. In mid-1987 the State Water Transport Company had thirty-seven boats, most built with help from Vietnam. There are state warehouses at Savannakhét, Xénô, and Vientiane, in addition to a number of ports. River transportation has improved as government policy has emphasized expanded trade with Vietnam and with rural regions.

CIVIL AVIATION

Lao Aviation, the national airline, services domestic and foreign points from Wattai Airport, the primary airport, located outside Vientiane. Domestic air service was already somewhat well developed prior to the beginning of the Indochina War years and limited international service from the 1950s. Lao Aviation has domestic flights to provincial capitals including Louangphrabang, Louang Namtha, Pakxé, Saravan, and Xiangkhoang. Improvements in civil air service are encouraged by the government as a way to boost tourism and commercial appeal. New airports and renovations-- primarily expansion projects, so as to have the capability to handle larger aircraft--are planned for Khamkeut, Louang Namtha, Louangphrabang, Oudômxai, and Phôngsali, but as of mid-1993, work had not begun. International service is provided to Hanoi, Bangkok, Saigon, Phnom Penh, and Kunming and Guangzhou in China. Flights to Burma, Chiang Mai (Thailand), Hong Kong, Singapore, and Taipei are in the planning stages. Lao Aviation has formed a joint venture with firms from Australia, Thailand, and the United States to increase and upgrade its international flights.

TELECOMMUNICATIONS

In mid-1994 the Lao telecommunications system was rudimentary, with a telephone system that serves primarily government offices and broadcast facilities in only a few large towns. In 1986 there were approximately 8,000 telephones for the entire country, or fewer than 2 telephones per 1,000 people. There reportedly was a substantial expansion of telephone lines in Vientiane beginning in 1989, but no updated figures were available.

One powerful amplitude modulation (AM) station is located in Vientiane; the other nine AM stations are low-powered transmitters scattered in other cities. Seven shortwave stations broadcasting in six tribal languages reach remote areas, including one that broadcasts in Cambodian, French, Thai, and Vietnamese to neighboring countries in Southeast Asia. The capital also has two lower-power television transmitters and one frequency modulation (FM) station. The number of radios increased from 350,000 in 1980 to 520,000 in 1990.

The first domestic television service was established in 1983, and the second, in 1988, broadcasting from Savannakhét. Southern Laos receives transmissions from Thailand, and all of Laos receives satellite-relayed transmissions from a ground satellite station linked to Intersputnik from the former Soviet Union. There were about 31,000 television sets in 1990.

International communications improved greatly with the installation in 1990 of a new satellite ground station. In 1991 agreements were concluded with China and France to relay their broadcasts to Laos by satellite.

THE BANKING SYSTEM

In March 1988, Decree 11 on the reform of the banking system was passed, separating commercial bank functions from central bank functions. The Vientiane branch of the old State Bank, the Banque d'État de la République Démocratique Populaire du Laos (RDPL), became the central monetary agency. In June 1990, the Central Banking Law was passed, establishing the Bank of the Lao People's Democratic Republic, or Central Bank, to replace the State Bank. Under this law, the Central Bank assumes responsibility for regulation and supervision of commercial and regional banks; maintenance of foreign exchange reserves; issuance and supervision of money for circulation; licensing, supervision, and regulation of financial services; and management of the monetary and credit system. The Central Bank has about ninety regional branches; as of 1991, the government was considering separating these branches into three regional banks, serving the southern, northern, and central regions.

Other branches of the former State Bank were transformed into autonomous commercial banks to promote private investment. These banks are responsible for accepting savings deposits from enterprises, government departments, and individuals, and for granting credit to state entities, joint ventures, and individuals for capital investment and business start-ups or expansion. Commercial banks are restricted from granting credit to economic units experiencing deficits and losses. These banks do not receive subsidies, although they do render 60 percent of their profits to the government.

By 1991 Laos had seven commercial banks, including the Joint Development Bank--a Lao-Thai joint venture--and six wholly stateowned banks. Government policy encourages privatization of these six banks. However, in part because of the absence of laws governing banking activities and in part because of the relatively small size of the economy, foreign bankers do not express much interest in these ventures.

The Foreign Trade Bank (Banque pour le Commerce Extérieur Lao-- BCEL), a subsidiary of the Central Bank, is the country's foreign exchange and foreign trade bank. By Decree 48 of July 1989, the Central Bank is assigned sole responsibility for setting and managing the exchange rate. BCEL was granted autonomy in November 1989 and was charged with handling foreign exchange transactions relating to trade; as of 1991, BCEL had arrangements with sixtyfour banks internationally. However, a Foreign Exchange Decree was scheduled to go into effect soon after 1991, allowing all commercial banks already authorized to deal in foreign exchange to carry out foreign exchange transactions themselves, thus removing BCEL's monopoly on such activities. Information on the status of this decree was unavailable as of mid-1994.

Responsibility for state-owned enterprise debts was transferred to the commercial banks, giving them enormous liquidity problems. To alleviate the precarious situation, in 1989 the government allowed foreign banks to begin operations in Laos. That October the Joint Development Bank became the first private commercial bank permitted to operate since 1975, followed soon thereafter by the Thai Military Bank. In addition, new reform measures stipulate that enterprises will have to clear all debts owed to the banks before being considered for new loans. In 1990 the Asian Development Bank granted Laos a soft loan of US$25 million to recapitalize the banking system.

Interest rates on commercial bank deposits with the Central Bank are uniform across the country and are generally higher than rates for enterprises depositing at the commercial banks. After August 1989, only minimum interest rates are set by authorities; banks are allowed to set specific rates on their own. Interest rates on deposits vary from bank to bank, depending on the type and currency of deposits. The annual rate on kip deposits at the end of 1991 was between zero and 1.2 percent for most banks; fixed deposits in kip earned between 16 and 24 percent annually, and deposits in United States dollars at some banks, including BCEL, earned 7 percent annually. Rates for loans depend on the term and currency of the loan and on the sector for which the investment is intended. Loans for the agriculture and forestry sectors carry rates ranging from 7 to 12 percent, for example, and loans for the services sector carry rates between 12 and 30 percent.

MONEY AND PRICES

By Decree 14 of March 1988, prices of most goods are no longer set by the government; exceptions include basic utility and mineral prices. Instead, a new system of "unified prices"--free market prices--was instituted. As a result, prices of rationed and subsidized goods such as rice, sugar, cloth, and petroleum increased, and procurement prices were raised by 50 percent to 100 percent.

In addition, in 1988 the wages of state employees, previously paid through coupons redeemable for subsidized goods at state stores, began to be gradually remonetized. Very high inflation rates soon caused a real drop in annual wages, however, and low rates of tax collection gave the government less revenue to spend on wages. As a result, large arrears built up on salaries that are quite small. In 1990 salaries were increased by 83 percent, and arrears began to be paid off, contributing to the increase of 65 percent in government expenditure. Once paid, however, salaries almost immediately go again into arrears. Moreover, the salary increase is not sufficient for state employees to recoup real losses from inflation.

For additional analytical, business and investment opportunities information, please contact Global Investment & Business Center, USA at (703) 370-8082. Fax: (703) 370-8083. E-mail: ibpusa3@gmail.com Global Business and Investment Info Databank - www.ibpus.com

FOREIGN TRADE

Foreign trade figures for Laos do not reflect the large volume of illegal trade in opium and other products, mostly with Thailand; some estimates put smuggling at half of all trade, legal and illegal. Although Laos continued to run a trade deficit throughout the 1980s and early 1990s, the volume of trade increased substantially during the latter half of that period, as a result of increased production of exportable goods, the shift in trade patterns from the Soviet bloc to the convertible currency bloc, especially Thailand, and the removal of many regulations on trade, as the government continues to implement the orders of the New Economic Mechanism. Despite these improvements, however, by 1990 exports still financed only about 40 percent of imports

Principal exports are hydroelectricity and timber and wood products. In addition, much smaller quantities of coffee, gypsum, and tin concentrates are exported. The composition of major export commodities did not change throughout the 1980s; however, the relative importance of the commodities did. In 1987 lower export earnings from hydroelectricity precipitated a shift toward exports of forestry products. The value of hydroelectricity exports decreased from US$30 million in 1986 to US$12 million in 1987, while the value of timber and wood exports increased from US$8 million to US$33 million. Timber and wood products thus replaced hydroelectricity as the major export, and despite restrictions on logging and high export taxes implemented in 1989-- which decreased its share of total exports by 36 percent-- timber and wood products remained the major export through 1992.

IMPORTS

Although the level of imports remained relatively stable beginning in the mid-1980s, droughts and the subsequent need to import rice influenced import totals. Principal imports include manufactured goods, including transport equipment; food items, including rice; and fuel. According to 1986 UN statistics, manufactured goods accounted for 53.5 percent of imports--of which 14.1 percent was transport equipment; food items for 20.8 percent-- of which 16.2 percent was cereals, including rice, and 18.9 percent for petroleum. Limited information shows that the composition of imports did not change significantly through 1989. A substantial portion of imports is linked to aid programs, although a government source indicated that these imports accounted for a slowly decreasing share of total imports\

TRADE PARTNERS

Although the overall composition of trade did not change significantly throughout the 1980s and early 1990s, the direction of trade did change. Until 1989 major trading partners were from nonconvertible currency areas--mainly China, the Soviet Union, and Vietnam; Laos also traded with Bulgaria, Czechoslovakia, Mongolia, and Poland. From 1984--the first year with accurate data--to 1988, the nonconvertible currency area accounted for over half of all imports. Although the nonconvertible currency area never had a monopoly on exports (mostly because the largest export until 1987, hydroelectricity, was sold only to Thailand) it accounted for over half of the total trade volume through the end of the decade. However, following the easing of some trade restrictions in 1988 and the improvement of relations with Thailand, including a reduction in the Thai list of 273 strategic goods in which trade has been prohibited, the pattern of trade began to shift in favor of the convertible currency area. Bilateral trade with Thailand increased 26 percent over 1987, and imports from the nonconvertible currency area dropped to about 35 percent of total imports.

Eager to avoid Thai domination of its foreign trade, Laos sought to improve relations with China, and in December 1989, the two countries signed their first bilateral agreement in a decade,

For additional analytical, business and investment opportunities information, please contact Global Investment & Business Center, USA at (703) 370-8082. Fax: (703) 370-8083. E-mail: ibpusa3@gmail.com Global Business and Investment Info Databank - www.ibpus.com

including notes on cross-border trade. As a result, trade with China grew by roughly 40 percent in 1990. Despite the positive effect of this move on the growth of regional trade, new agreements with members of the former Soviet bloc work against the trend. In 1990, at a Soviet-Lao Cooperation Commission meeting, it was determined that henceforth Soviet exports and loans would be paid for in convertible currencies at world prices. Previously, payments had been made in nonconvertible currencies and often on barter terms. Trade with Vietnam also shifted to a hard currency basis. In addition, the eventual disintegration of the Soviet Union clinched the shift in trade patterns toward the convertible currency area: in 1991 trade with the nonconvertible area accounted for just 2 to 3 percent of total imports and total exports. The convertible currency area was more than able to make up for this loss: trade volume actually increased that year, although by only 4.3 percent.

Major trading partners from the convertible currency area include Britain, France, Japan, Malaysia, Singapore, and Thailand. Of these, Malaysia, Singapore, and Thailand accounted for roughly 45 percent of imports from 1970 to 1978; their share increased to about 51 percent by 1987. Similarly, Japan's share of imports from the convertible currency area increased from 7 percent in 1978 to 19 percent in 1987. The United States accounted for less than 1 percent of imports from the convertible currency area in 1987, although the LPDR's first trade mission to the United States in 1991 signaled its eagerness to expand trade. Three Asian countries- -Malaysia, Singapore, and Thailand--accounted for 65 percent of Laos's exports to the convertible currency area in 1987, up from 43 percent in 1978. This increase in regional trade made up for the decrease in the shares in exports from the United States and Japan: from 33 percent to 6 percent for Japan, and from 9 percent to 4 percent for the United States. Thailand's removal of the ban on trade in strategic goods in late 1989 gave regional trade another boost.

TRADE POLICY

Trade policy prior to the introduction of the New Economic Mechanism had been highly restrictive, revolving around the centralized allocation of goods for export. In 1988, however, in line with the New Economic Mechanism, the government began to progressively decentralize some of its trade-oriented responsibilities, including planning and arranging trade contracts with foreign suppliers. Trade, controlled by the ministries of trade and finance, is conducted by about twenty-four state trading companies and some provincial trading companies. Several measures promulgated in March 1988 modified trade policy. According to Decree 16, the government became the sole exporter through state import-export organizations. Under Decree 13, the State Committee for Foreign Economic Relations and Trade, provincial administrative committees, and municipalities are empowered to supervise the management and control of import and export activities. The decree also authorizes trade agents at LPDR embassies worldwide to make direct trade contacts.

Decree 18 identifies a number of "strategic" goods, including coffee, tobacco, wood products (such as timber, sawn wood, pressed wood, and rattan), other forestry products (such as benzoin and sticklac), and minerals, for which the state has an export monopoly: in short, all the major export commodities. Only the central government's import-export organization, the Lao ImportExport Company (Société Lao Import-Export), and certain provincial and state enterprises are permitted to export these goods to fulfill national trade agreements with the nonconvertible currency area. All importing units are required to submit plans for their trading operations to the State Committee for Foreign Economic Relations and Trade in order to formulate the national importexport plan. However, importers are permitted to trade in all commodities not on the strategic or restricted lists. Under Decree 18, export businesses are permitted to export goods on the strategic list directly, after national requirements have been met. The decree thus considerably liberalizes trade regulations. The main reason for the restriction on trade in strategic goods is that the government has to plan its supply of export goods to coincide with its multiyear

For additional analytical, business and investment opportunities information, please contact Global Investment & Business Center, USA at (703) 370-8082. Fax: (703) 370-8083. E-mail: ibpusa3@gmail.com Global Business and Investment Info Databank - www.ibpus.com

trade arrangements with the nonconvertible currency area countries. After 1990, however, this issue was moot because as the trade volume with these countries dropped to a negligible amount.

The import of certain items, including automobiles and military vehicles, fertilizers, drugs, and "decadent cultural products and pictures," is subject to quotas and other restrictions. In addition, trade in certain goods is entirely prohibited, including poisons, weapons, and other goods related to national security.

At the end of the 1980s, the authority of the Lao Import-Export Company had begun to diminish, because import-export licenses were being granted to increasing numbers of private organizations.

TRANSIT

Because Laos is a landlocked country, its foreign trade volume is highly dependent on transit routes through neighboring countries. Bangkok serves as the major port, but the Vietnamese ports of Da Nang--the most distant from Vientiane at 1,000 kilometers--and Cua Lo--the closest to Vientiane at 460 kilometers- -are also used. The Express Transit Organization of Thailand has a monopoly on the LPDR's transit business through Thailand, initially imposed as a way to regulate trade in strategic goods. Transshipment of goods through Vietnam and especially Thailand increased the prices of Laos's goods greatly--by as much as 60 percent, or, according to some sources, as much as 300 percent-- severely reducing the competitiveness of export commodities on the world market. In December 1991, and again in the fall of 1993, Cambodia offered Laos the use of its seaport at Kompong Som, but Cambodia's poor infrastructure and lawlessness make this an empty gesture.

As of 1991, limitations on trade resulting from transshipment began to ease. Plans were made to establish a Thai-Lao joint venture responsible for handling transit goods to Laos, with the potential of cutting transit costs in half. To further reduce the Thai company's monopoly on transshipment of goods to Laos, Thai import duties on more than twenty agricultural goods, including one of Laos's major exports, coffee, were reduced from a 40 to 80 percent range to a maximum of 20 percent. By 1991 Thailand had expanded from three to eight the number of approved border transit points with Laos. Completion of the first bridge over the Mekong, which opened in April 1994, is likely to further encourage regional trade.

DIRECT FOREIGN INVESTMENT

The Foreign Investment Law of July 1988 is modeled on legislation that has already been adopted in Vietnam and China. Laos seeks to encourage foreign investment as a means of facilitating economic development as called for by the New Economic Mechanism. The government hopes that foreign investment projects will help to shift the economy from a subsistence to a commodity production basis by improving the management skills of the labor force; introducing advanced technology to the manufacturing sector; fostering economic, scientific, and technological cooperation with other countries; and increasing the production of goods for export.

The Foreign Investment Law allows investors to enter into three types of investment arrangements. The first type of arrangement, contractual or cooperative businesses, entails investment in existing state or private companies, or with Laotian individuals; in this way, the law is more liberal than comparable legislation in either Vietnam or China. The second type of arrangement, joint ventures, requires foreigners to invest a minimum of 30 percent of total capital.

In general, terms for either of these arrangements are not to exceed twenty years. The third type of arrangement, private ventures, requires foreigners to invest 30 percent of total capital, up to a maximum of 100 percent. Terms are generally limited to fifteen years. Tax exemptions or reductions for joint ventures and private enterprises are available for two to six years after the first year of profit, depending on the size of the investment, the volume of goods exported as a result of the project, the location of the project, and the sector on which it focuses.

Tax incentives--a reduction of 2 to 5 percent in the profit tax--are also used to encourage foreign investment. In order to qualify for the reduction, a foreign investment project has to meet three of the following criteria: the project will export more than 70 percent of the goods it produces; will obtain domestically more than 70 percent of the raw materials it uses; will use advanced technology; will aim to overcome unfavorable natural or socioeconomic conditions; will contribute to national economic development despite low profit margins; or will be established before 1995. The Foreign Investment Law allows foreign investors to remit profits to the countries of their choice; in addition, it prohibits the nationalization of their capital and property.

Other laws also seek to facilitate foreign investment. In early 1989, Decree 27 established the Foreign Investment Management Committee to centralize foreign investment approval procedures, thus enabling the Foreign Investment Law to be implemented. The Lao Chamber of Commerce was established in January 1990 to assist in attracting new business ventures. Private domestic and foreign investments have been encouraged by the gradual improvement of the legal environment, including the passage of laws regarding property rights (1990), contractual obligation (1990), inheritance (1990), crime (1990), civil procedures (1990), and labor (1991). The 1991 approval of the constitution, which protects the right to private ownership, is also an important factor in encouraging foreign investment. Also, as of late 1993, an arbitration law was being drafted that will provide a legal mechanism for the settlement of disputes. There was an informal arbitration procedure, but the lack of a law or decree made decisions nonbinding.

PROSPECTS FOR GROWTH

By the start of the 1990s, Laos had obtained some impressive results from the implementation of economic reforms under the New Economic Mechanism. The experiment in cooperative farming had ended as an ideological failure, and although rice harvests had reached self-sufficiency levels, they still depend to a large degree on favorable weather conditions. New decrees guarantee farmers the right to long-term use and transfer of property. In response to the encouragement of the manufacturing and services sectors through privatization, investment promotion, and other means, these sectors have slowly begun to supplant agriculture's share of GDP. The private retail sector has blossomed. Removal of restrictions on interregional transit and improvement of foreign relations with Thailand have fueled growth in the transport subsector, simplified trade activities, and are likely to reduce the prices of many goods. The potential for tourism as a foreign exchange earner has brightened as foreign investors join with Laotian companies to provide improved aviation and tourism services. The opening of the Friendship Bridge between Thailand and Laos symbolizes the new relationship with countries outside the former Soviet bloc: trade with and aid from both developed and neighboring countries have increased. Despite an inflationary surge in the late 1980s, the reduction of credit to money-losing state-owned enterprises and a tight monetary policy helped to bring inflation down to more manageable levels in the early 1990s. Tax reform has also worked to slow the increase in the fiscal deficit.

Despite these successes, however, many of the troubles that saddled Laos at the beginning of the 1990s remain. Perhaps the two most crucial constraints continue to be a poorly educated and trained labor force and a limited, poorly maintained transportation network with endemic problems. Many of Laos's most experienced and educated citizens had fled the country in the late 1970s, and the poorly run and underfunded educational system is inadequate to make up for this important loss of managerial and technical skill. Similarly, insufficient investment in operations and maintenance over the years has resulted in a road system poorly equipped to handle the increased traffic that liberalization precipitated. Without a better educated and trained labor force and an improved infrastructure, measures to increase foreign investment and encourage export-oriented production are not likely to yield sustainable economic progress. Even the push to privatize stateowned enterprises and encourage efficient, profit-oriented production depend upon the availability of trained managers to direct production. Thus, the sustainability of reforms implemented by the start of the 1990s depends, at least in part, upon the ability of the government to turn its attention to the long-term infrastructure and human capital requirements of a market-based economy.

For additional analytical, business and investment opportunities information, please contact Global Investment & Business Center, USA at (703) 370-8082. Fax: (703) 370-8083. E-mail: ibpusa3@gmail.com Global Business and Investment Info Databank - www.ibpus.com

STRATEGIC AND PRACTICAL INFORMATION FOR EXPORT-IMPORT OPERATIONS

GEOGRAPHY AND CLIMATE

I. BASIC COUNTRY DATA	
Location:	Between latitudes 140 54'N and 220 30'N and between longitudes 1000 05' E to 1070 38'E. Altitude between 200 and 2,820 metres.
Area:	236,800 km2
Land boundaries:	Total of 5,080 km (China 505 km, Cambodia 435 km, Viet Nam 2,069 km, Myanmar 236 km and Thailand 1,835 km)
Population:	5.6 million (2003)
	Female: 2.8 million
	Male: 2.8 million
Population density:	24.0 inh/km2
	Urban population: 20 per cent
Capital:	Vientiane
Administrative Division:	Three regions, 16 provinces, 1 capital city, 1 special zone and 142 districts
Time zone:	Add seven hours to Greenwich Mean Time
Principal languages:	Lao (official language)
	English and French also used for business purposes
Principal religions:	Buddhism (90 per cent)
Information technology:	Computer ownership per 100 inhabitants: 0.27
	Telephone lines per 100 inhabitants: 1.307
	Cell phone subscribers per 100 inhabitants: 1.935
Education and literacy:	Adult literacy rate stands at 65 per cent
	Female: 53 per cent
	Male: 72 per cent
Currency:	Kip
Measures:	Metric system
Business hours:	The work week in the Lao People Democratic Republic is a five-day week from Monday to Friday. Hours of business are usually as follows: 0800 to 1200 hours and 1300 to 1600 hours
Holidays:	1 January: New Year
	20 January: Army Day
	8 March: Women's Day – a holiday for women only
	14 to 16 April: Lao New Year's Day
	1 May: Labour Day
	2 December: National Day
Telecommunications:	Internet users per 100 inhabitants: 0.27
	Internet hosts per 10,000 inhabitants: 0.012
	Internet cafes per 10,000 inhabitants: 0.452

	Number of websites in English and other languages: over 100
	National bandwidth within country: 100 Mbps in Vientiane and 34 Mbps in the provinces
	National bandwidth to and from the country: 10 Mbps
Credit cards:	VISA and MasterCard are accepted
Airlines:	Lao Airlines. Main international airlines are Bangkok Airways, Thai Airways International, China Southern Airlines, Vietnam Airlines
Airports:	Wattay International Airport (Vientiane); Luang Prabang International Airport; Pakse International Airport
Railway network:	There is no railway network yet
Road network:	Road network is of about 32,624.8 km
Shipping:	No port within the country border
Exchange rate:	Kip 10,300.00 = US$ 1 (March 2005)

Lao People's Democratic Republic is a landlocked country, located in the centre of the Mekong subregion. Its land extends approximately 1,000 km north-south and between 120 km and 400 km from east to west. The country is bordered by China to the north, Viet Nam to the east, Cambodia to the south, Thailand to the west and Myanmar to the north-west.

The Annamite Cordillera runs along on the east side while the Mekong River runs along the west side of the south and central part of the country. About 75 per cent of the country is mountainous with Mount Phou Bia the highest point at 2,821 m of altitude. The remaining 25 per cent is lowlands adjacent to the Mekong River, which runs for 1,865 km from north to south.

The Lao People's Democratic Republic experiences two seasons – rainy season (April–October) and cool dry season (November–March). The average temperature is about 26 degrees centigrade, but may rise up to 38 degrees centigrade in April. In the mountainous areas, the weather is cold from December to February and temperatures can be as low as about 15 degrees centigrade.

HISTORY

The first recorded history of the Lao People's Democratic Republic began with the unification of the country in 1353 and the establishment of Luang Prabang as the capital. From then on, the country was ruled by kings and in the sixteenth century Buddhism was established as the predominant religion of the country. In the eighteenth century, the country entered a period of decline caused by dynastic struggles and conflicts with Burma (Myanmar), Siam (Thailand), Viet Nam and the Khmer kingdom.

At the end of the nineteenth century the French integrated the country into the French empire as directly ruled provinces, except for Luang Prabang, which was ruled as a protectorate. Lao independence was recognized by the Geneva Agreements on Indo-China in 1954. The Lao People's Democratic Republic was established in 1975.

POPULATION

The country has a population of about 5 million inhabitants comprising about 47 different ethnic groups. Each tribe has its own distinctive customs, dialects and costumes. The population density of 24 persons per square kilometre is one of the lowest in the region. The urban population is 20 per cent, and the major cities are Vientiane, the capital, Savannakhet, Pakse and Luang Prabang. About 73 per cent of the population lives in rural areas and is engaged in the agriculture, fishery and forest sector. Of the population, 44.1 per cent is under 14 years of age. The annual population growth rate is 2.8 per cent.

D. Languages and communication

Lao is the national language. Other languages used are English, French and various ethnic languages. The media are state-controlled. The Lao News Agency provides daily news in Lao, English and French at the following website: http://www.kpl.net.la.

The most popular English newspaper is the *Vientiane Times* (http://www.vientianetimes.org.la/). The French weekly newspaper is *Le rénovateur* (http://www.lerenovateur.org/hebdo/hebdo.htm).

ECONOMY

The transition from a centrally planned economy to a market-oriented economy started in the mid-1980s. However, these reforms stalled during the regional crisis in 1997 and the country struggled with some macroeconomic problems which were successfully stabilized at the beginning of 2000. Then the Government went through several consultative processes to issue the National Growth and Poverty Eradication Strategy, which articulates the country's development framework for poverty reduction.

However, the country's economic development status remains among the lowest in the world. The UNDP's Human Development index, which integrates longevity and health, knowledge and standard of living in its measures of development, ranked the Lao People's Democratic Republic 135 out of 177 countries in 2002.

GOVERNMENT

The Lao People's Democratic Republic is ruled by the Lao People's Revolutionary Party (LPRP). The main decision-making body is the Political Bureau, which is comprised of nine members chosen by the Central Committee. In 1991, the LPRP adopted the constitution, which was last amended in 2003.

The National Assembly has 99 members elected by secret ballot to 5-year terms (next election due in 2007). The National Assembly meets twice a year and approves all laws, although the executive branch retains the authority to issue binding decrees. The National Assembly elects the President, the Prime Minister and the Council of Government (Cabinet) composed of 12 ministries.

The government structure includes also a judicial branch comprised of district and provincial courts and a national supreme court. Administratively, the country is divided into 16 provinces, Vientiane Capital City and one special zone.

NATURAL RESOURCES

Forests cover about 47 per cent of the country, comprising a wide variety of tree species suitable for commercial purposes such as energy consumption and exports. In an effort to conserve forest resources, some protective measures have been implemented to manage commercial logging operations.

The country has large untapped hydropower potential. The exploitation of natural resources for hydroelectric power production is evaluated in the light of potentially serious environmental implications. Mineral resources such as tin and gypsum are extracted mainly for domestic use in the construction sector. Exploration for oil and gas has produced limited results. There are deposits of gemstones such as sapphire, zircon, amethyst and gold as well as minerals such as copper and iron ore in the country.

PARTICIPATION IN REGIONAL AND MULTILATERAL AGREEMENTS

The Lao People's Democratic Republic is a member of the United Nations Economic and Social Commission for Asia and the Pacific (ESCAP), the United Nations Development Programme (UNDP), the United Nations Conference on Trade and Development (UNCTAD), the United Nations Educational, Scientific and Cultural Organization (UNESCO), the United Nations Industrial Development Organization (UNIDO), the Food and Agriculture Organization of the United Nations (FAO), the International Fund for Agricultural Development (IFAD), the International Labour Organization (ILO), the International Telecommunication Union (ITU), the World Intellectual Property Organization (WIPO), the World Health Organization (WHO) , the World Meteorological Organization (WMO) and the World Tourism Organization (WTO).

The Lao People's Democratic Republic is also a member of the Asian Development Bank (ADB), the International Bank for Reconstruction and Development (IBRD), the International Monetary Fund (IMF), the International Development Association (IDA), the Multilateral Insurance Guarantee Agency (MIGA), the International Civil Aviation Organization (ICAO), the Mekong River Commission (MRC) and the Universal Postal Union (UPU).

The Lao People's Democratic Republic's participation in subregional trade cooperation includes its membership in ASEAN since 1997 and ASEAN Free Trade Area (AFTA). In this context, the Government has made progress in lowering import tariffs in line with its plans to join the ASEAN Free Trade Area in 2006. The Lao People's Democratic Republic has until 2008 to lower tariffs to below 5 per cent. In April 1997, the Lao People's Democratic Republic signed a trade and cooperation agreement with the European Union. It is also a member of the Asia-Pacific Trade Agreement, formerly the Bangkok Agreement.

The country is in the process of acceding to the World Trade Organization (WTO), the Lao People's Democratic Republic Working Party at the WTO was established on 19 February 1998. The Memorandum on the Foreign Trade Regime was circulated in March 2001 and the replies to questions from Members in October 2003. The first Working Party meeting took place on 28 October 2004.

The Lao People's Democratic Republic is also engaged in bilateral trade-related agreements at both the regional and global levels (see tables 1 and 2).

Trade agreements with non-Asian countries

Country	Type of agreement	Date of agreement

For additional analytical, business and investment opportunities information,
please contact Global Investment & Business Center, USA
at (703) 370-8082. Fax: (703) 370-8083. E-mail: ibpusa3@gmail.com
Global Business and Investment Info Databank - www.ibpus.com

Argentina Belarus Bulgaria United States
of America

Trade Trade Trade Trade

11 December 2002 30
August 2001 16 February
1990 18 September 2003

For additional analytical, business and investment opportunities information,
please contact Global Investment & Business Center, USA
at (703) 370-8082. Fax: (703) 370-8083. E-mail: ibpusa3@gmail.com
Global Business and Investment Info Databank - www.ibpus.com

PRACTICAL INFORMATION FOR EXPORT AND INVESTMENTS

STARTING BUSINESS IN LAOS

BASIC STEPS

No.	Procedure	Time to Complete	Associated Costs
1	Apply for a Name Reservation Certificate It is required to obtain a Name Reservation Certificate from the Enterprise Registry Office ("ERO") within the Ministry of Industry and Commerce ("MOIC"). All companies are required to obtain a Name Reservation Certificate before applying to the ERO for an Enterprise Registration Certificate. A completed Application for Reservation of Company Name, listing three potential names for the company to be established, and a signed Contract of Incorporation (if there are multiple shareholders) in the format approved by the MOIC must be submitted to the ERO in order to obtain a Name Reservation Certificate.	1 day	LAK 10,000
2	Apply for an Enterprise Registration Certificate and apply for tax registration certificate Founders shall complete the application form for enterprise registration in the MOIC standard application form attaching the following required documents: (i) 3 copies of the Contract of Incorporation, (ii) 3 original copies of the signed Articles of Association in the MOIC standard template, (iii) 3 copies of the resolution of founders of the company, (iv) 3 copies of the Power of Attorney in the MOIC standard template (if another person is assigned to submit the application), (v) 3 copies of ID card/passport of founders or business licenses for entities, (vi) 6 photos size 3cmx4cm of the nominated Managing Director. Once the company obtains the Enterprise Registration Certificate, it shall thereafter register its Articles of Association with the State Assets Management Department (SAMD), Ministry of Finance. For registration the following are required: letter request, the original signed Articles of Association, and copy of ERC. Enterprises operating in the Lao PDR are subject to direct and indirect taxes. Direct taxes are profit tax,	1 week for compamy registration and 2 weeks for tax registration	See procedure details

For additional analytical, business and investment opportunities information, please contact Global Investment & Business Center, USA at (703) 370-8082. Fax: (703) 370-8083. E-mail: ibpusa3@gmail.com Global Business and Investment Info Databank - www.ibpus.com

No.	Procedure	Time to Complete	Associated Costs
	income tax and fees; and indirect taxes are business turnover tax, value-added tax and use tax. Value added tax replaced the business turnover tax. A Tax Registration Certificate is neither issued nor required to be renewed annually. The fee for the Tax Registration Certificate depends on the annual income of the Company. The fee for a company with an annual business turnover of US $113,000 is LAK 983,018,852. The application fee is LAK 25,000. The company shall complete the application for the Tax Identification Number Certificate and enterprise registration in the standard form attach with the required documents and submitted at the Tax Authority, who will consider the application and issue the Tax Identification Number Certificate. The application for tax certificate can be submitted at the same time as the company registration (at the One-stop shop). Cost details: LAK 10,000 (Incorporation form) + LAK 70,000 (Application form) + LAK 300,000 (Registration service fee) + LAK 25,000 (Registration form for taxes) + LAK 100,000 (Tax certificate)		
3	Apply for an Operating License from relevant Ministry Upon obtaining the Enterprise Registration Certificate, Tax Identification Number Certificate, and enterprise registration number with the Tax Authority, the company shall complete the application form for factory operation with the DICV standard form and required documents. These are submitted at the DICV, which will consider the application and require inspection of the location of the factory before issuing the license.	2-3 weeks	LAK 50,000
* 4	Obtain Approval of Content on the Company Signage and the Company Signage Building Permit The company must obtain content approval and a building permit. For the content approval application, the company must complete the application form in MICT standard form and provide the following: (i) the name of the company in Lao, enterprise code provided under the enterprise registration certificate, office location and contact detail of the company; (ii) the color in red for the letters, and yellow for the background (these colors applied to domestic companies); and (ii) the size shall not exceed	5 days (simultaneous with previous procedure)	LAK 10,000

No.	Procedure	Time to Complete	Associated Costs
	2mx4m. For the building permit, the company must complete the application form and attach the signage layout indicating the location and size, and copy of the company's licenses.		
5	Carve a company seal The application form for making the company seal is LAK 10,000. The cost for the certificate authorizing the design in LAK 60,000. The carving of a seal in Lao language only is LAK 50,000 (the carving of a seal in Lao and in another language is LAK 53,000). The total time takes around 45 days.	45 days	LAK 120,000 for Lao language and LAK 123,000 for Lao and other languages
6	Register the workers for social security The application form to register workers for social security insurance is available at the agency in charge of registration. Employees and employers must participate in the compulsory social security regime. They may not enter into mutual agreements to avoid participation in the social security regime. The social security regime for company employees is established on the principle of state-guaranteed insurance. Contributions to the social security regime are paid by both the employers and employees: 5.0% of gross salary is to be contributed for social security by the employer and another 4.5%, by the employee. The maximum ceiling for calculating these contributions is LAK 2, 00,000 (5% and 4.5% of LAK 2,000,000).	7 days	no charge

To receive a foreign investment license (FI License) in all sectors, except the mining, hydropower and forestry sectors, a foreign investor must submit the following to the DDFI:

Fully and correctly completed application form (available from the DDFI)

Projected assets and liabilities, pro forma income statement for five years

Bio data of the investor

Support of financial capacity of the investor to undertake the proposed investment

Application fee (US$100 for projects with invested capital less than US$1 million; and US$200 for projects with capital exceed US$1 million)

Four copies of all of the above

The Screening Division of the DDFI reviews the application form for completeness and accuracy. The investor is contacted to supply necessary additional information or to clarify issues arising from the application. The application is then forwarded to the relevant line ministries.

When the ministries have formulated a position on the application, the application is brought before the Board Meeting for decision. Under the FI Law, this process is required to take a maximum of 60 days.

INVESTMENT INCENTIVES

Tax and Duty Incentives

The DDFI automatically awards all approved foreign investors an incentive tax rate of 20 percent, compared to the general tax rate of 35%. Unlike most other countries, this 20 percent rate applies to foreign investment in all sectors of the economy and does not depend on company or performance. Foreign investors must pay a 10 % dividend withholding tax. Foreign investors and expatriate personnel pay a flat 10 % personal income tax.

There is a minimum tax on all companies (unless tax holidays are granted) of 1% of turnover, i.e., foreign-owned companies pay either 20 % tax on profits or 1% tax on turnover, whichever is greater. In special cases, primarily for hydroelectric projects or resource-based development projects, tax holidays can be negotiated.

As an incentive to all foreign investors, a duty of only 1% is charged for imports of capital equipment, spare parts, and other means of production. No duties or import turnover taxes are payable on any imported inputs for export production. Foreign investors whose products substitute for imports can negotiate incentive duties and turnover taxes on imported inputs on case by case basis.

At present, an administrative ruling of the Minister of Finance allows all imports subject to incentive duty rates to be free of turnover tax and excise tax. Producers, whose output is sold on both the domestic and export markets, pay no duty on the inputs for export production and a negotiated rate on inputs for import substituting production. This simple system obviates the necessity of instituting cumbersome duty drawback systems or creating free trade or export processing zones.

In the future, however, the government may move to a system in which foreign investors face the same tax and tariff incentives as do domestic investors. Under this system, investment in "promoted industries" would receive tax and duty reduction incentives, but investment in other sectors would pay the normal corporate profit tax, turnover tax and duty rates.

Non-tax incentives

The government provides the following incentives to all foreign investors:

Permission to bring in foreign nationals to undertake investment feasibility studies.

Permission to bring in foreign technicians, experts, and managers if qualified Lao nationals are not available to work on investment projects.

Permission to lease land for up to 20 years from a Lao national and up to 50 years from the government.

Permission to own all improvements and structures on the leased land, transfer leases to other entities, and permission to sell or remove improvements or structures.

Facilitation of entry and exit visa facilities and work permits for expatriate personnel.

The government also offers guarantees against nationalization, expropriation, or requisition without compensation.

Under the FI Law, the government does not offer incentives of import protection (in the form of increasing duties or banning imports) for import substituting investments and it does not provide measures to restrict further entry to reduce competition for current investors. The policy of not reducing market competition as an incentive for investors is not a feature of the foreign investment systems of most other countries, such as Thailand and Vietnam, in the region.

Site development

Building Permits

Individuals or organizations that wish to construct or to do major repair work must apply for a permit to the Provincial Department of Communications, Transportation, Post and Construction (DCTPC). The application documents to be submitted in 4 copies are the following:

A standard application form available from the DCTPC

A certificate of residence from administrative authorities

A certified land title document, land use permit, and site permit attached to a plan for the structure

A situation plan

A construction plan

A septic tank plan

Before they can be submitted to the DCTPC, a legally recognized design company must approve these documents. The Provincial DCTPC (where appropriate) will notify the applicants within 45 days of the results of the examination of the application. The examination of the application form is made in conjunction with other relevant government agencies such as:

The Land Department

The Ministry of Interior

The Institute of Urbanism

Once a building permit has been assigned, it is be valid for 3 months. During the construction, the DCTPC will carry out inspections of the construction site to ensure construction activities are in accordance with the building permits and plans.

Environment Assessments

According to the Regulations on the Monitoring and Control of Wastewater Discharge, the buildings and factory facilities sites must be inspected twice per year to ensure that they are in conformity with the standards of wastewater discharge. After each inspection, a certificate is issued to the owners of buildings and sites. In cases of non-compliance, appropriate measures are imposed.

The draft environmental law requires an Environmental Impact Assessment to be made for large projects using natural resources. What constitutes a "large project" has not been specified.

Operating Permits

In case of construction of a plant, once the plant is finished, it requires a license from the Ministry of Industry and Handicraft to commence operations. The Ministry of Industry and Handicraft will make an inspection of the plant before it issues the license. At this time, all documentation is once again reviewed to check if it is complete.

Water Connections

The state enterprise Nam Papa Lao or its branches in the provinces provide water connections. Connection times vary from location to location. However the approximate time is 15 days. Individual households or production facilities wishing to have water connections to their sites must apply to Nam Papa Lao or its provincial branches (for projects located in the provinces). The documentation required is:

Standard application form available from Nam Papa Lao

Building permit

Approved construction plan

Electricity Connections

In October 1997 the electricity tariff was adjusted. Under this new tariff schedule, the electricity tariff varies from user to user. The highest tariff applies to entertainment businesses. They pay 100 kip per kwh. The lowest tariff is 10 kip per kwh and applies to small businesses with a simple accounting system.

Electricity connections are provided by legally recognized construction design companies. The documentation required is:

Application form from the Ministry of Industry and Handicraft

Foreign investment license

Building permit

Tax license

After the Ministry of Industry and Handicraft approves the application, foreign investors must contact one of the approved construction design companies to survey the site and make a price quotation for an electricity connection. The price and the time required for connections vary from location to location and also depend upon the size of the transformer and electricity phase (1, 2 or 3 phases).

The approximate time to get an electricity connection is 1-2 months for households and two to three months for plants.

Telephone Connections

Telephone connections are provided by Lao Telecom. Lao Telecom is a joint venture between a Thai investor and the Lao government. From major cities, international access via IDD is straightforward, fast and efficient. Sound produced over the lines is good and disconnects are rare. Rates for international calls, though still relatively expensive, have steadily lowered over the past few years.

Lao Telecom can usually provide a line within 2 weeks if lines adjacent to the property are in place. The connection fee is approximately $150 but can vary from location to location depending on the distance from the main switchboard in different areas.

The application process is straightforward. Foreign investors fill out an application form that includes the location where telephone hook-up is to be provided. After receiving the application, Lao Telecom will survey the location and prepare a quotation.

Forms of investment

Forms of Business Organization

Under the Business Law (1994), the Ministry of Trade and Tourism (MTT), Department of Enterprise Registration is responsible for registering all businesses in a Company Register. The Business Law makes no distinction between foreign and domestic companies. There are several types of business forms in Laos from which an investor may choose:

Representative office
Branch office
Sole Trader
Partnership
Limited Company
Public Company

Private-State Mixed Enterprise

The Business Law regulates the formation, conduct of affairs, and liquidation of all companies. (The Bankruptcy Law of 1994 also deals with liquidations.) In order for a company to be considered as a lawfully established juristic entity, it must be properly registered with the MTT and obtain an Enterprise Registration Certificate . If no errors or omissions are made in the application form or in the documentation submitted, the application will be processed within 10 to 30 days.

Most importantly, a foreign investor must first obtain a Foreign Investment License (FI License) before applying for a Business License. The Articles of Association of a foreign investor will

For additional analytical, business and investment opportunities information,
please contact Global Investment & Business Center, USA
at (703) 370-8082. Fax: (703) 370-8083. E-mail: ibpusa3@gmail.com
Global Business and Investment Info Databank - www.ibpus.com

already have been vetted and approved by the Department of Domestic and Foreign Investment (DDFI) as part of the approval process to obtain a FI License.

Representative and Branch Offices

The Business Law does not mention either representative offices or branch offices. Many branch and representative offices have been established in Laos. The FI Law permits the establishment of both representative offices and branch offices in Laos. The DDFI has standard descriptions for both these forms of business operations. Under the DDFI interpretation of a representative office, such an office cannot conduct business on its own, but must refer all business operations to units outside the country.

A foreign enterprise established in Lao PDR may be either a new company or a branch office of a foreign company. A branch office of a foreign company may have the Articles of Association of the parent company or separate Articles of Association providing they are consistent with the laws and regulations of the Lao PDR. The procedures for registering a branch office are the same as for any other type of company. A branch office is regarded as the same legal entity as its parent company. The parent company, therefore, can be held responsible for all liabilities of the branch in Laos.

Partnership

A partnership can be formed between two or more partners to carry out business. There is no capital requirement for a partnership. The partners each may contribute funds, capital equipment, land, patents and trademarks, and technological know-how based on a formula to which they have agreed. The partnership can be managed by either or all of the partners or by a designated manager. All partners are jointly and severally liable for the liabilities of the partnership.

Limited Liability Company

A limited liability company is comprised of from one to twenty shareholders. It must have a registered capital of at least kip 5,000,000 ($US470 as of April 2003) with at least half of the registered capital paid up upon registration of the company and the remaining capital paid up within two years of such registration. A limited liability company must establish reserve funds appropriated at 5 to 10% from its net profit. The shares of a limited liability company must all have the same value and are transferable only upon approval of two-thirds of the shareholders. A limited liability company must hold a general shareholder meeting at least once a year. One or more managers, chosen at a general shareholder meeting, may manage the company. The manager may bind the company and may be liable to the company and third parties for his or her wrongful acts.

A one-person limited liability company is a business unit created by a single person. It must have capital of at least 5,000,000 kip. This person is responsible for the company□s liabilities only up to the extent of the company's registered capital.

A limited liability company is the most common structure for conducting business in Laos. By law, a company is regarded as a juristic person that has the right to own property and carry out business under its name. Its liabilities to others are separate from those of its shareholders.

Sole Trader Enterprise

A sole trader enterprise is a business entity with a minimum registered capital of 1,000,000 kip created by one person who is fully liable for the activities of the entity. The owner of such a business acts on behalf of the entity and may assign a manager to run the business.

Public Company

A public company can be created by a minimum of seven shareholders. All shares in the company must have equal value. Shareholders in public companies are liable up to the limit of their unpaid capital contribution. Shares in public companies may be paid in cash or in kind. The maximum value of each share is 10,000 kip. A public company's registered capital must be 50,000,000 kip or greater.

The management of a public company is conducted by the Executive Council, which includes 5 to 17 members, including one or two workers□ representatives. A public company must hold an ordinary general meeting of shareholders at least once each year. Shareholders and proxies representing two-thirds of the shares can call an extraordinary general meeting upon first notification or half of the shareholders on second notification.

Shares of public companies may be sold to outsiders as well as inside shareholders. Shares in a public company are transferable. At present, however, there is no stock market in Laos. A public company is incorporated in a similar manner to a private company. A limited company may be transformed into a public company. Unlike a private company, a public company may issue debentures and shares to the public.

Mixed Enterprise

A Joint-Venture enterprise is a joint enterprise between the state on one side, and other forms of private business entities on the other side. In mixed enterprises, the state must hold at least 51% of the shares. Mixed enterprises are regulated by the same rules as public companies with the following exceptions:

The government has the decision over the transfer of shares owned by the state;

The private shares are managed as shares of public companies;

The share certificates are transferable;

The Chairman of the Board of Director is appointed by the Minister of Finance and the Vice-Chairman is selected by the private party and approved by the inister of Finance;

The President of the Board of Directors has a casting vote.

SELLING TO THE LAO PEOPLE'S DEMOCRATIC REPUBLIC

IMPORT POLICY, REGULATIONS AND PROCEDURES

A. General

The Ministry of Commerce has the role of managing the overall development of commerce throughout the country. One of the main tasks is to study and establish policy, laws and decrees concerning commerce development during each planning period, for submission to the Government and approval by the National Assembly.

The Customs Department under the Ministry of Finance is responsible for collecting import-export taxes in accordance with the law. Import and export activities are regulated by the Customs Law (1994).

The division of authority between the central Government and provincial authorities is regulated by decree No. 10 of the Council of Ministers, 12 March 1988, which describes the three administrative levels that are responsible for their own planning, implementation and distribution of benefits, namely, the central level, the local level provinces and districts, and the grass-roots level (companies, enterprises and state farms).

Any individual or legal entity that has been registered with a business licence (for further details on the registration process, please refer to Part 4, section II) is allowed to import goods according to the related laws and regulations.

On 10 June 2004, the Prime Minister issued Decree No. 12 in order to stop the excessive inspection and levying of fees on goods entering or leaving the country as well as the movement of goods within the country.

B. IMPORT APPROVAL

Any individual or firm seeking to import goods is required to make a six-month or one-year plan for each commodity, which is to be submitted to the Trade Section of the province, the Vientiane municipality, or the special region for acknowledgement and then to the Trade Section of the control unit in order to obtain the import approval.

As part of the import licence applications process, importers should submit a list of goods for import. The list may consist of one or many goods according to their capacity. Once approved, the list of goods is part of the import licence. The import operation should then be conducted in accordance with the list of goods as specified on the import licence, as well as the terms of the sell-buy contract.

C. LICENSING, QUOTAS AND PROHIBITIONS

Imports of goods controlled by the Government are subject to an import permit delivered by the Ministry of Commerce/provincial offices or related line Ministries as listed in table 3.

Table 3. Import authorization

Commodity	Permits issued by

For additional analytical, business and investment opportunities information, please contact Global Investment & Business Center, USA at (703) 370-8082. Fax: (703) 370-8083. E-mail: ibpusa3@gmail.com Global Business and Investment Info Databank - www.ibpus.com

Commodity		Permits issued by
All petroleum fuel products (27.10)	x x x	Foreign Trade Department, Ministry of Commerce Department of Intellectual Property Standardization and Metrology, Science Technology and Environment Agency Trade Section of Provinces, Vientiane Municipality or Special Region.
Gas (27.11)	x x	Foreign Trade Department, Ministry of Commerce Trade Section of Provinces, Vientiane Municipality or Special Region
All kinds of vehicles except bicycles and ploughs (87.02-11:87.16).	x x	Foreign Trade Department, Ministry of Commerce Department of Transport, Ministry of Communications, Transport, Post and Construction
Parts of all kinds of vehicles except bicycles and ploughs (87.02-11:87.16)	x x x	Department of Industry - Handicraft, Ministry of Industry and Handicrafts Foreign Trade Department, Ministry of Commerce Department of Transport, Ministry of Communications, Transport, Post and Construction
Valuable decorative objects (Diamond 721.02)	x	Foreign Trade Department, Ministry of Commerce
All kinds of minerals (25.02-22;25.24-30;26.01-21)	x x	Department of Geology - Mines, Ministry of Industry and Handicrafts Trade Section of Provinces, Vientiane Municipality or Special Region
Cement (25.23)	x x	Department of Intellectual Property Standardization and Metrology, Science Technology and Environment Agency Trade Section of Provinces, Vientiane Municipality or Special Region
Iron and steel (72.01–29)	x x	Department of Intellectual Property Standardization and Metrology, Science Technology and Environment Agency Trade Section of Provinces, Vientiane Municipality or Special Region
Edible meat or other parts of animals, fresh or frozen (02.01-10)	x	Food and Drug Department, Ministry of Health
Fish, crab, shellfish, prawn, fresh or frozen (03.01-07)	x	Food and Drug Department, Ministry of Health
Different kinds of dairy products (04.01-06)	x	Food and Drug Department, Ministry of Health
All kinds of finished food products, including canned food and fruit	x	Food and Drug Department, Ministry of Health
All kinds of desserts	x	Food and Drug Department, Ministry of Health
Food colouring	x	Food and Drug Department, Ministry of Health
All kinds of preservative substances	x	Food and Drug Department, Ministry of Health
Sweetening substitutes	x	Food and Drug Department, Ministry of Health

Commodity		Permits issued by
All kinds of drinks (22.01-09)	x	Food and Drug Department, Ministry of Health
Ducks' eggs, hens' eggs (04.08-08)	x	Food and Drug Department, Ministry of Health
Food seasoning (fish sauce, soy sauce. monosodium glutamate	x	Food and Drug Department, Ministry of Health

sauce, monosodium glutamate and others)		
Medicine for humans	x	Food and Drug Department, Ministry of Health
Medical equipment	x	Curative and Therapy Department, Ministry of Health
Animal food	x	Department of Livestock and Fisheries, Ministry of Agriculture and Forestry
Animal medicine	x	Department of Livestock and Fisheries, Ministry of Agriculture and Forestry
Animals products	x	Department of Livestock and Fisheries, Ministry of Agriculture and Forestry
Animals and all kinds of animal breeds	x x	Department of Livestock and Fisheries, Ministry of Agriculture and Forestry Trade Section of Provinces, Vientiane Municipality or Special Region
Agricultural products	x x	Department of Agriculture, Ministry of Agriculture and Forestry Trade Section of Provinces, Vientiane Municipality or Special Region
Raw material and semi-finished products for use by factories	x	Department of Industry - Handicraft, Ministry of Industry and Handicrafts
All kinds of fertilizers	x x	Department of Forestry, Ministry of Agriculture and Forestry Trade Section of Provinces, Vientiane Municipality or Special Region
Insecticides	x	Department of Forestry, Ministry of Agriculture and Forestry
Video cassettes, tape cassettes, CDs, film, etc.	x	Mass Media Department, Ministry of Information and Culture
Luxury sets such as for games	x	Mass Media Department, Ministry of Information and Culture
Equipment for sculpture, drawing and carving	x	Mass Media Department, Ministry of Information and Culture
Printed matter, reference books, periodicals and so on	x	Publishing and Library Department, Ministry of Information and Culture
Sport guns and rifles	x x	Department of Sports, Ministry of Information and Culture Trade Section of Provinces, Vientiane Municipality or Special Region
Chemicals	x x x x	Department of Intellectual Property Standardization and Metrology, Science Technology and Environment Agency (for chemicals that affect the environment only) Foreign Trade Department, Ministry of Commerce Department of Industry - Handicraft, Ministry of Industry and Handicrafts Trade Section of Provinces, Vientiane Municipality or Special Region
Valuable objects (gold bars, silver bars)	x	International Department, Bank of Lao PDR
Telephone sets, fax machines and other communication equipment	x x	Posts and Telecommunications Department, Ministry of Communications, Transport, Post and Construction Trade Section of Provinces, Vientiane Municipality or Special Region

Source: **Ministry of Commerce, Regulation No. 0285/MOC.FTD of 17 March 2004.**

Some quantitative restrictions are currently applied on the following products, which account for 45 per cent of imports:

x fuel and lubricants
x construction steel
x cement
x rice
x motor vehicles
x electricity
x tobacco
x timber products

The prohibition of imports applies to prohibited business activities, which are those involving private sector activities related to national security, poisons, poisonous chemicals, arms production and any professions or products monopolized by the State. According to Ministry of Commerce notification No. 0284/MOC.TFD of 17 March 2004, the list of goods prohibited for import effective 3 May 2004 is as follows:

1. **Any kind of explosive, weapons and war vehicles.**
2. **Different chemical substances that may be used to make explosives, weapons and war vehicles.**
3. **Any kind of drug products.**
4. **Any kind of products affecting the traditions of the country.**
5. **Industrial disposal and chemical products dangerous for public health and environment.**
6. **Antiques and sacred religious objects.**
7. **Food, medicine and medical equipment under strict control by a ministry concerned.**
8. **Wildlife, aquatic animals and their parts, which are forbidden by domestic law and under the international treaty signed by the Lao People's Democratic Republic.**
9. **All types of right-hand drive vehicles.**
10. **Toys affecting children's attitude, development and safety and peace of the country.**
11. **Literature, pornographic printed matter and other publications that go against the laws of the Lao People's Democratic Republic.**
12. **Second-hand goods that the Government has banned from import.**
13. **Bank notes printing equipment.**
14. **Toxic insecticides, which are prohibited by the related sectors.**
15. **All types of log, sawed timber (processed timber), wood and forestry products that are banned according to internal regulations.**

D. IMPORT REQUIREMENTS

Most import activities require the opening of a letter of credit through a foreign exchange bank. The same information as the notes on the import licence form must be used for the letter of credit. The amount of the letter of credit should not exceed the authorized amount and should be expressed in the same currency as the one specified in the import licence.

Lao sanitary and phytosanitary measures regulations and standards are based on the relevant international standards in order to control the risk to humans, animal and plant from pests and diseases, disease-causing organisms and pesticide contamination. In the case of imports of live animals, a certification that appropriate vaccinations have been undertaken is required. For imports of plants and foodstuffs, depending upon the origins, a phytosanitary certificate is required.

Goods imported through land border should be transported along routes determined by the authorities and declared to the nearest customs office or entry point. The use of other routes is not allowed and any violation will be considered as voluntary tax evasion.

Goods transported by air should be accompanied by air waybills certified by airline officers. At the landing to the point of entry airport, airline officers should present such air waybills to the airport customs for registration in the warehouse as detailed in the customs declarations.

Goods imported by boat on international rivers should be accompanied by shipping documents. Such documents should be certified by the ship's owner and contain all information as required in the forms. Crafts sailing on international rivers, whether transporting shipments or not, should only stop at ports where customs stations are established. The craft's owner should immediately declare the shipment to the customs officers after the craft's arrival or before its departure.

As for temporary transport, goods classified under the regime of temporary importation include: x Imported goods for any purpose and then re-exported in the original quantity and condition; x Imported goods for processing, assembly into finished products, improvement and repair, and then re-exported.

For the temporary importation of goods, importers should sign a contract in the temporary import declaration whereas such goods shall be re-exported or entered in the warehouse system or in the duty free zone pending their re-export and shall fully comply to the conditions provided by the law and regulations on temporary importation. In addition, the goods classified under the temporary import regime will be exempted from duty upon their importation and re-exportation according to outlined regulations and principles.

E. PACKING AND LABELLING REQUIREMENTS

There are no special packing requirements for import shipments. As a precaution against smuggling, imported goods should bear the importer's name on the label. Food distributed directly to consumers in the country must carry Lao language wording in a font and size that it is clearly visible. Foreign language wording is also permitted.

F. Inspections

Pre-shipment inspection is not used. Upon receipt of the shipments, the customs house inspector will verify that the contents of the shipments correspond with the description in the import licence.

REGISTRATION

If you are an importer wishing to import commercial goods into Laos you should, first of all, be a company registered with the *Ministry of Industry and Commerce Department of Enterprise Registration and Management,*

PROHIBITED GOODS

Before importing goods into Laos you should ensure that they do not fall into the category of prohibited goods. Prohibited goods cannot be imported, exported, transited, sold or circulated in

Laos. Among prohibited goods are weapons, narcotics, psychotropic substances and hazardous chemical substances. You should refer to the specific laws and regulations that cover these prohibitions. The goods prohibited for imports are listed in *Notification No. 0973, Annex 1*.
If in doubt you should seek advice from the *Department of Customs* or from the *Department of Import and Export* (DIMEX) of the *Ministry of Industry and Commerce*.

1. PROHIBITED GOODS ON IMPORT

No.	HS Code	Goods	Purpose	Regulation	Supervising authority
	NA	Chemicals of high-level danger used in industries	For protection of health, safety of human and environment	At present the governing regulation is being drafted and expected to be issued by March 2011. Decree on Import and Export of Goods No. 114/GoL dated 6 April 2011.	Ministry of Industry and Commerce (Industry Department)
	8710.00.00 9301 9302.00.00 9306	Bullets and weapons of all kinds (except for explosives used in industries) and war vehicles	For public order and national security	Articles 76 & 77 of Criminal Law No. 12/NA, dated 09 November 2005. Prime Minister's Decision on the Control and Use of Explosives in Lao PDR No. 39/PM, dated 12/7/2001.	Ministry of National Defense (Advisory Major Department)
	1211.40.00 1211.30 1211.90.12 1207.91.00 1302.11 2939.11.00 2939.19.00 2939.91.10	Opium Opium balls, poppy seeds Opium poppies, other finished and dried opium poppies made from coco leaves, marihuana in various forms, cocaine and their derivatives	For public order and national security	Article 146 of Criminal Law No. 12/NA, dated 09 November 2005. Law on Narcotic Drugs. Decree implementing Law on Narcotic Drugs No. 076/PM, dated 20/2/2009.	Ministry of Public Security (Narcotic Drug Control Police) Prime Minister's Office (Narcotic Drug Control and Inspection Authority)
	NA	Destructive fishing tools	For sustainable conservation of aquatic fauna and environment	Fisheries Law.	Ministry of Agriculture and Forestry (Department of Livestock and Fishery)

NA	Pornographic medias / materials	For protection of fine tradition	Law on Printings No. 05/NA, dated 9 December 2008.	Ministry of Information and Culture (Media Department)
3215.19.00 4802.62.90 8443.19.00 8454.30.00	Banknote paper, banknote ink, banknote printer and coin making machine	For financial stability	Article 4 scope of rights of banks, Law on Bank of Lao PDR No. 05/NA. dated 14 /10/1999.	Bank of Lao PDR (Stock-Monetary Department)

2. PROHIBITED GOODS ON EXPORT

No.	HS Code	Goods	Purpose	Regulation	Supervising authority
	9705.00.00 9706.00.00	Archeological objects including Buddha statues, angel statues and holy objects, national heritages with historical and cultural values of 50 years old or older.	For protection of national artistic and cultural heritage "protection of valuable national artistic, historical and archeological heritage" in compliance with Article XX (f) of GATT 1994.	Article 15 of Customs Law. National Heritage Law. Article 2 Edict on Preservation of National cultural, historical and natural heritage.	Ministry of Information and Culture (Heritage Department)
	2834	Bat guano / manure	For protection of natural resources	Article 29, Agriculture Law, No. 01/98.NA, dated 10/10/1998. Order of the Minister of Agriculture and Forestry on the Control and Use of Bat Guano in the Country No. 0613/MoAF.05, dated 08/7/2005.	Ministry of Agriculture and Forestry (Agriculture Department)

IMPORT LICENSE

For certain types of products it is necessary to obtain an import license from DIMEX. Depending on the product, the license can be either automatic or non-automatic. The rules about licensing are governed by *Notification No. 0076* and trader can find the list of products requiring licensing in its *Annexes* as well as a list of supporting documents required.

If a product is not subject to licensing or to specific sanitary/phytosanitary or technical measures, trader can proceed with the importation of the product by submitting a declaration directly to Customs.

EXPORT-IMPORT LICENCE APPLICATION

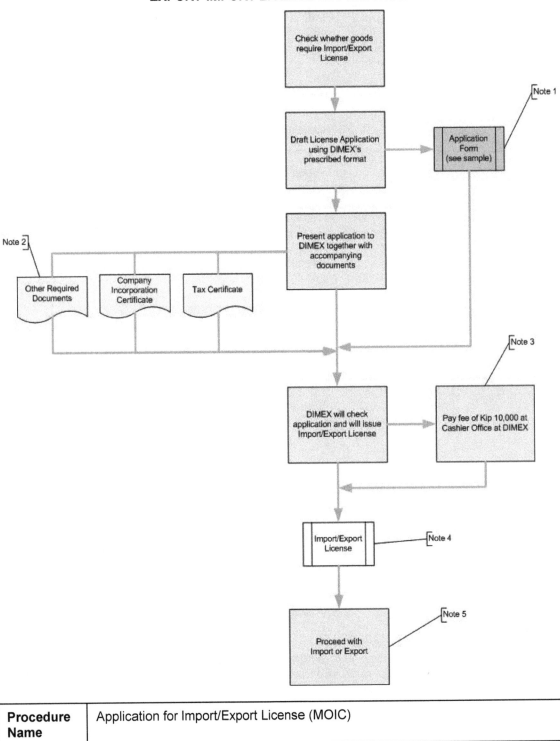

Procedure Name	Application for Import/Export License (MOIC)

Description	This procedure is used to obtain an Import License or an Export License from DIMEX/MOIC or from your nearest provincial office of the Ministry of Industry and Commerce for goods for which a license is required.
	Import or Export licenses can be automatic or non-automatic. Automatic licenses will be granted in any case provided the normal statutory requirements are satisfied. Non-automatic licenses may be granted depending on a determination made by DIMEX. This is usually when an import quota is involved.
	The procedure below is the same, except for the documents that need to be presented, for applying for an Import License or an Export License.
	Please refer to Decree on Import Export No. 114 for the rules governing import and export licensing.
	NOTE 1
	The application form is a free format letter but a template is available from DIMEX.
	NOTE 2
	The documents required to be presented in order to obtain an import or export license vary according to the product and may need to be obtained from other ministries.
	Import of Cement for Project Use
	You must submit to DIMEX an Annual Import Plan and an approval letter from the Ministry of Planning and Investment. Click here to view the procedure to obtain this document.
	Import of Steel for Project Use
	You must submit to DIMEX an Annual Import Plan and an approval letter from the Ministry of Planning and Investment. Click here to view the procedure to obtain this document.
	Import or Export of Diamonds
	In order to import or export diamonds certain specific documents need to be presented to DIMEX in order to prove their origin. These documents are listed in Notification No. 588/MOC.FTD.
	Import or Export of Wood Products
	In order to obtain an Export License for wood products subject to non-automatic licensing (see Notification 076/MOIC.DIMEX) it is necessary to

show to DIMEX the purchase agreement, a log list, a wood concession receipt.

In order to obtain an Export License for wood products subject to automatic licensing (see Notification 076/MOIC.DIMEX) it is necessary to show to DIMEX the purchase agreement, a Certificate of Origin issued by the Ministry of Agriculture and Forestry, the export stamp logbook and a log list.

In order to obtain an Import License for wood products subject to automatic licensing (see Notification 076/MOIC.DIMEX) it is necessary to show to DIMEX an export permit from the country of origin, a Certificate of Origin issued by the relevant authority in the country of origin (e.g. MAF), a quotation and/or contract of sale documents with a product list.

Import of Motor Vehicles for Project Use

You must submit to DIMEX a quotation for the vehicle/s to be imported and a permit obtained from the Ministry of Planning and Investment. Click here to view the procedure to obtain this document.

Import of Petroleum Products for Project Use

You must submit to DIMEX an approval letter from the Ministry of Planning and Investment. You must also submit an import log book or certificate from the border control officer that shows the importations made against the import plan. In the case of import for project use it is not necessary to submit a Tax Certificate.

Import of Gas Products for Project Use

You must submit to DIMEX an approval letter from the Ministry of Planning and Investment. Click here to view the procedure to obtain this document. You must also submit an import log book or certificate from the border control officer that shows the importations made against the import plan. In the case of import for project use it is not necessary to submit a Tax Certificate.

NOTE 3

The Import License form must be purchased by paying a fee of KIP 10,000 to the Finance Division of the Ministry of Industry and Commerce.

NOTE 4

The format of the Import License varies according to the product.

NOTE 5

	The trader can proceed with the normal import or export procedure.
Category	Import/Export

The following form/s are used in this procedure

Title	Description	Created Date	Updated Date	Issued By
Import Application Form	This form is a template that a trader can use to create an import declaration. The application can be drafted on the trader's own paper.	25-01-2012	20-06-2012	Ministry of Industry and Commerce

This procedure applies to the following measure/s:

Name	Measure Type	Agency	Description	Comments	Legal Document	Validity To
Requirement to obtain automatic import license - Road Vehicles	Licensing Requirement	Ministry of Industry and Commerce	Road vehicle, except road vehicle with three wheels (87.04.31) Please check the relevant law for a list of the documents required to submit an import application.	For statistical purpose	Decision on the Management of Importation and Distribution of Vehicles in Lao PDR No. 0919/MOIC.DIMEX	31-12-9999
Requirement to obtain automatic import license - Petroleum and Gas	Licensing Requirement	Ministry of Industry and Commerce	Petroleum and Gas	For statistical purpose	Notification No. 0076/MoIC.DIMEX - Annex A List on Goods subject to Automatic and Non-automatic Import Licensing	31-12-9999
Requirement to obtain automatic import license - Logs, trunks, etc.	Licensing Requirement	Ministry of Industry and Commerce	Logs, trunks, barks and transformed timber	For statistical purpose	Notification No. 0076/MoIC.DIMEX - Annex A List on Goods subject to Automatic and Non-automatic Import Licensing	31-12-9999

Name	Measure Type	Agency	Description	Comments	Legal Document	Validity To
Requirement to obtain automatic import license - Unmilled rice, etc.	Licensing Requirement	Ministry of Industry and Commerce	Unmilled rice, low standard rice, premium rice, semi-milled or fully milled rice whether filtering or not. This license is obtained from the Provincial Office of MOIC.	For statistical purpose	Notification No. 0076/MoIC.DIMEX - Annex A List on Goods subject to Automatic and Non-automatic Import Licensing	31-12-9999
Requirement to obtain automatic import license - Steel bars and transformed steel	Licensing Requirement	Ministry of Industry and Commerce	Steel bars and transformed steel. This license is obtained from the Provincial Office of MOIC.	For statistical purpose	Notification No. 0076/MoIC.DIMEX - Annex A List on Goods subject to Automatic and Non-automatic Import Licensing	31-12-9999
Requirement to obtain automatic import license - Cement, mortar and concrete	Licensing Requirement	Ministry of Industry and Commerce	Cement, mortar, concrete. This license is obtained from the Provincial Office of MOIC.	For statistical purpose	Notification No. 0076/MoIC.DIMEX - Annex A List on Goods subject to Automatic and Non-automatic Import Licensing	31-12-9999
Requirement to obtain automatic import license - Printing products	Licensing Requirement	Ministry of Information, Culture and Tourism	Printing products	For statistical purpose	Notification No. 0076/MoIC.DIMEX - Annex A List on Goods subject to Automatic and Non-automatic Import Licensing	31-12-9999
Requirement to obtain automatic export license - Logs, trunks, timber, etc.	Licensing Requirement	Ministry of Industry and Commerce	Logs, trunk, bark, transformed timber and semi-finished timber from plantations	For monitoring the conformity of the implementation the Chain of Custody System (CoC)	Notification 0076/MoIC.DIMEX - Annex B List of Goods subject to Automatic and Non-automatic Export Licensing	31-12-9999
Requirement	Licensing	Ministry of	Unmilled	For statistical	Notification	31-12-

Name	Measure Type	Agency	Description	Comments	Legal Document	Validity To
to obtain automatic export license - Unmilled rice, etc.	Requirement	Industry and Commerce	rice, low standard rice, premium rice, semi-milled or fully milled rice whether filtering or not. This license is obtained from the Provincial Office of MOIC.	purpose	0076/MoIC.DIMEX - Annex B List of Goods subject to Automatic and Non-automatic Export Licensing	9999
Requirement to obtain non-automatic export license - Logs, trunks, timber, etc.	Licensing Requirement	Ministry of Industry and Commerce	Logs, trunk, bark, transformed timber and semi-finished timber from natural forest	For monitoring the conformity of the implementation the Chain of Custody System (CoC)	Notification 0076/MoIC.DIMEX - Annex B List of Goods subject to Automatic and Non-automatic Export Licensing	

SANITARY AND PHYTOSANITARY REQUIREMENTS

If the goods trader intend to import are subject to sanitary and phytosanitary measures you will have to comply with the special regulations relating to those products.

Normally, trader may need to get a permit from the *Ministry of Agriculture and Forestry* either from the *Livestock Department* or from the *Plant Quarantine* department depending on what you are intending to import. A detailed description of the procedures and documentation required can be found on the *Procedures* page of this website.

Lao PDR has established an *SPS Enquiry Point* as required by the WTO *SPS Agreement.* Trader can contact the *SPS Enquiry Point* if you have any questions regarding sanitary and phytosanitary requirements.

TECHNICAL REQUIREMENTS

For certain types of products it may be necessary to obtain a permit that certifies that these products conform to certain technical standards. These technical regulations are administered by the *Ministry of Science and Technology*.

Trader can find out on this website which commodities are subject to these requirements by using the search facilities on the *Commodity Search* page. A detailed description of the procedures and documentation required can also be found on the *Procedures* page of this website.

For additional analytical, business and investment opportunities information, please contact Global Investment & Business Center, USA at (703) 370-8082. Fax: (703) 370-8083. E-mail: ibpusa3@gmail.com Global Business and Investment Info Databank - www.ibpus.com

Lao PDR has established a *TBT Enquiry Point* as required by the WTO *TBT Agreement*. Trader can contact the *TBT Enquiry Point* if you have any questions regarding technical standards.

IMPORT DECLARATION

All goods imported into Laos must be declared and duty is payable on them unless they are covered by an exemption or a suspension.

A declaration is made by submitting a duly completed and signed *ACDD Form* together with the following minimum supporting documents:

- A commercial invoice or contract of sale document from the supplier of the goods

- Transport documents such as Bill of Lading or Air Way Bill

- Packing List (if available)

- Certificate of Origin. This should have been supplied to you by the exporter.

- Any import licenses or permits obtained from other ministries depending on the type of goods you are importing

Declarations can be submitted at your regional Customs office. *Click here* to see a list of all the Customs offices where trader can submit a declaration and clear your goods.

A declaration must be submitted within 15 days from the date of lodgment with Customs of the transport documents (e.g. manifest) notifying Customs of the arrival of the cargo (see *Transport*).

Currently, at the Thanaleng border post only, all Customs declarations must be submitted via the Asycuda automated system. *Click here* to view the procedure for submitting declarations through Asycuda. In future, Asycuda will be rolled to all other border posts nation-wide. Until then, at these border posts, the normal procedure applies. *Click here* to view the normal procedure. Certain penalties may apply if you do not submit a declaration in time

ADVANCE DECLARATION

In order to facilitate the process of clearing imports trader can submit a pre-arrival Customs declaration. This can be done within 7 working days prior to the date of arrival of the goods following the same procedures as a normal declaration. Trader can pay the duties at the time of arrival of the goods.

CUSTOMS BROKER

Trader may engage a Customs Broker to carry out the import formalities on your behalf. For information pertaining to brokers *click here*. ***Top***

CLASSIFICATION AND VALUE

For additional analytical, business and investment opportunities information, please contact Global Investment & Business Center, USA at (703) 370-8082. Fax: (703) 370-8083. E-mail: ibpusa3@gmail.com Global Business and Investment Info Databank - www.ibpus.com

Customs duty is payable on imported goods as a percentage of their declared value. The rate of duty payable on goods imported into Laos varies according to the commodity and the country of origin.

Commodities are classified using the 8-digit *Harmonized System (HS) Code* which is maintained and, from time to time, amended by the World Customs Organization (WCO). The Lao tariff classification conforms with ASEAN's AHTN standard (*ASEAN Harmonized Tariff Nomenclature*).

It is your responsibility to declare the correct classification, origin, value and quantity of the goods you are importing. If in doubt please seek advice from the Department of Customs.

The basis for the calculation of duties is the actual transaction value of the goods (as evidenced by the commercial invoice or other contract of sale document). If the value of the goods cannot established by this method Customs will attempt to establish the value of the goods using 5 more methods in line with *Article 7 of the General Agreement on Tariffs and Trade* (GATT 1947).

PAYMENT OF DUTIES

Once a declaration has been submitted and accepted by Customs, Customs will be required to pay the duties. At the major border posts you will be able to pay for duties at a bank nearby. Present the receipt to Customs in order to receive your clearance. At other border posts only cash is accepted and trader can pay for duties at the Customs cashier. *Top*

GOODS IMPORTED UNDER WAREHOUSE REGIME

Goods can be imported into Laos under the *Warehouse Regime* if you are not intending to release them for circulation into Laos immediately. Duty will be suspended for the period the goods are in the warehouse and will be payable when the goods are finally released into circulation.

You must submit an import declaration under the *Warehouse Regime* when you bring the goods into the warehouse and a normal Import declaration when you want to bring them into circulation. There are different types of warehouse. Please refer to *relevant article of the Customs Law*. Warehouses have to be approved by the Ministry of Finance.

TEMPORARY IMPORTS

Goods can be imported under the *Temporary Imports* regime under the following circumstances:

- Goods necessary for the manufacture, processing, assembly, transformation or repair of items which will subsequently be re-exported ("inward processing")

- Vehicles imported for the purpose of project supervision or for tourism or business visits as long as they are re-exported by the allotted time

- Materials required for project supervision purposes

- Exhibition, educational or scientific materials

For these types of import you must submit a declaration under *Temporary Imports* regime. No duties are payable on these imports.

In all the above cases certain documents or permits must be obtained from the relevant authority and presented to Customs. Before importing goods under this regime please contact Customs to obtain advice as to what documentation will be required for your specific circumstances.

To import a vehicle into the country for the purpose of a temporary visit you need to make a declaration under the Temporary Imports regime to Customs at the border crossing. You must present a valid registration certificate for that vehicle. Vehicles imported under this regime must be re-exported within the allotted timeframe or a penalty will be liable.

For goods imported for exhbition purposes a bond is payable to Customs which is refunded when the goods are re-exported. *Top*

EXEMPTIONS

Exemption from Customs duties and other obligations are available for diplomatic missions, for goods imported under a government investment promotion scheme or for certain economic zone and for other goods to be imported under certain circumstance. *Click here* to see a list of goods eligible for these exemptions.

Please contact Customs to find out what is required to take advantage of these exemptions.

Personal belongings of passengers arriving in Laos are also exempt from Customs duties. For specific limits concerning these goods please refer to section on *Passengers* on this website.

TARIFF SCHEDULE – CUSTOMS

A. GENERAL

As part of the Ministry of Finance, the Lao Customs Department is responsible for ensuring that all legislation governing the importation and exportation of goods into and out of the Lao People's Democratic Republic are fully complied with. The Lao Customs Department is also responsible for ensuring that all applicable duties and taxes have been paid.

B. CLASSIFICATION

The Lao People's Democratic Republic uses the Harmonized Commodity Description and Coding System, generally referred to as the Harmonized System, or HS, at an eight-digit level.

C. CUSTOMS DUTIES

Customs duties are calculated ad valorem on c.i.f. value of imports. The tariffs rate range from 0 to 40 per cent and the weighted average tariff is 14.7 per cent. The overall tariff structure is low tariffs on investment goods and inputs for industry and higher tariffs on non-essential goods. Imports, which are inputs into productive foreign investments, attract a special rate of 1 per cent.

The following products are exempted from import duty: certain types of food for travellers; certain family implements when changing residence; certain types of materials obtained from inheritance;

For additional analytical, business and investment opportunities information,
please contact Global Investment & Business Center, USA
at (703) 370-8082. Fax: (703) 370-8083. E-mail: ibpusa3@gmail.com
Global Business and Investment Info Databank - www.ibpus.com

belongings and presents of governmental delegations returning from abroad; certain types and quantity of personal belongings of Lao students, pupils, civil servants and diplomats imported after termination of studies, training or civil service abroad; fuel remaining in tanks of motor vehicles; fuel for international flights by Lao and foreign airplanes on the basis of agreement or mutual compensation; non-salable samples; present, assistance materials, loans or debt servicing by the Government; humanitarian assistance materials; specific defence and police equipment; certain types of necessary religious items based on the approval of the state agency concerned.

In 1997, the Lao People's Democratic Republic became a member of ASEAN[1] and committed to fully implement the ASEAN Free Trade Area (AFTA) in 2008. The backbone of AFTA is tariff reduction through the mechanism of the common effective preferential tariff (CEPT). Under CEPT, tariffs on goods traded within the ASEAN region will be reduced to 0-5 per cent by the year 2008 for the Lao People's Democratic Republic. By 2010-2015, the ASEAN countries have agreed to enact zero tariff rates on virtually all imports from the four newer ASEAN members, including Lao People's Democratic Republic.

ASEAN's newer members, namely Cambodia, the Lao People's Democratic Republic, Myanmar and Viet Nam, have already moved almost 80 per cent of their

[1] ASEAN member countries are Brunei Darussalam, Cambodia, Indonesia, the Lao People's Democratic Republic, Malaysia, Myanmar, the Philippines, Singapore, Thailand and Viet Nam.

products into their respective CEPT Inclusion Lists. Of these items, about 66 per cent already have tariffs within the 0-5 per cent tariff band.

Under CEPT, goods are classified in four categories, as follows:

1. Inclusion List: goods that will have a 0 or 5 per cent tariff rate by the deadline for each country. The Lao People's Democratic Republic has until 2008 to bring down the tariff of 98 per cent of the products in the Inclusion List to duty of no more than 5 per cent.
2. Temporary Exclusion List: sensitive goods that are temporarily excluded from the Inclusion List, and will be subject to 0 or 5 per cent tariff rates within the following seven years. For the Lao People's Democratic Republic, the deadline to transfer the items under the Temporary Exclusion List into the Inclusion List is 2005.
3. Sensitive List: goods that are given a longer time frame to transfer to the Inclusion List (2015 for the Lao People's Democratic Republic), including unprocessed agricultural products.
4. General Exceptions List: goods that are not subject to tariff reduction or elimination for reasons of national security, human, animal and plant life and health, including articles of artistic, historic and archaeological values.

The Inclusion List of the Lao People's Democratic Republic consists of 3,551 tariff lines (about 84 per cent of total tariff lines). The Inclusion List covers 2,967 tariff lines. Import duties on products in the Inclusion Lists of the Lao People's Democratic Republic will be eliminated not later than 1 January 2008. Flexibility, however, will be allowed for import duties on some sensitive products which will be eliminated not later than 1 January 2015. The full 2002 CEPT package for the Lao People's Democratic Republic is available at:

http://www.aseansec.org/economic/afta/2002_cept_package/LaoPDR2002.zip

For additional analytical, business and investment opportunities information, please contact Global Investment & Business Center, USA at (703) 370-8082. Fax: (703) 370-8083. E-mail: ibpusa3@gmail.com Global Business and Investment Info Databank - www.ibpus.com

The Lao People's Democratic Republic is a member of the Asia-Pacific Trade Agreement, but does not have a national schedule or concession for the five other countries, namely Bangladesh, China, India, the Republic of Korea and Sri Lanka.

D. TAXES AND SURCHARGES

The excise tax is calculated on the customs value plus import duty and other fees if these exist. According to the Tax Law, the rates of the excise tax are the following:

Alcohol or alcoholic drinks (above 15 degrees) 40 per cent

Beer, wine and other drinks (below 15 degrees) 30 per cent

Bottled soft drinks and other vitamin drinks 20 per cent

Packed and unpacked cigarettes, cigars 10 per cent

Perfumes and cosmetics 10 per cent

Most import duty rates are set at 5 or 10 per cent. Administrative fees are at a rate of 5 per cent ad valorem on equipment and materials.

FOREIGN EXCHANGE REGIME

A. GENERAL

Reform of the Lao economy began in 1986 when the Government adopted the New Economic Mechanism programme, with the main purpose of gradually transforming its centrally planned economy into a market-oriented economy. Elements of this programme that have been particularly important to private sector growth include legal reform, trade policy reform, banking reform and privatization of State-owned enterprises.

During the 1990s, the Lao People's Democratic Republic moved away from the mono-bank system by separating central banking from commercial banking and allowing joint venture and foreign banks to operate in the country.

The Bank of the Lao People's Democratic Republic, as central bank, has a mandate equivalent to ministry status. Its role is to assist the Government in maintaining the stability of the domestic currency and keep inflation low for the economy. Among other duties, the Bank is also responsible for supervision and participation in the Foreign Exchange Inter-bank Market to stabilize the activities of this market and according to the laws and conducts the exchange rate policy in a market-oriented manner by managing the spread between the bank and the parallel market rates at a rate of less than 1 per cent.

B. CURRENCY CONVERTIBILITY

The use of foreign exchange is largely for external payment. Domestic goods and service payments shall be made in kip except for duty free shops where payment in both foreign currency and kip is allowed. Other cases should be authorized by the Government based on the proposal of the Bank of the Lao People's Democratic Republic.

Purchase of foreign currency by the commercial banks or foreign shops amounting to or more than US$ 10,000 shall go along with source proof of the foreign exchange. Individuals or juristic persons can have deposit accounts in kip and in foreign currencies at the commercial banks.

C. FOREIGN EXCHANGE ALLOCATION

The commercial banks or authorized money changers shall sell foreign currency to the public according to their capacity, but the sale shall not be more than US$ 2,000 or its equivalent for one person for the purpose of health treatment and travelling and this shall go along with proof of the using purpose as indicated in Article 5 of the Instruction on Implementation of Decree Law on Management of Foreign Currency and Precious Metals NO 02/BOL.29/09/2003

Tourists and foreign visitors who want to change their money back to foreign currency must present the proof of having exchanged their foreign currency at a money changer or commercial bank in the Lao People's Democratic Republic within the period of their tour or visit.

Individuals or juristic persons who have invested in the Lao People's Democratic Republic who want to transfer the approved profit, dividend, capital and interest received from their business operation to their home country or a third country shall apply to the commercial bank with the following documents:

-**Application for transfer;**

-**Evidence of bringing in the capital certified by the Bank of the Lao People's Democratic Republic;**

-**Account statement issued by the commercial bank.**

-**Tax payment certification;**

-**Decision of the board or shareholders on the dividend of the company**

The commercial bank is responsible for considering the application and responding officially within no more than 5 working days from the date the fully completed application has been received. Approval can also be granted to send a large amount of capital back to a home country or to a third country in multiple transactions. The Bank of the Lao People's Democratic Republic shall cooperate with the related commercial bank to process the transfer in a timely manner.

D. MONEY AND FINANCE MEASURES

The methods of payment used in trade transactions are the standard international methods, namely, letter of credit, draft, wire transfer and direct payment order via post to the bank concerned.

E. BANKING

Currently, the banking system comprises four State-owned banks, three joint-venture banks, seven branches of foreign commercial banks and one representative office (see table 4). There are no domestic private banks.

Major commercial banks in the Lao People's Democratic Republic IV. DOCUMENTS

Bank	Ownership/ status
Agricultural Promotion Bank Banque pour le Commerce Extérieur Lao Ltd. Lao May Bank Ltd. Lan Xang Bank Ltd. Lao-Viet Bank Vientiane Commercial Bank Joint Development Bank Bangkok Bank Public Company Ltd. Krung Thai Bank Public Company Ltd. Siam Commercial Bank Public Company Ltd. Thai Military Bank Public Company Ltd Thai Farmers Bank Public Company Ltd. Bank of Ayuddhya Public Company Ltd. Public Bank Berhard Public Company Ltd. Standard Chartered Bank	State-owned commercial bank State-owned commercial bank State-owned commercial bank State-owned commercial bank Joint-venture bank Joint-venture bank Joint-venture bank Branch of foreign commercial bank Branch of foreign commercial bank Branch of foreign commercial bank Branch of foreign commercial bank Branch of foreign commercial bank Branch of foreign commercial bank Branch of foreign commercial bank Representative office

IMPORTING FROM LAOS

The declaration form or single administrative document (SAD) is used for all customs transactions: import, export or transit. It must be duly completed to be accepted by Lao Customs authorities.

The Declaration of Goods Form must be accompanied by a bill of lading and a detailed customs declaration form. All types of import goods should be declared in detail and according to the tariff code, even if they are duty exempted. Detailed declarations should be handed over to the customs station within 10 days from the registration of warehouse entry exclusive of public holidays.

Regime/code description of types of transactions to be registered in the declaration form

10 Exportation of domestic goods

14 Exportation under a drawback regime

20 Temporary exportation

35 Re-exportation

40 Importation of goods for home consumption.

4A Importation of goods for diplomatic use, returning residents and humanitarian assistance; samples, educational materials and certain religious articles.

4B Goods ex-warehoused to duty free shops

4C Goods ex-warehoused for exportation out of the Lao People's Democratic

Republic

45 Home consumption of goods after temporary admission

47 Home consumption of goods entered under a warehousing regime

50 Temporary importation

62 Re-importation of goods exported temporarily

70 Warehousing of goods

80 Transits

Source: Lao Customs.

A pro-forma invoice is required for the establishment of a letter of credit. The following documentation is required to enable goods to be cleared through Lao Customs:

A. DOCUMENTS REQUIRED FOR IMPORTS

Document	Number of copies	Body concerned
Bill of lading/Air waybill Certificate of origin Form D, if required Commercial invoice Single administrative document Import permit Packing list Other permits, as required	3 2 2 3 sets 1 2	Shipping company/airline company Ministry of Commerce/ LNCCI Importer Customs department Line ministries (see table 3) Importer Ministries concerned

To qualify for ASEAN-CEPT treatment, products must be included in the CEPT products coverage list and comply with the ASEAN rules of origin (40 per cent local content). Once a product qualifies for CEPT, a proof of origin has to be issued for it to be recognized by the customs authorities in the country giving preference. This proof is the Certificate of Origin (Form D). The Rule of Origin Division under the Foreign Trade Department, the Ministry of Commerce is responsible for the issuance of the Certificate of Origin Form D.

Before applying for CEPT Form D, enterprises should inform the Ministry of Commerce of their capacity of production and export in each period, and their need for imported raw materials for the production of finished goods to be distributed either domestically or exported. They should also submit the application for registration with their business documents and tax registration documents.

Thereafter, the Ministry of Commerce together with the Committee of Inspection, consisting of representatives from the Ministry of Industry and Ministry of Finance (Customs Department), conduct a factory visit to assess whether the company in question has the capabilities, personnel and machinery. If it is approved, the enterprise must submit a cost statement for pre-exportation verification of the origin of products to the Rule of Origin division with the following documents:

(1)**Commercial Invoice and Packing List of the products;**
(2)**Production cost declaration document;**
(3)**Certificate of Origin of imported material, Form D;**
(4)**Customs declaration document.**

These documents must be submitted at least one week before the shipment of products. After receiving these documents, he Rule of Origin Division has to conduct a verification and before giving approval must ensure that these products are qualified for CEPT concession and have also complied with the rules of origin.

For further details on the issuance of Form D and the methods of ASEAN content calculation, please refer to the Ministry of Commerce website at: http://www.mot.gov.vn/Laowebsite/vbdetail.asp?id=7/23/1997

B. SPECIAL REQUIREMENTS

For most products there are no special requirements. If live animals are imported for sale and not for use as food, then a medical certificate from a veterinarian is required.

In addition to the import permit, certain types of products require authorization from other ministries, as follows:

x Ministry of Health: gives the authorization for drugs for local sale

x Ministry of Agriculture: gives the authorization for fertilizers and agricultural chemicals

x Ministry of Transport and Communications: responsible for checking standard techniques of the vehicles and gives the authorization for cars and other vehicles.

If claiming duty and tax exemptions apply, documents authorizing such exemptions must be presented with the declaration.

MARKETING AND DISTRIBUTION

A. MARKET REGULATIONS AND PRODUCT STANDARDS

The metric system is commonly used in the Lao People's Democratic Republic. Therefore all weights are expressed in kilograms and tons.

The Government is developing market regulations and product standards. The Standards and Quality Division of the Department of Intellectual Property, Standardization and Metrology is the government office in charge of product standards. The address is as follows:

Standards and Quality Division Department of Intellectual Property, Standardization and Metrology Nahaidio Rd, Vientiane - P.O. Box 2279 Lao People's Democratic Republic Tel.: +856-21 240784 Fax: +856-21 213472

Within the framework of the ASEAN Consultative Committee on Standards and Quality (ACCSQ), all member countries have accomplished the harmonization of standards for the 20 priority products and 81 standards for Safety and Electromagnetic Compatibility. In this context, the Lao People's Democratic Republic has approved the following standards: Portland cement P425 and P525, and nails.

Additionally, in 2004, the Lao People's Democratic Republic completed new national quality standards, which now cover a total of 11 products as follows:

1. Green coffee
2. Mixed cement
3. Gasoline
4. Diesel
5. Deformed steel bars
6. Round steel bars
7. Instant Lao coffee
8. Portland cement
9. Zinc
10. Nails
11. Brick
12. Construction steel.

B. PORT FACILITIES AND TRADING ROUTE

The Greater Mekong Subregion generally lacks adequate transportation infrastructure. The Lao People's Democratic Republic is a landlocked country and transportation costs as well as tariff and non-tariff barriers in the transit country might increase the final cost of imported goods.

The Lao People's Democratic Republic does not currently have a railway system, which hinders trade and the exploitation of minerals. Moreover, of the 32,624 kilometres of road in the country, around 4,000 kilometres are paved. In 1994 the Friendship Bridge was opened as a link across the Mekong River between the Lao People's Democratic Republic and Thailand.

Transit routes and border crossing in the Lao People's Democratic Republic are s follows:

(a)Route 3: Kunming-Yuxi-Yuanjiang-Mohei-Simao-Xiaomenyang-Mohan (China) - Boten-Houayxay (Lao People's Democratic Republic)-Chiang Khong-Chiang Rai-Tak-Bangkok (Thailand)
(i) Border crossing: Mohan (China) – Boten (Lao People's Democratic Republic)
(ii) Border crossing: Houayxay (Lao People's Democratic Republic) – Chiang Khong (Thailand)
(b)Route 9: Phitsanulok-Khon Kaen-Kalasin-Mukdahan (Thailand)-Savannakhet-Dansavanh (Lao People's Democratic Republic)-Lao Bao-Dong Ha-Hue-Da Nang (Viet Nam)

(i) Border crossing: Mukdahan (Thailand) – Savannakhet (Lao People's Democratic Republic)

(ii) Border crossing: Dansavanh (Lao) – Lao Bao (Viet Nam)

Thailand, the State enterprise Express Transport Organization has the monopoly in transporting goods to the border of the Lao People's Democratic Republic. In addition, the Government of Thailand lists certain items for which transit is not permitted. The number of those items has been reduced from 61 to 29.

GOVERNMENT PROCUREMENT AND STATE-OWNED ENTERPRISES

A. GOVERNMENT PROCUREMENT

The Government of the Lao People's Democratic Republic has regulated its procurement activities with Decree No. 31/ PM of 9 January 2004on Government Procurement of Goods, Construction, Maintenance and Services and Decree No. 0063/ MOF of 12 March 2004 on Implementing Rules and Regulation.

Decree No. 31/PM applies to government entities at the central, provincial and local levels; to State-owned enterprises, and joint ventures in which the Sate holds a share.

The following is a reference list of suppliers and contractors:

(1)

Each year, the Ministry of Finance, in cooperation with the component authorities, shall maintain the list of firms, enterprises, joint ventures, individuals and foreign contractors and suppliers participating in public procurement that have experience, qualifications and financial stabilities.

(2)

The reference list of contactors and suppliers will demonstrate their stability and qualifications according to the Public Procurement Degree. Registration of contractors and suppliers on the reference list is not a prerequisite for bidding. Other interested bidders shall be given an equal opportunity of submitting bids. Post-qualification of successful bidders shall be undertaken prior to awarding the contract.

As a reference for the assessment of bidders' qualifications, the Ministry of Finance is entrusted to issue each year a list of enterprises with their capacity, experience and financial situation, as well as to publicize the criteria for inclusion in such a list.

Procurement methods used in the Lao People's Democratic Republic are:

- Public bidding

- Limited bidding

- Direct contracting

- Price comparison.

The selection of consultant services is carried out under the following procedure:

1. The main procedure is Quality and Cost-based Selection Method. This method uses a competitive process among short-listed firms that takes into account the quality of the proposal of the cost of services in the selection of a successful firm. The short list of up to six (6) firms and not less than three (3) is compiled from different sources of information.
2. Quality-Based Selection is appropriate for complex or highly specialized assignments for which it is difficult to define precise items of reference and the required input from the consultants that have a high downstream impact and in which the objective is to have high-quality expertise.
3. Fixed budget, least-cost selection based on consultants' qualifications and single-source selection may be used as specified in the Implementing Rules and Regulation.

In the case of large-scale, technically complex and high-value projects, the suitability of bidders is evaluated prior to carrying out the bidding.

Threshold values of each form of bidding are set by the Ministry of Finance periodically as appropriate and in accordance with the socio-economic context.

In any form of bidding, except for direct contracting and price comparison, bidders are required to provide bid securities, which must be effective for 30 days longer than the validity of the bid. Bids are effective for at least 30 days since the day of opening.

Bid validity. Bidders are required to submit bids valid for a period specified in the tender documents, which shall be sufficient to enable the comparison and evaluation of bids and obtain the necessary approval so that the contract can be awarded within that period.

B. STATE-OWNED ENTERPRISES

State-owned enterprises (SOEs) have been a central feature of the Lao People's Democratic Republic economy. However, during the 1990s, the Lao People's Democratic Republic made significant progress in reforming SOEs by closing down, leasing, merging and selling a large number of them. Although the number of SOEs has been reduced, they still play an important role in the economy.

Decree No. 17 of the Council of Ministers of 16 March 1990 called for the privatization of SOEs. The Government has classified 31 SOEs (7 central and 24 provincial) for sale and liquidation in addition to the 9 SOEs that are currently undergoing restructuring (see table 5). Prime Minister Notice No. 058/ CPMO and No. 059/CPMO of 15 January 2004 adopted the key elements for the SOEs restructuring plans.

Table 5. SOEs undergoing restructuring

Large SOEs	Other SOEs
Agriculture Industry Development Import-Export State Owned Enterprise (DAI) Bolisat Phatthana Khet Phoudoi (BPKP) Development of Agricultural-Forestry and Industry (DAFI) Lao Airlines Lao State Fuel Enterprise Nam Papa Laos	Agro-industrial Development Company (DAI) Bridge-Road Construction No. 13 Company Lao Import-Export Trading Company Pharmaceutical Factory 3

Source: **Ministry of Finance. Currently, the situation of the large SOEs is as follows:**

x Lao Airlines: The Government has decided to propose conversion of Lao

Airlines into a joint-venture entity and is currently seeking a partner.

Discussions are under way with a regional airline.

x Bolisat Phatthana Khet Phoudoi: Most of the non-core business activities

have been proposed for sale or liquidation. Wood processing and construction activities continue to operate although independent audits are

expected to draw a clear picture. The tourism centre is reported to have

been separated and it is being run as a State-owned entity.

x Nam Papa Laos: The asset revaluation has been completed and the

company has started implementing its restructuring plan.

x Pharmaceutical Factory 3: The revaluation of assets and the accounting

audit have been completed.

Most of the infrastructure services in the Lao People's Democratic Republic (electricity, water, telecommunications and aviation) are provided by SOEs although there are more and more private sector firms providing these services.

PRINCIPAL IMPORT ITEMS

Table 6. Direction of imports (Millions of United States dollars)

1998		1999	2000	2001	2002	2010
Thailand	411.3	452.0	419.1	451.7	444.0	501.8
Viet Nam	80.7	181.8	77.7	70.8	76.8	87.6
China	19.6	24.4	33.9	59.9	59.7	108.1
Singapore	22.1	37.0	32.9	28.9	29.1	22.4
Japan	21.0	24.9	23.6	13.0	19.6	16.7
France	6.2	7.6	27.5	8.5	8.9	11.8
Hong Kong, China	8.7	11.0	7.9	10.1	6.1	8.2
Australia	2.3	2.5	4.2	8.3	12.6	9.5
Republic of Korea	5.3	11.9	4.9	6.9	5.0	5.6
Germany	15.4	9.5	3.6	7.4	4.1	5.9
World Total	644.6	808.9	685.9	719.4	730.9	844.9

BUYING FROM THE LAO PEOPLE'S DEMOCRATIC REPUBLIC

I. EXPORT POLICY, REGULATIONS AND PROCEDURES

A. General

The export of goods from the Lao People's Democratic Republic requires a series of procedures including the conclusion of an export contract, the issuance of export approval and customs clearance and shipment. Most Lao export transactions are made under a Letter of Credit.

The Prime Minister's Order No. 24/PM of 22 September 2004 on facilitating import and export procedures and domestic movements of goods mandates relevant ministries and local administration to review and streamline import-export procedures and to facilitate the movements of goods across the country. It has a mandate to avoid burdensome and lengthy technical certification by relevant authorities. The Order reinforces the implementation of single-window service at border checkpoints, which is composed of customs, commerce and other technical regulation authorities.

The Ministry of Commerce issues annual regulations to implement the Prime Minister's Decree 24/PM of 22 September 2004 and Notification No. 1691/PMO of 7 October 2004. The current regulation is the Order on import and export No. 0962/MOC.FTD of 13 October 2004. It reinforces the single-window service by coordinating with line agencies. It also has a mandate to streamline and facilitate import and export procedures particularly for trading businesses located along the borders.

The export procedure is rather simple. The exporters can go directly to the Customs checkpoint to undergo clearance, except gold and copper which require an export licence.

B. Export approval

Some commodities are subject to an export authorization delivered by the Ministry of Commerce/provincial offices or/and related line ministries as listed in table 7.

The relevant agencies produce their list of exports, subject to control for the purpose of technical regulations, health, information and culture, agriculture and forestry, industry and handicraft.

In some cases the Government conducts inspections of designated export items prior to shipment. Export inspection is not required for all commodities but is required for the export of precious stones such as cut diamonds.

Procedures of inspection can be classified under four categories: quality of packaging, condition of material, design and manufacturing method.

Table 7. Export authorization

Commodity	Permits issued by
Valuable objects (Diamond 721-02)	x Foreign Trade Department, Ministry of Commerce
All kinds of minerals (25.02-22;25.24-30; 26.01-21)	x x Department of Geology - Mines, Ministry of Industry and Handicrafts Trade Section of Provinces, Vientiane Municipality or Special Region
Plant seeds	x Department of Agriculture, Ministry of Agriculture and Forestry
Domestic animals and animal products	x Department of Livestock and Fisheries, Ministry of Agriculture and Forestry
Wood products	x Department of Forestry, Ministry of Agriculture and Forestry
Wild forestry products	x Department of Forestry, Ministry of Agriculture and Forestry

Source: **Ministry of Commerce, Regulation No. 0285/MOC.FTD of 17 March 2004.**

For additional analytical, business and investment opportunities information, please contact Global Investment & Business Center, USA at (703) 370-8082. Fax: (703) 370-8083. E-mail: ibpusa3@gmail.com Global Business and Investment Info Databank - www.ibpus.com

C. Licensing, quotas and prohibitions

An enterprise can export all kinds of commodities as long as they are not on the list of goods prohibited or restricted through quotas. According to Ministry of Commerce notification No. 0284/MOC.TFD of 17 March 2004, the list of goods prohibited for export effective 3 May 2004 is as follows:

PROHIBITED GOODS FOR EXPORT

1. Any kind of explosives, weapons and war vehicles.
2. Any kind of chemical substances that may be used to produce explosives, weapons and war vehicles.
3. Any kind of addictive drugs.
4. Any kind of cultural antiques or products related to the tradition of the nation.
5. Wildlife, aquatic animals and their parts which are forbidden by domestic law and any international convention signed by the Lao People's Democratic Republic.
6. All type of logs, sawn wood, rattan and unprocessed Ketsana wood.
7. Wild forestry products such as orchids, Bialai, Chandai and others prohibited according to internal law.
8. Sulphur (bat manure).
9. Equipment for printing of bank notes.

D. Other requirements

The Committee for Food and Drug Control is responsible for quality control of goods. Quality control is required for food, drinks and medicines. A veterinary certificate is required for the export of live animals.

E. Documentary evidence under trade agreements and preferential schemes

As a least developed country, the Lao People's Democratic Republic receives tariff preferences from different countries. However, Lao exporters still face difficulties in making use of the preferences due to a number of constraints such as certification of products/ origin, quality, transport costs, customs clearance and local capacity.

The Lao National Chamber of Commerce and Industry (LNCCI), provides access to the documents and forms required to export under the non-different preferential schemes. See annex 1 for samples of the following:

-certificate of origin for exports of wood and agricultural products;

-certificate of origin for exports of textiles outside the EU;

-certificate of origin and export license for exports of textiles to the EU.

ASEAN INTEGRATION SYSTEM OF PREFERENCES

Beginning on 1 January 2002, ASEAN adopted the ASEAN Integration System of Preferences (AISP) scheme whereby preferential tariffs are offered to the newer members by the older members on a voluntary and bilateral basis.

AISP is implemented based on products proposed by Cambodia, the Lao People's Democratic Republic, Myanmar and Viet Nam (CLMV countries). About 1,117 tariff lines from these CLMV countries are eligible for tariff preferences in Brunei Darussalam, Indonesia, Malaysia and Thailand. Thus far, Malaysia, the Philippines and Thailand have issued their legal enactments to implement the AISP.

Under the AISP, Malaysia has offered the Lao People's Democratic Republic preferential treatment on 12 products, which include agriculture, wood, plastics, ceramics, articles of iron and electrical products. This year, at the request of the Lao People's Democratic Republic, Malaysia will add 73 products to the list, including vegetable, wooden furniture, textiles and garments. Companies from the Lao People's Democratic Republic should make use of the AISP privileges to increase their share of Malaysia's growing imports

The Philippines has granted preferential tariffs on 12 products for the Lao People's Democratic Republic and 62 products for all CLMV countries, as per Presidential Executive Order No. 448 dated 22 July 2005 (see http://www.tariffcommission.gov.ph/EO%20448.htm).

2. Australia

As of 1 July 2003, Australia has allowed the entry of goods manufactured or produced in least developed countries free of import duty. Two categories of goods, namely, raw products and manufactured goods, will be considered for the purposes of duty-free entry.

Goods are the manufacture of a least developed country if:

(a)
The last process in the manufacture of the goods was performed in a least developed country;

(b)
The allowable factory cost of the goods is not less than 50 per cent of the total factory cost of the goods.

Before claiming duty free entry, importers need to obtain sufficient evidence that the goods meet the rules of origin for least developed countries. For example, importers could obtain a declaration from the producer or manufacturer of the goods.

However, a declaration from a supplier that is not the producer or manufacturer of the goods is not sufficient evidence that the goods meet the rules of origin for least developed countries.

3. Bangkok Agreement

As a least developed country member of the Asia-Pacific Trade Agreement, the Lao People's Democratic Republic enjoys preferential access to certain member countries, such as India, the Republic of Korea and Sri Lanka. Further details are available at http://www.unescap.org/tid/apta.asp.

4. Canada

In January 2003, the Government of Canada launched its initiative to eliminate all duties and quotas on most imports from the 48 least developed countries. Implementation of the initiative involved a number of new measures for imports of textiles and apparel products, as well as the enactment on February 2004 of Bill C-21 extending the General Preferential Tariff (GPT) scheme and the Least Developed Country Tariff (LDCT) legislation for a further 10 years until June 2014.

Currently, most products from the least developed countries can be imported duty free and quota free under Canada's LDCT. This initiative also allows products that are not currently covered by the LDCT to be imported without duty or quota, provided they meet the rules of origin.

In order to benefit from this initiative, the Government of the Lao People's Democratic Republic signed a Memorandum of Understanding on market access with the Government of Canada in March 2003.

Canada Customs has created a new certificate to reflect the rules of origin. Importers must have the proof of origin at the time a product is imported if preferential treatment under the LDCT is to be claimed. The exporter in the country where the goods were finished should issue Form A, Certificate of Origin, (http://www.cbsa-asfc.gc.ca/E/pub/cm/d11-4-4/d11-4-4-e.html#P415_57022) or the Exporter's Statement of Origin (http://www.cbsa-asfc.gc.ca/E/pub/cm/d11-4-4/d11-44-e.html#P452_61587). Either document may be used to support a claim for preferential treatment for goods imported under the GPT and, with the exception of textile and apparel goods, under the LDCT.

Textile and apparel products exported from least developed countries are eligible for duty free treatment provided they have been manufactured or formed from inputs from any of the 48 eligible least developed countries, or they have been formed from inputs from the GPT beneficiary countries, provided the value added in the exporting least developed country is at least 25 per cent. For more information on the specific rules of origin, please consult the appropriate official publication in the *Canada Gazette*, Part II of 1 January 2003. at:

http://canadagazette.gc.ca/partII/2003/20030101/pdf/g2-13701.pdf.

The Certificate of Origin for textile and apparel goods originating in a least developed country, importers in Canada must use the Form B255, Certificate of Origin - Textile and Apparel Goods Originating in a Least Developed Country (http://www.cbsa-asfc.gc.ca/E/pbg/cf/b255/README.html), when claiming the LDCT for textile and apparel goods classified within Chapters 50-63 (textile and apparel goods) of the Harmonized System of Tariff Classification.

5. European Union

As a least developed country, the Lao People's Democratic Republic benefits from preferential access to the EU market under different schemes and agreements, such as the GSP, the EU-Lao People's Democratic Republic agreement on trade in textile products, the regional accumulation advantage and the Everything but Arms initiative.

A. GSP scheme

Under the EU GSP scheme, certificates of origin Form A (http://europa.eu.int/comm/taxation_customs/resources/documents/guide-annex_4-en.pdf) are issued by the EU-recognized competent governmental authorities of the exporting country (usually ministerial bodies) if they determine that the exports meet the

requirements of the rules of origin. In the Lao People's Democratic Republic, the competent authority is the Foreign Trade Department.

Under certain conditions, an invoice declaration may be submitted instead of a certificate of origin Form A. Such an invoice declaration may be made by an approved exporter or by any other exporter for any consignment of a total value up to 6,000 euros. The declaration may be made on an invoice, a delivery note or any other commercial document that describes the products concerned in sufficient detail to be identified.

B. EU-Lao People's Democratic Republic agreement on trade in textiles

The access of Lao textile exports to the EU single market was given a further boost when the EU-Laos Agreement on Trade in Textile Products became effective in December 1998.

Under this agreement, certain products are allowed to enter the EU free of quantitative limits (see Annex I of the agreement). Quantitative restrictions could be established if the EU determines that the level of imports in a given category exceeds certain rates in relation to the level of imports in the preceding year.

Products covered by the agreement require a specific certificate of origin, which must always be certified by the Lao competent authorities and must conform to the model set out in the Protocol to the agreement. This certificate of origin is not required if the textile products are already covered by the GSP scheme, in which case they only require certificate of origin Form A, as mentioned above.

Similarly to products under the GSP scheme, goods included in Groups III, IV and V in Annex I of the agreement may be introduced into the EU on the production of a declaration by the exporter on the invoice or other commercial document stating that the products originate in the Lao People's Democratic Republic.

The EU-Lao People's Democratic Republic Agreement on Trade in Textile Products establishes a double-checking system for certain categories of textiles (see Annex II of the agreement), some of which are subject to quantitative restrictions or quotas.

Since January 2005, the double-checking system of an export license has been abolished.

C. Regional cumulation advantage

A further and permanent relaxation of the Preferential Rules of Origin was introduced in January 1999 when the EU granted the Regional Cumulation advantage (http://europa.eu.int/comm/trade/issues/global/gsp/eba/ug.htm).

This advantage - reserved for members of regional groupings such as ASEAN

- allows the Lao People's Democratic Republic to consider intermediary inputs, such as fabric imported from another ASEAN country, as having been produced in the Lao People's Democratic Republic.

D. Everything but Arms

The Lao People's Democratic Republic also benefits from the EU Everything but Arms (http://europa.eu.int/comm/trade/issues/global/gsp/eba/index_en.htm) initiative introduced in March 2000. This scheme allows the duty and quota free export to the EU of all products from least developed countries with the exception of arms and munitions.

6. Japan

The Japan GSP scheme is used by the Lao People's Democratic Republic to export handicrafts, natural mushrooms, textiles and wood products.

7. United States of America

The Government of the United States launched the GSP in 1976 and it now offers duty-free treatment for more than 4,650 products from 144 designated countries and territories throughout the world. The GSP scheme has been renewed periodically since, most recently in 2002 when the Government enacted the necessary legislation to extend the GSP program until 2006.

Until December 2004, the United Stated did not have normal trade relations with the Lao People's Democratic Republic. On 4 February 2005, the Government of the United States granted permanent normal trade relation status to the Lao People's Democratic Republic and enacted legislation to normalize trade relations. The Lao People's Democratic Republic-United States of America Bilateral Trade Agreement (http://www.bilaterals.org/IMG/pdf/US-LA_FTA.pdf) was concluded in 1997 and signed on 18 September 2003.

The agreement is intended to promote trade cooperation between the two countries and help to remove all obstacles and non tariff on a reciprocal basis, The main concept of normal trade relations and bilateral trade agreements focuses on market access, transparency and national treatment making it easier for the Lao People's Democratic Republic to export to the American market at a favourable tariff rate. It is also hoped that it will encourage both nationals and foreign investors to invest in the Lao People's Democratic Republic.

EXPORT CHARGES

Export taxes are assessed based on the quantity, volume, weight, price and other factors multiplied by a fixed rate or a percentage. Export valuation is based on the f.o.b. price at the Lao People's Democratic Republic border. No export duties are levied.

SETTLEMENTS OF BILLS, LETTER OF CREDIT

Any of the standard international methods of payment may be used in the Lao People's Democratic Republic (draft, wire transfer or payment order) but most export transactions are made under letter of credit.

DOCUMENTS

Document	Number of copies	Body concerned

Application for export permit Bill of 5 2 1 1 1 1 1 1 lading/air waybill Commercial 1 invoice Single Administrative Document Export licence, if required Export permit GSP Form A Other permits, as required Packing list	Exporter Shipping company/airline company Exporter Customs department Ministry of Commerce, Provincial trade officer Ministry of Commerce, Provincial authorities Ministry of Commerce, Foreign Trade Department Ministries concerned Exporter

Source: LNCCI/ MOC.

STATE MONOPOLY FOR EXPORT ITEMS

The state monopoly for the export of strategic items has been abolished, although a number of products perceived as strategic remain under government price control.

Group	Product	Items
Group 1	Energy	1 item: fuel and gas
Group 2	Construction materials	4 items: steel bars, cement, roof tiles and galvanized sheets
Group 3	Agricultural	2 items: fertilizer and animal food
Group 4	Foods	6 items: rice, sugar, beef, pork and eggs

Source: World Bank Economic Monitor, **May 2004 and Ministry of Commerce.**

VI. PRINCIPAL EXPORT ITEMS

Over the past decade, the structure of exports from the Lao People's Democratic Republic has changed from commodity-based to more process-based exports (see table 8).

Table 8. Composition of exports, by principal commodities

(Millions of United States dollars)

1998		1999	2000	2001	2002	2003
Wood products	115	55	73	79	71	61
Electricity	67	91	112	106	104	92
Coffee	48	15	12	15	9	10
Garments	70	66	92	99	100	93

Source: **Based on data from ADB.**

Exports from the Lao People's Democratic Republic depend heavily on two neighbouring countries, Viet Nam and Thailand, which represents around 40 per cent of the country's total exports. Exports to the European Union account for about 25 per cent of the total.

Table 9. Direction of exports

(Millions of United States dollars)

1998		1999	2000	2001	2002	2003
Viet Nam	119.5	179.4	96.1	61.9	67.1	76.6
Thailand	28.8	51.6	68.9	81.0	85.0	94.4
France	23.3	18.2	27.1	33.7	33.8	33.5
Germany	21.4	27.0	20.8	25.5	22.0	25.2
Belgium	12.8	13.5	13.6	10.4	13.6	17.6
United Kingdom	7.7	12.5	7.2	9.3	13.4	14.1
Netherlands	5.4	8.9	10.0	9.7	10.6	10.2
Italy	9.5	5.9	9.2	10.9	10.1	10.3
Japan	17.8	12.3	10.9	6.3	6.1	7.3
China	7.2	8.7	4.9	6.8	8.8	10.2
Total, world	370.8	462.5	389.7	375.4	396.0	441.6

Source: **Based on data from ADB.**

References for part three: buying from the Lao People's Democratic Republic

Australia Customs http://www.customs.gov.au/webdata/resources/notices/ACN_03412.pdf
Canada Border Service Agency http://www.cbsa-asfc.gc.ca/import/accountingintroe.html#P305_26310 Canada Department of Foreign Affairs and International Trade http://www.dfaitmaeci.gc.ca/tna-nac/ldc_back-en.asp , http://www.dfait-maeci.gc.ca/tna-nac/socialen.asp#development

Department of Foreign Trade: 'What and how to do business in the Lao People's Democratic Republic' (1998) EU bilateral relations with Lao People's Democratic Republic

http://europa.eu.int/comm/external_relations/lao/intro/

EU Delegation to Lao People's Democratic Republic

http://www.dellao.cec.eu.int/en/eu_laos_sea/laos_trade.htm EU textiles sector http://trade-info.cec.eu.int/textiles/legis_texts.cfm EU trade and development http://europa.eu.int/comm/trade/miti/devel/index_en.htm EU User's guide to the EU GSPs, Special Arrangements for Least Developed Countries

http://europa.eu.int/comm/trade/issues/global/gsp/eba/ug.htm EU-Laos Agreement on Trade in Textile Products http://tradeinfo.cec.eu.int/doclib/html/111335.htm
http://www.customs.gov.au/site/page.cfm?u=5337
http://www.customs.gov.au/webdata/resources/notices/ACN_03412.pdf Lao-U.S. Trade Agreement http://www.bilaterals.org/IMG/pdf/US-LA_FTA.pdf LNCCI
http://www.lncci.laotel.com/Lao%20Import%20&%20Export.htm MOC Lao People's Democratic Republic

http://www.mot.gov.vn/Laowebsite/vbdetail.asp?id=0203/MOC.TFD

U.S.Department of State http://www.state.gov/r/pa/ei/bgn/2770.htm
U.S.Embassy in Lao People's Democratic Republic http://usembassy.state.gov/laos/

U.S.Federal Register, 11 February 2005
http://a257.g.akamaitech.net/7/257/2422/01jan20051800/edocket.access.gpo.gov/2005/pdf/0
5 -2723.pdf
U.S.Trade Representative

http://www.ustr.gov/Trade_Development/Preference_Programs/GSP/Section_Index.html

World Bank Economic Monitor, May 2004

http://siteresources.worldbank.org/INTLAOPRD/Resources/2935821096519010070/lao_eco
n_monitor_may2004.pdf

INVESTING IN THE LAO PEOPLE'S DEMOCRATIC REPUBLIC

I. FOREIGN INVESTMENT POLICY AND REGULATIONS

Since the adoption of the New Economic Mechanism (NEM) in 1986 and the Constitution in 1991, the Lao People's Democratic Republic has promulgated a number of laws and regulations which promote foreign investment and form the legal basis for the development of the private sector.

The policy framework for foreign investment in the Lao People's Democratic Republic is based on the new Law on the Promotion of Foreign Investment (2004) effective 14 January 2005 (which replaced the Law on the Promotion and Management of Foreign Investment of 1994), the Business Law (1994), the Customs Law (1994), and the Tax Law (1995).

The Law on the Promotion of Foreign Investment states the forms of acceptable foreign investment as well as the rights, benefits and obligations that come with each type of investment. It also explains the responsibilities of the Committee for Promotion and Management of Investment (CPMI) at the central and provincial levels. The law excludes indirect investment, such as loans, aid and general buying and selling of commodities.

The Government's role is that of a facilitator to help create an enabling environment for expanding private investment, both domestic and foreign. The CPMI is acting as a one-stop service on investment issues and the coordinating body with sectoral organizations at the central level and provincial levels.

Foreign investment is welcome in all production, businesses, sectors and zones of the country except in business activities which are (a) detrimental to national security, (b) cause a negative impact on the environment in the present or long term and (c) detrimental to health or national customs and traditions.

The Lao People's Democratic Republic has concluded bilateral investment agreements with the following 20 countries:

Bilateral Investment Agreements

Australia	Germany	Singapore

China	India	Sweden
Cuba	Indonesia	Switzerland
Democratic People's	Malaysia	Thailand
Republic of Korea	Mongolia	United Kingdom
Denmark	Republic of Korea	United States of America
France	Russian Federation	Viet Nam

A separate bilateral agreement for the avoidance of double taxation has been signed with Thailand.

Foreign direct investment (FDI) in the Lao People's Democratic Republic has shown substantive growth in recent years. In 2003-2004,[2] actual investment increased almost 20 per cent with regard to the period 2002-2003, from US$ 150 million to US$ 180 million. Approved investment grew by 8 per cent during the same period.

Investment has flowed into the following sectors: garments, wood processing, tourism, hydropower generation and mining. Of these, the industrial sector (mining, handicrafts and wood processing) has been the main recipient of FDI over the past years, accounting for almost 70 per cent of the total FDI approvals. Agriculture and services sectors made up for 25 per cent of total FDI approvals each.

During the period 2003-2004, the main foreign investors in the Lao People's Democratic Republic were Australia (US$ 293 million), Viet Nam (US$ 63 million), Thailand (US$ 51 million), Switzerland (US$ 30 million) and China (US$ 28 million). Other investors are France, Malaysia, Netherlands, the Republic of Korea, Singapore and the United States of America.

As the role of the public private sector dialogue was recognized as one of the most effective ways to promote better understanding between the Government and the business community, in March 2005 the Government signed a Memorandum of Understanding with the International Finance Cooperation (World Bank Group) and Mekong Private Sector Development Facility (MPDF) to launch the Lao Business Forum to be organized twice a year. The first meeting took place on 9 March 2005.

II. INVESTMENT PROCEDURES

A foreign investor has the following choices when investing in the Lao

People's Democratic Republic:

x Business cooperation by contract;

x Joint ventures between foreign and domestic investors, where foreign equity should not be less than 30 per cent of the registered capital;

x One hundred per cent foreign-owned enterprises.

A. Foreign investment licence

Foreign companies or investors who wish to invest in the Lao People's Democratic Republic should fill out an application form available at the one-stop service of CPMI at the central or provincial levels. Application forms are free of charge.

The competed application must be submitted to CPMI with the following

attachments:

x Copy of the passport

x Resume of the foreign investor

x Feasibility study or business plan

x Statement certifying the legal and financial status of the legal entity

x In the case of a joint venture, a copy of the joint venture agreement.

[2] World Bank, Economic Monitor, November 2004.

Upon receipt of an application with the above-listed attachments, CPMI would coordinate with relevant sector and local authorities, when necessary, to consider and respond in writing to the foreign investor pursuant to the following time frame:

x Project falling in the lit of promoted activities: 15 working days

x Project falling in the lit of open activities with conditions: 25 working days

x Project involving the grant of a concession: 45 working days

Foreign investors who qualify shall obtain a foreign investment licence as well as an enterprise registration certificate and a tax registration certificate from CPMI. The activity must start within 90 days from the date of receipt of the investment licence, otherwise the licence shall be terminated.

Since August 2004,[3] the Department of Domestic and Foreign Investment (DDFI) operating under the Prime Minister's Office, acts as a one-stop service to foreign investors by providing information and assistance during the investment process. DDFI is a central government agency under the supervision of CPMI. The DDFI web page offers information on how to conduct business in the Lao People's Democratic Republic, laws and regulations, start-up procedures, as well as access to investment application forms required.

At the central level, CPMI is designing and planning the foreign investment policies while at the provincial level it is responsible of implementing the policies within its jurisdiction.

B. Business registration

Under the Business Law (1994), Domestic Trade Department Business Registration Division of the Ministry of Commerce (MOC) is responsible for registering all businesses in a company register. The Business Law makes no distinction between foreign and domestic companies.

A Guiding Order has established a provision of two days for the registration of local businesses in the trade sector at one of the following three levels: central (MOC), provincial and district. The application must include:

x an application form

x personal biography

x a statement of criminal records No. 3

x a copy of ID card and three 3x4 photographs

x financial statement

x charter by-law approved by trade agency (for entity as company only).

There is a division of tasks for business registration approval between different levels of government agencies as follows:

x MOC registers foreign companies (with registered capital of

US$ 200,000 or more), enterprises dealing with imports of vehicles and

fuel and exports of wood and wood products, State enterprises and joint ventures established at the central level.

[3] See PM Decision No. 43/PM of 27 August 2004 on the new procedure for registration and approvals of FDI.

x Provincial trade authorities provide registration to foreign investors (with registered capital below US$ 200,000), enterprises in the agricultural, industrial and services sectors, trading firms, state enterprises and joint ventures established by local governments.

x District offices can register and manage retail stores, shops, small supermarkets and other small services.

For further information concerning investment policy, regulations of the Lao People's Democratic Republic and to obtain an application form, trader may contact:

Investment Promotion Division Luang Prabang Road Vientiane 01001 Tel.: (856-21) 222 690, (856-21) 215 491 E-mail: fimc@laotel.com URL: http://invest.laopdr.org

III. INVESTMENT INCENTIVES AND SPECIAL PROMOTION ZONES

The Government of the Lao People's Democratic Republic offers incentives to foreign investors according to specific activities and zones. According to the Law on the Promotion of Foreign Investment, the promoted activities are the following:

1. Production for export;
2. Activities relating to agriculture or forestry, and agricultural, forestry and handicraft processing activities;
3. Activities relating to industrial processing, industrial activities using modern techniques and technology, research and development, and activities relating to the protection of the environment and biodiversity;
4. Human resource development, skills development and public health;
5. Construction of infrastructure;
6. Production of raw materials and equipment to be supplied to key industrial activities;
7. Development of the tourism industry and transit services.

The three promoted zones identified by the law, based on geographical location and socio-economic conditions in the zones, are:

Zone 1: Mountainous, plain and plateau zones with no economic infrastructure to facilitate investment.

Zone 2: Mountainous, plain and plateau zones with a moderate level of economic infrastructure suitable to accommodate investment to some extent.

Zone 3: Mountainous, plain and plateau zones with good infrastructure to support investment.

A. Duties and tax incentives

According to the Law on the Promotion of Foreign Investment (2004), the foreign investment enterprises investing within the promoted activities and zones as listed above are entitled to the following duty and tax incentives:

Zone 1: Profit tax exemption for 7 years and a concessional 10 per cent profit tax rate after the exemption period.

Zone 2: Profit tax exemption for 5 years followed by a reduced profit tax rate of 7.5 per cent for 3 years and after a concessional 15 per cent profit tax rate.

Zone 3: Profit tax exemption for 2 years followed by a reduced profit tax rate of 10 per cent for 2 years and after a concessional 20 per cent profit tax rate after the exemption period.

The starting date for the profit tax exemption is the date the foreign investment enterprise carries out operations, while for tree plantation activities it is the date the enterprise starts to make a profit.

In addition, foreign investors investing in the listed promoted activities are entitled to the following incentives: x During the tax exemption and reduced tax periods, the enterprise is exempted from the minimum tax; x The profit used for the expansion of licensed business activities are exempted from profit tax during the accounting year;

x Exemption from import duties and taxes on: + Equipment, spare parts and vehicles directly used for production; + Raw materials not available domestically or that exist but are insufficient in number and semi-finished products imported for manufacture or processing for re-export; and x Exemption from export duty on exported products.

Additionally, raw materials and semi-finished products imported for manufacture assembly or processing for import substitution will be exempted or allowed a reduced rate of import duties and taxes.

B. Non-tax incentives

The Government provides the following non-tax incentives to all foreign investors: x Right to employ foreign technicians, experts and managers but should not

exceeding 10 per cent of the enterprise's labour force x Investment term is up to 75 years x Personal income tax at a flat rate of 10 per cent x Foreign investors are also allowed to expatriate their earnings back home

or to a third country.

The Government also offers guarantees against nationalization, expropriation or requisition without compensation.

For further details on investment incentives, please refer to the DDFI website at http://invest.laopdr.org/.

C. Special economic zone

Approximately 500 km south of Vientiane, the province of Savannakhet is located along the East-West Economic Corridor (EWEC) linking Myanmar, Thailand, Lao People's Democratic Republic and Viet Nam (Road No. 9). EWEC crosses the Indo-China peninsula and forms a land bridge between the South China Sea and the Andaman Sea. The reconstruction of Road No.9 in Savannakhet province was completed in mid-2004. A free traffic system and operation of a single custom inspection point of the corridor among the countries concerned should be implemented soon.

According to Prime Minister Decree No. 148/PM on the establishment of the Savan-Seno Special Economic Zone (SSEZ) located in Savannakhet province dated 29 September 2003, the zone composes the following:

x Site A (305 ha), located immediately upstream of Savannakhet capital city

in Khanthabouly district, next to the new Mekong River Bridge,

x Site B (20 ha) in Seno town located 28 km East from site A, at the junction

between the National Road No. 13 and National Road No. 9.

The main objectives of SSEZ are:

x To attract and promote investment

x To create jobs and upgrade labour skills

x To develop and modernize the country industrialization

x To become a trade and service hub on EWEC The categories of business activities to be developed in SSEZ are the following:

x Export Processing Zone

x Free Trade Zone

x Free Service and Logistic Centre (which should include tourism, banking and other activities)

According to Prime Minister Decree No. 177/PM on the management regulations and incentive policies regarding SSEZ dated 13 November 2003, the SSEZ governance is the responsibility of SSEZ Authority. The primary function of the Authority is to ensure prompt and transparent authorization of licensing of investment in the zone and to provide investors and developers with all the necessary facilities and assistance, including processing of their investment requests through a One-Stop Station Service. SSEZ has an autonomous budget and full responsibility in the management, design and construction of the Zone.

Interested investors should submit the investment application form directly to SSEZ. The approval or rejection of the application and granting of the licence would be done within 5 working days.

For further details on investment possibilities in SSEZ please contact: Savan-Sena Special Economic Zone Authority

P.O. Box 200 Phetsalad Road, Khanthabouli District Savannakhet

Tel./Fax: (856 41) 251487 E-mail: sonphet@laotel.com Website: www.invest.laopdr.org

IV. TAXATION

All persons or legal entities consuming goods or services, conducting business, performing independent professions and generating income in the Lao People's Democratic Republic are subject to pay taxes.

According to the Tax Law of 1995, the tax system of the Lao People's Democratic Republic consists of direct and indirect taxes as follows:

Indirect taxes	Direct taxes	Other taxes
Excise tax	Income tax	Fees/charges
Turnover tax	Profit tax	Minimum tax
	Social security tax	

Enterprises operating in the country must pay one of the following two taxes, whichever produces the higher tax return, the minimum tax, at a flat rate of 1 per cent of gross profit or the profit tax, based on net profit.

The latest legislations relevant to taxation are the Prime Minister Decree No. 241 dated 25 December 1998 and the Ministry of Finance Decree No.1 dated 4 January 1999.

A. Excise tax

Excise tax is an indirect tax collected on certain types of goods. As specified in article 23 of the Tax Law, 1995, goods subject to excise tax include fuel (2-23 per cent), alcohol (30-40 per cent), tobacco products (30 per cent) and cosmetics (10 per cent).

B. Turnover tax

Turnover tax is collected on imports and the sale of general imported or locally produced goods. In addition, general services, constituting the supply of labour to others against a service fee as compensation, are also subject to turnover tax. Rates of turnover tax are 5 or 10 per cent.

Payment is made to the relevant tax authorities on a monthly basis, before the tenth day of the following month. Deductions are made from these monthly turnover taxes if the importer has already paid at the port of entry. Paid taxes are carried forward to the next month if necessary. Goods, whether imported or locally produced, constructions or services that are used by the operator are also subject to turnover tax.

Importers of goods for re-export to third countries, export-oriented producers or providers of services which have been subjected to turnover taxes at the port of entry are entitled to deduct these payments from the taxes payable at the next import of goods, raw materials, etc.

Imports on equipment, means of production, spare parts and other materials used in the operation of foreign investors' projects or in their productive enterprises are taxed at a uniform flat rate of 1 per cent of the imported value. Raw materials and intermediate components, imported for the purpose of processing and then exported, are exempt from such import duties.

C. Income tax

This is a direct tax collected from income generated in the Lao People's Democratic Republic. Taxable income includes: x Income from salaries such as wages, bonuses, position bonuses and other material benefits, including benefits-in-kind

x Income from movable assets, such as dividends or other benefits for shareholders of a company, loan interest and guarantee fees or other liens

x Income from the lease of assets

x Income from patents or other rights, including lease of rights, production formulae, trademarks and copyrights.

Certain types of income are exempt from tax. These include social insurance and salaries of foreign experts involved in projects in the Lao People's Democratic Republic.

A salary tax on earnings of foreign personnel is levied at a flat rate of 10 per cent on gross income, including most benefits-in-kind. It is paid on a monthly basis through withholding at payment. Foreign personnel receiving salaries abroad are liable to pay income tax in the Lao

People's Democratic Republic when they reside in the country for over 180 days in a given tax year.

Salary tax is levied at a progressive rate of up to 45 per cent on gross income of local personnel. Salary and wage earners are entitled to deduct 200,000 kip from their monthly salary in the computation of tax payable. This deduction is an allowance for "expenses for living costs".

D. Profit tax

Taxes on profits are set at 35 per cent on net profits for all Lao business enterprises and for foreign business enterprises, please see details in chapter III of this part. Taxable profit includes:

x **Profit from business generated from agro-forestry, industrial and handicraft production, the exploitation of natural resources, import/export, wholesale or retail trade and general services**

x **Profit from independent professionals**

x **Certain expenses can be deducted when determining annual profit. These include:**

- **General expenses in business activities, including utility costs, travel and entertainment, advertising, salaries, lease costs and insurance**
- **Expenses on travel and entertainment - these are only deductible up to a limit of 0.2 per cent of turnover**
- **Expenses on gifts, allowances, presents and prizes - these are only deductible up to a limit of 0.15 per cent of turnover**

x Depreciation, which can be claimed on a straight line or cost reduction method. In the year of acquisition or disposal, depreciation can be claimed for the portion of the year the asset was owned

x Reserves for unexpected expenses and risks relating to items such as valuation of inventory or receivables.

Profit taxes, income taxes on salaries, salaries paid to partners in partnerships, luxury expenses and interest payments to shareholders are examples of non-deductible expenses. Individuals receiving income from business profits are entitled to an annual deduction of 1,200,000 kip.

The profit tax is remitted on a quarterly basis, based on estimated profit or the prior year's profit. Tax returns are made to the tax authorities prior to the fifteenth day of the month following the end of each quarter. The balance of the Profit or Minimum Tax due should be remitted before 15 April of the following year. If the quarterly profit tax is overpaid, the amount is not refunded in cash but can be deducted from future profit tax calculations. Tax can also be payable on a lump-sum basis.

E. Value added tax

Following recommendations by the IMF, the Government has pledged to introduce a value added tax regime, which will replace the turnover tax. This is partly designed to offset the anticipated loss of customs revenue as tariffs are lowered in line with the commitments of the Lao People's Democratic Republic with ASEAN-AFTA. The value added tax would be introduced in 2007.

The Tax Law sets out a simple system of tax payment which associates turnover tax and profit tax into one payment. The simple system of tax payment requires an agreement between the tax authority and the taxpayer. The agreement becomes effective within one year of the signature of the contract. In order to cancel the agreement, the taxpayer should inform the tax authority 60 days before expiration of the contract. The tax authority may cancel the agreement at any time if it is discovered that the taxpayer has violated the limits of business operations stated in the contract.

Rates for the simple system of tax payment

Rates for each type of activities			
Estimated annual income	(percentage)		
(kip)	Production, construction and	Trade restaurants transport	Services and
Less than 2,000,000 Kip	1	2	3
2,000,001 - 4,000,000	2	3	4
4,000,001 - 8,000,000	3	4	5
8,000,001 - 12,000,000	4	5	6
12,000,001 - 16,000,000	5	6	7
16,000,001 - 20,000,000	6	7	8
20,000,001 - 24,000,000	7	8	9

Source: **Tax Law 1994, p. 29**

V. FOREIGN EXCHANGE

The policy framework for foreign exchange is based on the following laws and regulations: Law on the Bank of the Lao People's Democratic Republic, No. 05/LNA, dated 14 October 1995 and the amended version No. 05/LNA, dated 14 October 1999 as well as the Presidential Decree No. 01/OP dated 9 August 2002 on governing the management of foreign exchange and precious metals.

The national currency is the kip. Official currency exchange facilities are provided by a range of Lao banks, including the *Banque du Commerce Extérieur* or at a foreign exchange bureau licensed by the Bank of the Lao People's Democratic Republic.

All foreign enterprises are considered to be Lao residents for the purpose of foreign exchange. They must deposit all foreign exchange earnings into accounts with banks in the Lao People's Democratic Republic and cannot open accounts abroad except where deemed necessary.

In conformity with the law and regulations governing the management of foreign exchange and precious metals, foreign investors may repatriate earnings and capital from their foreign investments to their own home countries or third countries. They may do this through a Lao bank or a foreign bank established in the Lao People's Democratic Republic, using the exchange rate prevailing on the date of repatriation, as quoted by the Bank of Lao People's Democratic Republic.

Foreign personnel with foreign investments may also repatriate their earnings, after paying Lao personal income taxes and all other taxes due. After paying the annual profit tax, foreign investors have to devote 5 per cent of their profit each year to various reserve funds designed to ensure that enterprises continuously improve their efficiency, in accordance with the enterprise's policy and Articles of Association.

VI. LABOUR ISSUES

A central piece of legislation covering labour and employment in the Lao People's Democratic Republic is the Labour Law, 1994. The law covers the rights and obligations of employees and employers.

A. Main provisions under the Labour Law, 1994

Working hours	Prohibition of work in excess of 8 hours per day, 6 days per week or 48 hours per week; for workers in jobs in hazardous or unpleasant -abnormally hot or cold, or underground - environments, a maximum of 6 hours per day or 36 hours per week applies. Shift workers are entitled to a 45-minute meal break. Production workers are entitled to rest for at least 5-10 minutes every two hours.
Overtime	Maximum overtime of 30 hours per month, with a maximum of 3hours in each period. Overtime rates are 150 per cent of the standard rate if worked by day and 200 per cent if worked by night. If overtime is worked on Saturdays, Sundays or public holidays these rates are 250 per cent by day and 300 per cent by night (unless workers' contracts already require them to work on those days).
Minimum age	The minimum age of employment is 15 years. Between the ages of 15 and 18 the maximum work week is 6 hours per day or 36 hours per week; workers under 18 may not perform hazardous or arduous work.
Wages	Fixed salaries or wages must be paid at least monthly; hourly wages must be paid at least every 16 days.
Holidays	Workers are entitled to 15 days' holiday per year, or 18 days per year if performing arduous or hazardous work; these are in addition to official holidays or weekly rest days.
Sick leave	Workers are entitled to a maximum of 30 days sick leave per year upon presentation of a medical certificate.
Maternity	Women may take 90 days paid maternity leave. The law also prohibits work involving heavy lifting or long periods of continuous standing during pregnancy and for the 6 months after a pregnancy.
Retirement	The law provides for company pensions for long service and retiring employees and bonuses for elderly employees. The retirement age is 60 years for men and 55 years for women. Workers who have reached retirement age, have completed 25 years of service and have paid social security contributions for 25 years are entitled to a pension upon retirement. The ages and time periods are reduced by 5 years each for those in hazardous or arduous occupations.

For injuries sustained while performing occupational duties at the workplace, the employer or the social security fund shall bear the costs of treatment and hospitalization. Where a worker dies through occupational injury, the employer shall pay at least 6 months' salary to cover funeral expenses and pay a lump-sum benefit to the beneficiaries of the deceased. Workers who sustain an occupational injury are also entitled to full salary for up to 6 months and 50 per cent of their salary for a further 18 months. After 18 months, benefits are granted under the social security system.

Source: DDFI website at http://invest.laopdr.org/labour%20law.htm.

B. Labour contract

The Labour Law requires a written contract between an employer and an employee. In limited circumstances, a verbal contract is possible, for example for temporary or daily work or employment involving only a small amount of work. The contracts can be for a fixed term or indefinite period.

A probationary period is allowed to determine workers' ability to perform their duties. The period lasts a maximum of 30 days for work requiring no experience or specialized skills and a maximum of 60 days in other cases. The probationary period can be extended by a maximum of 30 days. Probation can be terminated at any time, but 3 days (or 6 days for skilled workers) notice must be given.

As for the termination of the contract, if workers are employed on an indefinite contract, 45 days notice must be given to skilled workers and 15 days to other workers. Workers may be dismissed in the case of inadequate skills or if there is a need to reduce the total number of workers.

In the case of dismissal to reduce staff numbers, dismissed workers are entitled to compensation according on their length of service. In the case of dismissal because of wrongdoing by the worker (e.g. dishonesty, deliberate damage to employer's property, or unexplained absences of four consecutive days), the employer has the right to terminate the contract with 3 days notice. However, the employer must also notify the trade union or worker's representative in the labour unit and the local labour administration.

C. Social security

The Social Security Decree came into force in June 2001 and is being introduced gradually. It applies to:

x Employees of State-owned enterprises, private enterprises and joint enterprises

x Enterprises that employ 10 or more employees

x An enterprise that has less than 10 employees, but is a branch of a larger enterprise If an enterprise is subject to the Social Security Decree, but later reduces its number of employees to less than the minimum requirement, it must still maintain its application of the Social Security Decree. However, the Government has set a ceiling where the deductions will cease to apply. Salaries above 1 million kip per month will be ignored for Social Security. As a result, the maximum charge will be 50,000 kip per month from employers and 45,000 kip per month from employees.

The employer is responsible for ensuring that the payments are made, by withholding the employee's contribution from wages.

VII. DISPUTE SETTLEMENT

As a member of ASEAN, the Lao People's Democratic Republic adheres to the ASEAN Protocol on Enhanced Dispute Settlement Mechanism signed in Vientiane on 29 November 2004, which provides rules and procedures on dispute settlements for all member States.

The Labour Law makes a distinction between (a) disputes over rights: disputes concerning the provisions of the Labour Law, labour regulations, employment contracts, labour unit regulations, etc; (b) disputes over interests: claims on the employer for new benefits or rights.

In the case of dispute over rights, the parties are encouraged to resolve the claim between themselves. If this is not possible then the worker is entitled to submit the claim to the labour administration for conciliation. If the dispute still cannot be resolved, the claim can be submitted to the People's Court.

The above also applies in respect of disputes over interests. If the labour administration fails to resolve the dispute, then the case goes to the Labour Dispute Arbitration Committee for a final decision.

In practice, Lao courts appear to do all they can to resolve disputes by arbitration. It is therefore rare for any case going to a Lao court to be resolved quickly and according to the strict letter of a contract.

VIII. PROTECTION OF PROPERTY RIGHTS

The Government is engaged in the modernization of its industrial property administration and in the early stages of developing its legal and procedural system for the protection of intellectual property.

Trademarks, patents, industrial design and copyrights are governed by the following legislative framework: x Decree of the Prime Minister on Trademark Registration, No. 06/PM, 18 January 1995 x Regulation on Registration of Trademarks, No. 466/STEA-PMO, 7 March 2002 x Decree of the Prime Minister on Patents, Industrial Designs and Utility Models, January 2002 x Regulation on the Implementation of the Decree on Patents, Industrial Designs and Utility Models, 2 July 2002 x A new Decree on Industrial Property Matters has been drafted and submitted to the Prime Minister's Office for approval.

Since 1999, the Science, Technology and Environment Agency (STEA), attached to the Prime Minister's Office, is responsible for the protection of intellectual property rights in the Lao People's Democratic Republic as well as for the improvement of the country's ability to adhere to conventions and international protocols.

Within the STEA, the Department of Intellectual Property, Standardization and Metrology (DISM) gives guidance on trademark registration and is also responsible for drafting Industrial Property laws. DISM also registers trademarks for use within the Lao People's Democratic Republic. The Intellectual Property division within this Department is responsible for the protection of patents, petty patents, industrial designs and trademarks.

For additional analytical, business and investment opportunities information, please contact Global Investment & Business Center, USA at (703) 370-8082. Fax: (703) 370-8083. E-mail: ibpusa3@gmail.com Global Business and Investment Info Databank - www.ibpus.com

Lao People's Democratic Republic signed the World Intellectual Property Organization (WIPO) Convention in January 1995 and the Paris Convention (Industrial Property) in October 1998. WIPO's contribution is playing a vital role in the establishment of an intellectual property system in the country. The Lao People's Democratic Republic plans to join the ASEAN Trademark and Patent Common Filing System and is actively participating in the ASEAN Cooperation on Intellectual Property.

A. Trademarks

Trademark indicates a sign used to mark goods or services to designate the goods and services as belonging to the owner of the created trademark.

Enforcement measures consist of administrative measures or claims and disputes that can be resolved by mediation through the DISM or the Economic Arbitration Committee; or/and judicial procedures for intellectual property protection, which can involve both the Civil Code and the Penal Code.

There are designated government offices which act as enforcement agencies for intellectual property rights in the country. For further details on enforcement and designated agencies, please refer to the STEA website at: http://www.stea.la.wipo.net/enforcement/index.html

The application for the registration of a trademark should contain:

x An application for the registration of trademark
x Some specimens of the trademark
x A power of attorney if application is made through an authorized representative
x A list of the goods or services with the description of characteristics and quality that are to bear the mark and other necessary relevant documents
x The rules governing the use of the mark (in case of a collective mark)
x The receipt of the prescribed charges for trademark registration and other services

An individual or legal entity who has been assigned the right to use the trademark should request to register trademark in the Lao People's Democratic Republic. An application may contain permission of the owner of the trademark, defining the characteristics and quality of goods and services bearing the mark. In the case of partial assignments, the agreement shall provide for the right of the owner of trademark to verify the quality of goods or services.

The request to register a trademark should be forwarded to STEA, which reviews the application, undertakes the substantial examination, issues the certificate of registration, records the mark on the Trademark Registry and publishes the registered mark on the Official Trademark Gazette. The certificate of registration of the trademark will be for a period of 10 years starting from the filing date of the application for registration and may be renewed every 10 years.

The fees for trademark registration, as set out in the Guidance on Registration of Trademark in the Lao People's Democratic Republic, are as follows:

For additional analytical, business and investment opportunities information,
please contact Global Investment & Business Center, USA
at (703) 370-8082. Fax: (703) 370-8083. E-mail: ibpusa3@gmail.com
Global Business and Investment Info Databank - www.ibpus.com

Type of services for trademark registration or renewal	Fee (in US dollars)
Trademark registration or trademark renewal Consultation Verification Application Search of Trademark Modification of items on application Licensing Cancellation Duplication of a registration certificate Issuance of certified document relating to the trademark registration or renewal Publication of the result of trademark registration or renewal	80 per mark 5 per mark 5 per mark 2 per mark 10 per mark 10 per mark 40 per mark 20 per mark 10 per mark 5 per one copy 20 per one copy

Source: STEA website at http://www.stea.la.wipo.net/trademark/fees.html.

For a list of trademark agents, go to http://www.stea.la.wipo.net/trademark/list.html.

B. Patents, petty patents and industrial designs

The owner of a patent, petty patent or an industrial design, before allowing another person to use such patent, petty patent or industrial designs in the Lao People's Democratic Republic, should notify STEA by written declaration.

1. Patents and petty patents

As defined in Decree No. 01/PM January 2002, a "patent" indicates the title granted to protect an invention whereas an "invention" indicates an idea of an inventor which permits in practice the solution to a specific problem in the field of technology. A "petty patent" indicates the title granted to protect device whereas a "device" indicates a technical creation utilizing rules of nature.

The application for a patent or a petty patent should be filed with STEA and should contain the following:

x A request, which should include a petition to the effect that a patent be
   granted, the name of and other prescribed data concerning the applicant,
   the inventor and the agent, if any, and the title of the invention
x A description
x One or more claims
x One or more drawings, if required
x An abstract.

At the request of the registry, the applicant will furnish the date and number of any application for a patent or petty patent filed in a foreign country, particularly relating to the same inventions as that claimed in the application filed in the Lao People's Democratic Republic.

The documents to be submitted regarding the foreign applications are as follows:

x A copy of certified results of any search or examination carried out in respect of the foreign application

x A copy of the patent granted on the basis of the foreign application

x A copy of any final decision refusing the grant of patent requested in the foreign application

After examination, if the application fulfils all conditions established in the regulations, the Registry Unit will notify the applicant to pay the prescribed fee, it will publish it to the public and issue a certificate of the grant of the patent.

A patent will expire 20 years after the filing date of the application. A petty patent will expire 7 years after the filing date of the application. In order to maintain the patent and/or petty patent, an annual fee should be paid in advance by the owner of the patent. For details on fees derived from registration and maintenance of patents (petty patens and industrial designs), please refer to the table below.

2. Industrial designs

An "industrial design" indicates any composition of lines or colours or any three-dimensional form, whether or not associated with line or colours, which can serve as a pattern for a product of industry or handicraft or give a special appearance to such a product, and appeals to and is judged by the eye.

The application for registration of an industrial design should contain: x A request x Drawings, photographs or other adequate graphic representations and an

indication of the kind of products for which the industrial design is to be used x A specimen of the article embodying the industrial design, where the industrial design is two-dimensional x A statement justifying the applicant's right to the registration of the industrial design, where the applicant is not the creator

An industrial design will expire 5 years after the filing date of the application and may be renewed for 2 continuous periods. Each period takes 5 years, where the application for renewal will apply for 90 days before expiry.

Table 10: Registration and maintenance fees for patent, petty patent and industrial design

Types of services	Registration fees (in US dollars)		
	Patent	Petty patent	Industrial design
Official fee for granting Application form for registration of Consultation Request against registration Amendment of application Licensing Duplicate Publication	30 per one item 20 per one item 10 per one item 20 per one item 10 per one item 40 per one item 10 per one copy 40 per one item	30 per one item 10 per one item 10 per one item 10 per one item 10 per one item 40 per one item 10 per one copy 30 per one item	20 per one item 10 per one item 10 per one item 10 per one item 10 per one item 40 per one item 10 per one copy 30 per one item
Maintenance fees (in US dollars)			
	Patent	Petty patent	Industrial design

Starting the	5th year	2nd year	2nd year
Official fee Services fee	30 per one item 20 per one item	15 per one item 10 per one item	10 per one item 5 per one item
For the following years, please refer to regulation No. 322/STEA-PMO, July 2002			

An individual or a legal entity who is the owner of a patent, petty patent or industrial design can apply for settlement of dispute relating to the infringement of his or her registered invention, device and industrial design with STEA. An individual or a legal entity who is the owner of a patent, petty patent or industrial design has the right to propose the method of settlement of dispute and claim for damages from another person who infringes on the rights of the invention.

References for part four: investing in the Lao People's Democratic Republic

Austrade, Lao People's Democratic Republic country profile

http://www.austrade.gov.au/australia/layout/0,,0_S2-1_-2_-3_PWB192923-4_-5_-6_7_,00.html Customs Law, 1994 http://invest.laopdr.org/customs%20law.htm DDFI, Business Guide http://invest.laopdr.org/business%20guide.htm DDFI, FI law, http://invest.laopdr.org/investment%20law.htm DDFI, SEZs http://invest.laopdr.org/specialper cent20zone.htm STEA http://www.stea.la.wipo.net/aboutdism/index.html Tax Law, 1995 http://invest.laopdr.org/tax%20law.htm Trademark Decree, 1995 http://www.stea.la.wipo.net/download/decree.zip http://invest.laopdr.org/trademark%20decree.htm

UNCTAD, Country Fact Sheet on FDI, November 2004 WIPO Guide to Intellectual Property Worldwide, Country Profiles (Last updated May 2004)

http://www.wipo.int/about-ip/en/ipworldwide/pdf/la.pdf World Bank – Doing Business Database http://rru.worldbank.org/DoingBusiness/ World Bank, Lao People's Democratic Republic Economic Monitor, May 2004

http://siteresources.worldbank.org/INTLAOPRD/Resources/2935821096519010070/lao_econ_mo nitor_may2004.pdf

World Bank, Lao People's Democratic Republic Economic Monitor, November 2004

http://siteresources.worldbank.org/INTLAOPRD/Resources/2935821096519010070/lao_econ_mo nitor_nov2004.pdf

PRACTICAL INFORMATION FOR STARTING AND CONDUCTING BUSINESS IN LAOS [2]

DOING BUSINESS IN LAO PDR

MARKET OVERVIEW

• The Lao market economy has grown at a nearly 7% clip for the last decade and

is heading into a new phase of regional and global integration. After acceding to the World Trade Organization in 2013, Laos looks to the ASEAN Economic Community as a marker for its next set of economic policy and trade development goals.

• The Lao government suffered through a fiscal and monetary crisis in 2013 and into 2014, brought about by poor budgetary processes, uncontrolled investment in infrastructure, and a large raise for civil servants. Government fiscal and budgetary policy formulation and implementation remain weak but the government is taking steps to address some deficiencies.

• Laos is one of five remaining communist countries in the world and this legacy continues to weigh on both governance and the economy. The Lao economic model bears some relation to its Chinese and Vietnamese counterparts, in that it has implemented market-based economic practices while maintaining a very high degree of political control. Laos is politically stable.

• Laos and the United States signed a bilateral trade agreement in 2005, although the terms of the agreement are still being implemented in Laos, with U.S. assistance.

Since 2005 trade has increased from $14 million to $55 million per year in 2013. Vietnam, China and Thailand have dominant trade and investment roles in the Lao economy, with participation in certain sectors by Korea, France, Japan, Australia, Malaysia and Singapore. Bilateral trade between Laos and Thailand, its largest trading partner by far, totaled $5 billion in 2012.

• Laos' GDP was an estimated $11.1 billion in 2013, up 8.1 percent from the prior year. The Lao economy is projected to grow at 8 percent annually through 2020. Inflation was 6.4 percent in 2013.

• The Lao population was estimated at 6.6 million in 2013. Approximately 70 percent of the workforce is employed in agriculture, mostly in small scale farming. The Lao population is young, with more than half under 20 years of age.

• GDP per capita continued to rise in 2013, edging up to $1,587. The country has a small but growing middle class concentrated mostly in the capital and larger cities.

• Laos ran a projected trade deficit of approximately $2.9 billion in 2013, with merchandise imports of $6.9 billion, exports of $3.4 billion and net services of $539 billion. Laos imported $24 million worth of goods from the United States and exported $30 million to the United States in 2013. Top U.S exports to Laos in the past include precious

---

[2] US Departmetn of Comemrce materials

For additional analytical, business and investment opportunities information, please contact Global Investment & Business Center, USA at (703) 370-8082. Fax: (703) 370-8083. E-mail: ibpusa3@gmail.com Global Business and Investment Info Databank - www.ibpus.com

stones, machinery, metals and vehicles. Top U.S. imports from Laos have been garments, chemicals, plastics and precious stones.

> • The Lao Trade Portal, established in 2012, has information for exporters and importers at: http://www.laotradeportal.gov.la/index.php?r=site/index

Useful Web links:

Lao Chapter of The American Chamber of Commerce: http://amchamlao.com/
Lao Trade Portal: http://www.laotradeportal.gov.la/index.php?r=site/index
U.S. Embassy in Vientiane, Laos: http://vientiane.usembassy.gov/
U.S. Census Trade data: http://www.census.gov/foreign-trade/statistics/country/
CIA World Factbook: https://www.cia.gov/library/publications/the-world- factbook/geos/la.html

MARKET CHALLENGES

• Commercial law and the commercial court system in Laos are developing slowly and are not transparent. Business disputes are rarely adjudicated in favor of the foreign investor. Sanctity of contract is not well understood in Laos and concessions or property rights granted by the government are liable to overlap or conflict with other claims.

• Customs procedures are improving but remain opaque. Customs clearance speed has improved markedly in recent years with the introduction of automated customs procedures, dropping from an average 18 hours in 2010 to 11 hours in 2012. The cost for a standard shipping container fell from $2100 to $1900 in 2013 but remains more than twice the regional average for East Asia and the Pacific.

• Despite government efforts to establish "one stop service" for business registration and licensing, procedures for investment are cumbersome and approvals often do not occur within stated times or rules.

• Human resources are not well developed in Laos, and employers frequently have a difficult time finding and retaining qualified employees. For skilled employees, the labor market offers frequent incentives to change employers.

Tax administration is consistently cited as one of the largest barriers to commerce in Laos in surveys of small and medium enterprises.

• The World Bank's "Doing Business" project compares Laos with 185 other economies at: http://www.doingbusiness.org/ExploreEconomies/?economyid=107 • Corruption is a major problem and seriously hampers the efficient operation of the Lao economy and society. Competitors from countries without the legal or moral sanctions against corrupt practices have a major advantage in securing government approvals and concessions. Frequent bribes and payoffs are an accepted part of Lao business culture. http://cpi.transparency.org/cpi2012/results/

MARKET OPPORTUNITIES

• Increases in disposable income and a slowly expanding middle class mean that the consumer and services sectors are likely to experience continued growth in the future.

• The power sector is open to foreign investment, with many international firms represented. Hydropower, coal, and transmission infrastructure will be the focus of increasing investment by the GOL as it develops its power industry.

• Laos has a very poorly developed infrastructure with virtually no rail, few decent roadways, and underdeveloped medical, water and sewage systems. The GOL is likely to make investments in these areas in coming years in keeping with it's ambitious goal of graduating from Least Developed Country status by 2020.

• The minerals and mining sector is a major driver of growth in Laos. Commodities prices in recent years have favored Lao and copper producers. Other mineral resources include bauxite and potash.

• The Lao government has targeted tourism, especially ecotourism, as a major area of future growth, and in 2013 it was Laos' second largest source of foreign exchange after mining, earning an estimated $550 million.

MARKET ENTRY STRATEGY

• American companies considering investments in Laos are advised to visit the country several times, as personal relationships are key to locating suitable Lao business partners and avoiding misunderstandings. Many foreign businesses take on a Lao partner or agent.

• The American Chamber of Commerce (AMCHAM) in Laos was established in 2012. Foreign businesses can also apply for membership in the Lao National Chamber of Commerce and Industry. http://www.lncci.laotel.com/

• In addition to AMCHAM, there are business chambers or associations from China, France, Australia-New Zealand, Japan, Vietnam, Taiwan, India, Korea, and the European Chamber of Commerce and Industry.

LAOS INVESTMENT AND BUSINESS CLIMATE - STRATEGIC INFORMATION AND CONTACTACT FOR STARTING BUSINESS IN LAOS

Contact Point
Matt Younger
Economic and Commercial Officer
American Embassy Vientiane, Rue Bartholonie, That Dam, Lao PDR
856-21-26-7156
youngermb@state.gov

After a decade-long experiment with a pure Marxist economy following the founding of the Lao People's Democratic Republic, the Lao PDR launched the "New Economic Mechanism" in 1986. Since that time, the country has gradually implemented the reforms and built the institutions necessary to a market economy. Over the last thirty years, the trend has been slow but steady progress, culminating in accession to the World Trade Organization in February, 2013. Since 2009, annual GPD growth has averaged approximately eight percent.

In order to meet the requirements for entry to the WTO, Laos engaged in major reforms of its economic and trade laws and regulations. The Lao government is now working to implement the commitments embodied in those laws, and to meet the 2015 goal for creation of the ASEAN Economic Community (AEC), which will further liberalize the trading environment and economy. Additionally, WTO and AEC requirements reinforce fuller implementation of the conditions of the 2005 U.S.-Laos Bilateral Trade Agreement.

Economic progress and trade expansion in Laos remain hampered by a low level of human resource development, weak education and health care systems, and a poor, although improving, transportation infrastructure. Institutions, especially in the justice sector, are a work in progress, and regulatory capacity is low. Additionally, increasing corruption has recently become a major concern, and the country has suffered through fiscal and monetary crises in the past year. The Lao economy is highly dependent on exploitation of natural resources, particularly in copper mining and hydropower. Although the services and industrial sectors have grown in recent years, the economy is in need of further diversification, and the majority of the Lao population is still employed in agriculture.

According to the 7th National Socio-Economic Development Plan (NSEDP) 2011-2015, Laos seeks to continue an annual economic growth rate in the neighborhood of 8%. To accomplish this, the government of Laos estimates that it needs approximately US$15 billion of total investment in the next five years, US$7 to US$8 billion of which it plans to source from foreign and domestic private investment. The plan directs the government to formulate "policies that would attract investments in addition to attracting Overseas Development Assistance; begin to implement public investment and investment promotion laws; and increase cooperation with friendly countries and international organizations."

1. OPENNESS TO, AND RESTRICTIONS UPON, FOREIGN INVESTMENT

The government of Lao PDR (GOL) officially welcomes both domestic and foreign investment as it seeks to graduate from Least Developed Country status by the year 2020. The pace of foreign investment has increased over the last several years. Mining and hydropower compose eighty percent of Foreign Direct Investment (FDI). China, Vietnam, Thailand Korea, and Japan are the largest sources of foreign investment.

The 2010 Law on Investment Promotion introduced uniform business registration requirements and tax incentives that apply equally to foreign and domestic investors. Foreigners may invest in any sector or business except those that the government deems to be detrimental to national security, health or national traditions, or to have a negative impact on the natural environment. There are no statutory limits on foreign ownership or control of commercial enterprises, but in practice, many companies seek a local partner. Companies involved in large FDI projects, especially in mining and hydropower, often either find it advantageous or are required to give the government partial ownership, frequently with money borrowed from the investor or multilateral institutions.

Foreign investors seeking to establish operations in Laos are typically required go through several steps prior to commencing operations. In addition to an investment license, foreign investors are required to obtain other permits, including; an annual business registration from the Ministry of Industry and Commerce; a tax registration from the Ministry of Finance; a business logo registration from the Ministry of Public Security; permits from each line ministry related to the investment (i.e., Ministry of Industry and Commerce for manufacturing; Ministry of Energy and Mines for power sector development); appropriate permits from local authorities; and an import-export license, if applicable. Obtaining the necessary permits can pose a challenge, especially in areas outside the capital. In 2013, the Lao government began allowing businesses to apply for tax registration at the time of incorporation, slightly simplifying the business registration process.

The Lao government has attempted to streamline business registration through the use of a "one-stop shop" model. For general business activities, this service is located in the Ministry of Industry and Commerce. For activities requiring a government concession, the service is located in the Ministry of Planning and Investment. For Special Economic Zones (SEZ), one-stop registration is run through the Secretariat to the Lao National Committee on Special Economic Zones (SNCSEZ) in the Office of the Prime Minister. According to PM Decree 177, the Savan-Seno SEZ authority is required to establish one-stop service to facilitate the issuing of investment licenses and improve the efficiency of business operations. In practice, it appears as though SEZ applications involve several different permissions and vary widely across SEZs. For clarification of one-stop shop procedures it is recommended that investors contact the SNCSEZ directly at: **sez@sncsez.gov.la**

Foreign partners in a joint venture must contribute at least thirty percent (30%) of the venture's registered capital. Capital contributed in foreign currency must be converted into kip based on the exchange rate of the Bank of the Lao People's Democratic Republic on the day of the capital contribution. Wholly foreign-owned companies may be either a new company or a branch of an existing foreign enterprise. Throughout the period of operation of a foreign investment enterprise, the assets of the enterprise must not be less than its registered capital.

Individual companies in the petrochemical industry are required to file an annual import plan. The government controls the retail price and profit margins of gasoline and diesel. Government documents articulating the restrictions and explaining the policy are difficult to obtain. Goods prohibited for import and export range from explosives and weapons, to literature that presents a negative view of the Lao government, to certain forestry products and wildlife. Agriculture production and most manufacturing production are private. State-owned enterprises (SOEs) currently account for only one percent of total employment. Over 90% of manufacturers have fewer than 10 employees. Equity in medium and large-sized SOEs can be obtained through a joint venture with the Lao government.

Although accurate statistics are difficult to obtain, there is no question that foreign investment has trended dramatically upward over the last several years, going from $1.2 billion in 2012 to $1.8 billion in 2013. There are also small but growing signs of growth in higher-quality FDI, focused on manufacturing, largely through one Special Economic Zone in the southern part of the country.

Measure	Year	Rank or value	Website Address
TI Corruption Perceptions index	2013	(140 of 177)	http://cpi.transparency.org/cpi2013/results/
Heritage Foundation's Economic Freedom index	2013	(144 of 178)	http://www.heritage.org/index/ranking
World Bank's Doing Business Report "Ease of Doing Business"	2013	(159 of 189)	http//doingbusiness.org/rankings
World Bank GNI per capita	2012	USD 1270	http://data.worldbank.org/indicator/NY.GNP.PCAP.CD

TABLE 1B – 2014 Lao PDR Millennium Challenge Scorecard:

MCC Scorecard Categories	Year	Percentage Score	Raw Score

MCC Government Effectiveness	FY 2014	56%	.04
MCC Rule of Law	FY 2014	60%	.07
MCC Control of Corruption	FY 2014	40%	-.13
MCC Fiscal Policy	FY 2014	49%	-3.1
MCC Trade Policy	FY 2014	12%	58.6
MCC Regulatory Quality	FY 2014	44%	-0.09
MCC Business Start-Up	FY 2014	23%	0.771
MCC Land Rights and Access	FY 2014	66%	0.68
MCC Natural Resource Protection	FY 2014	81%	93.9
MCC Access to Credit	FY 2014	36%	22
MCC Inflation	FY 2014	72%	4.3

The Millennium Challenge Corporation, a U.S. Government entity charged with delivering development grants to countries that have demonstrated a commitment to reform, produced scorecards for countries with a 2012 per capita gross national income (GNI) or $4,085 or less. A list of countries/economies with MCC scorecards and links to those scorecards is available here: **http://www.mcc.gov/pages/selection/scorecards**. Details on each of the MCC's indicators and a guide to reading the scorecards are available here: **http://www.mcc.gov/documents/reports/reference-2013001142401-fy14-guide-to-the-indicators.pdf**

2. CONVERSION AND TRANSFER POLICIES

In 2013, Laos suffered fiscal and monetary difficulties which resulted in low levels of foreign reserves. In response, the Bank of the Lao PDR (BOL) imposed daily limits on converting funds from Lao Kip into U.S. Dollars and Thai Baht, leading to difficulties in obtaining foreign exchange in Laos. The BOL also imposed restrictions on loans made in USD and Baht, limiting them to businesses which generated foreign currency. There were no reports of restrictions on, or difficulties in, repatriating or transferring funds associated with an investment.

In order to facilitate business transactions, foreign investors generally open commercial bank accounts in both local and foreign convertible currency at domestic and foreign banks in Laos. The Enterprise Accounting Law places no limitations on foreign investors transferring after-tax profits, income from technology transfer, initial capital, interest, wages and salaries, or other remittances to the company's home country or third countries provided that they request approval from the Lao government. Foreign enterprises must report on their performance annually and submit annual financial statements to the Ministry of Planning and Investment (MPI).

The Bank of Lao PDR manages the Lao currency, the kip, under a managed floating exchange rate in which it seeks to maintain its value in a band of plus or minus five percent around the nominal exchange rate with the U.S. dollar and Thai baht. Lao PDR is listed as a high-risk jurisdiction for money laundering/combating the financing of terrorism by the Financial Action Task Force (FATF) and has strategic deficiencies in its AML/CFT regime. In 2013, the Bank of Lao PDR agreed with the Asia Pacific Group, a regional FATF-body, to implement an action plan to address AML/CFT deficiencies.

3. EXPROPRIATION AND COMPENSATION

Foreign assets and investments in Laos are protected by laws and regulations against seizure, confiscation, or nationalization except when deemed necessary for a public purpose, in which case foreign investors are supposed to be compensated. Revocation of an investment license cannot be appealed to an independent body, and companies whose licenses are revoked must then quickly liquidate their assets.

Since 2012, Sanum Investments, a subsidiary of Lao Holdings, Inc., a company incorporated in Aruba and owned by American citizens, has been involved in a business dispute with its Lao partner. Thus far, court decisions in the case have been uniformly in favor of the Lao partner and could be construed as implicitly forcing local ownership. In addition, the company was subjected to audits and tax enforcement decisions that Sanum has alleged amount to expropriation. Sanum filed a case against the Lao PDR at the World Bank's International Center for the Settlement of Investment Disputes in 2012.

4. DISPUTE SETTLEMENT

The Lao judicial system is not independent and faces challenges in meeting the needs of a modern market economy. Contract law in Laos is lacking in many areas important to trade and commerce. While it does provide for sanctity of contracts, in practice contracts are subject to political interference and patronage. A contract can be voided if it is disadvantageous to one party, or if it conflicts with state or public interests. Foreign businessmen have described contracts in Laos as being considered "a framework for negotiation" rather than a binding agreement. Although a commercial court system exists, in practice most judges adjudicating commercial disputes have little training in commercial law. Those considering doing business in Laos are strongly urged to contact a reputable law firm for additional advice on contracts.

According to the Law on Investment Promotion, investors should resolve disputes in the following order: mediation; administrative dispute resolution; dispute resolution by the Committee for Economic Dispute Resolution; and finally, litigation. However, due to the poor state of the Lao legal system and low capacity of most Lao legal administrators, foreign investors are generally advised to seek arbitration outside the country.

Laos is not a member of the International Center for the Settlement of Investment Disputes. It became a party to the New York Convention of 1958 on the Recognition and Enforcement of Foreign Arbitral Awards on September 15, 1998, but Laos has never been asked to enforce a foreign arbitral award. Laos is a member of the United Nations Convention on International Trade Law.

In disputes involving the Ministry of Planning and Investment, decisions can only be appealed back to the Ministry itself. There is no separate independent body. Thus a company which feels it is receiving unfair treatment from the government has no independent recourse. Lao laws often contradict each other and lack implementing regulations. Some laws have been officially translated into English, including the business, tax, bankruptcy, customs, and secured transaction laws. The reliability of unofficial translations varies considerably. Application of Lao law remains inconsistent and knowledge of the laws themselves is often limited (especially outside the capital). The existence of a large number of government decrees, sometimes unpublished, further complicates the situation.

A commercial court does exist in Laos. Laos has no anti-trust statutes. The bankruptcy law permits either the business or creditor the right to petition the court for a bankruptcy judgment, and allows businesses the right to request mediation. There is no record of foreign-owned enterprises, whether as debtors or as creditors, petitioning the courts for a bankruptcy judgment.

5. PERFORMANCE REQUIREMENTS AND INVESTMENT INCENTIVES

Laos does not impose performance requirements and its regulations appear to be broadly consistent with WTO Trade Related Investment Measures (TRIMs), although it has notified the WTO that it will avail itself of transition periods for least-developed countries in completely phasing out local content and export performance requirements. Foreign investors are encouraged to give priority to Lao citizens in recruiting and hiring. Foreign personnel can be hired, although they may not normally exceed 10% of the enterprise's total labor force, with exceptions for skilled labor or politically important projects. Before bringing in foreign labor, foreign enterprises must apply for work permits from the Ministry of Labor and Social Welfare. A list of foreign personnel must also be submitted to MPI.

Laos grants incentives for foreign investment depending on industry sectors and activities promoted by the government, and the level of infrastructure and socio-economic development in specific geographic zones. Under Articles 49, 50 and 51 of the Law on Investment Promotion, the government defines agriculture, industry, handicraft and services as promoted activities.

Investment promotion is divided into 3 levels: Level 1 - high, Level 2 - medium and Level 3- low. Additionally, the country is divided into three promotion zones. Zone 1 is defined as areas lacking in socio-economic infrastructure – primarily mountainous and remote areas – and is assigned a high level of investment promotion. Zone 2 applies to areas with socio-economic infrastructure that is partially able to facilitate investments and is given medium priority. Zone 3 has infrastructure available to support investments and is assigned a low level of investment promotion.

In Zone 1, Level 1 investments receive profit tax exemptions for 10 years, Level 2 investments for 6 years and Level 3 investments for 4 years.

In Zone 2, Level 1 investments receive profit tax exemptions for 6 years, Level 2 investments for 4 years and Level 3 investments for 2 years.

In Zone 3, Level 1 investments receive profit tax exemptions for 4 years, Level 2 investments for two years and Level 3 investments for 1 year. Profit tax exemptions in all zones start from the date the enterprise commences operations.

Incentives related to customs duties, access to finance, and other taxes are described in Articles 52, 53 and 54 of the Law on Investment Promotion. As of 2011, foreign investors and workers must pay an income tax of 24% to the Lao Government, unless they are citizens of a country with which the Lao Government has signed a double-taxation agreement. Previously, this rate was 10%.

The United States does not have a double-taxation agreement with Laos. Article 67 of the Law on Investment Promotion stipulates that foreign investors and their families, including foreign professionals and foreign employees of an enterprise, may obtain multiple entry visas with a maximum term of five years. The government routinely approves long-term residence in the Lao PDR for foreign investors.

The government began replacing the turnover tax with a Value Added Tax (VAT) in 2010. Foreign investors are not required to pay import duty on equipment, spare parts and other materials used in the operation of their enterprises. Raw materials and intermediate goods imported for the purpose of processing and re-export are also exempt from import duties. Raw materials and intermediate goods imported for the purpose of import substitution are eligible for import duty reductions on a case-by-case basis.

Foreign enterprises are also eligible for profit tax and import duty reductions or exemptions on an individual basis, if the investment is determined by the GOL to benefit to Laos' socio-economic development. To date the Lao Government appears to have honored its incentives. Annual business license renewal is contingent upon certification that corporate income taxes have been paid. Investors report difficulties in obtaining tax certifications in a timely manner.

6. RIGHT TO PRIVATE OWNERSHIP AND ESTABLISHMENT

The GOL recognizes the right of private ownership, and foreigners may transfer shares of a foreign-invested company without prior government approval. However, the business law requires that all shareholders be listed in the articles of association, and changes in the articles of association of a foreign-invested company must be approved by Ministry of Planning and Investment. Thus, transferring shares in a foreign-invested company registered in Laos does require the indirect approval of the government.

7. PROTECTION OF PROPERTY RIGHTS

Foreign investors are not permitted to own land in fee-simple. However, Article 58 of the Law on Investment Promotion stipulates that foreign investors with registered investment capital of US$500,000 or above are entitled to purchase land use rights of less than 800 square meters in order to build housing or office buildings. The GOL grants long-term leases, and allows the ownership of leases and the right to transfer and improve leasehold interests. Government approval is not required to transfer property interests, but the transfer must be registered and a registration fee paid.

A creditor may enforce security rights against a debtor and the concept of a mortgage does exist. Although the GOL is engaged in a land parceling and titling project through the Ministry of Natural Resources and Environment, it remains difficult to determine if a piece of property is encumbered in Laos. Enforcement of mortgages is complicated by the legal protection given mortgagees against forfeiture of their sole place of residence.

Laos provides for secured interest in moveable and non-moveable property under the 2005 Law on Secured Transactions and a 2011 implementing decree from the Prime Minister. In 2013, the State Assets Management Authority at the Ministry of Finance launched a new Secured Transaction Registry (STR), intended to expand access to credit for individuals and smaller firms. The STR allows for registration of movable assets such as vehicles and equipment so that they may be easily verified by financial institutions and used as collateral for loans.

Intellectual Property: A government reorganization in 2011 created the Ministry of Science and Technology, which controls the issuance of patents, copyrights and trademarks. Laos is a member of the ASEAN Common Filing System on patents but lacks qualified patent examiners. Since Thailand and Laos have a bilateral Intellectual Property Rights (IPR) agreement, in principle a patent issued in Thailand would also be recognized in Laos.

Copyright protection in Laos is weak. There is no system to issue copyrights in Laos, only a certification of copyright information. Laos is a member of the World Intellectual Property Organization (WIPO) Convention and the Paris Convention on the Protection of Industrial Property but has not yet joined the Bern Convention on Copyrights.

In 2011 the National Assembly passed a comprehensive revision of the Law on Intellectual Property which brings it into compliance with WIPO and Trade-Related Aspects of Intellectual Property standards (TRIPS). The consolidation of responsibility for IPR under the Ministry of Science and Technology is a positive development, but it lacks enforcement capacity.

For additional information about treaty obligations and points of contact at local IP offices, please see WIPO's country profiles at **http://www.wipo.int/directory/en/**.

Embassy point of contact: Matt Younger **youngermb@state.gov**

8. TRANSPARENCY OF THE REGULATORY SYSTEM

Principal laws, regulations, decrees and guidelines governing international trade and investment are available to the public, although not all have been officially translated into English. Laws and their schedules for implementation are customarily published in Lao daily newspapers, and relevant line ministries are beginning to put laws and regulations on websites.

The National Assembly includes a step for public consultations in the legislative process prior to sending laws to the Prime Minister for consideration. However, a highly centralized decision-making process, combined with difficulties in obtaining information, can make the regulatory system appear arbitrary and inscrutable. The government purports to seek the advice given of the business community through the Lao Business Forum.

In 2012, the National Assembly passed the Law on Making Legislation, which requires 60-day periods for public comment and regulatory impact assessment notes of all new draft legislation. In 2013, the Lao Official Gazette opened online, a landmark achievement in legal transparency for the country. The gazette will facilitate the 60-day comment period, and the Ministry of Justice has committed to publishing all current Lao laws on the site. The gazette can be accessed here: **http://laoofficialgazette.gov.la/index.php?r=site/index**

9. EFFICIENT CAPITAL MARKETS AND PORTFOLIO INVESTMENT

Laos does not have a well-developed capital market, although government policies increasingly support the formation of capital and free flow of financial resources. Due to a monetary and fiscal crisis in 2013, there have been liquidity concerns, particularly related to foreign currency. The soundness of the banking system also appears to have suffered in the past year due to lending to off-budget infrastructure projects, and there are reports of some companies in the construction sector facing asset seizures by commercial banks.

The largest denomination of currency is 100,000 kip (about $12.50). Credit is generally not available on the local market for large capital investments, although letters of credit for export can sometimes be obtained locally. In January 2014, Laos issued a second round of government bonds denominated in Thai Baht, raising approximately $90 million. Its first foreign currency denominated bond sale, also in Thai Baht, raised $49 million in 2013.

The banking system is under the supervision of the Bank of Lao PDR, and includes 32 banks with assets of approximately US$6.8 billion. Private foreign banks can establish branches in all provinces of Laos. Domestic credit growth has been very high in the last decade and remained so at 31% year-over-year through September 2013. The BOL reports an increase in ATMs from 442 in 2012 to 622 through the middle of FY 2013. Technical assistance to Laos' financial sector has led to some reforms but overall capacity within the governance structure remains poor.

The Lao Securities Exchange (LSX) began operations in 2011 with two stocks listed, both of them state-owned – the Banque Pour l'Commerce Exterieur (BCEL), and electrical utility Electricity du Laos (EDL). In 2013, the LSX listed a third company that runs exhibitions and convention centers and appears to be largely privately-held. In 2012, the GOL increased the proportion of shares that foreigners can hold on the LSX from 10 to 20 percent.

10. COMPETITION FROM STATE-OWNED ENTERPRISES

The GOL maintains ownership stakes in key sectors of the economy such as telecommunications, energy, finance, and mining. Where state interests conflict with private ownership, the state is in a position of advantage.

In 2011, under the auspices of the Ministry of Post and Telecommunications, four large telecoms with high state ownership stakes cut service to a foreign-owned telecom in retaliation for alleged marketing violations. In 2012, private carrier Lao Central Airlines opened service on international and domestic routes, challenging the monopoly previously enjoyed by state-owned Lao Airlines.

There are reportedly 139 State-Owned Enterprises in Laos with $2.4 billion in assets. The government appears to be considering methods to increase private ownership in some SOE such as Lao Airlines, potentially through listing on the LSX.

11. CORPORATE SOCIAL RESPONSIBILITY

Corporate Social Responsibility is not yet well understood and recognized by Lao producers and consumers, but protection of the environment and mitigation of social impacts are stressed by some foreign companies, particularly in the natural resources and energy sectors.

12. POLITICAL VIOLENCE

Laos is a peaceful and politically stable country. The risk of political violence directed at foreign enterprises or businesspersons is low.

13. CORRUPTION

Corruption is a serious problem in Laos and appears to be growing alongside the economy. The GOL has developed several anti-corruption laws but enforcement remains weak, with no high-profile cases ever having been brought to trial. According to the State Inspection Authority, the Lao Government has prosecuted some individuals for corruption but it cannot publicize the information. In September 2009, Laos ratified the United Nations Convention Against Corruption.

The State Inspection Authority, located in the Prime Minister's Office, is charged with analyzing corruption at the national level and serves as a central office for gathering details and evidence of suspected corruption. Additionally, the State Inspection Department in each Ministry is responsible for combat internal ministry corruption. Laos is not a signatory to the OECD Convention on Combating Bribery. Both giving and accepting bribes are criminal acts punishable by fine and/or imprisonment. Foreign businesses frequently cite corruption as an obstacle to operating in Laos. Officials commonly accept bribes for the purpose of approving or expediting applications.

In 2014 an asset declaration regime entered into force for government officials requiring them to declare income, assets and debts for themselves and their family members. Assets over $2500

For additional analytical, business and investment opportunities information,
please contact Global Investment & Business Center, USA
at (703) 370-8082. Fax: (703) 370-8083. E-mail: ibpusa3@gmail.com
Global Business and Investment Info Databank - www.ibpus.com

are required to be disclosed, including land, structures, vehicles and equipment, as well as cash, gold, and financial instruments. However, the effectiveness of this program has yet to be determined.

14. BILATERAL INVESTMENT AGREEMENTS

Laos has bilateral investment agreements with Australia, Burma, Cambodia, China, Cuba, Denmark, France, Germany, India, Indonesia, Japan, Kuwait, Malaysia, Mongolia, Netherlands, North Korea, Pakistan, Philippines, Russia, South Korea, Singapore, Sweden, Switzerland, Thailand, the United Kingdom, and Vietnam. On February 1, 2005 a Bilateral Trade Agreement (BTA) came into force between the U.S. and the Government of Laos. Laos and the United States do not have a bilateral taxation treaty.

15. OPIC AND OTHER INVESTMENT INSURANCE PROGRAMS

The United States and Laos signed an Overseas Private Investment Cooperation (OPIC) agreement in March 1996. OPIC does not have any projects ongoing in Laos but the potential exists in the Lao economy for OPIC involvement. In 1998 Laos signed an agreement with the Multilateral Investment Guarantee Agency (MIGA). The Lao kip is not an internationally traded currency and fluctuated in a narrow range against the U.S. dollar in 2012.

16. LABOR

70% of Laos' work force is engaged in subsistence agriculture. There are shortages in skilled labor across virtually the entire economy. The lack of a skilled workforce is consistently cited by foreign and domestic companies as the main constraint to growth. The estimated migration of Lao labor to Thailand numbers in the hundreds of thousands. At the same time, Laos has in recent years received a large influx of labor from China and Vietnam who largely come to work with Chinese and Vietnamese companies. Generally, the current extremely tight labor market places labor-management relations on a somewhat equal footing; if employees are not satisfied at their current job, they simply leave.

The 1994 labor law provides for the formation of trade unions; specifies working hours and compensation standards; allows for maternity leave and benefits; workers' compensation and retirement benefits; and establishes procedures for labor dispute resolution. There are, however, no unions independent of the Lao Federation of Trade Unions, a Communist Party organization. In January 2012, the Lao government raised the minimum wage for unskilled workers to US$78 per month based on a six-day, eight hour per day work week. Reforms to the labor law passed in 2014 contained the first mention in Lao law of collective bargaining, but the country still lacks freedom of association for labor, independent unions, or a detailed framework for independent collective bargaining. There is virtually no avenue for, or risk of, labor strikes in Laos currently. In 2014, Laos approved a national plan of action to combat the worst forms of child labor and the Ministry of Labor and Social Welfare is working to improve its capacity for labor inspections.

Laos has human resource deficiencies in virtually all sectors. English is not widely spoken. In 2012, about 16 percent of the population age 15 and above remained illiterate. The shortage of skilled labor is particularly acute in high-tech sectors. The country has a few technical colleges, one scientific research facility-- the National Institute of Hygiene and Epidemiology--and almost no effective post-graduate degree programs.

The Lao Government has dedicated few of its own resources to improve the country's education system and tends to rely heavily on international donors for support; there are a few state training programs and some foreign funded programs. Potential investors should note the need to dedicate substantial resources, both human and capital, to train employees. It is not unusual for foreign investors to bring in Thai managers due to a lack of skilled local personnel.

17. FOREIGN TRADE ZONES/FREE PORTS

The Foreign Investment Law allows for the establishment of Special Economic Zones (SEZ) and Specific Economic Zones as an investment incentive. Prime Ministerial Decree 443 on Special Economic Zones and Specific Economic Zones was issued in 2010 and provides guidance on the establishment of the zones.

Special Economic Zones are intended to support development of new infrastructure and commercial facilities and include incentives for investment. Specific Economic Zones are meant to develop existing infrastructure and facilities and provide a lower level of incentives and support than Special Economic Zones. Laos plans to construct 25 special and specific zones in the next ten years via foreign direct investment of US$3 billion.

There are currently 10 different economic zones across the country, including: Savan-Seno Special Economic Zone, Golden Triangle Special Economic Zone, Boten Beautiful Land Specific Economic Zone, Vientiane Industrial and Trade Zone, Saysettha Development Zone, Phoukyou Specific Economic Zone, Thatluang Lake Specific Economic Zone, Longthanh – Vientiane Specific Economic Zone, Dongphosy Specific Economic Zone and Thakhek Specific Economic Zone.

The Savan-Seno Special Economic Zone in Savannakhet province is legitimately developing as a production, supply, and distribution center with increasingly sophisticated manufacturing businesses and advanced infrastructure. Other SEZ's in the northern part of the country have experienced problems associated with casino gambling, prostitution and drug trafficking.

Lao laws pertaining to trade are supposedly applied uniformly across the entire customs territory of Laos, including all sub-central authorities, special economic zones, specific economic zones and border trade regions. In reality, however, customs practices vary widely at ports of entry in the provinces. Centralization of customs collection by the central government has led to more uniform practices and increased the flow of customs revenue to the central government. In order to comply with National Single Window requirements under the ASEAN Single Window, in 2012 Laos began operating the Automated System for Customs Data (ASYCUDA) at the busiest point of cross-border trade, the Lao-Thai Friendship Bridge linking Vientiane with Thailand and has slowly expanded the use of ASYCUDA at other border crossings as well.

18. FOREIGN DIRECT INVESTMENT AND FOREIGN PORTFOLIO INVESTMENT STATISTICS

Key Macroeconomic data, U.S. FDI in host country/economy

	Bank of the Lao PDR Annual Report		USG or international statistical source		USG or international Source of data (Source of Data: BEA; IMF; Eurostat; UNCTAD, Other)
Economic Data	Year	Amount	Year	Amount	

Host Country Gross Domestic Product (GDP) (Millions U.S. Dollars)	2012	9100	2012	9400	http://www.worldbank.org/en/country
Foreign Direct Investment	Ministry of Planning and Investment		USG or international statistical source		USG or international Source of data: BEA; IMF; Eurostat; UNCTAD, Other
U.S. FDI in partner country (Millions U.S. Dollars, stock positions)	3.513	NA	Insert 2012	Amount 0	(BEA) click selections to reach. Bureau of Economic Analysis Balance of Payments and Direct Investment Position Data U.S. Direct Investment Position Abroad on a Historical-Cost Basis By Country only (all countries) (Millions of Dollars)
Host country's FDI in the United States (Millions U.S. Dollars, stock positions)	NA	NA	NA	NA	(BEA) click selections to reach Balance of Payments and Direct Investment Position Data Foreign Direct Investment Position in the United States on a Historical-Cost Basis By Country only (all countries) (Millions of Dollars)
Total inbound stock of FDI as % host GDP (calculate)	Insert 2012	Amount 20.3%	Insert (Year)	Amount	

LAWYERS IN LAWS - IMPORTANT CONTACTS

There are a limited number of independent lawyers in Laos. A lawyer seeking to represent a foreign citizen in a criminal matter may need to obtain prior permission from the Ministry of Justice.

The U.S. Embassy in Vientiane, Laos assumes no responsibility or liability for the professional ability or reputation of, or the quality of services provided by, the following persons or firms. Inclusion on this list is in no way an endorsement by the Department of State or the U.S. Embassy. Names are listed alphabetically, and the order in which they appear has no other significance. The information in the list on professional credentials, areas of expertise and language ability are provided directly by the lawyers; the Embassy is not in a position to vouch for such information. You may receive additional information about the individuals on the list by contacting the local bar association or the local licensing authorities.

1.   Mr. William GREENLEE, Jr.
Tel: 856-21-242-068
  856-21-242-069
856-21-242-070
DFDL Mekong Law Group   Fax: 856-21-218-422
PO Box 2920

Vientiane, Lao PDR   Website:www.dfdl.com
    Email: Laos@dfdl.com
      William.Greenlee@dfdlmekong.com
Languages: English, Mandarin, Thai, Bahasa Indonesian
Areas of Expertise: Banking/Financial, Commercial/Business, Foreign Investments, Marketing, Patents/Trademarks/Copyrights, Damages, Collections, Contracts, Transportation, Corporations, Foreign Claims, Estates, Taxes, Government Relations, Labor

2. Mr. Brennan COLEMAN
Tel: 856-21-242-068
856-21-242-069
856-21-242-070
DFDL Mekong Law Group   Fax: 856-21-218-422
PO Box 2920   Cell: 856-20-7878-7699
Vientiane, Lao PDR   Website: www.dfdl.com
            Email: Brennan.Coleman@dfdl.com

Languages: English
Areas of Expertise: Banking/Financial, Commercial/Business, Foreign Investments, Marketing, Patents/Trademarks/Copyrights, Damages, Collections, Contracts, Transportation, Corporations, Foreign Claims, Taxes, Government Relations, Labor

3. Mr. Somphou KEOMOUNMANY   Tel: 856-21-454-300
Ban Naxay, Xaysettha District   Cell: 856-20-5562-6676
Vientiane, Lao PDR   Email:bearsomphou@yahoo.com
Languages (in addition to Lao): English
Areas of Expertise: Child Custody, Child Protection, Marriage/Divorce, Patents/Trademarks/Copyrights, Contracts, Labor

4. Mr. Viengsavanh PHANTHALY   Tel: 856-21-330470
Ban Phonpapao, Sisattanak District   Cell: 856-20-5422-3377
Vientiane, Lao PDR   Email: vlaw@live.com
            v.phanthaly@vlaw.la
            www.vlaw.la
Languages (in addition to Lao): English, Vietnamese, Thai, Japanese
Areas of Expertise: Family, Adoptions, Marriage/Divorce, Insurance, Banking/Financial, Commercial/Business, Foreign Investments, Marketing, Patents/Trademarks/Copyrights, Civil, Criminal, Damages, Contracts, Transportation, Corporations, Foreign Claims, Estates, Taxes, Government Relations, Labor, Immigration, Accidents

5. Mr. Sabh PHOMMARATH   Cell: 856-20-2220-2297
Ban Anou, Chanthabury District   Email:sabhpr123@gmail.com
Vientiane, Lao PDR
Languages (in addition to Lao): English, French, Thai
Areas of Expertise: Family, Marriage/Divorce, Foreign Investments, Marketing, Civil, Criminal, Contracts

6. Mr. Veng SAYSANA   Cell: 856-20-5561-2883
Ban Naxay, Xaysettha District   Email:vengsaysana@yahoo.com
Vientiane, Lao PDR
Languages (in addition to Lao): English, French
Areas of Expertise: Family, Adoption, Child Custody, Parental/Child Abduction, Child Protection, Marriage/Divorce, Banking/Financial, Commercial/Business, Foreign Investments, Marketing,

Patents/Trademarks/Copyrights, Civil, Criminal, Damages, Narcotics, Collections, Contracts, Corporations, Aeronautical/Maritime, Estates, Government Relations, Labor

7. Mr. Vannloh SISOPHA   Tel: 856-21-218-426
128 Saigon Rd.   Cell: 856-20-5582-8178
            Email:vannloh@gmail.com
Ban Anou, Chanthabury District
Vientiane, Lao PDR
Languages (in addition to Lao): English, French
Areas of Expertise: Family, Commercial/Business, Civil, Criminal

8. Mr. Douangsim SOUPHANTHONG   Cell: 856-20-5561-8379
Lao Bar Association, Ban Anou
Vientiane, Lao PDR
Languages (in addition to Lao): French, limited English
Areas of Expertise: Family, Adoption, Child Protection, Marriage/Divorce, Foreign Investment, Civil, Criminal, Damages, Contracts, Government Relations, Labor, Immigration, Accidents

9. Mr. Mixay THEPMANY
Ban Savang, Chanthabury District   Cell: 856-20-5567-6383
Vientiane, Lao PDR   Fax: 856-21-219051
                                    Email: mthepmany@yahoo.com
Languages (in addition to Lao): English, French, Thai
Areas of Expertise: Family, Adoption, Child Custody, Child Protection, Marriage/Divorce, Commercial/Business, Foreign Investments, Civil, Criminal, Contracts, Labor

10. Mr. Sysavong VITHASAY
Ban Phayawath, Sisattanak District   Fax: 856-21-353953
Vientiane, Lao PDR   Cell: 856-20-5551-4259
Languages (in addition to Lao): French, Thai, limited English
Areas of Expertise: Family, Marriage/Divorce, Commercial/Business, Foreign Investments, Marketing, Civil, Criminal, Damages, Narcotics, Contracts, Labor

11. Mr. Manolin THEPKHAMVONG
Ban Sapanthong-kang, Sisattanak District
Vientiane, Lao PDR   Email: m.thepkhamvong@vlaw.la
Languages (in addition to Lao): English, Thai
Areas of Expertise: Family, Civil, Criminal, Damages, Public Interest, land, environment protection, water and water recourses, narcotic, woman and children protection.

SELLING U.S. PRODUCTS AND SERVICES - PRACTICAL INFORMATION

USING AN AGENT OR DISTRIBUTOR

Employing a Lao agent or finding a Lao business partner is a frequently used method for developing contacts with Lao businesses, customers and government officials. There are also a number of expatriate Lao who are either American citizens or legal permanent residents, and who may be able to assist business startup.

Numerous import-export companies are based in Vientiane and in the cities located at or near border crossings in the provinces of Luang Namtha, Bokeo, Bolikhamxay, Khammouane, Savannakhet and Champasack.

Most import-export companies are ill-equipped to handle large-scale distribution. U.S. firms looking for a distributor or an agent in a particular province should contact the provincial branch of the Lao National Chamber of Commerce (LNCC) at http://www.laocci.com/ and the Trade and Investment Department of the respective province for assistance in identifying viable business partners.

ESTABLISHING AN OFFICE

Foreign investors seeking to establish operations in Laos are required to obtain a foreign Investment and Business license, an enterprise registration certificate, and a tax registration certificate.

Depending on the size of the investment, investors first submit project proposals to the "One Stop Shop" Unit in the Department of Investment Promotion (DIP) in the Ministry of Planning and Investment (MPI), or to the Investment Promotion in General Business Department at the Ministry of Industry and Commerce.

http://www.moic.gov.la/contact.asp

DIP screens projects for financial and technical feasibility before forwarding them to relevant line ministries for review. Depending on the size of the investment, they are then sent to the Prime Minister's Office (PM) or "Government Office" for adjudication.

In addition to the investment license, foreign investors are required to obtain other permits, including; an annual business registration from the Ministry of Industry and Commerce; a tax registration from the Ministry of Finance; a business logo registration from the Ministry of Public Security; permits from each line ministry related to the investment (e.g., Ministry of Industry and Commerce for manufacturing; Ministry of

Energy and Mines for power sector development); appropriate permits from local authorities; and an import-export license, if applicable. Obtaining the necessary permits can pose a challenge, especially in areas outside the capital.

The GOL is supposed to respond to proposed new business investment within 15–45 working days. Foreign enterprises must begin business activities within 90 days from the date of receipt of an investment license, or the license is subject to termination

FRANCHISING

Franchising is a relatively untested business model in Laos and the country has no specific law regulating franchises. In 2012, a team of American, Thai, and Lao investors added a second location to the first fast food franchise in Laos, originally opened in 2010. In 2014, Dairy Queen franchises opened at Wattay International Airport and in downtown Vientiane.

DIRECT MARKETING

For additional analytical, business and investment opportunities information,
please contact Global Investment & Business Center, USA
at (703) 370-8082. Fax: (703) 370-8083. E-mail: ibpusa3@gmail.com
Global Business and Investment Info Databank - www.ibpus.com

Direct marketing in Laos may have increased potential, as an estimated 65 in 100 persons have mobile cellular subscriptions, and an estimated 7 of 100 persons are internet users. Although the road network is improving, there is limited postal coverage. The literacy rate is officially estimated to be 80% for those older than 15 years.

JOINT VENTURES/LICENSING

Care in selection of suitable business partners for joint ventures is crucial in Laos. As in

other countries in the region, joint venture partners can contribute local knowledge of language and culture, local contacts and access to human resources. There can also be challenges in a joint venture arrangement, including different management styles, different cultural expectations and difficulty in exiting business arrangements with a local partner.

Lao foreign investment law recognizes joint ventures, but requires the foreign partner to contribute at least thirty percent of registered capital. Capital contributed in foreign currency must be converted into Kip based on the exchange rate of the Bank of the Lao People's Democratic Republic on the day of the capital contribution.

Foreign partners' equity may be foreign currency, plant and equipment, capital goods, technology, and/or skills and management. Lao partners (including the Lao government) may contribute money, land, water rights, natural resources, and/or capital goods. The value of the inputs and assets of each side are assessed at international market rates and converted into local currency at the prevailing exchange rate on the date of equity payment.

Licensing arrangements also require a trustworthy Lao partner and opportunities should be thoroughly researched with, among others, the Lao government and the Lao National Chamber of Commerce.

SELLING TO THE GOVERNMENT

The Lao Government is a leading consumer of goods and services, but procurement procedures are opaque. The national budget is heavily financed by Official Development Assistance (ODA), and donors commonly encourage government purchases from their home industries as part of aid deals. Laos is not a party or an observer to the WTO Agreement on Government Procurement.

Most business opportunities involving Lao Government entities are associated with donors and their development projects. Contracts in support of these projects are often advertised for bid in the English-language newspapers (Vientiane Times and KPL).

http://www.vientianetimes.org.la/ and http://www.kplnet.net/

These bidding events have not been verified as open and fair, as no American company has reported success through this channel. However, niche opportunities are known to exist for direct private sales to government entities with past examples in such areas as telecommunications and aviation.

DISTRIBUTION AND SALES CHANNELS

Generally, import-export wholesale companies import goods into Laos and sell goods to retailers. Goods may enter Laos by air, road, or (less formally) by river. There is just one active railroad in

For additional analytical, business and investment opportunities information,
please contact Global Investment & Business Center, USA
at (703) 370-8082. Fax: (703) 370-8083. E-mail: ibpusa3@gmail.com
Global Business and Investment Info Databank - www.ibpus.com

Laos, a short spur line from Nong Khai, just across the river in Thailand, which began operations in 2009.

The lack of a well-developed road system and basic infrastructure in many areas makes distribution outside of the main urban areas in Vientiane, Luang Prabang, Savannakhet, and Pakse difficult, time-consuming, and costly. Road improvements are ongoing, with several decent roads in the northern provinces and along the southern corridor connecting Thailand, Laos and Vietnam. However, Laos is still operating a mid- twentieth century distribution and logistics network, with large inventories on hand. Use of modern logistics techniques such as just-in-time supply would likely be difficult given the current state of the Lao infrastructure.

SELLING FACTORS/TECHNIQUES AMERICAN PRODUCTS GENERALLY ENJOY A GOOD REPUTATION FOR TECHNOLOGICAL SOPHISTICATION AND

high quality in Laos. The consumer products of Laos' regional neighbors are far better known, however, and the Lao market can be difficult for American products due to their relatively high prices.

To compete successfully, some US firms have combined routine advertising with workshops, training programs, trade shows, and product launching events for wholesalers and distributors, as well as customers. The Thai and Lao languages are not identical but are very similar. Thai products with Thai language packaging are ubiquitous in Laos and most educated Lao can read Thai, so Thai language packaging often suffices. American products that include Lao-language packaging and/or promotional materials are likely to be positively received.

ELECTRONIC COMMERCE

Electronic commerce is not widely used in Laos, due to underdevelopment of the telecommunications infrastructure and the low rate of formal banking and credit card use. Broadband internet access is widely available in Vientiane. The Lao government passed a law on electronic transactions in 2012, paving the way for future growth in electronic commerce.

TRADE PROMOTION AND ADVERTISING

Advertising and trade promotion are important marketing tools for American products.

Since nearly all Lao who own televisions watch Thai advertisements, a good reputation and strong advertising campaign in Thailand will likely have a positive effect on Lao consumers as well.

Many companies advertise in two Lao local newspapers, Vientiane Mai, a Lao language newspaper, and the Vientiane Times, an English language newspaper. A brief listing of major newspapers, business journals, radio, television stations and business advertising companies follows. All newspapers and television stations are state owned, and all communications are state controlled:

Major Newspapers:

Vientiane Times (English Language) http://www.vientianetimes.org.la/
Lao News Agency, KPL (English Language) http://www.kplnet.net/
Pasaxon (Lao Language) http://www.pasaxon.org.la

Vientiane Mai (Lao Language) http://www.vientianemai.net
Vientiane Thurakit Sangkhom (Lao Language)

Target Business Magazine
Lao National Radio c/o Ministry of Information and Culture: nationalradio@hotmail.com
Lao National Television 1 and 3 Lao National Television 1 and 3 Lao National Television 1 and 3
Lao Star Television http://www.laostartv.com/
Lao International Trade, Exhibition, and Conference Center (ITECC) http://www.lao- itecc.la/

PRICING

Lao consumers are sensitive to price due to low levels of disposable income. The Lao

government continues to control the retail price of gas and diesel, as well as a number of

other "sensitive" goods. As a new member of the World Trade Organization in 2013, price
controls as well as unwieldy import restrictions in Laos should decline in the future. Although the
Government often discusses the need to control food prices, in practice markets set the price. A
value added tax (VAT) came into force in January 2010 although the state of implementation is
uneven.

SALES SERVICE/CUSTOMER SUPPORT

Customer support and service tend to be the province of large multinationals such as automobile
manufacturers, which offer excellent in-country support. In general, attitudes towards customer
service, especially at the retail level, are still in the developing stages.

Availability of spare parts is limited and replacement/replenishment is slow.

PROTECTING YOUR INTELLECTUAL PROPERTY

Protecting Your Intellectual Property in Laos

Several general principles are important for effective management of intellectual property ("IP")
rights in Laos. First, it is important to have an overall strategy to protect your IP. Second, IP is
protected differently in Laos than in the U.S. Third, rights must be registered and enforced in
Laos, under local laws. Your U.S. trademark and patent registrations will not protect you in Laos.
There is no such thing as an "international copyright" that will automatically protect an author's
writings throughout the entire world. Protection against unauthorized use in a particular country
depends, basically, on the national laws of that country. However, most countries do offer
copyright protection to foreign works under certain conditions, and these conditions have been
greatly simplified by international copyright treaties and conventions.

Registration of patents and trademarks is on a first-in-time, first-in-right basis, so you should
consider applying for trademark and patent protection even before selling your products or
services in the Lao market. It is vital that companies understand that intellectual property is
primarily a private right and that the US government generally cannot enforce rights for private
individuals in Lao PDR. It is the responsibility of the rights' holders to register, protect, and
enforce their rights where relevant, retaining their own counsel and advisors. Companies may
wish to seek advice from local attorneys or IP consultants who are experts in Lao law. The U.S.

For additional analytical, business and investment opportunities information,
please contact Global Investment & Business Center, USA
at (703) 370-8082. Fax: (703) 370-8083. E-mail: ibpusa3@gmail.com
Global Business and Investment Info Databank - www.ibpus.com

Commercial Service can provide a list of local lawyers upon request:
http://laos.usembassy.gov/legal_assistance.html

While the U.S. Government stands ready to assist, there is little we can do if the rights holders have not taken these fundamental steps necessary to securing and enforcing their IP in a timely fashion. Moreover, in many countries, rights holders who delay enforcing their rights on a mistaken belief that the USG can provide a political resolution to a legal problem may find that their rights have been eroded or abrogated due to legal doctrines such as statutes of limitations, laches, estoppel, or unreasonable delay in prosecuting a law suit. In no instance should U.S. Government advice be seen as a substitute for the obligation of a rights holder to promptly pursue its case.

It is always advisable to conduct due diligence on potential partners. Negotiate from the position of your partner and give your partner clear incentives to honor the contract. A good partner is an important ally in protecting IP rights. Consider carefully, however, whether to permit your partner to register your IP rights on your behalf. Doing so may create a risk that your partner will list itself as the IP owner and fail to transfer the rights should the partnership end. Keep an eye on your cost structure and reduce the margins (and the incentive) of would-be bad actors. Projects and sales in Laos require constant attention. Work with legal counsel familiar with Lao laws to create a solid contract that includes non-compete clauses, and confidentiality/non-disclosure provisions.

It is also recommended that small and medium-size companies understand the importance of working together with trade associations and organizations to support efforts to protect IP and stop counterfeiting. There are a number of these organizations, both Lao and U.S.-based. These include:

- The U.S. Chamber and local American Chambers of Commerce

- National Association of Manufacturers (NAM)

- International Intellectual Property Alliance (IIPA)

- International Trademark Association (INTA)

- The Coalition Against Counterfeiting and Piracy

- International Anti-Counterfeiting Coalition (IACC)

- Pharmaceutical Research and Manufacturers of America (PhRMA)

- Biotechnology Industry Organization (BIO)

IP Resources

A wealth of information on protecting IP is freely available to U.S. rights holders. Some excellent resources for companies regarding intellectual property include the following:

- For information about patent, trademark, or copyright issues -- including enforcement issues in the US and other countries -- call the STOP! Hotline: 1-866-999-HALT or register at www.StopFakes.gov .

• For more information about registering trademarks and patents (both in the U.S. as well as in foreign countries), contact the US Patent and Trademark Office (USPTO) at: 1-800-786-9199.

• For more information about registering for copyright protection in the US, contact the US Copyright Office at: 1-202-707-5959.

• For more information about how to evaluate, protect, and enforce intellectual property rights and how these rights may be important for businesses, a free online training program is available at www.stopfakes.gov .

• For US small and medium-size companies, the Department of Commerce offers a "SME IP Advisory Program" available through the American Bar Association that provides one hour of free IP legal advice for companies with concerns in Brazil, China, Egypt, India, Russia, and . For details and to register, visit: http://www.abanet.org/intlaw/intlproj/iprprogram_consultation.html

• For information on obtaining and enforcing intellectual property rights and market-specific IP Toolkits visit: www.StopFakes.gov This site is linked to the USPTO website for registering trademarks and patents (both in the U.S. as well as in foreign countries), the U.S. Customs & Border Protection website to record registered trademarks and copyrighted works (to assist customs in blocking imports of IP-infringing products) and allows you to register for Webinars on protecting IP.

• The U.S. Commerce Department has positioned IP attachés in key markets around the world. You can get contact information the IP attaché who covers Laos at: peter.fowler@trade.gov

DUE DILIGENCE

Due diligence is key in the Lao market. Companies are advised to make numerous trips

to Laos prior to investing in order to meet both with potential partners and with relevant

government officials. Working with a local lawyer (see below) is recommended.

LOCAL PROFESSIONAL SERVICES

The legal community is small in Laos and it is wise to ask for recommendations. Please see the following website for information on local professional services: http://laos.usembassy.gov/attorneys.html

WEB RESOURCES

Lao National Chamber of Commerce and Industry (LNCCI): http://www.lncci.laotel.com/

The Ministry of Science and Technology: http://www.laopdr.gov.la/ePortal/nbocompany/listdivisions.action?contentType=4&contentGroupId=11565&organizationContentId=18065&subType=100&request_locale=en_US

For additional analytical, business and investment opportunities information, please contact Global Investment & Business Center, USA at (703) 370-8082. Fax: (703) 370-8083. E-mail: ibpusa3@gmail.com Global Business and Investment Info Databank - www.ibpus.com

Lao Bar Association: http://www.laobar.org/welcome.php

Lao Ministry of Industry and Commerce: http://www.moic.gov.la/contact.asp

For additional analytical, business and investment opportunities information,
please contact Global Investment & Business Center, USA
at (703) 370-8082. Fax: (703) 370-8083. E-mail: ibpusa3@gmail.com
Global Business and Investment Info Databank - www.ibpus.com

LEADING SECTORS FOR EXPORT AND INVESTMENT

TOURISM INFRASTRUCTURE AND RESORTS

Unit: USD thousands

	2011	2012	2013 (estimated)	2014 (estimated)
Total Market Size	406,000	514,000	550,000	

The tourism industry in Laos is developing rapidly, with particular emphasis on eco- tourism. The major tourist destination is the world heritage site and ancient capital of Luang Prabang. Eco-tourism featuring the undeveloped Lao countryside is gaining in popularity.

WEB RESOURCES

Information on Luang Prabang: http://whc.unesco.org/en/list/479

Lao Ministry of Information, Culture and Tourism:
http://www.ecotourismlaos.com/worldheritagesites.htm

ARCHITECTURE, CONSTRUCTION AND ENGINEERING SERVICES

Laos has an underdeveloped infrastructure, including its road networks, and its public water and electricity systems. Transportation projects will be high demand as the country modernizes. There are also several large construction projects ongoing in the capital of Vientiane, including office buildings and shopping malls.

Chinese, Vietnamese and Thai companies are the most active participants in infrastructure development in Laos. The Lao government makes use of donor funding, development banks and other financing methods to pay for infrastructure projects. Laos is undergoing development of its airport and aviation system, including provincial airports.

Laos is seeking to modernize and integrate its electrical grid in the next decade as it seeks to meet its goal of supplying Thailand and Vietnam with electricity exports, while at the same time providing electricity to 90 percent of the population by 2020. To do this it will need to invest in modern power distribution and power management equipment and expertise.

WEB RESOURCES

World Bank:
http://web.worldbank.org/WBSITE/EXTERNAL/COUNTRIES/EASTASIAPACIFICEXT/LAOPRDE XTN/0,,menuPK:293689~pagePK:141159~piPK:141110~theSitePK:293684,00.html

Asian Development Bank: http://beta.adb.org/countries/lao-pdr/main

PHARMACEUTICALS, MEDICAL SUPPLIES AND MEDICAL EQUIPMENT

The health care system in Laos is very rudimentary but developing. Maternal and child health is an important priority for the GOL as it seeks to graduate from Least Developed Country status by

2020. The Ministry of Health controls the import of medical equipment, supplies and pharmaceuticals. Refurbished medical equipment and low-cost pharmaceuticals are market possibilities.

TRADE REGULATIONS, CUSTOMS AND STANDARDS

IMPORT TARIFFS

The Lao import tax system aims to promote importation of inputs for investment and production while protecting domestic production and limiting luxury imports. Foreign investors do not pay import duty on imports of capital machinery and equipment for production, or on spare parts.

Raw materials and intermediate goods needed for export production are also exempt.

Raw materials and intermediate goods imported for import substituting industries can be accorded special treatment based on an incentive agreement.

There are standard ASEAN import tariff rates varying from zero, to40 percent, excluding non-ASEAN countries and according to the Tariff Nomenclature of Lao PDR based on ASEAN Harmonized Tariff Nomenclature (AHTN 2007/1). These published rates are levied by the Customs Department.

Excise tax ranges from 5-90% on many goods. The Lao government has phased out turnover taxes over the last several years and replaced them with a Value Added Tax (VAT) regime. Additional tax information can be found at the Tax Department, Ministry of Finance, http://www.mof.gov.la/?q=en/node/989

TRADE BARRIERS

The Lao Government has simplified its tariff structure and is gradually amending non-tariff barriers. The Bilateral Trade Agreement with the United

States lowers tariffs on a range of American products and offers importers the ability to appeal tariff decisions they feel are improper.

IMPORT REQUIREMENTS AND DOCUMENTATION

Application for an import license must be made to the provincial trade authority where the importing enterprise is located. An import/export license is valid for the life of the business, but investors must periodically notify the authorities that they intend to continue operating their businesses. The Lao Government offers quotas for importing duty-free vehicles to qualifying individuals and companies.

For general goods, importers are required to have the following documentation for each shipment: 1) invoice; 2) packing list; 3) transport documents; 4) bill of lading; and 5) a customs clearance report. Importers of raw materials for re-export are required to have the same documents as other importers, except for a contract and import license.

Automobile importers, individuals or companies, unless they have obtained duty free status, must pay an import tax, excise tax, VAT, and, potentially, a tax for luxury goods.

For additional analytical, business and investment opportunities information, please contact Global Investment & Business Center, USA at (703) 370-8082. Fax: (703) 370-8083. E-mail: ibpusa3@gmail.com Global Business and Investment Info Databank - www.ibpus.com

Exporters should have the following documents when applying for an export declaration:

1) an application for export declaration; 2) an import/export license (only for goods under control of the ministry or government, e.g. rough or polished diamonds); 3) an invoice of goods; 4) a packing list; 5) a certificate of country of origin and generalized system of preferences certificate of origin if applicable; 6) phyto-sanitary certificate for food exports; and 7) industrial products certification for industrial products.

To import or export pharmaceuticals, food, or chemical products, in addition to the aforementioned documents, the importer must obtain a license from the Food and Drug Control Import Division of the Food and Drug Department of the Ministry of Public

Health. Pre-shipment inspection is required for exported goods in accordance with the requirements of the destination country. Laos has no special labeling or marking requirements.

U.S. EXPORT CONTROLS

Several United States export controls apply to Laos. For the most part, these export controls fall under the categories of National Security licensing requirements and the Chemical Weapons Convention. For detailed information regarding U.S. export controls please contact the Bureau of Industry and Security within the U.S. Department of Commerce at http://www.bis.doc.gov

TEMPORARY ENTRY

Products imported for the purposes of processing, assembly into finished products, or for exhibition and subsequent re-export, are exempt from duty. Trans-shipment of goods through Laos requires the same documents normally needed for import and export. Goods traveling through Laos are not subject to import or export taxes.

LABELING AND MARKING REQUIREMENTS

Laos has no laws governing product labeling and marking. Prohibited and Restricted Imports In February 2010, the Lao government launched the Decree on Import and Export Licensing procedures of Controlled Goods, No. 180 PMO, in a bid to comply with the World Trade Organization (WTO) and World Customs Organization (WCO) rules. Laos also began implementing the Notification for Goods Subject to Non-Automatic Import and Export Licensing and Goods Subject to Automatic Import and Export Licensing, No 2151/MOIC.

For more information, please contact the Department of Import and Export Management: http://www.moc.gov.la/default.asp

CUSTOMS REGULATIONS AND CONTACT INFORMATION

Please see: http://laocustoms.laopdr.net/laws_and_regulations.htm

The Lao Trade Portal, established in 2012, has extensive information for exporters and importers: http://www.laotradeportal.gov.la/index.php?r=site/index

EXPORT-IMPORT STANDARDS

Laos has no specific law on standards for imported or exported goods. Imported goods are allowed to enter based on the certification of the country of export.

STANDARDS ORGANIZATIONS

Laos currently has no independent standards organizations. In 2011, the Department of Standards and Metrology in the Ministry of Science and Technology was established as an independent department alongside the Department of Intellectual Property.
http://www.laotradeportal.gov.la/index.php?r=site/displayb&id=220

NIST Notify U.S. Service

Member countries of the World Trade Organization (WTO) are required under the Agreement on Technical Barriers to Trade (TBT Agreement) to report to the WTO all proposed technical regulations that could affect trade with other Member countries. Notify U.S. is a free, web-based e-mail subscription service that offers an opportunity to review and comment on proposed foreign technical regulations that can affect your access to international markets. Register online at Internet URL: review and comment on proposed foreign technical regulations that can affect your access to international markets. Register online at Internet URL:

CONFORMITY ASSESSMENT

Laos currently has no conformity assessment.

PRODUCT CERTIFICATION

Laos currently has no product certification.

ACCREDITATION

Laos currently has no accreditation bodies.

PUBLICATION OF TECHNICAL REGULATIONS

Laos currently does not publish technical regulations, although the Official Gazette, designed to publish all proposed and enacted legislation, is currently under development.

LABELING AND MARKING

According to regulation 027/CFDC, all foodstuffs imported into Laos for consumer use must be labeled in accordance with Food and Drug Control Department requirements.

In practice, this requirement does not appear to be enforced.

CONTACTS

Department of Standards and Metrology: Department of Intellectual Property.
http://www.laotradeportal.gov.la/index.php?r=site/displayb&id=220

U.S. Embassy Vientiane Economic and Commercial Officer: youngermb@state.gov

TRADE AGREEMENTS

Laos acceded to the World Trade Organization (WTO) in 2013, and is working towards meeting the requirements of the ASEAN Economic Community by 2015.

The following countries have granted Generalized System of Preference (GSP) status to Laos: Canada, Japan; Australia (no import tax); European Union; South Korea; Norway and Switzerland. Lao PDR is currently under review for eligibility for U.S. GSP status, which would remove import tariffs for over 5000 products exported to the United States from Laos.

Laos has also signed trade agreements with 15 countries, including: Vietnam; China; Cambodia; Burma; Thailand; North Korea; Mongolia; Malaysia; Russia; India; Belarus; Argentina; the United States; Kuwait and Turkey.

WEB RESOURCES

http://www.nist.gov/notifyus/
http://laocustoms.laopdr.net/laws_and_regulations.htm
http://www.moc.gov.la/default.asp
http://www.laotradeportal.gov.la/index.php?r=site/displayb&id=220

TRADE AND PROJECT FINANCING

HOW DO I GET PAID (METHODS OF PAYMENT)

Depending on the size of the transaction, payment can be made using EFT, cash, or letter of credit.

HOW DOES THE BANKING SYSTEM OPERATE

The Lao banking sector is growing rapidly, with 35% credit growth year-on-year through June 2013. New private and foreign banks

provide modern banking options to Lao and foreign businesses, with a total of 32 banks licensed through 2014. Laos does not have a

national deposit insurance system and supervisory standards are low. Technical

expertise and the range of services offered at domestic banks are limited. While it

continues to receive outside assistance, central bank (Bank of Lao PDR) supervision of the sector remains somewhat weak.

According to the Asia Pacific Group, the regional arm of the Financial Action Task Force (FATF), there are a large volume of illicit proceeds generated in the Lao PDR. The Lao government is taking steps in 2014 to address deficiencies in the anti-money laundering (AML) framework and enforcement. These include drafting a new AML/Counter Financing of Terrorism law, with international assistance. Although the law should address most FATF requirements, enforcement will likely remain weak, and Laos is at risk of being downgraded by the FATF in the future. This may affect the ease with which international banking transactions are conducted in Laos.

FOREIGN-EXCHANGE CONTROLS

Lao law maintains that payment for goods and services should be in Lao, vice foreign, currency. Debts should not be paid in foreign currency within the Lao PDR except for cases in which the Bank of the Lao PDR has proposed such a transaction and the Lao Government has approved. In practice, the Lao economy is highly dollarized and Thai baht or American dollars (as well as Chinese Yuan in northern areas) are frequently used for private transactions involving imported goods.

A holder of foreign exchange who needs to make payments within the Lao PDR can exchange for Kip at a commercial bank or at a foreign exchange bureau licensed by the Bank of the Lao PDR. Those who need to use foreign exchange for any of the objectives stipulated in Lao law, such as payment for imported goods, may purchase foreign exchange at a commercial bank or a foreign exchange bureau.

In order to facilitate business transactions, foreign investors generally open commercial bank accounts in both local and foreign convertible currency at domestic and foreign banks in Laos. Australian, Vietnamese, Thai, Cambodian, Malaysian, Chinese and French banks currently have a presence in Laos. Bank accounts must be maintained in accordance with the Enterprise Accounting Law.

The law places no limitations on foreign investors transferring after-tax profits, income from technology transfer, initial capital, interest, wages and salaries, or other remittances to the company's home country or third countries so long as they request approval from the Lao government. These transactions are conducted at the official exchange rate on the day of execution, upon presentation of appropriate documentation.

Supply of foreign exchange has in the past been limited in Laos, which imposed a de facto limit on repatriation of capital.. Foreign enterprises must report on their performance

annually and submit annual financial statements to the Ministry of Planning and

Investment (MPI).

In 2013, Laos suffered fiscal and monetary difficulties which resulted in low levels of foreign reserves. In response, the Bank of the Lao PDR (BOL) imposed daily limits on converting funds from Lao Kip into U.S. Dollars and Thai Baht, leading to difficulties in obtaining foreign exchange in Laos. The BOL also imposed restrictions on loans made in USD and Baht, limiting them to businesses which generated foreign currency. There were no reports of restrictions on, or difficulties in, repatriating or transferring funds associated with an investment.

U.S. BANKS AND LOCAL CORRESPONDENT BANKS

There are no U.S. banks operating in Laos. BCEL has correspondence arrangements

with the following banks (US dollars):

Bank	Country
Joint Stock Commercial Bank for Foreign Trade of Vietnam	Vietnam
Bank of Tokyo-Mitsubishi UFJ, LTD	Japan
Industrial and Commercial Bank of China (Head Office Beijing CN)	China
Credit Suisse	Switzerland
Sumitomo Mitsui Banking Corporation	Japan
Wells Fargo	USA
Standard Chartered Bank	Singapore
Standard Chartered Bank	USA

PROJECT FINANCING

On June 12, 2009 President Obama issued a Presidential determination that Laos and

Cambodia would no longer be classified as "Marxist-Leninist countries" as defined in the

Export Import Act. This determination opened the door for Ex-Im Bank activity in those

two countries.

An Overseas Private Investment Cooperation (OPIC) agreement was signed in 1996,

and an agreement with the Multilateral Investment Guarantee Agency (MIGA) in 1998. In

1998, the government signed an agreement with the Mekong Project Development

Facility (MPDF), a multi-donor funded operation managed by the International Finance

Corporation (IFC). The MPDF is designed to promote the establishment and expansion

of privately owned, small and medium-sized enterprises, as well as joint venture projects

with significant local private participation in Laos, Cambodia, and Vietnam.

The World Bank (WB) and the Asian Development Bank (ADB) are very active in Laos

and are often involved in providing financing or guarantees for major projects.

WEB RESOURCES

Export-Import Bank of the United States: http://www.exim.gov

Country Limitation Schedule: http://www.exim.gov/tools/country/country_limits.html

OPIC: http://www.opic.gov

Trade and Development Agency: http://www.tda.gov/

SBA's Office of International Trade: http://www.sba.gov/oit/

USDA Commodity Credit Corporation: http://www.fsa.usda.gov/ccc/default.htm

U.S. Agency for International Development: http://www.usaid.gov

(Insert a link to the applicable Multilateral Development Bank here and any other pertinent web resources.)

EXPORT DOCUMENTS AND PROCEDURES

PART I : DOCUMENTATION

- Cargo Control Document
- Invoice
- Declaration Form
- Certificate of Origin

You will be able to obtain release of your goods upon presentation of a fully completed declaration package consisting of the following:

1. 3 copies of the cargo control document
2. 2 copies of the invoice
3. 2 carrier advice notes
4. 2 copies of any permit issued by a relevant Ministry or Department
5. 2 certificates of origin showing origin of goods
6. 3 sets of the declaration form

CARGO CONTROL DOCUMENT

A cargo control document in the form of an airway bill for goods arriving by air or a manifest for goods arriving by highway or river will be sent to you together with an advice note issued by the carrier to inform you that a shipment has arrived and is awaiting customs clearance.

You will need the cargo control number from the airway bill or manifest to complete the appropriate field on the declaration form.

Three copies of the cargo control document and two copies of the advice note must accompany the declaration form.

INVOICE

For all shipments entering or leaving Lao PDR, a commercial invoice which indicates the buyer and seller of the goods, the price paid or price payable, and an adequate description of the goods including quantity of the goods contained in the shipment, should be produced to support the declaration. The invoice must be prepared by the exporter. Locally produced invoices are not acceptable. Click here to download an invoice sample

Declaration Form

Certificate of origin

PART II :CLASSIFICATION OF GOODS

- Harmonized System

General Information on the Harmonized Commodity Description and Coding (HS) Based Tariff

The H.S. based tariff is logically structured and divided into twenty-one sections. For the most part, commodities are arranged in these sections according to the decree of manufacture or processing.

Within the twenty-one sections there are 99 chapters. Chapter 77 is reserved for possible future expansion. The last chapter, 99 is set aside for special use by individual countries.

Chapters are arranged according to levels of processing, with primary commodities classified in the earlier chapters and technically more complex products treated later on.

Each chapter begins with a title page. Section and chapter legal notes precede certain chapters and sections. However, these notes only define the scope and limits of the chapter and sections they precede. Following the chapter notes, you will find the classification numbers of all products covered by the chapter.

For additional analytical, business and investment opportunities information,
please contact Global Investment & Business Center, USA
at (703) 370-8082. Fax: (703) 370-8083. E-mail: ibpusa3@gmail.com
Global Business and Investment Info Databank - www.ibpus.com

STRUCTURE OF THE CLASSIFICATION NUMBER

Classification in the HS is a systematic process. To use this process, it is essential to understand the structure of the classification number.

With the entry of Lao PDR in ASEAN, the classification number consists of eight digits. This eight-digit number is sub-divided at various levels to provide greater details and definitions for a product than the previous level at the six digits.

Each level is identified as follows:

01.01 HEADING
01.01.20 1st SUB-HEADING
01.01.20.00 2sd Sub-Heading

International Lao and ASEAN
Requirement Requirement

The first six digits represent the international portion of the classification number and are the numbers that will be used by all countries acceding to the Harmonized System. The last two digits reflect the Lao and ASEAN requirements for tariff and statistical purposes.

The structure of the classification number, i.e., the breakdown of the number by heading, and sub-headings is the basis for classifying your product in the H.S. Once a product has been located in a heading, an appropriate eight-digit number of sub-headings within the selected heading must be determined.

PART III : VALUE FOR DUTY

- Transaction Value Method
- Other Methods of Valuing Imports
- Importer's Responsibility
- Importer's Rights

The Lao PDR system of valuing imported goods is known as the transaction value system. It is based on an internationally approved set of rules, under the General Agreement on Tariffs and Trade. The system is now used by most trading nations and provides for a fair and uniform means of valuing goods for customs duty.

The transaction value system stipulates that the transaction value method must be used whenever possible. This value method bases the customs value on the price paid by the importer to the exporter for the imported goods. If the transaction value method cannot be used, one of the other five methods must be used, in the sequence presented. These other methods are known as

- Transaction value of identical goods
- Transaction value of similar goods
- Deductive value
- Computed value
- Flexible value

For additional analytical, business and investment opportunities information,
please contact Global Investment & Business Center, USA
at (703) 370-8082. Fax: (703) 370-8083. E-mail: ibpusa3@gmail.com
Global Business and Investment Info Databank - www.ibpus.com

TRANSACTION VALUE METHOD

1. The transaction value method will be used for valuation of most imported goods, except in situations where there is a relationship between the importer and exporter that may influence the value, or where the imported goods are rented or leased, or are sent on consignment, or where the exporter imposes certain conditions such as restricting the trading level or the area of resale, or barter trade.

2. When using the transaction value method, the following costs must be included in the customs value:
- Transportation costs to Lao PDR
- Insurance costs
- Packing, packaging and special handling costs
- Fees paid to the exporters for royalties, licenses, etc.
- Storage charges in the country of export that are paid by the importer
- All escalation costs charged after the goods are ordered
- All selling costs such as commissions, etc that are charged to the importer
- Assists are goods or services supplied by the importer to the exporter free or at a reduced cost that were used in the production of the goods.

3. Costs which may be deducted from the customs value are:
- Discounts for volume purchases, payment for the goods in advance or within an agreed period (such discount must be shown on the invoice and granted before importation)
- If goods were sold by the exporter on a duty and tax paid basis, deduct the amount paid for duties and taxes
- Amount paid to the exporter for work that will be performed in Lao PDR, such as construction, erection, assembly, maintenance or technical assistance related to the imported goods (such costs must be shown separately on the invoice or in a contract)

OTHER METHODS OF VALUING IMPORTS

The five other methods of valuation are more complex and the necessary information may not be readily available. The following is therefore only for the importer's information and, if it is necessary to apply these methods the importer may wish to consult with a customs officer to determine the value for duty.

IDENTICAL OR SIMILAR GOODS METHOD

Under these methods the value for duty is based on the customs value of other identical or similar goods which have been previously exported to Lao PDR, at or about the same time as the goods being imported. The customs value can be adjusted to allow for differences in the trade level of purchases and in the cost of transportation. It is unlikely that the importer will be able to use these methods, as it requires information on values declared to customs for imports of identical or similar goods. Values for duty under these methods is therefore usually calculated in conjunction with the assistance of a customs officer.

DEDUCTIVE VALUE METHOD

Under the deductive value method, the value for duty is based on the most common selling price of goods imported into Lao PDR. From this resale price is deducted an amount which represents the average profit and general expenses involved in selling the goods in the Lao PDR. Included in the general expenses involved in the expenses will be items such as Lao PDR duties and taxes, all transportation, warehousing, selling and distribution costs, also any packaging or further processing costs in Lao PDR, should also be deducted in calculating the value for duty.

The purpose behind this method is to determine what the cost of the goods would have been had they been purchased, in the same condition as when imported, from an unrelated exporter. This method would only be used in situations such as goods being imported on consignment or barter trade.

COMPUTED VALUE METHOD

The computed value method is the cost of production of the imported goods, plus an amount for normal profit and general expenses experienced by the exporter, when selling the same type of goods to importers in Lao PDR.

As most exporters are reluctant to release this information, the use of this valuation method will generally be limited to those importers who are related to the exporter and where the exporter is the manufacturer of the goods being appraised.

FLEXIBLE METHOD

If the other methods of valuation can not be used, the flexible method must be applied. This method does not provide specific rules, but stipulates that the rules of one of the other five methods is applied in a flexible manner and that the information used is available in the Lao PDR.

IMPORTER'S RESPONSIBILITY

The importer of commercial goods into Lao PDR is responsible for the self-assessment of the duty and tax liabilities on all goods imported. This means that the importer or his authorized agent must prepare all necessary documents for presentation to customs.

CUSTOMS' RESPONSIBILITY

Customs is responsible to ensure that all legislation governing the importation and exportation of goods into and out of the Lao PDR have been fully complied with. Customs is also responsible to insure that all applicable duties and taxes have been paid. Customs will also review customs declarations after release of the goods and may issue notices for payment of additional, duties and tax as a result of the review, or reassessment of value or redetermination of tariff.

IMPORTER'S RIGHTS

An importer has the right to request customs to reconsider any reassessment of value and any redetermination of tariff classification. Further, the importer has the right to appeal the customs reassessment notice to higher authorities.

PART IV : CODING INSTRUCTIONS

Annex
I List of Customs Offices and Codes
II List of Country and Currency Codes
III List of Regional Customs Offices and Addresses

THE DECLARATION FORM

The declaration form or single administrative document is used for all customs transactions; import, export or transit. It must be complete to be acceptable in customs.

Click here to view a sample form

THE DECLARATION FORM HAS THREE SEGMENTS.

1. In the first section(Boxes No.1-23) enter general information on importer, exporter and declarant as well as transport and transaction details.

2. In the second section (Boxes No.24-42) enter details on the item declared, including amount of duties and taxes payable or exempted.

3. Summary of Payment and Responsibility of Declaration Section.

It is presented in the form of (i.) a header sheet, which is used to declare importation, exportation or in transit information for each commodity item (ii.) continuation sheets to declare other commodity items and (iii.) section sheet for official use.
Note. Declaration forms are on sale at all Regional Customs offices.
Instructions to fill each box of the form.

BOX NO.1 DECLARATION REGIME

Inscribe one of the following codes to identify the type of transaction the declaration is for:

Regime Code Description
10 Exportation of domestic Goods
14 Exportation under a drawback regime
20 Temporary Exportation
35 Re-Exportation
40 Importation of goods for Home consumption.
4A Importation of goods for diplomatic use, returning residents, and humanitarian assistance; samples, educational materials and certain religious articles.
4B Goods ex-warehoused to duty free shops
4C Goods ex-warehoused for exportation out of Lao PDR
45 Home Consumption of Goods after temporary admission
47 Home Consumption of Goods entered under a warehousing regime
50 Temporary Importation
62 Re-Importation of Goods Exported temporarily
70 Warehousing of Goods
80 Transit

Office Codes.

Enter the code of the office where the declaration is presented. See Annex I for a list of all customs offices and their codes.

MANIFEST /AIRWAY BILL NUMBER.

Enter the cargo control number from the air waybill if the goods arrive or leave by air or from the manifest if goods arrive or leave by any other mode of transport.
Declaration Number and Date.

Customs will assign the declaration number and the date when the declaration is presented and registered with customs.

BOX NO.2 EXPORTER AND ADDRESS

If you enter goods for exportation, indicate your name and address as well as the taxpayer identification number (TIN) issued by the Tax Department. If you have not yet been issued a TIN please obtain a number from the nearest tax office and use it on all subsequent customs declarations. Also include your office telephone number. For diplomatic and personal exportations, leave the number field blank.

BOX NO.3 GROSS MASS KG.

Indicate the gross weight in kilograms of the entire consignment of goods as declared on the manifest or air waybill.

BOX NO.4 ITEMS

Indicate the total number of items as shown on the invoice.

BOX NO.5 TOTAL PACKAGES.

Indicate the total number of packages as declared on the manifest or airway bill. In case of bulk cargo, indicate BULK only.

BOX NO. 6 IMPORTER AND ADDRESS

If you enter goods for importation, indicate your name and address as well as the taxpayer identification number (TIN) issued by the Tax Department. If you have not been issued a TIN please obtain a number from the nearest tax office and use it on all subsequent customs declarations. Also include your office telephone number. For diplomatic and personal importations, leave the number field blank.

BOX NO.7 CONSIGNEE.

If you are importing goods on behalf of another person, or the other party holds title to the good at time of importation indicate the name and address of the consignee as well as the TIN issued by the Tax Department. Please contact the nearest tax office for a number and use on all subsequent declarations, or obtain the TIN number from the consignee if one has been issued to the consignee by the tax department. For diplomatic importations, leave the number field blank.

Box No.8 Declarant.

If you are a licensed agent authorized to transact business in customs, enter the TIN issued by the Tax Department. If you do not have a TIN, contact the nearest tax office.

Box No.9 Country of Consignment/Destination.

For importation, indicate the country and the code from where the goods have been consigned. For exportation, indicate the country and the code to where the goods are exported or re-exported.

See Annex II: List of Country and Currency Codes.

Box No.10 Type of License.

Indicate the type of trade or industry license held by you.

Box. No.11 Delivery Terms.

Indicate the terms of delivery of goods either CIF for importation, or FOB for exportation.

Box No.12 Total Invoice in Foreign Currency.

For importation, indicate the total amount of the invoice in foreign currency. See list of Country and Currency Codes in Annex II.

Box No.13 Total Invoice in Local Currency.

Enter here the total value of the invoice in Kip by converting the value declared in box No. 12 with the rate of exchange indicated in box No.16. If there is only one item, this value should correspond to the value declared in box no.38. If there are many items, the total value should correspond to the total of values declared in all the boxes no.38 on the Continuation sheets.

Box No.14 Total FOB (Exports)

Indicate the FOB value of the goods in foreign currency.
(if known)

Box No. 14 Total FOB (Imports)

Enter the FOB value in foreign currency. (if known)

Box No.15 Total FOB Ncy (Import/Export)

For import, leave blank.
For export, indicate the FOB value of the goods in Kip.

Box No.16 Rate of Exchange.

Indicate the rate of exchange of the foreign currency to the Kip and the code of the foreign currency. (The exchange rate shall be that which is in force at time of importation, unless otherwise advised).

Box No.17 Mode of Transport.

Indicate the mode of transport, the voyage number. Also the country code of the nationality of the aircraft, truck or ship.
(if known)

The codes for mode of transport are:

SEA 1
RAIL 2
ROAD 3
AIR 4

Box No.18 Port of Loading/Unloading.

For imports indicate the name and the code of the foreign country where goods are loaded,
For exports, indicate the name and the code of the foreign country where goods are destined.

See Annex II for a list of Country Codes.

Box No.19 Place of Shipping/ Landing.

For imports, indicate the place in Lao PDR where goods have arrived. At export, or re-export, indicate the place in Lao PDR from where the goods are exported or re-exported.

Box No.20 Entry/Exit Office.

Indicate the code of the Lao customs office where the declaration is presented for clearance.

In a transit operation, indicate the code of the customs office where the transit operation commences. Also indicate the code of the exit customs office where the transit operations is to be terminated.

Box No.21 Identification Warehouse (Leave blank until bonded warehouses are established)

Indicate the code of the bonded warehouse where goods are to be warehoused or ex-warehoused.

Box No.22 Financial and Banking Data.

For additional analytical, business and investment opportunities information, please contact Global Investment & Business Center, USA at (703) 370-8082. Fax: (703) 370-8083. E-mail: ibpusa3@gmail.com
Global Business and Investment Info Databank - www.ibpus.com

Indicate the terms of payment of the transaction, as well as the name of the bank and the branch where payment for the commercial transaction is made.

Box No.23 Attached Documents.

Indicate the codes of attached documents, which support your declaration. (Documents must be originals or certified as true copies).

1234567891011 InvoiceManifestAirway billPacking ListCertificate of Origin (If required)Phytosanitary Certificate (If required)Import Permit from Ministry of Trade (If required)Import permit from Ministry of Agriculture (If required)Import Permit from Ministry of Heath (If required) Authorization from Department of Transport (If required)If claiming duty and tax exemptions, documents authorizing such exemptions must be presented with the declaration.

Box No.24 Marks, Numbers and Description of Goods

Indicate the marks and numbers of the packages as shown on the manifest or airway bill.

If goods arrive or leave by containers, indicate the container number as shown on the manifest.

The total number of packages should correspond to the total number of packages indicated in box No.5.

Give a detailed description of the goods. Avoid, as far as possible, trade names. Except in the case of vehicles and electronic devices, provide make and model.

Box No.25 No. of Items.

Indicate the number of items on the invoice.

Box No.26 Tariff Code

Indicate the classification code of the commodity imported. This classification code in based on the AHTN and must be eight digits.

Box No.27 Customs Procedure Codes.
(Leave blank at this time)

Box No.28 Country of Origin/Destination

For imports, indicate the code of the country of origin of the goods imported, if the country of origin of the goods is different from the country where the goods have been consigned.

Box No.29 Zone.
It the goods originate from ASEAN member countries and are supported by a certificate of origin enter ASEAN. For other countries enter GEN. At export enter XPT.

Box No.30 Valuation Code

Indicate the code of the valuation method used to determine the customs value for duty.

There are six valuation methods and coded as follows:

Valuation Method Code
Transaction Method 1
Identical Goods Method 2
Similar Goods Method 3
Deductive Method 4
Computed Method 5
Flexible Method 6

Note: The transaction valuation method must be used as the primary method for valuation if possible.

Box No.31 Gross Mass.

Enter the gross weight in kilograms for the item on the first page only. The total weight of all items on the continuation sheets in the declaration should be equal to the weight declared in box no.3 of the general segment.

Box No.32 Net Mass.

Enter the net weight of the goods in kilograms for each item declared. If a continuation sheet is used a net mass must be inscribed for each item.

Box No.33 FOB Foreign Currency.

Enter the FOB value of the item in foreign currency (if known).

Box No.34 FOB Local Currency, only if transport and insurance are not prepaid by exporter. If prepaid, enter the value that includes transportation and insurance.

Enter the FOB value of the item in Kips, only if transport and insurance are not prepaid by exporter. If prepaid, enter the value that includes transportation and insurance.

Box No. 35 Freight.

Enter the amount of freight paid or payable for the item in Kip. For a shipment of various items, the freight charges are apportioned according to freight paid or payable and by weight. If freight is prepaid by exporter and included in the value, mark the box "Prepaid".

Box No.36 Insurance.

Enter the amount of insurance in Kip for the item.

For a shipment of various items, the insurance paid or payable is to be apportioned.

If the insurance is prepaid by the exporter and included in the value, mark the box "prepaid"

Box No.37 Other Costs.

Enter other costs and expenses incurred for the import of goods and paid to the exporter for the imported goods.

Box No.38 Customs Value in Local Currency.

Enter the customs value for the item, which is the total of values of boxes 33, 34, 35 and 36.

Box No. 39 Supplementary Unit/Quantity.

Some of the most common international units of quantity are as follows:

Unit Code
Cubic Metre MTQ
Gigawatt-hour GWH
Hundred CEN
Kilogram KGM
Litre LTR
Metre MTR
Number NMB
Number of packs NMP
Square Metre MTK
Ten TEN
Ten Pairs TPR
Thousand MIL
Tonne TNE

Enter any of the code, which describes the unit quantity of goods imported/exported. If the units of imports or exports are not included in this list, consult a customs officer for more detailed lists.

Box No.40 Duty Payable.

Enter the amount of duties and taxes payable for the item declared per category of duty, tax and excise.

Enter also the taxable base for each category of duty, tax and excise. Duty rate is calculated on the Customs value. The tax is calculated on the customs value plus the duty payable. The excise tax is calculated on the customs value plus duty payable plus tax payable.

For other items of the declaration, on the continuation sheets enter the duty, tax and excise payable.

Box No.41 Permit Numbers.

Enter permit number and date of issue for the shipment, if required.

Box No.42 Previous Declaration.

If the declaration refers to a previous declaration, the registration number and date of the previous declaration is entered here.

For additional analytical, business and investment opportunities information, please contact Global Investment & Business Center, USA at (703) 370-8082. Fax: (703) 370-8083. E-mail: ibpusa3@gmail.com Global Business and Investment Info Databank - www.ibpus.com

Present a copy of the previous declaration with the declaration you have just prepared.

Responsibility of Declaration

You must enter your full name, indicate the capacity in which you are acting. And sign the declaration.

You must also indicate the mode of payment by which duty and taxes are to be paid.

After you have completed your declaration, trader can now lodge it at the designated customs office where your goods are held.

After customs review and approval of the declaration, please make the payment of all applicable duties and taxes, and present a copy of the payment receipt to the customs office where the declaration was presented.

On receipt of the customs release note, present the release note to the warehouse keeper for delivery of the imported goods and sign for receipt of the goods or have the carrier sign for receipt.

FOREIGN INVESTMENT OPPORTUNITIES IN LAOS

FOREIGN INVESTMENT LICENSED IN LAOS

Rank	Countries	Number of Projects	Investment in US $ x 1000	Percentage
1.	Thailand	233	$2,278,289	44.78%
2.	USA	39	1,482,717	29.14
3.	R. Korea	17	394,785	7.76
4.	France	68	312,806	6.15
5.	Malaysia	11	188,731	3.71
6.	Australia	41	134,026	2.63
7.	Taiwan	31	64,764	1.27
8.	Norway	1	56000	1.10
9.	China	61	38,921	0.76
10.	UK.	13	28,685	0.56
11.	Hong Kong	23	28,266	0.56
12.	Canada	13	17,914	0.35
13.	Russian	12	17,564	0.35

For additional analytical, business and investment opportunities information, please contact Global Investment & Business Center, USA at (703) 370-8082. Fax: (703) 370-8083. E-mail: ibpusa3@gmail.com Global Business and Investment Info Databank - www.ibpus.com

14.	Singapore	16	12,217	024
15.	Japan	17	7,913	0.16
16.	Indonesia	2	5,140	0.10
17.	DPK Korea	1	3300	0.06
18.	Germany	7	3,019	0.06
19.	Vietnam	10	2,724	0.05
20.	Macao	2	2,560	0.05
21.	Sweden	7	2,203	0.04
22.	Italy	6	1,973	0.04
23.	Holland	3	770	0.02
24.	New Zealand	5	734	0.01
25.	India	2	645	0.01
26.	Belgium	2	500	0.01
27.	Denmark	6	406	0.01
28.	Switzerland	2	240	0.00
29.	Ukraine	1	200	0.00
30.	Austria	3	172	0.00
31.	Myanmar	3	65	0.00
	Laos' Shares		1,158,400	
	TOTAL:	658 projects	US$6,246,649,000	100%

SELECTED BUSINESS AND INVESTMENT OPPORTUNITIES

AGRO-FORESTRY SECTOR

Agriculture : The economic growth of the Lao PDR **Depends to a large extend,** upon the, performance of the Agricultural sector which contributed in 1993 for 56% of the GDP and employed about 0% of the labor force.

Coffee is by far the most promising **product for export.** In 1992, export of coffee accounted for around 80% of the export value in the agricultural sector and contributed for 7.4% of the total export value of the country. Export also includes several annual and perennial corps of limited quantities.

The Lao PDR has the **highest potential land/person** in the Greater Mekong Subregion large and unexploited fertile land and favorable climatic conditions, particularly in the **boloven basaltic**

For additional analytical, business and investment opportunities information, please contact Global Investment & Business Center, USA at (703) 370-8082. Fax: (703) 370-8083. E-mail: ibpusa3@gmail.com Global Business and Investment Info Databank - www.ibpus.com

plateau. This could offer promising **opportunities** for low-intensive investment in the **agro-processing industry** for export based on annual and perennial crops.

The on-going improvement of main National Roads linking major provinces, together with the high rate of urbanization have created **favorable conditions** for investment in the **import-substitution** agro-processing industries.

Forestry : It has been estimated that the Lao PDR has **the highest ratio** of forest to total area in ASIA. Wood products including lumber are one of the main **export earning** of Lao PDR. In 1993, it accounted for **22% of the total export value.** In view of the long term sustainable development and the preservation of the environment, the Government has been implementing the policy of striking **a balance** between exploitation and conservation and shifting from exports of logs and lumbers towards the **promotion of wood** processing. Due to **shortage** of capital and the technical know-how in the country, the development of wood processing subsector also needs the investment and the introduction of new technology of the **foreign investors.**

ENERGY SECTOR

Electricity requirements in the region-. are increasing rapidly it has been predicted that 23,958 MW of new generation will be needed between now and year 2000. Lao PDR. is rich in energy resources: **Hydropower, coal, oil and gas. The uneven distribution** of the energy resources among the countries, particularly the hydropower resources : Countries with higher power demand have limited resources while those with limited requirements are well endowed with the hydropower resources.

Lao PDR has a hydropower potential of about **15,000 MW** within its territory. Up to now, slightly over 1% of the total potential has been developed with 70 to 75% of the production exported to Thailand.

With the huge resources located close to the biggest power demand country in the subregion **(Thailand)** and the low domestic demand, the hydropower sector will continue to be **one of the main foreign exchange earning of Lao PDR.**

Without other financial sources than **The public investment funds and the external soft loan** the hydropower development would provably continue with the similar **slow rate** as experienced in the eighties. This would lead to a loss of opportunity for foreign exchange earning badly needed for development of other sectors.

On the basis of the above and in line with the new economic policy, the Government has begun, since the beginning of the nineties, **to seek participation of foreign investors** for projects beyond the financial capacity of the public and soft loan investment.

Within the short timeframe, experiences have proven that such policy is correct and several projects with the aggregate generation capacity about **10 times higher than the existing capacity** are being implemented in 1994 and expected to be completed by **the 2000** as shown 'm the attached figure.

The funds for these projects are from both the private sector **(BOT schemes)** for large schemes and soft loan for small/medium schemes. Agreements between the Government and the developers have been signed for most of the BOT schemes of the 1994-2000 peroid.

All the a above-mentioned BOT schemes have a provision for **equity sharing by the government** ranging from 25% to 60%.

Information given in following tables and figures are aimed to show the potential and the relative advantages of the hydropower resources in Lao PDR. It also indicates the, long-term forecast of power and electric energy demands of the countries in the Greater Mekong Subregion.

MINING SECTOR

Foreign investment is particularly sought in the Mining Sector because of its capital-intensive investment combined with scarce domestic financial resources and its high potential for export.

In 1991, the foreign investment in this sector was ranked second in terms of aggregate value (about 25% of the total).

Fiscal regulations such royalty rate, income taxes and incentives in the Mining Sector are widely recognized as **competitive** by international standard. This indicates the firm commitment and strong support of the Government to **pave the way** for foreign investment in the sector.

The following location maps of various minerals and fossil fuels such as coal lignite, oil and natural gas show that the country possess huge mineral resources.

Market for fossil fuel in **Thailand** is tremendous as the country has to import about **60% of its requirements.** This would be an area of **high prospects** for foreign investors. Recently, an agreement was signed with private investors to implement a **lignite power plant** project in Hongsa (Northwest of Lao PDR) for exporting the electricity to Thailand.

In the **short-term,** other minerals having high prospects for export would be gemstones which require simple extraction equipment and could be easily transported.

Some **medium-and long-term** investment opportunities offered by the Ming Sector would be :

    a). **The potash production** in the **Vientiane** province, the largest known deposits in the subregion with the estimated reserves exceeding by far those in Thailand;

    b). The significant **iron ore** deposits in the province of **Xiengkhouang,** the occurrences of **base metals** (components needed for steel) and the planned hydropower development on the Nam Ngum river, both in the northeast of Vientiane and in Xiengkhoang Province, suggest the region could provide opportunities for both iron ore and steel export;

    c). The **boloven** basaltic plateau in the southern Laos well endowed with both the competitive **hydropower** potential and **bauxite** might also offer opportunities for aluminum melting plants.

Having been fully aware that the absence of railways and inadequacy -of the road network are the major constraints for the development of the Mining Sector, the Government is now seeking all financial means to develop the transport sector including the **concession arrangement** with private investors Mining and transport development could be tied together in a **Single package** for concession arrangement.

For additional analytical, business and investment opportunities information,
please contact Global Investment & Business Center, USA
at (703) 370-8082. Fax: (703) 370-8083. E-mail: ibpusa3@gmail.com
Global Business and Investment Info Databank - www.ibpus.com

ROADS

The Second and Third conferences in Subregion Economic Cooperation have identified the following priority projects in the road subsector :

a). Upgrading of the **Ho Chi Minh City- Phnom Penh- Bangkok road connection,** including possible extension to Vung Tau in Vietnam;

b). Construction of a **Thai- Lao PDR- Vietnam east-west Corridor;**

c). Development of a good quality road linking **Chiang Rai-Kunming via Myanmar;**

d). Development of a good quality road linking **Chiang Rai-Kunming via Lao PDR;** and

UPGRADING KUNMING -LAOSHIO ROAD SYSTEM.

RAILWAY, WATER AND TRANSPORT SUB-SECTOR

The Subregion Transport Sector Study by ADB considers 3 projects in railway subsector, 2 in the water transport subsector and 2 in the air transport subsector which are directly concerned Lao PDR.

a). **Projects in railway subsector** :

- Yunnan Province- Thailand Railway Project with two out of three optimal via Lao PDR.

- Extension Thailand Railway to Lao PDR (150 km) through the firstinternational Mekong bridge.

- Construction of new railway line from Lao PDR's Xiengkhouang Province to a Cualo port in Vietnarn mainly for export of iron ore.

b). **Water Transport Subsector** :

- Upper Mekong River Navigation Improvement Project.

- Southem Lao PDR- Cambodia River Navigation Improvement Project.

c). **Air Transport Subsector** :

- Project to upgrade the airport in Lao PDR

- Project to Establish New Subregional Air Routes involving Luang Prabang.

TOURISM AND HOTEL SECTOR

Within the Subregion, links and networks in the tourism sector **already exist** : Government-to-government and the commercial sector.

The commun interest among all six countries is to promote nature and culture types of tourism. The major problem is the **gaps** in most countries in the **basicinfrastructure** and **support services** necessary for maximizing tourism potential.

The subregional cooperation will primarily focus on :

1. **Promoting the Subregion as a tourism destination.**
2. **Establishing Subregional Tourism Forum.**
3. **Training the trainers in the basic craft skills of tourism.**
4. **Training the Resource Management in Conservation and Tourism.**
5. **mekong River Tourism Promoting Study.**

TRANSPORT

In most countries, transportation infrastructures are inadequate and are considered as a **major impediment** to trade , cooperation and the exploitation of rich mineral resources, particularly those located in the hinterlands.

Further major commitments are required before minimum standards can be satisfies and most of the shortcomings could only be addressed by **cooperation efforts**.

Through several meetings and consultations, the six countries have agrees that :

a). **Priority** should be on to the improvement and rehabilitation of existing facilities and Subregional projects on which there is already agreement among the countries directly concerned;

b). **The formulation of projects** should consider trade generation impacts, especially considering the economic transformation taking place in the Subregion;

c). Transport projects should be **implemented in sections or stretches** in order to facilitate project(s) implementation and provide immediate benefits;

d). Given financial constraints, **criteria** for project(s) selection will need to be established, including consideration of the subregional versus national character of the project and financial resources available.

TRADE AND SERVICES SECTOR

Most of the countries trade more often with countries outside the subregion than within.

However, trade and investment **within the subregion** are being **development steadily** owing to the growing openness and revitalization of the economies, and the favorable legal and regulatory framework for local and foreign investors.

The countries in the subregion have many **commun problems** (such as severe infrastructure shortage) and also commun goals (such as outward-oriented economy and promotion of the participation of private sector). All countries recognize that the attraction of foreign investor **depend to a great extend** on the trade and investment environment.

For additional analytical, business and investment opportunities information, please contact Global Investment & Business Center, USA at (703) 370-8082. Fax: (703) 370-8083. E-mail: ibpusa3@gmail.com Global Business and Investment Info Databank - www.ibpus.com

The cooperation aiming at improving the Trade and Investment Climate in the Subregion would enable investors to consider their own strategies in the **subregional context** which is more attractive than the national context. Projects and initiatives emerged from the Third Conference on the Economic Cooperation in the Greater Mekong Subregion includes :

    (a) Two Projects aiming at Facilitating and Enhancing Trade Flows
    (b) Three Projects aiming at Improving Investment Climates
    (c) Two Projects on Building a Strong Science and Technology Base
    (d) One Project aiming at Increasing the Role of Private Sector

IMPORTANT BUSINESS AND INVESTMENT OPPORTUNITIES

20 MILLION ENVIRONMENT & SOCIAL PROGRAM

1. The proposed USD20 million loan project for Lao's Environment and Social program project is expected to be approved by the Asian Development Bank's (ADB) Board on **December 6, 2001**. This cable is intended to:

-- Alert Embassies and AID missions to ADB-financed projects, and

-- Provide U.S. businesses with as much lead time as possible concerning procurement and consulting opportunities.

-- For more information on this project or ADB lending opportunities, firms should contact Ms. Chantale Wong, Alternate U.S. Executive Director, Asian Development Bank at phone no. (63-2) 632-6051, and fax no. (63-2) 632-4003 or Mr. Stewart Ballard, The U.S. Commercial Liaison Office for the ADB at telephone nos.: (63-2) 887-1345 to 46 and fax no. (63-2) 887-1164. For in-country inquiry, please contact Mr. Scott Rolston, Commercial Officer, American Embassy, Vientiane; Tel.: (856-21) 212-581; Fax: 212-584.

2. For post, USADB requests AmEmbassy and AID mission views on the Project before **December 06, 2001** based on currently available information.

A. PROJECT RATIONALE:
- Lao People's Democratic Republic (Lao PDR) is a small landlocked country, characterized by its mountainous terrain, low population density, limited skilled human resources, and a wealth of natural resources and environmental assets. As natural resources underpin economic development and poverty reduction prospects) the Government attaches priority to conserving the environment and ensuring the environmental and social sustainability of all development activities.

- Improving environmental management and social safeguards performance has been the subject of considerable policy dialogue and technical assistance. Enactment of the Environment Protection Law (EPL) in 1999 was a breakthrough. Together with environmental provisions in laws on electricity, roads, land, water resources, and forests, the EPL provides a framework for implementing safeguards. However, effective enforcement requires the adoption of enabling regulations, compliance mechanisms, and measures to enhance Government capacity and financial sustainability. Without this, the integration of environmental management and social safeguard issues across sectors will remain elusive.

- The Government aims to go beyond case-by-case remedial action on environment and social impacts towards a pro-active approach that integrates these concerns within national, sectoral, and area-based planning. The Government has sought Asian Development Bank (ADB) assistance to develop and implement a program aimed at shifting the country onto a more sustainable development trajectory, focusing initially on the energy and transport sectors. This will require five closely related sets of constraints to be addressed: (i) incomplete policy and regulatory framework; (ii) lack of implementation capacity at sectoral and provincial levels; (iii) inadequate compliance and enforcement mechanisms; (iv) absence of integrated area-based planning frameworks to guide investments in energy and transport; and (v) insufficient attention to sustainable finance for environment management.

B. PROJECT OBJECTIVES:
- The objective is to support the Government's policy reform agenda for improved environmental management and social safeguards in the energy and transport sectors. The scope covers five closely linked priority areas for policy action: (i) strengthening national policy and regulatory framework for environment management and social safeguards; (ii) enhancing policy implementation measures and capacity at sectoral and provincial levels; (iii) improving compliance and enforcement; (iv) promoting river basin management as a multi-sectoral and integrated planning framework for energy and transport development; and (v) establishing sustainable financing mechanisms, including an environment fund.

C. PROJECT DESCRIPTION:
- The Environment and Social Program (the Program) will assist the Lao PDR implement a targeted policy reform agenda for environmental management and social safeguards in the energy and transport sectors, focusing on hydropower and roads, with a proposed program loan of USD20.0 million.

D. EXECUTING AGENCY:
- The Science, Technology and Environment Agency (STEA) will be the Executing Agency for the Program, in close coordination with the Committee for Planning and Cooperation (CPC), Ministry of Finance (MOF), Ministry of Communication, Transport, Post and Construction (MCTPC), Ministry of Industry and Handicrafts (MIH), and Ministry of Agriculture and Forestry (MAF). STEA will have overall responsibility for ensuring effective implementation of the Program. MOF will monitor the use of loan proceeds and counterpart funds.

E. TOTAL PROJECT COST: USD20.0 million

F. PROGRAM PERIOD AND TRANCHING:
- The Program period will be 36 months (FY2002- FY2004). The proposed loan is to be disbursed in three tranches. The first tranche of USD5.0 million will be made available upon loan effectiveness, while the second tranche of USD10.0 million will be disbursed within 14 months after the first tranche, subject to the Government's compliance with the conditions set for the release of that tranche. A third tranche of USD5.0 million will be made available when the Government establishes a proposed environment fund during the 36 months of loan utilization.

G. PROCUREMENT:
- The proceeds of the loan will finance the full foreign exchange costs, excluding local duties and taxes, of imports procured in and from ADB's member countries, other than those specified in the list of ineligible items and those financed by other multilateral and bilateral official sources. Procurement of eligible items under ADB's loan will be based on

normal commercial practices for procurement by the private sector or standard Government procurement procedures acceptable to ADB for procurement by the public sector. In the case of goods commonly traded on international commodity markets, procurement will be done in accordance with procedures appropriate to the trade and acceptable to ADB.

H. COUNTERPART FUNDS:
- The Government will use counterpart funds generated by the loan to (i) finance additional public investment costs in transport and power projects to ensure strengthened social and environment safeguards; (ii) build institutional capacity to plan, design, and enforce environment and social safeguards; (iii) provide local counterpart resources for development projects aimed at river basin planning and management; (iv) address mitigation costs of existing infrastructure where social and environment costs were not adequately addressed; and (v) establish an environment fund.

I. CONSULTING SERVICES:
- No consulting services are required under the Program.

J. PROJECT BENEFITS:
- Program benefits include: (i) reducing the environmental and social costs of projects developed with inappropriate safeguards; (ii) increasing equity and resource use efficiency by internalizing social and environmental considerations in sector development; (iii) reducing the costs associated with "fixing" environmental and social problems resulting from inadequate regulatory framework and weak enforcement of safeguards; (iv) attracting increased commercial investment in infrastructure development; and (v) ensuring more sustainable and less risky project designs that better reflect local concerns, needs, and opportunities.

- The Program will also contribute to the country's poverty reduction goals. Improved environmental management will help maintain and enhance the livelihood base of the rural poor. Land use planning and watershed management will improve prospects for sustainable use of natural resources. Road transport developed, conceived within an area based planning framework, will directly benefit isolated communities through improved market linkages and access to services. Over the medium term, it is expected that revenues from hydropower projects will also allow the government to increase the share of public expenditure allocated to health, education and social development. Introduction of social safeguards in infrastructure development will ensure that vulnerable groups are not impoverished or marginalized by adverse impacts.

PREPARATORY TECH ASSISTANCE PROJECTS

This report alerts U.S. firms to US$3.6 million in new, potential national procurement of consulting services under the Asian Development Bank's (ADB) technical assistance (TA) grant programs. Opportunities are reported for Azerbaijan, India, Laos, Maldives, and Pakistan. In 2000, U.S. firms, including many small consulting firms, succeeded in winning USD 57 million ADB-funded national technical assistance contracts out of a total ADB-financed consulting budget of USD 348 million.

The ADB selects a consultant for a TA grant based on its prior Expression of Interest (EOI). An EOI can be transmitted on-line through the ADB's website (www.adb.org); afterward it will be acknowledged automatically. Firms may opt to send a hardcopy follow-up EOI addressed to Mr. S. Thuraisingham, Manager, Consulting Services Division, with a copy to the ADB Project Officer. The EOI should relate a firm's experience and expertise to the ADB project. It is important for a

U.S. firm to emphasize its similar project experience in the country or in a similar geographic area rather than presenting a general profile of its consulting activities. A separate EOI should be submitted for each project. The project name indicated in the EOI should exactly match that listed in the ADB Business Opportunities publication to avoid confusion.

To be considered for employment, consultants must register on the ADB's DACON (Data on Consulting Firms) and DICON (Data on Individual Consultants)
Systems, otherwise, their EOIs will not be accepted. DACON and DICON registration can now be done on-line at www.adb.org/consulting.

Firms may also send a notification copy of their EOIs to the U.S. mailing address for the U.S. Commercial Liaison Office for the ADB, Attention: Stewart Ballard, Senior Commercial Officer, PSC 500 Box 33, FPO AP 96515-1000, or to the same office at its international mailing address: 25th Floor Ayala Life-FGU Center, 6811 Ayala Avenue, Makati City, Metro Manila, Philippines 1226; Phone: (63-2) 887-1345; Fax: (63-2) 887-1164; E-mail: manila.adb.office.box@mail.doc.gov. This office works closely with the Office of the U.S. Executive Director to the ADB to increase American awareness of, and participation in, the ADB's activities.

The projects listed in this cable are now being actively processed by the ADB. For more information on these projects, the name of the ADB project officer is indicated in the project brief. The U.S Commercial Liaison Office is ready to provide assistance to U.S. firms upon request. (Please see paragraph 4.)

The following TA projects will be listed for the first time in the January 2002 issue of the Asian Development Bank's (ADB) Business Opportunities (ADBBO). (Note: The ADBBO is also available on the ADB's website <http://www.adb.org>.

NAME OF PROJECT: GMS: Northern Economic Corridor
Project No.: LAO34231-01
Executing Agency: Ministry of Communication, Transport, Post and Construction, Lanexang Avenue, Vientiane, Lao PDR
Fax: 856-21-414132
Tel. No.: 856-21-412741
TA Amount: US$600.0 Thousand
Sector/Subsector: Transport and Communications/Roads and Road Transport

Objectives and Scope: The Project will help to improve access and potential market linkages of a remote area of the Lao PDR to two large and growing economies in the region. Two main objectives of this TA are (i) to assist the Government to update all project parameters of the pre-feasibility study for the existing road in the Lao PDR from Houei Sai to Boten, and (ii) to prepare a pre-investment study to determine feasibility of developing a viable economic corridor. The TA will adopt a holistic approach to plan integrated development of the region. It will undertake surveys and hold stakeholder consultations with potential business leaders and private investors to identify projects and investment opportunities. The pre-investment study will also identify policy, institutional and human resource constraints and suggest an action plan to develop this region into a vibrant economic corridor.
Consulting Services: The TA is expected to commence in January 2002 and completed by December 2002 and will have duration of 12 months.

The TA will involve a total of 66 person-months of consulting services, divided between international (about 18 person-months) and domestic (about 48 person-months) consultants. The TA will be implemented with a multidisciplinary team of international and domestic consultants, headed by an economist as team leader with the main output related to update the cost estimates and providing overall supervision of the TA. Other expertise and skills required for the TA include engineers, environmental, social and resettlement experts, transport economist, business economist, and financial analyst. Familiarity with transport and communication sectors and region's economies, especially of the private sector operations will be essential.

Recruitment of Consultants: No action has yet been taken to recruit consultants.
Environmental Analysis: Required
Project Processing Stage:
SRC Completed: 3 Dec 2001
Project Officer: Rita Nangia (632-6801)
Transport and Communications Division West
In-country Commercial Officer: Scott Rolston, Commercial Officer, U.S. Embassy, Vientiane; E-mail: RolstoSL@state.gov.

NAME OF PROJECT: Northern and Central Water Supply and Sanitation Sector
Project No.: LAO34197-01
Executing Agency: Ministry of Communication, Transport, Post and Construction, Lane Xang Avenue, Vientiane
TA Amount: USD700.0 Thousand

Sector/Subsector: Social Infrastructure/Water Supply and Sanitation
Objectives and Scope: The ensuing Project will address the Government's highest priorities in the water supply sector and will help in its long-term vision of providing safe and convenient water supplies and sanitation facilities to 80 percent of all urban communities as contained in the Government's Sector Investment Plan. The Project will identify the demand for expanded urban water supply and sanitation services in the selected small urban communities, develop selection criteria for the participation of urban communities, develop strategies to strengthen the regulatory framework and build institutional capacity, and prepare new investment project covering a number of small urban communities in the Northern and Central regions.

Consulting Services: Consulting services yet to be determined.
Recruitment of Consultants: Requirements for consulting services to be completed during Fact-finding Mission.
Environmental Analysis: Not Required

Project Processing Stage:
Beginning of Fact-finding Mission: Jan 2002.
Project Officer: Keiichi Tamaki (632-6843)
Water Supply, Urban Development and Housing Division West
In-country Commercial Officer: Scott Rolston, Commercial Officer, U.S. Embassy, Vientiane; E-mail: RolstoSL@state.gov.

U.S.$37 MILLION VIENTIANE URBAN INFRASTRUCTURE & SRV PROJ

. The proposed USD 37 million loan project for Laos' Vientiane Urban Infrastructure and Services project is expected to be approved by the Asian Development Bank's (ADB) Board on August 23, 2001. This report is intended to:

-- Alert Embassies and AID missions to ADB-financed projects, and

-- Provide U.S. businesses with as much lead time as possible concerning procurement and consulting opportunities.

-- For more information on this project or ADB lending opportunities, firms should contact Ms. Cinnamon Dornsife, U.S. Executive Director, Asian Development Bank at phone no. (63-2) 632-6051 and fax no. (63-2) 632-4003 or Mr. Stewart Ballard, The U.S. Commercial Liaison Office for the ADB at telephone nos.: (63-2) 887-1345 to 46 and fax no. (63-2) 887-1164. For in-country inquiry, please contact Ms. Patricia Mahoney, American Embassy, Vientiane; Tel.: (856) 21-212581; Fax: 856) 21-212584; e-mail: mahoneypa@vientiwpoa.us-state.gov.

2. For post, USADB requests AmEmbassy and AID mission views on the Project before August 23, 2001 based on currently available information.

A. BACKGROUND

- Current deficiencies in urban infrastructure and services in Vientiane impede economic growth and undermine the quality of life of the urban residents. especially the poor. Despite the recent investments in primary road and drainage networks, the poor condition of secondary and tertiary infrastructure constrains the full potential of and benefits from recent improvements to primary infrastructure and services. The inadequate infrastructure and services at community level has a particularly adverse impact on the lives of the poor, the majority of whom live in low-lying land, flooded for most of the year. Sustained growth and the quality of life of the residents are further constrained by the present urban institutional framework and nascent urban management that are still evolving in the process of ongoing reforms for decentralization. While considerable progress has been made toward a decentralized form of urban governance and development of Vientiane Urban Development Administration Authority (VUDAA) as a new entity responsible for urban management in Vientiane, the extent of further reforms yet needed to fully achieve decentralized urban governance requires extensive and long-term support. There is a need at this stage to shift the focus of efforts to secondary and tertiary infrastructure and services to ensure that environmental improvements are felt by all, especially the poor. Equally important is the further progress in the decentralization process and development of VUDAA with adequate management systems and skills and financial resources.

B. PROJECT OBJECTIVES

- The Project aims to improve the quality of life of the urban residents and especially the poor and enhance urban productivity and economic growth in Vientiane urban area. To this end, the Project has two specific objectives. One is to support decentralization and urban governance reforms and the process toward an autonomous, well-functioning, and self-sufficient urban local government that is capable of planning, managing, and financing urban development and providing services in a sustainable manner. The second is to target investments in infrastructure and services to maximize the utility of existing infrastructure by completing the remaining gaps and focussing on secondary and tertiary level infrastructure and services. The Project represents AD6's second investment in the Vientiane urban area, and builds on lessons learned from the experience of the first intervention, Vientiane Integrated Urban Development Project.

The scope of the Project includes (i) Part A: citywide urban infrastructure and services, comprising critical missing links of primary and secondary roads and drainage, efficiency improvements in solid waste management, traffic management and safety , and institutional infrastructure and maintenance improvements; {ii) Part B: village area improvements (VAI), adopting a demand-led and participatory approach, seeking as a prerequisite the willingness of villages to participate in and contribute to a portion of the cost of the improvements, and combining community infrastructure and services with community-level capacity building and awareness raising in environmental health, participatory local planning and community-based infrastructure development and service delivery; and (iii) Part C: a comprehensive capacity building program to support the accomplishment of the urban policy and institutional reform agenda, and enhance planning, operation and maintenance, revenue mobilization and financial management capabilities of VUDAA.

C. PROJECT DESCRIPTION

- The Project is designed to improve the urban environment in Vientiane and reinforce the Government's reforms for effective and responsive urban management. It combines physical infrastructure and service improvements with interventions for decentralized urban governance and extensive capacity building of VUDAA. Physical investments consist of improvements to drainage, roads, traffic management and safety, solid waste management, and sanitation. The Project incorporates a social strategy to ensure active participation of the urban communities in the implementation of the Project and effective targeting of the poor and vulnerable. The Project area covers a hundred urban villages with a population of about 162,000 residents within Vientiane that falls under the jurisdiction of VUDAA.

D. EXECUTING AGENCY
- Vientiane Prefecture (the Provincial Government of
- Vientiane City)
- Contact: Mr. Thongmy Phomvisay, President
- Fax: 856-21-212104

E. TOTAL PROJECT COST: USD 37.0 MILLION

- Foreign Exchange : USD 20.0 million
- Local Currency: USD 17.0 million

F. MEANS OF FINANCING
- Bank Loan: USD 25.0 million
- Government and Community: USD 7.6 million
- AFD Cofinancing: USD 4.4 million

G. PROCUREMENT
- Procurement will be carried out by VUDAA. All procurement will follow the ADB's Guidelines for Procurement. International competitive bidding (ICB) procedures will be used for major civil works contracts estimated to cost over USD 1.0 million and for supply contracts estimated to cost over USD 500.000. For civil works, with a value up to USD 1.0 million, local competitive bidding (LCB) procedures will be used. The package of work per village under VAI component is relatively small ranging from USD 30,000 to USD 100,000. The works are labor-intensive and do not require sophisticated technologies. Therefore, for the works, estimated to cost less than USD 50,000 and where the capacity of the community to undertake the works is adequate, community participation in procurement will be applied.

H. CONSULTING SERVICES
- The selection and engagement of consultants under the loan will be in accordance with ADB's Guidelines on the Use of Consultants and other arrangements satisfactory to ADS for engaging domestic consultants. A team of consultants with a total input of 270 person-months (76 international and 194 domestic) is required to assist PIMU in overall Project implementation management, detailed engineering design, construction supervision, demand-led village area improvements, and development of legal and financial reforms for decentralized governance. Additionally, services of domestic consultants are required to assist in community preparation and awareness program and construction supervision. A further 191 person-months of consultancy inputs, including 173 person-months (65 international and 108 local) for capacity building and 18 person-months (5 international and 13 local) for traffic management and safety components will also be provided under a parallel financing arrangement funded by AFD.

For additional analytical, business and investment opportunities information,
please contact Global Investment & Business Center, USA
at (703) 370-8082. Fax: (703) 370-8083. E-mail: ibpusa3@gmail.com
Global Business and Investment Info Databank - www.ibpus.com

I. PROJECT BENEFITS

- The Project will benefit about 162,000 Vientiane urban residents, 18 percent of whom belong to low-income groups. The overall population will benefit from the Project directly or indirectly through upgrading of roads, improved traffic and safety conditions, and enhanced urban management capacities within VUDAA, leading to sustainable delivery of urban services. The Project will directly improve the living conditions of 81,000 residents of Vientiane through improved community infrastructure and services under VAI, a partially coincident 60,000 people through drainage improvements, and 50,000 people through improved solid waste collection and disposal. The Project will promote good governance through supporting decentralized urban governance and empowerment of village communities in local planning, project implementation, and operation and maintenance of urban infrastructure and services.

3. For U.S. businesses and consultants: The shorlisted consultants will receive a request for proposals, selection of and contract negotiation with the firm submitting the best technical proposal will be completed, and preparation of bid specifications and contract documents will begin.

- Potential equipment suppliers and contractors should maintain regular contact with the executing agency and its consultants so that they may act quickly when tenders or prequalification notices are issued. Procurement notices and prequalification announcements are also released by the U.S. Commercial Liaison Office for the ADB and the Commerce Business Daily. These are also published on http://www.adb.org.

NEW ADB LOAN PROJECTS

. This report alerts U.S. firms to USD 101.2 million in new, potential national procurement of goods and services in Cambodia, Laos, and Nepal. These opportunities are an example of the many procurements financed by Asian Development Bank (ADB) loans to 33 ADB member developing countries. In 2000, U.S. contractors and equipment suppliers succeeded in winning USD 196 million in such national procurements as well as another USD 153 million in national consulting services financed by ADB loans.

This report notifies prospective U.S. exporters early on the current formal consideration of development projects by the ADB Board of Directors. Generally tender documents are issued 12-24 months later. Interested prospective U.S. contractors and equipment suppliers should contact the persons listed below to position themselves for future opportunities. U.S. consultants should contact the persons listed below and submit an Expression of Interest (EOI) to the national executing agency to market their firms' expertise and experience on similar past projects.

3. U.S. Consultants must also register with the ADB DACON (Data on Consulting Firms) system. DACON registration may now be completed on-line at <http://www.adb.org/consulting/dacon>. For loan projects, primary responsibility for hiring consultants rests with the executing agency in the borrowing country. A good way to facilitate contact with the executing agency is by working with the appropriate U.S. Commercial Service officer listed below.

4. Firms may also send a notification copy of their EOIs to U.S. Commercial Liaison Office for the ADB, Attention: Stewart Ballard, Senior Commercial Officer, PSC 500 Box 33, FPO AP 96515-1000, or to the same office at its international mailing address: 25th Floor Ayala Life-FGU Center, 6811 Ayala Avenue, Makati City, Metro Manila, Philippines 1226; Phone: (63-2) 887-1345; Fax: (63-2) 887-1164; E-mail: manila.adb.office.box @mail.doc.gov. This office works closely with the Office of the U.S. Executive Director to the ADB to increase American awareness of, and participation in, the ADB's activities.

5. The projects listed in this cable are now being actively processed by the ADB. For more information on these projects, the name of the ADB project officer is indicated in the project brief. The U.S Commercial Liaison Office is ready to provide assistance to U.S. firms upon request. (Please see paragraph 4.)

6. The following loan projects will be listed for the first time in the August 2001 issue of the Asian Development Bank's (ADB) Business Opportunities (ADBBO). (Note: The ADBBO is also available on the ADB's website <http://www.adb.org>.

7. LOAN PROJECTS FOR CAMBODIA, LAOS, AND NEPAL

A. CAMBODIA
NAME OF PROJECT: Rural Development
Project No.: CAM34207-01
Executing Agency: Ministry of Rural Development
Contact: His Excellency Ngy Chanphal, Undersecretary
Fax: 855-23366-790
Loan Amount: USD 25.0 Million
Sector/Subsector: Agriculture and Natural Resources/ Irrigation and Rural Development

Objectives and Scope: The project will target poor, rural populations in selected rural areas where significant number of soldiers will be demobilized and will settle in host communities. Activities in support of area development would include rural infrastructure (rural roads, water supply, village-level social infrastructure), facilitating provision of social services (rural finance, skill training, microenterprise development) through existing provider programs, institutional strengthening and capacity building.

Procurement:
Goods: To be determined.
Services: To be determined.

Environmental Category: B

Project Processing Stage:
Fact-Finding in Field: 2 Jul 2001
Project Officer: Alain Goffeau (632-6955)
Agriculture and Rural Development Division West
In-country Commercial Officer: Bruce Levine, Economic and Commercial Officer, American Embassy Phnom Penh

LAOS
NAME OF PROJECT: Second Education Quality Improvement Project
Project No.: LAO31345-01
Executing Agency: Ministry of Education
Department of Planning and Cooperation
Vientianne
Contact: Dr. Sikhamtath Mitaray, Director
Fax: 856-21-216006
Tel. No.: 856-21-217927

Loan Amount: USD 20.0 Million

Sector/Subsector: Social Infrastructure/Education
Objectives and Scope: The Project will: (i) improve the relevance, quality and efficiency of primary and secondary education, by providing teacher training programs, and by introducing measures to improve the professional status and development of teachers; (ii) expand access to and improve retention in primary schools in the poor, underserved areas, by constructing new complete and/or multigrade schools, and renovating existing schools; and (iii) strengthen the institutional capacity to manage education at the MOE, PES, DEB, village/community, and school levels.

Procurement:
Goods: None.
Services: To be determined.
Environmental Category: C
Project Processing Stage:
Appraisal Completed: 15 Jun 2001
Project Officer: Yasushi Hirosato (632-6949)
Education, Health and Population Division West
In-country Commercial Officer: Patricia Mahoney, Commercial Officer, American Embassy Vientiane

USD 1.55 MILLION ADB BUSINESS OPPORTUNITIES

1. This report alerts U.S. firms to USD 1.55 million new, potential national procurement of consulting services under the Asian Development Bank's (ADB) technical assistance (TA) grant programs. Opportunities are reported for Cook Islands, Laos, and Nepal. In 2000, U.S. firms, including many small consulting firms, succeeded in winning USD 57 million ADB-funded national technical assistance contracts out of a total ADB-financed consulting budget of USD 348 million.

2. The ADB selects a consultant for a TA grant based on its prior Expression of Interest (EOI). An EOI can be transmitted on-line through the ADB's website (www.adb.org); afterward it will be acknowledged automatically. Firms may opt to send a hardcopy follow-up EOI addressed to Mr. S. Thuraisingham, Manager, Consulting Services Division, with a copy to the ADB Project Officer. The EOI should relate a firm's experience and expertise to the ADB project. It is important for a U.S. firm to emphasize its similar project experience in the country or in a similar geographic area rather than presenting a general profile of its consulting activities. A separate EOI should be submitted for each project. The project name indicated in the EOI should exactly match that listed in the ADB Business Opportunities publication to avoid confusion.

3. Although not required for employment, consultants should register on the ADB's DACON (Data on Consulting Firms) and DICON (Data on Individual Consultants) Systems, otherwise, their EOIs will not be accepted. DACON and DICON registration can now be done on-line at www.adb.org/consulting.

4. Firms may also send a notification copy of their EOIs to the U.S. mailing address for the U.S. Commercial Liaison Office for the ADB, Attention: Stewart Ballard, Senior Commercial Officer, PSC 500 Box 33, FPO AP 96515-1000, or to the same office at its international mailing address: 25th Floor Ayala Life-FGU Center, 6811 Ayala Avenue, Makati City, Metro Manila, Philippines 1226; Phone: (63-2) 887-1345; Fax: (63-2) 887-1164; E-mail: manila.adb.office.box @mail.doc.gov. This office works closely with the Office of the U.S. Executive Director to the ADB to increase American awareness of, and

participation in, the ADB's activities.

5. The projects listed in this cable are now being actively processed by the ADB. For more information on these projects, the name of the ADB project officer is indicated in the project brief. The U.S Commercial Liaison Office is ready to provide assistance to U.S. firms upon request. (Please see paragraph 4.)

6. The following TA projects will be listed for the first time in the July 2001 issue of the Asian Development Bank's (ADB) Business Opportunities (ADBBO).
(Note: The ADBBO is also available on the ADB's website http://www.adb.org.

7. PROJECT PREPARATION TECHNICAL ASSISTANCE
FOR COOK ISLANDS, LAOS, AND NEPAL

COOK ISLANDS
NAME OF PROJECT: Outer Islands Development
Project No.: COO29645-01
Executing Agency: Ministry of Finance and Economic
Management
TA Amount: USD 250.0 Thousand
Sector: Others
Objectives and Scope: To prepare a project to help accelerate outer islands development.
Procurement: About 10 person-months of international consultants and 10 person-months of domestic consultants.
Status of Consulting Services: No action has yet been taken to recruit consultants.
Environmental Analysis: Not Required
Project Processing Stage: Beginning of Fact-finding Mission: Sep 2001.
Project Officer: Michel D. Latendresse (632-6129)
Pacific Operations Division
In-country Commercial Officer: c/o AmConsul Auckland

LAOS
NAME OF PROJECT: Northern Community-Managed Irrigation Sector Project
Project No.: LAO34188-01
Executing Agency: Department of Irrigation
Vientiane, Lao PDR
Contact: Mr. Phuovieng Latdavong,
Permanent Secretary
TA Amount: USD 700.0 Thousand

Sector/Subsector: Agriculture and Natural Resources/ Irrigation and Rural Development
Objectives and Scope: The objective of the TA is to prepare a follow-on sector investment project which will address the poverty reduction, environmental protection and gender issues through the development of community-managed irrigation (CMI) schemes in selected northern provinces. CMI development demonstrated the effectiveness to increase the yields of rice and other value crops and to reduce the shifting cultivation under the ongoing Project (ADB's Community-Managed Irrigation Sector Project: Loan No. 1488-LAO). The TA will comprise the following major activities: (i) review relevant water sector policies; (ii) review the lessons learnt from ongoing Projects; (iii) undertake institutional capacity analyses of organizations; (iv) determine the northern provinces to be included in the proposed project by taking into consideration the stakeholders' demand, Government's strategy, implementation capacity, etc.; (v) review and upgrade the completed appraisal studies on sample subprojects; (vi) conduct a social and

environmental assessment of sample subprojects with particular emphasis on poverty reduction and environmental protection; (vii) analyze the cost effectiveness and financial sustainability; and (viii) develop a sector investment package and necessary supporting mechanism for sustainable and affordable CMI considering all above. The investment package may have sustainability of CMI schemes in the following components: (i) community mobilization and training; (ii) development of community-managed irrigation schemes; and (iii) institutional support for CMI development.

Procurement: The TA work will be carried out by a team of experts from an international consulting firm in association with domestic consultants.
Other details of consulting services to be required will be determined during the fact-finding mission. Procurement of one service vehicle will be proposed to facilitate the work of the consultants.
Status of Consulting Services: No action has been taken to recruit consultants.
Environmental Analysis: Required
Project Processing Stage:
Fact-Finding in Field: 11 Jun 2001
Project Officer: Toshio Kondo (632-6779)
Forestry and Natural Resources Division West
In-country Commercial Officer: Patricia Mahoney, Commercial Officer, AmEmbassy Vientiane

NEPAL
NAME OF PROJECT: Third Irrigation Sector
Project No.: NEP33209-01
Executing Agency: Department of Irrigation, Kathmandu
Jawalakjel, Lalitpur
Fax: 977-1-537169
E-mail: doi@jwlk.mos.com.np
TA Amount: USD 600.0 Thousand

Sector/Subsector: Agriculture and Natural Resources/ Irrigation and Rural Development
Objectives and Scope: Farmer-managed irrigation schemes are a major focus of the Government's irrigation strategy. This PPTA will prepare a sector project to cover about 300 small farmer-managed irrigation schemes covering about 40,000 ha for as many households.

Main components of the project will include water users' associations mobilization and training, construction and rehabilitation of irrigation schemes, provision of vehicles and equipment to the executing agency, staff training and capacity building for both the Department of Irrigation and Agriculture. The TA will develop specific intervention package including measures for improving sector policy, plan, and institutions through (i) water sector policy and institutions/review; (ii) assessment of ongoing Second Irrigation Sector Project; and (iii) feasibility study of sample subprojects.

Procurement: A total of about 45 person-months (pms) of consulting services' inputs : (i) 15 pms of international consultants including water resource institutional specialist (Team Leader); water resource engineer; resource economist; agronomist; environmental and social specialists; and (ii) 30 pms of water resource planner (Deputy Team Leader); water resource institutional specialist; agronomist; agricultural economist; environmental, social and poverty specialists.

Status of Consulting Services: No action has yet been taken to recruit consultants.

Environmental Analysis: Required
Project Processing Stage:
Beginning of Fact-finding Mission: Jul 2001.
Project Officer: Kenichi Yokoyama (632-6937)
Forestry and Natural Resources Division West
In-country Commercial Officer: John Dyson, Political/Economic Officer, AmEmbassy Kathmandu

PRIMARY HEALTH CARE EXPANSION PROJECT

The proposed loan grant application for Lao for the Primary Health Care Expansion Project is expected to come to the ADB Board in about five weeks. This cable is intended to:
Alert Embassies and AID missions to upcoming ADB-financed projects, and
Provide U.S. businesses with as much lead-time as possible concerning procurement and consulting opportunities. For more information on this project of ADB lending opportunities, firms should contact Ms. Cinnamon Dornsife, U.S. Executive Director, Asian Development Bank at phone no. (63 2) 632 6051 and fax no. (63 2) 632 4003 or Mr. Alex Severens, The U.S. Commercial Liaison Office to the ADB. For in-country inquiry, please contact Ms. Trish Mulhoney of AmEmbassy Vientiane at telephone nos.: (856 21) 212581, 212582, 212585 and fax no.: 212584.

2. For Post: USADB requests AmEmbassy and AID Mission views on the said Project on or before August 20 based on currently available information.

Background: With a per capita income of $283 and half of the population living in poverty, Lao PDR is one of the poorest countries in the Asia and Pacific Region. The rural poor, in particular women and children, ethnic minorities and other vulnerable groups living in the inaccessible northern hills suffer from extremely poor health. Life expectancy of only 51 years is the lowest in the region. Most sickness and deaths are from common communicable diseases such as malaria, acute respiratory infections, diarrhea and measles, most of which are preventable or easily curable. Maternal and infant mortality and fertility are among the highest in the region, yet maternal and child health and family planning services are not readily available. The existing network of health facilities has inadequate coverage and mainly provides a limited range of curative services of often sub-standard quality. Much as half of the rural population does not have access to preventive and promotive services and first referral care, in particular in the northern hills.

The Government, as a cornerstone of its social policy, accords high priority to the improvement of the health status of the population. Primary health care (PHC) has been identified as the most cost-effective approach to provide basic health services. The Government recently approved a PHC policy that aims to make a basic package of health care available to the entire population, and restructured Ministry of Health (MOH) in support of PHC. The Government has requested Asian Development Bank (ADB) to support expansion and improvement of PHC delivery, strengthen PHC planning and management, and develop an effective financial mechanisms. The Project is specially designed to improve the health status of women and children, ethnic minorities and the rural poor.

Project Objectives: The Project will contribute to the Government's goals of improving the health status and reduce poverty of the population of Lao PDR. The Project will improve PHC for the rural poor by (i) expanding and improving the quality of PHC in the northern region, and (ii) strengthening the institutional capacity of PHC.

The Project will target women and children, ethnic minorities and the rural poor by (i) increasing their physical, social and financial access to essential services, (ii) focusing on interventions and diseases that affect them disproportionally, and (ii)improving the quality of services for these groups. The Project will give priority to cost-effective interventions benefiting women and children including health promotion, reproductive health care, prevention and treatment of common infections and micronutrient deficiencies, and first referral services.

Component 1 will develop PHC in the northern provinces by (i) increasing access to PHC at health center and village levels; (ii) improving the quality of PHC including training of ethnic minority staff, (iii) strengthening maternal and child health and family planning services, and (iv) supporting village health care and promotion.

Component 2 will strengthen the institutional capacity for PHC nationwide by (i) strengthening PHC coordination; (ii) standardizing management systems; (iii) supporting staff development and training for PHC management; and (iv) testing innovating financing approaches.

Project Description: The Project will develop primary health care (PHC) in the eight northern provinces of Bokeo, Louang-Namtha, Phongsali, Houaphan, Louangphrabang, Xiangkhoang, Oudamxai, and Xaignabouri. It will improve access to and quality of essential preventive, promotive and curative health services at village, health center and district levels in 34 underdeveloped districts with a total population of 0.9 million, and improve referral services for 1.7 million people. It will also strengthen the institutional capacity of the MOH and all Provincial Health Offices to plan, manage, monitor and finance PHC.

Executing Agency:

Ministry of Health
PHC Extension Project
Contact: Dr. Prasongsidh Boupha, Project Director
Fax No.: (856 21) 223146
Tel.No.: (856 20) 518422

Total Project Cost: $25.0 million (Foreign Exchange: $8.4 million; Local Currency: $16.6 million)

Procurement: All ADB-financed procurement for the Project will be in accordance with ADB's Guidelines for Procurement. Related equipment and material will be combined into packages to simplify procurement. Supply contracts costing more than $500,000 equivalent or less will follow international shopping procedures, except for some equipment and supplies like hostel beds and furniture that are locally manufactured and unlikely to attract foreign suppliers. These will be procured through local competitive bidding in accordance with Government procedures acceptable to ADB. Packages of less than $100,000 may be procured on a direct purchase basis. Equipment and materials required at provincial level and costing less than $10,000 may be procured by the PIO according to Government procedures acceptable to ADB.

The Project includes construction of 41 health centers and seven hospitals and renovation or upgrading of six health centers and 17 hospitals. The health facilities are located in remote and scattered locations and are unlikely to attract international bidders. Civil works contracts will be awarded according to local competitive bidding procedures acceptable to ADB. However, if any package is estimated to cost $1.0 million or more, international competitive bidding procedures will be followed.

g.) All consultants financed under the loan will be selected and engaged in accordance with ADB Guidelines on the Use of Consultants and other procedures acceptable to ADB on the recruitment of domestic consultants. Six international and six domestic individual consultants and one domestic firms will be provided. The international consultants will include chief technical adviser (36 person-months), education and training specialist (6 person-months), management specialist

(12 person-months), health sector financing specialist (6 person-months), procurement specialist (6 person-months), and architect (6 person-months). Domestic consultants will include education and training specialist (72 person-months), management specialist (72person-months), health sector financing specialist (72 person-months), accountant (72 person-months), procurement specialist (72 person-months), and architectural monitoring and evaluation specialist (72 person-months). A domestic firms will be contracted for five years for building design and construction supervision.

For US Businesses and Consultants: The loan is now at a point where, shortly after ADB Board approval, shortlisted consultants will receive a request for proposals, selection of and contract negotiation with the firm submitting the best technical proposal will be completed, and preparation of bid specifications and contract documents will begin.

Potential equipment supplies and contractors should maintain a regular contact with the executing agency and its consultant so that they may act quickly when tenders or prequalification notices are issued. Procurement notices and prequalification announcement are also released by the U.S. Commercial ADB Liaison Office and made available on the National Trade Data Bank (NTDB) and the Commerce Business Daily. These are also published on the Asian Development Bank's homepage, http//www.adb.org.

IMPORTANT LAWS AND REGULATIONS AFFECTING BUSINESS

LAW ON THE PROMOTION AND MANAGEMENT OF FOREIGN INVESTMENT IN LAO PDR[3]

SECTION ONE: GENERAL PROVISIONS

Article I : The Government of the Lao People's Democratic Republic encourages foreign persons, either individuals or legal entities, to invest capital in the Lao People's Democratic Republic (hereinafter "the Lao PDR") on the basis of mutual benefit and observance of the laws and regulations of the Lao PDR. Such persons hereinafter shall be referred to as "foreign investors ".

Article 2 : Foreign investors may invest in and operate enterprises in all fields of lawful economic activity such as agriculture and forestry, manufacturing, energy,, mineral extraction, handicrafts, communications and transport. construction, tourism trade, services and others.

Foreign investors may not invest in or operate enterprises which are detrimental to national security, the natural environment, public health or the national culture, or which violate the laws and regulations of the Lao PDR.

Article 3 : The property, and investments in the Lao PDR of foreign investors shall be fully-protected by the laws and regulations of the Lao PDR. Such property and the investment may not be requisitioned. confiscated or nationalized except for a public purpose and upon payment of prompt, adequate and effective compensation.

SECTION TWO: FORMS OF FOREIGN INVESTMENT

Article 4 : Foreign investors may invest in the Lao PDR in either of two forms:

(1) A Joint Venture with one or more domestic Lao investors-; or
(2)   A Wholly Foreign-Owned Enterprise.

Article 5 : A Joint Venture is a foreign investment established and registered under the laws and regulations of the Lao PDR which is jointly owned and operated by one or more foreign investors and by one or more domestic Lao investors.

The organization, management and activities of the Joint Venture and the relationship between its parties shall be governed by the contract between its parties and the Joint Venture's Articles of Association, in accordance with the laws and regulations of the Lao PDR.

Article 6 : Foreign investors Who invest in a Joint Venture must contribute a minimum portion of thirty percent (30%) of the total equity investment in that Venture. The contribution of the Venture's foreign party or parties shall be converted in accordance with the laws and regulations of the Lao PDR into Lao currency at the exchange rate then prevailing on the date of the equity payment(s), as quoted by the Bank of the Lao PDR.

---

[3] National Assembly No. 01/94

For additional analytical, business and investment opportunities information, please contact Global Investment & Business Center, USA at (703) 370-8082. Fax: (703) 370-8083. E-mail: ibpusa3@gmail.com
Global Business and Investment Info Databank - www.ibpus.com

Article 7 : A wholly Foreign-Owned Enterprise is a foreign investment registered under the laws and regulations of the Lao PDR by one or more foreign investors without the participation of domestic Lao investors. The Enterprise established in the LAO PDR may be either a new company or a branch or representative office of a foreign company.

Article 8 : A foreign investment which is a Lao branch or representative office of a foreign company shall have Articles of Association which shall be consistent with the laws and regulations of the Lao PDR and subject to the approval of the Foreign Investment Management Committee of the Lao PDR.

u The incorporation and registration of a foreign investment shall be in conformity with the Enterprise Decree of the Lao PDR.

SECTION THREE: BENEFITS, RIGHTS AND OBLIGATIONS OF FOREIGN INVESTORS

Article 10 : The Government of the Lao PDR shall protect foreign investments and the property of foreign investors in accordance with the laws and regulations of the Lao PDR. Foreign investors may lease land within the Lao PDR and transfer their leasehold interests; and they may own improvements on land and other moveable property and transfer those ownership interests.

Foreign investors shall be free to operate their enterprises within the limits of the laws and regulations of the Lao PDR. The Government shall not interfere in the business management of those enterprises.

Article 11 : Foreign investors shall give priority to Lao citizens in recruiting and hiring their employees. However, such enterprises have the right to employ skilled and expert foreign personnel when necessary and with the approval of the competent authority of the Government of the Lao PDR.

Foreign investors have an obligation to upgrade the skills of their Lao employees , through such techniques as training within the Lao PDR or abroad.

u The Government of the Lao PDR shall facilitate the entry into, travel within, stay within, and exit from Lao territory of foreign investors, their foreign personnel, and the immediate family members of those investors and those personnel. All such persons are subject to and must obey the laws and regulations of the Lao PDR while they are on Lao territory.

Foreign investors and their foreign personnel working within the Lao PDR shall pay to the Lao government personal income tax at a flat rate of ten percent (10 %) of their income earned in the Lao PDR.

Article 13 : Foreign investors shall open accounts both in Lao currency and in foreign convertible currency with a Lao bank or foreign bank established in the Lao PDR.

Article 14 : In the management of their enterprises, foreign investors shall utilize the national system of financial accounting of the Lao PDR. Their accounts shall be subject to periodic audit by the Government's financial authorities in conformity with the applicable Lao accounting regulations.

For additional analytical, business and investment opportunities information,
please contact Global Investment & Business Center, USA
at (703) 370-8082. Fax: (703) 370-8083. E-mail: ibpusa3@gmail.com
Global Business and Investment Info Databank - www.ibpus.com

Article 15 : In conformity with the law and regulations governing the management of foreign exchange and precious metals, foreign investors may repatriate earnings and capital from their foreign investments to their own home countries or to third countries through a Lao bank or foreign bank established in the Lao PDR at the exchange rate prevailing on the date of repatriation. as quoted by the Bank of the Lao PDR.

Foreign personnel of foreign investments may also repatriate their earnings, after payment of Lao personal income taxes and all other taxes due.

Article 16 : Foreign investments subject to this law shall pay a Lao PDR'. annual profit tax at a uniform flat rate of twenty percent (20%), calculated in accordance with the provisions of the applicable laws and regulations of the Lao PDR.

Other Lao taxes, duties and fees shall be payable in accordance with the applicable laws and regulations of the Lao PDR.

For foreign investments involving natural resources exploitation and energy generation, sector-specific taxes and royalties shall be prescribed in project agreements entered into between the investors and the Lao Government.

Article 17 : Foreign investments shall pay a Lao PDR import duty on equipment, means of production, spare parts and other materials used in the operation of their investment projects or in their productive enterprises at a uniform flat rate of one percent (1%) of their imported value. Raw materials and intermediate components imported for the purpose of processing and then re-exported shall be exempt from such import duties. All exported finished products shall also be exempted from export duties.

Raw materials and intermediate components imported for the purpose of achieving import substitution shall be eligible for special duty reductions in accordance with the Government's applicable incentive policies.

Article 18 : In highly exceptional cases and by specific decision of the Government of the Lao PDR, foreign investors may be granted special privileges and benefits which may possibly include a reduction in or exemption from the profit-tax rate prescribed by Article 16 and/or a reduction in or exemption from the import-duty rate prescribed by Article 17, because of the large size of their investments and the significant positive impact which those investments are expected to have upon the socioeconomic development of the Lao PDR.

In the event of the establishment of one or more Free Zones or Investment Promotion Zones. the Government shall issue area-specific or general regulations or resolutions.

Article 19 : After payment of its annual profit tax, a foreign investor shall devote a portion of its profit each year to various reserve funds necessary for the operation and development of the enterprise in order to continuously improve the enterprise's efficiency, in accordance with the policy and the Articles of Association of the enterprise.

Article 20 : Foreign investments approved under this law shall at all times be operated in accordance with the laws and regulations of the Lao PDR . In particular, foreign investors shall take all measures necessary and appropriate to ensure that their investments' facilities, factories and activities protect the natural environment and the health and safety of the workers and the

For additional analytical, business and investment opportunities information,
please contact Global Investment & Business Center, USA
at (703) 370-8082. Fax: (703) 370-8083. E-mail: ibpusa3@gmail.com
Global Business and Investment Info Databank - www.ibpus.com

public at large, and that their investments contribute to the social insurance and welfare programs for their workers in conformity with the policy and the laws and regulations of the Lao PDR.

Article 21 : In the event of disputes between foreign parties within a foreign investment, or between foreign investors and Lao parties , the disputants should first seek to settle their differences through consultation or mediation.

In the event that they fail to resolve the matter , they shall then submit their dispute to the economic arbitration authority of the Lao PDR or to any other mechanism for dispute resolution of the Lao PDR, a foreign country or an appropriate international organization which the disputants can agree upon.

SECTION FOUR: THE ORGANIZATION OF FOREIGN INVESTMENT MANAGEMENT

Article 22 : The Government of the Lao PDR has established a State organization to promote and to manage foreign investment within the Lao PDR titled the Foreign Investment Management Committee (hereinafter called "the FIMC").

The FIMC is responsible for administration of this law and for the protection and promotion of foreign investment within the Lao PDR.

Article 23 : All foreign investments established within the Lao PDR shall be assisted, licensed and monitored through the "1-stop-service " of the FIMC, acting as the central focal point for all Government interactions with the investors, with the collaboration of the concerned ministries and the relevant provincial authorities.

Article 24 : A foreign investment shall be considered to be legally established within the Lao PDR only upon the investment's receipt of a written foreign investment license granted by the FIMC.

Article 25 : A foreign investor which seeks a license for a foreign investment shall submit to the FIMC an application and such supporting documentation as the FIMC may prescribe by regulation.

The FIMC may grant preliminary approval-in-principle for investment projects being specially promoted by the Government.

Article 26 : Upon receipt of a completed application and supporting documentation, the FIMC shall screen them, take a foreign-investment licensing. decision and notify the applicant of that decision within 60 days of the application's submission date.

Within this same overall 60-day period, concerned ministries and provincial authorities consulted by the FIMC for their views shall have a maximum of 20 days in which to reply.

Article 27 : Within 90 days of receiving its foreign investment license from the FIMC. a foreign investor shall register that license and commerce operation of its investment in conformity with the implementation schedule contained in the investment's feasibility study and with the terms and conditions of the license granted by FIMC, and in accordance with the laws and regulations of the Lao PDR.

Article 28 : The FIMC has responsibility to coordinate with other concerned ministries and provincial authorities in monitoring and enforcing the implementation of a foreign investment in

For additional analytical, business and investment opportunities information,
please contact Global Investment & Business Center, USA
at (703) 370-8082. Fax: (703) 370-8083. E-mail: ibpusa3@gmail.com
Global Business and Investment Info Databank - www.ibpus.com

conformity with the investment's feasibility study and with the terms and conditions of the investment license, and in accordance with the laws and regulations of the Lao PDR.

The concerned ministries and provincial authorities have the responsibility to perform their respective monitoring and enforcement obligations.

Article 29 : If a foreign investor violates the agreement and the terms and conditions of its foreign investment license or the laws and regulations of the Lao PDR, the investor shall be notified of the detected violation and shall be instructed to promptly desist. In the event the investor fails to desist or in case of a serious violation, the investor's foreign investment license may be suspended or revoked and the investor may additionally be subject to other sanctions under the applicable laws and regulations of the Lao PDR.

SECTION FIVE: FINAL PROVISIONS

Article 30 : This law shall come into force 60 days after its ratification.

Upon the entry into force of the present law, the foreign investment law of the Lao people's Democratic Republic No. 07/PSA dated 19 April 1988 shall cease to have effect, without prejudice to the rights and privileges granted to, and the obligations imposed upon, foreign investments under the law.No. 07/PSA.

Notwithstanding this provision, a foreign investor which received its license tender the prior law may elect to petition the FIMC in writing, within 120 days of the coming into force of this law, to become subject to the terms of this law. The FIMC may grant such petitions at its discretion. For a foreign investor whose petition is granted, the rights and benefits previously granted. and the obligations previously imposed under the law No. 07/PSA shall thereafter prospectively cease to have effect .

Article 31 : The Government of the Lao PDR shall, by decree, issue detailed regulations for the implementation of this law.

LAW ON THE PROMOTION AND MANAGEMENT OF FOREIGN INVESTMENT IN THE LAO PEOPLE'S DEMOCRATIC REPUBLIC

SECTION: GENERAL PROVISIONS

Article 1: The Government of the Lao people's Democratic Republic encourages foreign persons, either individuals or legal entities, to invest capital in the Lao People's Democratic Republic (hereinafter "the Lao PDR") on the basis of mutual benefit and observance of the laws and regulations of the Lao PDR. Such persons hereinafter shall be referred to as "foreign investors".

Article 2: Foreign investors may invest in and operate enterprises in all fields of lawful economic activity such as agriculture and forestry, manufacturing, energy, mineral extraction, handicrafts, communications and transport, construction, tourism, trade, services and others.

Foreign investors may not invest in or operate enterprises which are detrimental to national security, the natural environment, public health or the national culture, or which violate the laws and regulations of the Lao PDR.

Article 3: The property and investments in the Lao. PDR of Foreign investors shall be fully protected by the laws and regulations of the Lao PDR. Such property and investments may not be requisitioned, confiscated or nationalized except for a public purpose and upon payment of prompt, adequate and effective compensation.

SECTION TWO: FORMS OF FOREIGN INVESTMENT

Article 4: Foreign investors may invest in the Lao PDR in either of two forms:

1. A Joint Venture with one or more domestic Lao investors or (2) A Wholly Foreign-Owned Enterprise.
2. A Wholly Foreign-Owned Enterprise.

Article 5: A Joint Venture is a foreign investment established and registered under the laws and regulations of the Lao PDR which is jointly owned and operated by one or more foreign investors and by one or more domestic Lao investors.

The organization management and activities of the Joint Venture and the relationship between its parties shall be governed by the contract between its parties and the Joint Venture's Articles of Association, in accordance with the laws and regulations of the Lao PDR.

Article 6: Foreign investors who invest in a Joint Venture must contribute a minimum portion of thirty percent (30%) of the total equity investment in that Venture. The contribution of the Venture's foreign party or parties shall be converted in accordance with the laws and regulation of the Lao PDR into Lao currency at the exchange rate then prevailing on the date of the equity payment(s), as quoted by the Bank of the Lao PDR

Article 7: A wholly Foreign-Owned Enterprise is a foreign investment registered under the laws and regulations of the Lao PDR by one or more foreign investors without the participation of domestic Lao investors. The Enterprise established in the Lao PDR may be either a new company or a branch or representative of5ce of a foreign company.

Article 8: A foreign investment which is a Lao branch or representative office of a foreign company sha11 have Articles of Association which shall be consistent with the laws and regulations of the Lao PDR and subject to the approval of the Foreign investment Management Committee of the Lao PDR.

Article 9: The incorporation and registration of a foreign investment sha11 be in conformity with the Enterprise Decree of the Lao PDR.

SECTION THREE: BENEFITS, RIGHTS AND OBLIGATIONS OF FOREIGN INVESTORS

Article 10: The Government of the Lao PDR shall protect foreign investments and the property of foreign investors in accordance with the laws and regulations of the Lao PDR. Foreign investors may lease land within the Lao PDR and transfer their leasehold interests; and they may own improvements on land and other moveable property and transfer those ownership interests.

Foreign investors shall be free to operate their enterprises within the limits of the laws and regulations of the Lao PDR. The Government shall not interfere in the business management of those enterprises.

Article 11: Foreign investors sha11 give priority to Lao citizens in recruiting and hiring their employees. However, such enterprises have the right to employ skilled and expert foreign personnel when necessary and with the approval of the competent authority of the Government of the Lao PDR.

Foreign investors have an obligation to upgrade the skills of their Lao employees, through such techniques as training within the Lao PDR or abroad.

Article 12: The Government of the Lao PDR shall facilitate the entry into, travel within, stay within, and exit from Lao territory of foreign investors, their foreign personnel, and the immediate family members of those investors an those personnel. All such persons are subject to and must obey the laws and regulations of the Lao PDR while they are on Lao territory.

Foreign investors and their foreign personnel working within the Lao PDR shall pay to the Lao government personal income tax at a flat rate of ten percent (10%) of their income earned in the Lao PDR.

Article 13: Foreign investors shall open accounts both in Lao currency and in foreign convertible currency with a Lao bank or foreign bank established in the Lao PDR.

Article 14: In the management of their enterprises, foreign investors shall utilize the nationa1 system of financia1 accounting of the Lao PDR. Their accounts shall be subject to periodic audit by the Government's financial authorities in conformity with the applicable Lao accounting regulations.

Article 15: In conformity with the law and regulations governing the management of foreign exchange and precious metals, foreign investors may repatriate earnings and capital from their foreign investments to their own home countries or to third countries through a Lao bank or foreign bank established in the Lao PDR at the exchange rate prevailing on the date of repatriation, as quoted by the Bank of the Lao PDR.

Foreign personnel of foreign investments may also repatriate their earnings, after payment of Lao personal income taxes and all other taxes due.

Article 16: Foreign investments subject to this law shall pay a Lao PDR annual profit tax at e uniform flat rate of twenty percent (20%), calculated in accordance with the provisions of the applicable laws and regulations of the Lao PDR.

Other Lao taxes, duties and fees shall be payable in accordance with the applicable laws and regulations of the Lao PDR.

For foreign investments involving natural resources exploitation and energy generation, sector-specific taxes and royalties shall be prescribed in project agreements entered into between the investors and Lao Government.

Article 17: Foreign investments shall pay a Lao PDR import duty on equipment, means of production, spare parts and other materials used in the operation of their investment projects or in their productive enterprises as a uniform flat rate of one percent (1%) of their imported value. Raw materials and intermediate components imported for the purpose of processing and then re-exported shall be exempt from such import duties. All exported finished products shall also be exempted from export duties.

Raw materials and intermediate components imported for the purpose of achieving import substitution shall be eligible for special duty reductions in accordance with the Government's incentive policies.

Article 18: In highly exceptional cases and by specific decision of the Government of the Lao PDR, foreign investors may be granted special privileges and benefits which may possibly include a reduction in or exemption from the profit-tax rate prescribed by Article 16 and/or a reduction in or exemption from the import-duty rate prescribed by Article 17, because of the large size of their investments and the significant positive impact which those investments are expected to have upon the socio-economic development of the Lao PDR.

In the event of the establishment of one or more Free Zones or Investment Promotion Zones, the Government shall issue area-specific or general regulations or resolutions.

Article 19: After payment of its annual profit tax, a foreign investor shall devote a portion of its profit each year to various reserve funds necessary for the operation and development of the enterprise in order to continuously improve the enterprise's efficiency, in accordance with the policy and the Articles of Association of the enterprise.

Article 20: Foreign investments approved under this law sha11 at all times be operated in accordance with the laws and regulations of the Lao PDR. In particular, foreign investors sha11 take al1 measures necessary and appropriate to ensure that their investments facilities, factories and activities protect the natura1 environment and the health and safety of the workers and the public at large, and that their investments contribute to the socia1 insurance and welfare programs for their workers in conformity with the policy and the laws and regulations of the Lao PDR.

Article 21: In the event of disputes between foreign parties within a foreign investment, or between foreign investors and Lao parties, the disputants should first seek to settle their differences through consultation or mediation.

In the event that they fail to resolve the matter, they shall then submit their dispute to the economic arbitration authority of the Lao PDR or to any other mechanism for dispute resolution of the Lao PDR, a foreign country or an appropriate international organization which the disputants can agree upon.

SECTION FOUR: THE ORGANIZATION OF FOREIGN INVESTMENT MANAGEMENT

Article 22: The Government of the Lao PDR has established a State organization to promote and to manage foreign investment within the Lao PDR titled the Foreign Investment Management Committee (hereinafter called "the FIMC").

The FIMC is responsible for administration of this law and for the protection and promotion of foreign investment within the Lao PDR.

Article 23: All foreign investments established within the Lao PDR shall be assisted, licensed and monitored through the "1-stop-service" of the FIMC, acting as the central focal point for all Government interactions with the investors, with the collaboration of the concerned ministries and the relevant provincial authorities.

Article 24: A foreign investment shall be considered to be legally established within the Lao PDR only upon the investment's receipt of a written foreign investment license granted by the FMC.

Article 25: A foreign investor which seeks a license for a foreign investment shall submit to the FMC an application and such supporting documentation as the FMC may prescribe by regulation.

The FMC may grant preliminary approval-in- principle for investment projects being specially promoted by the Government.

Article 26: Upon receipt of a completed application and supporting documentation, the FIMC shall screen them, take a foreign-investment licensing decision and notify the applicant of the decision within 60 days of the application's submission date.

Within the same overall 60-day period, concerned ministries and provincial authorities consulted by the FIMC for their views shall have a maximum of 20 days in which to reply.

Article 27: Within 90 days of receiving its foreign investment license from the FIMC, a foreign investors shall register that license and commence operation of its investment in conformity with the implementation schedule contained in the investment's feasibility study and with the terms and conditions of the license granted by the FIMC, and in accordance with the laws and regulations of the Lao PDR.

Article 28: The FIMC has responsibility to coordinate with other concerned ministries and provincial authorities in monitoring and enforcing the implementation of a foreign investment in conformity with the investment's feasibility study and with the terms and conditions of the investment license, and in accordance with the laws and regulations of the Lao PDR. he concerned ministries and provincial authorities have the responsibility to perform their respective monitoring and enforcement obligations.

Article 29: If a foreign investor violates the agreement and the terms and conditions of its foreign investment license or the laws and regulations of the Lao PDR, the investor shall be notified of the detected violation and shall be instructed to promptly desist. In the event the investor fails to desist or in case of a serious violation, the investor's foreign investment license may be suspended or revoked and the investor may additionally be subject to other sanctions under the applicable laws and regulations of the Lao PDR.

SECTION FIVE: FINAL PROVISIONS

Article 30: This law shall come into force 60 days after its ratification.

For additional analytical, business and investment opportunities information, please contact Global Investment & Business Center, USA at (703) 370-8082. Fax: (703) 370-8083. E-mail: ibpusa3@gmail.com Global Business and Investment Info Databank - www.ibpus.com

Upon the entry into force of the present law, the foreign investment law of the Lao People's Democratic Republic No. 07/PSA dated 19 April 1988 shall cease to have effect, without prejudice to the rights and privileges granted to, and the obligations imposed upon, foreign investments under the law No. 07/PSA

Notwithstanding this provision, a foreign investor which received its license under the prior law may elect to petition the FIMC in writing, within 120 days of the coming into force of this law, to become subject to the terms of this law. The FIMC may grant such petitions at its discretion. For a foreign investor whose petition is granted, the right and benefits previously granted, and the obligations previously imposed under the law No. 07/PSA shall thereafter prospectively cease to have effect.

Article 31: The Government of the Lao PDR shall, by decree, issue detailed regulations for the implementation of this law.

NOTIFICATION ON PROCEDURE FOR BUSINESS REGISTRATION IN LAO P D R.

- According to additional announcement No.0530/MOC,dated 10/May/2002 & No.0538/MOC,dated 13/May/2002.
 Ministry of Commerce, Domestic Trade Department (Business Registration Division) hereby notify the procedures for Business Registration and documents required for Enterprises.
* Business Registration takes place at 3 Levels

I. MINISTRY (CENTER) LEVEL.

The following are required registered at the Ministry :
1. Foreign investment whose registered capital is more than $ 200.000.
2. Enterprises engaged in import of Vehicles, Gas and export of wood products .
3 . State enterprises and state-owned joint venture enterprises who obtained
     licenses from the Ministry.

II. PROVINCES, CAPITAL AND SPECIAL ZONE LEVEL.

1. Foreign investors whose registered capital is less than $199,999.
2. Enterprises regulated by or have dealings with other main sectors such as:
-     Agriculture, Industry and Services .
3. Commercial :Enterprises engaged in export--import trade out side administered by the Ministry will be transferred to provinces.
4. All enterprises who have license from provincial governments.

III. DISTRICTS LEVEL.

Small business enterprises who opera out side from the Ministry and Provincial jurisdiction should register with the district office these are:
1. Branches .
2. Small shops.
3. Others

DOCUMENTS TO BE COMPLETED BY FOREIGN INVESTORS

-   License from Foreign Investment Management Committee (FIMC)
-   Registration form .
-   Copy of passport.

- 3 photos of size 3x4 inches .
- Letter of authority from the manager of company .

DOCUMENTS TO BE COMPLETED BY DOMESTIC INVESTORS AND ENTERPRISES OTHER THAN COMMERCE.

- License from the concerned sector.
- Registration form .
- Curriculum Vitae (CV)
- Certificate of Assets
- Criminal noted No 3, copy of ID card,3 photos of size 3x4 inches

DOCUMENTS TO BE COMPLETED BY DOMESTIC INVESTORS AND CONTROLLED BY COMMERCE SECTORS:

- Registration form from commerce
- Curriculum Vitae (CV)
- Certificate of finance
- Criminal noted No 3 , copy ID card, 3 photos of size 3x4 inches .
- Regulation confirmed by commerce sector.
- Economic evaluation.

Fees. See Minister of Finance additional announcement No. 0341/MF,dated 21/02/2002 .
Notes 1: If all documents are complete as required , registration will be completed in 24 hours.
Notes 2: This notification translated from additional announcement No.0530/MOC,dated 10/May/2002 & No.0538/MOC,dated 13/May/2002.

NOTIFICATION ON LIST OF GOODS SUBJECT TO IMPORT-EXPORT CONTROL AND PROHIBITION

- According to the Decree on the import-export management, No 205/PMO of 11 October 2006 .
- According to the Regulation on the Import-Export Licensing of Controlled goods, No 106/MOC.FTD dated 25/1/2002.
- According to Prime Minister Order on import-export facilitation and distribution of goods throughout country No. 24/PMO,dated 24/09/2004..
- According to the list of goods needed approval from related government agencies.

The Minister of Industry and Commerce issues the notification on the list of goods subject to import-export control and prohibition, as follows:

I. GOODS SUBJECT TO IMPORT-EXPORT PROHIBITION

Goods subject to import – export prohibition are dangerous and have a severe effect on national security, peace and public safety in order to protect the social/public order; the standard of living; national cultures and traditions; human, animal and plant life or health; national treasures of artistic, historic or archaeological value; architectural value; and national resource preservation; to comply with the United Nations treaties and national laws and regulations. The list of goods subject to import-export prohibition includes:

A. There are five categories of goods subject to import prohibition
1. Guns, bullets, all kinds of explosives, war weapons and war vehicles
2. Opium seeds, opium flowers, cannabis
3. Dangerous pesticide
4. Game Machines that lead to bad attitudes

5. Pornography and literatures that affect on cultures and national security

B. There are nine categories of goods subject to export prohibition
1. Guns, bullets, explosives, war weapons and war vehicles
2. Opium seeds, opium flowers, cannabis
3. Animals and animal products which are prohibited to export according to the law
4. Log, timber and Akar wood from the forest
5. All kinds of orchids from the forest and Dracaena Loureiri
6. All kinds of rattan
7. Bat manure
8. Antique objects; national treasures of historic or archaeological and cultural value and naturally national historic objects.
9. Old/antique Buddha and angel images; and religiously respectful objects

II. GOODS SUBJECT TO IMPORT-EXPORT APPROVAL OR CERTIFICATE

Goods subject to import-export approval or certificate means that those need to get approval or certification from related government agencies prior to the import – export in order to comply with the national laws and international treaties that Lao PDR is a party member; to ensure the safety of use; to inspect the quality and standards; and to prevent epidemic disease. The List of goods subject to import – export approval is:

A. There are 25 categories of goods subject to import approval or certificate

1. Live animal, fish and aquatic animals
2. Animal meat and other parts for human consumption; and products from animals and processed products from animal meat.
3. Milk products
4. Rice in the husk (paddy); rice
5. Cereals, products from vegetables, other processing for human consumption
6. Beverage, alcohol and orange juice
7. Food for animals
8. Cements, mortars and concretes
9. Fuel
10. Gas
11. Chemicals that are reacted to Ozone and products contained such chemical substances
12. Bio-chemical products
13. Pharmaceutical products, medicine for human and animal as well as medical equipment
14. Chemical fertilizer
15. Some types of cosmetic
16. Pesticide and toxic products for mouse and germs /microbes / bacteria
17. Sawn wood processed by sawmill company
18. Log and seedling
19. Textbooks and books
20. Rough diamonds
21. Silver and gold
22. Steel (long and round piece of steel and other shapes)
23. All kinds of vehicles and parts (except bicycles and tractors)
24. Game machine
25. Explosive substances

B. There are seven categories of goods subject to export approval or certificate

1. Live animal, fish and aquatic animals
2. Rice in the husk (paddy); rice
3. Resin and forestry products
4. Mining
5. Wood and wooden products
6. Rough diamond
7. Gold and silver

Ministry of Industry and Commerce will regularly improve the notification on the list of goods subject to import – export control and prohibition, where it is appropriate, in order to facilitate the business and to comply with the international treaties that Lao PDR is a party member.

This Notification replaces the notification on List of goods subject to import-export prohibition N. 0284/MOC.FTD date 17/6/2004 and the notification on List of goods subject to import-export approval from trade and other related government agencies.

NOTIFICATION LIST OF PROHIBITED GOODS FOR IMPORT AND EXPORT

-   According to decree on export and import management no. 205/PMO, dated 11 October 2001;
-   According to decree on export and import licensing with trade sectors for control goods, no. 106/MOC.FTD, dated 25 January 2002;
-   According to notification on list of goods from related sectors.

Minister of Commerce issues the list of prohibited goods for import-export to notify the trade units, concerned organization and implementing as follow:

A.   Prohibited goods for importation:
1.   Any kind of explosive, weapons and armament
2.   Any kind of drug addict
3.   Any kind of products affecting tradition of the nation
4.   Industrial disposal and chemical product that dangerous for health and environment
5.   Antiques
6.   Food, medicine and prohibited doctor equipments from related sectors
7.   Wild life, aquatic animals and their parts which are forbidden by domestic law and international subcontract that Lao PDR had signed.
8.   All type of right hand side driving vehicles
9.   Toys affecting children attitude, growth, safety and peace of the society
10.   Literature work, nude publication and other that against Lao PDR
11.   Second hand goods that government banned from import
12.   Equipment for printing of bank note
13.   Dangerous insecticides which prohibited by related sectors
14.   All type of log, sawed timber (processed timber), wood and forestry product that banned according to internal regulation

B.   List of export prohibition goods
1.   Any kind of explosive, weapons and armament
2.   Any kind of drug addict
3.   Any kind of products affecting tradition of the nation
4.   Wild life, aquatic animals and their parts which are forbidden by domestic law and international subcontract that Lao PDR had signed

5. All type of log, sawed timber (processed timber), all type of rattan and unprocessed eaglewood
6. Forestry product such as: Orchids, Ã€Â®Ã‰Â¨-Ã¬Â¾Â¨, Ã•-Â´Ã±-Â¨Â¾Â¤, Â¥Ã±-ÃƒÂ© and etc that prohibited according to internal law
7. Sulfur (bat manure)
8. Equipment for printing of bank note

List of prohibited goods for import and export is goods that badly damaged and dangerous to economic and social situation, politic, peace, safety and traditional of the country. All type of goods mentioned above are prohibited to import and export with an exception to Article 8 of decree numbers 205/PMO, dated 10/11/01 on export and import management. The detail of procedures and regulations are requested to follow the regulation numbers 106/MOC.FTD, dated 25/01/2002 on export and import licensing with trade sectors for control goods.

So this notification is prepared to notify organizations, related business units and be strictly implemented.

REGULATION ON THE IMPORT AND EXPORT LICENSING PROCEDURES OF CONTROLLED GOODS FROM TRADE AUTHORITIES

- Pursuant to the Decree on the establishment and operation of the Ministry of Commerce and Tourism No. 24/PM, dated 24 March 1999
- Based on the Decree on import and export No. 205/PM, dated 11 October 2001

The Minister of Commerce sets out

CHAPTER I GENERAL PRINCIPLES

Article 1. Licensing
An import or export licensing is a measure to administer import and export of goods in the Lao PDR, with an aim:
- To control the implementation conditions, criteria of the applicants for import or export activities;
- To monitor the conditions and criteria of import or export applicants, and to collect statistics of controlled-good imports or exports;
- To avoid a severe adverse impact on domestic production or national balance of payments;
- To control the import or export of prohibited goods which are occasionally needed for import or export.

Article 2. Applicant
An applicant comprises of importer, exporter as specified in Article 9 and Article 10 of the Decree on Import and Export No. 205/PM, dated 11 October 2001.

Article 3. Goods subject to licensing
The goods subject to an import or export license are controlled goods by which the Minister of Commerce has specified the criteria for import or export. The importer or exporter must strictly follow every procedure and regulation in this Regulation and in the laws and regulations of relevant sectors.
The detail of goods items subject to import or export licensing will be announced later.

CHAPTER II LICENSING PROCEDURES

Article 4. Licensing authority

Importer or exporter who wishes to import or export goods subject to control is required to submit an application with trade authorities as follows:
- Prohibited goods: approval from the Ministry of Commerce with a permission from the Prime Minister;
- Some controlled goods: approval from the Ministry of Commerce;
- Other controlled goods: approval from trade services in provinces, Vientiane municipality, and special zones.

Article 5. Licensing procedures

A license needs to be acquired prior to the import or export where accompanying documents include:
- Business registration and tax certification;
- Application form;
- Buying or selling contract;
- Technical certification from relevant authorities.

Article 6. Licensing consideration

The consideration of licensing application shall be in time, simple, and transparent for importer or exporter who supplies all required documentation as specified in this regulation.

The delay of licensing process without justification or unjustified reasons is considered in breach of this regulation and penalties shall be applied case by case.

Article 7. Time validity of a license

How long a license is valid depends on types of imports or exports. Related authorities specified in Article 4 of this regulation shall determine the time validity of licensing.

CHAPTER III PENALTIES

Article 8. Breach of licensing regulation

An importer or export who does not adhere to this regulation shall not have the right to import or export.

Article 9. Fraud, claim and other breaches

Any act related to fraud, claim, and other breaches to acquire a licensing shall be penalized according to seriousness or is subject civil penalty.

CHAPTER IV FINAL PROVISIONS

The Foreign Trade Department acts as a focal point to coordinate with related authorities, including trade services in the provinces, Vientiane Municipality and special zones, to implement in detail and for effectiveness of this regulation. The list of additional or reducing imports or exports subject to licensing shall also be provided to the Ministry of Commerce in subsequent notification.

Article 11. Enforcement

This regulation shall be into force from its date of signatory. Any other provisions and regulations inconsistent with this regulation shall be nullified.

DECREE ON IMPORT AND EXPORT MANAGEMENT

- Based on the Law on the Government of the Lao PDR No. 01/95 dated 8 March 1995,
- Based on the Business Law No. 03/94/NA dated 18 July 1994,
- Based on the Decree on the Customs Law No. 04/94 dated 18 July 1994,
- Based on the proposal of the Minister of Trade No. 1165/MCT dated 9 October 2001,
- Based on the Decision of the Government Meeting in November 2001,

The Prime Minister of the Lao PDR has decreed:

SECTION I: GENERAL PROVISIONS

ARTICLE 1: FUNCTION OF THE DECREE

This decree has the function of stipulating management regulations on exports and imports in accordance with the laws, focused on production and export promotion, reasonable import control, promotion of international trade, improving living standards of people and active contribution to the national socio-economy.

ARTICLE 2: DEFINITION

"Export" means exports of goods from the Lao PDR to other country.
"Import" means imports of goods from other country to the Lao PDR.

ARTICLE 3: BASIC PRINCIPLE OF ORGANIZATION AND OPERATION

Any organization and operation of import and export within the Lao PDR shall be conducted strictly in accordance with this decree and other related laws and regulations.

SECTION II: GOODS CONTROL, CONTROLLED GOODS ON IMPORT AND EXPORT

Article 4: Goods Control

The government of the Lao PDR encourages export and import of all goods except those goods which are under state control specified in this decree or other related laws or regulations.

According to this decree, control on import or export of a certain goods means the implementation of measures on these goods as necessary to maintain the economic and social stability, to preserve the national culture and tradition, and to protect other benefits of the state and society.

Application of import control is to protect the domestic production and consumer, to prevent price speculation in the country, and to maintain equilibrium of imports and exports.

Application of export control is needed to prevent the shortage of goods and to accumulate stocks within the country to ensure the export of some goods according to the international agreements that the Lao PDR is a party.

Article 5: Measures of control

Import and export control may be conducted through the following measures:

- Prohibit import or export;

- Require import or export application;
- Demand documentation such as bill of origin and quality certificate of the imported or exported goods based on the agreement or traditional procedure of the international trade.
- Forbid or restrict import or export of some goods;
- Issue specific conditions for the business license;
- Charge import or export fees;
- Stipulate certain quality including amount, packing, type, kind, size, weight, price, trade name or brand, country of origin and export or import country,
- Apply other necessary measures on import and export such as equilibrium plan, customs and tax policy, organize related group or association.

The measures of control specified in this article, which may be in conflict with the laws and regulations of the international trade systems that the Lao PDR is committed to or is member of, will be cancelled.

Article 6:   Controlled Goods

Controlled Goods are those one which the measures are applied on import â€" export control as indicated in the article of this decree.

The list of controlled goods may be changed as necessary.

The Ministry of Commerce shall stipulate, cancel and apply the list and measures on controlled goods periodically, except those goods controlled by other sectors or being covered by other measures.

ARTICLE 7:   CONTROLLED GOODS UNDER OTHER SECTORS

Goods under control of other sectors are those under the direct management of the related sectors. Importer and exporter of those goods shall conduct business according to measures issued by the related sectors.

The goods mentioned in paragraph 1 above and controlled measures on them shall be stipulated and issued as necessary by the related sectors. Then the list of these goods shall be reported officially to the Ministry of Commerce to add to the list of goods under the state control.

The Ministry of Commerce shall announce this list to business entity and related sectors.

Article 8:   Permission Needed Goods

Goods that need to be permitted before import or export comprise forbidden goods and some controlled goods.

The Ministry of Commerce shall issue approval and lay down regulations on application procedures. The Ministry of Commerce has to coordinate with the related sectors and each approval shall be agreed by the Prime Minister.

SECTION III: IMPORTER AND EXPORTER

ARTICLE 9:   IMPORTER

Importer includes individual or juristic entity who has registered as a business according to this decree. Imported goods of these business entities are for sale within the Lao PDR.

Individual or juristic entity who has been registered with a business license may import some goods according to the related laws and regulation to serve their specific purpose as indicated in article 18 of this decree.

ARTICLE 10:   EXPORTER

Individual or juristic entity who hold a business license may operate the export business.

Article 11:   Importer or Exporter of Goods (for Self Consumption)

Importers or exporters of goods (for self consumption) are individual or organizations who have been authorized temporarily to bring in or out some goods for noncommercial purposes.

SECTION III: ESTABLISHMENT AND OPERATION OF THE EXPORT AND IMPORT BUSINESS

ARTICLE 12:   ESTABLISHMENT OF THE IMPORT COMPANY

Individual or juridic entities who want to set up a import company as indicated in the first paragraph of Article 9 above shall apply to the Commercial Section for establishment and business registration and to the Financial Section for tax registration.

ARTICLE 13:   ESTABLISHMENT OF THE EXPORT COMPANY

All business entities registered with a business license as indicated in Article 10 above can operate an export business.

Those who do not have a business license as specified in the first paragraph above, but want to operate an export business, shall apply for establishment as indicated in Article 12.

ARTICLE 14:   BUSINESS ORGANIZATION

The organization of the import or export company may be set up in accordance with the type and form as indicated in the Business Law.

ARTICLE 15:   REGISTERED CAPITAL

Registered Capital to set up an export or import business shall be undertaken as indicated in the Business Law, except for export or import of some commodities, for which the laws and regulations specify for a higher Registered Capital.

ARTICLE 16:   APPROVED GOODS ON THE LICENSE

Individual or juridic entity shall submit the goods list along with the application for a import business license. The applied list may consist of one or many goods according to its capacity.

Individual or juridic entity received the import license according to the first paragraph above may trade in export of any kind of goods, except those goods controlled by the state which require the export license, those forbidden by the state and others specified in the laws.

The list of approved goods shall be shown on the import license of importer who is dealing with specific goods, as specified in the second paragraph of Article 9.

The Ministry of Commerce shall indicate goods that require an export license.

ARTICLE 17: CONSEQUENCE FROM NON-OPERATION

A business license of the import or export business entity, which is not operative for one year after approval, will be cancelled , except when a reasonable reason has been reported to the Commercial Section before the end of the one year limit.

SECTION V: IMPORTATION

ARTICLE 18: IMPORT BY THE IMPORT COMPANY

Import by the import company shall be conducted in accordance with the following:

- import according to the goods list specified on the import license;
- holding of a sell-buy contract

ARTICLE 19: SPECIFIC PURPOSE IMPORT

Specific purpose importer has the rights to import equipment, machinery and raw materials which will be used directly in production or business based on plan adopted by the related sectors.

Article 20: Import Procedure

Import company or specific purpose importer who has complied with the conditions specified in this decree can submit the import document directly to the related office at the border station to bring in the goods.

Article 21: Import of goods (for self consumption)

Authorized import (for self consumption) shall be conducted in accordance with the list, limit, type and amount of goods indicated in the customs law.

SECTION VI: EXPORTATION

ARTICLE 22: EXPORT BY THE EXPORT COMPANY

Export by the export company shall be accompanied by the sell-buy contract with the foreign counterpart. For export of controlled goods, the company shall abide by the specific regulations on each controlled goods.

Article 23: Export Procedure

Exporters as indicated in Article 10 of this decree can submit export documents directly to the related office at the border station to bring out the goods.

Article 24: **Export for self consumption**

Authorized export for self consumption shall be conducted in accordance with the Customs Law.

SECTION VII: SANCTIONS

Article 25: Individual or juristic entity who breach the regulations on controlled goods, in addition to the withdrawal the license, shall be fined and be subject to legal proceedings.

ARTICLE 26: OTHER VIOLATIONS

Any violation of the importer, exporter and government officer such as falsifying documents or misuse of the position shall be punish according to the law.

SECTION VIII: FINAL PROVISION

ARTICLE 27: IMPLEMENTATION

The Prime Minister Office, the Ministry of Commerce, the Ministry of Finance, Ministries, comparable organizations, provinces, municipality and special zone shall implement this decree throughout the country.

ARTICLE 28: EFFECTIVENESS

This decree takes effect from its signature date. All promulgated decrees and regulations in conflict with this decree are herewith abrogated.

DECREE ON GOODS TRADING BUSINESS

- Based on the law on the Government of the Lao PDR No. 01/95 dated 8 March 1995,
- Based on the Business Law No. 03/94/NA dated 18 July 1994,
- Based on the Tax Law No. 04/95/NA dated 14 October 1995,
- Based on the proposal of the Minister of Trade No. 1165/MTT dated 9 October 2001,
- Based on the decision of the Government Meeting dated 25 December 2000.

The Prime Minister of the Lao PDR has decreed:

SECTION I: GENERAL PROVISIONS

ARTICLE 1: FUNCTION OF THE DECREE
This decree has the function of setting up management regulations on domestic goods trading business in accordance with the law, focused on sufficient goods circulation, promotion of goods production, price and exchange rate stabilization, improving living standard of people and active contribution to the national socio-economic development.

ARTICLE 2: GOODS TRADING BUSINESS
Goods Trading Business means business on goods traffic within the country which covers the first sale of local produced goods or imported goods through the last sale to the consumer of both whole and retail sale.

For additional analytical, business and investment opportunities information, please contact Global Investment & Business Center, USA at (703) 370-8082. Fax: (703) 370-8083. E-mail: ibpusa3@gmail.com Global Business and Investment Info Databank - www.ibpus.com

The first sale is the first ownership transfer of goods from the domestic producer or the importer to a person or entity against money or other benefit.

Article 3: Basic Principle of Organization and Operation

Any organization and operation of Goods Trading Business shall be conducted strictly in accordance with this decree and other related laws.

Section II: Management of Conditional Goods

Article 4: Management on Distribution of Conditional Goods

The Government of the Lao PDR promotes the circulation of any commodity liberally in accordance with the law, except commodities, that the government stipulates conditions on distribution in this decree and other laws and regulations related.

Management on distribution of Conditional Goods is the stipulation for the trading business of a certain commodity according to its nature, specific, important, affect, risk or danger.

Article 5: Control Measures of Conditional Goods

Conditional Goods may be controlled by one of the following measures:
- Forbid or restrict business on trading of some goods as necessary;
- Stipulate Registered Capital higher than indicated in the Business Law;
- Require certain qualification of the director, manager, owner or staff;
- Set up standard, quality of goods, trading mark, accounting and other;
- Indicate part which will be permitted for business;
- Set up the price limits and the margins of stocks accumulation periodically.

The measure indicated for a certain conditional goods should not hinder the mentioned business, which can have a negative effect on supply, price, money and competition at reasonable level.

ARTICLE 6: CONDITIONAL GOODS

Conditional Goods are those controlled by the measures in the above Article 5. The list of Conditional Goods may be change as necessary.

Designate the Ministry of Commerce to set up or cancel the list of Conditional Goods and to issue detail management measures for each type of commodity periodically, except those commodities managed by other sector or being covered by other measures.

Article 7: Conditional Goods under other sectors

Conditional Goods under other sectors are those under the direct management of the related sectors. Traders of those goods shall conduct business according to measures issued by the related sectors.

The related sectors shall set up and issue the type and detailed management measures of Conditional Goods mentioned in paragraph 1 above as necessary, then report its list of Conditional Goods officially to the Ministry of Commerce to compile into the list of Conditional Goods of the state.

Assign the Ministry of Commerce to announce this list of business entity and related sectors.

Article 8: Forbidden Goods Trading

Trading of Forbidden Goods shall be permitted by the Ministry of Commerce based on the agreement of the Prime Minister.

In case the Forbidden Goods are under direct management of the related sectors, the Ministry of Commerce shall coordinate with the related sectors before making proposal to the Prime Minister.

SECTION III: FOUNDATION AND OPERATION OF GOODS TRADING BUSINESS

ARTICLE 9: FOUNDATION

Individual or juristic entities who want to set up a Goods Trading Business shall apply to the Commercial Section for foundation and business registration and to the Financial Section for tax registration.

ARTICLE 10: REGISTERED CAPITAL

Registered Capital to set up a Goods Trading Business shall be undertaken as indicated in the Business Law, except for trading of some commodities which the laws and regulations specify for a higher Register Capital.

Article 11: Approved goods on the license

Individual or juristic entity who want to set up a Goods Trading Business may apply for trading of one or many kinds of commodities.

Article 12: Business Organization

The organization of Goods Trading Business may be set up in accordance with the type and form as indicated in the Business Law.

Article 13: Business Activity

Individual or juristic entities who have been licensed for Goods Trading Business may chose the form of trading according to capacity, but have to conduct business in accordance with the related regulations of the selected form of trading.

Article 14: Consequence from Non-operation

A business License of the Goods Trading Business entity, which is not operative for one year after approval, will be cancelled, except in case a reasonable reason has been reported to the Commercial Section before the end of the one year limit.

SECTION IV: SANCTION

ARTICLE 15: VIOLATION OF THE REGULATIONS ON CONDITIONAL GOODS

Individual or juristic entities who breach the regulations on Conditional Goods, in addition to the withdrawal the license, shall be fined and be subject to legal proceedings.

ARTICLE 16: OTHER VIOLATIONS

Any violation of trader and government officer such as false documentation and misuse of position shall be punished according to the law.

SECTION V: FINAL PROVISION

Article 17: Implementation

The Prime Minister's Office, the Ministry of Commerce, the Ministry of Finance, Ministries comparable organizations, provinces, municipality and special zone shall implement this decree throughout the country.

Article 18: Effectiveness

This decree takes effect from its signature date. All promulgated decrees and regulations in conflict with this decree are herewith abrogated.

For additional analytical, business and investment opportunities information, please contact Global Investment & Business Center, USA at (703) 370-8082. Fax: (703) 370-8083. E-mail: ibpusa3@gmail.com Global Business and Investment Info Databank - www.ibpus.com

DECREE ON TRADE COMPETITION

Based upon the Law regarding the Government No. 02/NA, dated 8 May 2003; Based upon the Business Law No. 03194/NA, dated 18 July 1994;

Based upon the proposal of the Minister of Commerce, No. 0713 /MOC.ERIT, dated 18 July 2003,

The Prime Minister issues
Decree:

CHAPTER I GENERAL PROVISIONS

Article 1   Objectives

This Decree is issued to define rules, measures and enforcement to regulate monopolization and unfair competition in trade of all forms, aiming to promote fair trade competition, protect the rights and legal interests of consumers and to encourage business activities in the Lao PDR to function efficiently in the market economy mechanism as determined by the Government of the Lao PDR.

Article 2   Definitions

In this Decree:

"acquisition" means the power in business management of one business entity by purchasing the property or buy all or part of the shares of another business entity;

"business person" means a person who sells goods, buys goods for further processing and sale or buys goods for resale or is a service provider;

"Commission" refers to the Trade Competition Commission;

"consumer" means any buyer and/or user of goods and services purchased from a seller;

"goods" refers to products designed for durable and non-durable consumption, including document certifying the ownership of these goods; "trade" means trade in goods and services;

"market dominance" means sales volume or market share of any goods or services of one or more business entities is above that prescribed by the Trade Competition Commission;

"merger" means two or more business entities coming together and forming into one business entity with the result the individual business entity will cease to exist;

"monopoly" means the dominance of the market individually or in collusion with other businesses;

"price" means price charged in the sale of goods and services;

"service" means accepting to perform or performing services, giving for use or interest in goods or any activity for payment in return or other consideration, except wages;

Article 3   Fundamental principle in competition

For additional analytical, business and investment opportunities information,
please contact Global Investment & Business Center, USA
at (703) 370-8082. Fax: (703) 370-8083. E-mail: ibpusa3@gmail.com
Global Business and Investment Info Databank - www.ibpus.com

Business activities of all sectors are equal under the law, they cooperate and compete with each other in a fair manner by in compliance with this Decree and concerned Laws and regulations.

Article 4   Scope of application

This Decree applies to the sale of goods and services in business activities.

CHAPTER 2 THE TRADE COMPETITION COMMISSION

Article 5   The Trade Competition Commission

The Trade Competition Commission shall consist of concerned parties of the trade sector and a number of relevantly experienced people.

The Minister of Trade, by virtue of his position, is the Chairman and appoints members of this Commission.

The Trade Competition Commission shall have its office and its permanent secretariat

within the Ministry of Commerce.

Articles 6   Rights and duties of the Commission

The Fair Trading Commission has the rights and duties as follows:

Determine rules on activities, rights and duties of the secretariat, and supervise the functioning of the secretariat;

Formulate and stipulate further regulations in enforcing this Decree;

Establish a sub-commission to implement a specific duty when necessary;

Consider submissions and give approval for any business person as stipulated in Article 13   of this Decree;

Determine and publish a list of parties and type of businesses as stipulated in Article 13 of this Decree;

Call on concerned persons for consultations, advice or clarification on any matter;

Monitor and control business activities and order any business entity to solve, change, suspend or stop its behavior that is unfair;

Determine market share, and the total volume amount of a business which is found to be dominating the market;

Determine market share or assets that are considered to dominate business management of another business entity;

For additional analytical, business and investment opportunities information,
please contact Global Investment & Business Center, USA
at (703) 370-8082. Fax: (703) 370-8083. E-mail: ibpusa3@gmail.com
Global Business and Investment Info Databank - www.ibpus.com

Consider complaints from business persons and consumers;

Submit to the concerned organizations to take measures for those who breach;

Coordinate with the media and concerned business entities to publicise various activities   and issues on matter relating to competition;

Implement any other duties and responsibilities as may assigned by the Government.

CHAPTER 3 COMPETITION IN TRADE

Article 7   Promoting a fair trade competition

The Government of the Lao PDR encourages business entities of all economic sectors to undertake businesses under competitive conditions with equality, fairness, and cooperation.

Article 8   Anti-monopoly

It is prohibited for a business person to perform any act stipulated in Articles 9, 10, 11 and 12 of this Decree so as to monopolize any market of goods and services.

Article 9   Merger and Acquisition

It is prohibited for a business person to monopolize the market in the form of a merger or acquisition that destroys competitors or substantially reduces or limits competition.

Article 10   Elimination of other business entities

It is prohibited for a business entity to act or behave so as to cause losses directly or indirectly, by such conduct as dumping, limiting or intervening with intent to eliminate other business entities.

Article 11   Collusion and Arrangements

It is prohibited for a business entity to collude or make arrangements to engage in unfair trade practices in any form, such as:

Price fixing, and fixing the sale and purchase price of goods and services;

Stocking goods, limiting, reducing the quantity or limiting the production, purchase, sale, distribution or import of goods and services;

Colluding in tenders for purchase, sale and supply of goods and services;

Fixing conditions that, directly or indirectly, force their customers to reduce production, purchase or sale of goods or the supply of services;

Limiting the customer's choice to purchase, sell goods and receive services;

Prohibiting their suppliers or retailers from purchasing or selling goods to other   business entities;

Entering into allocation arrangements of markets, customers or suppliers restricting competition;

Appoint, or give authority to an individual the for sole right to sell goods or supply services in one market;

Arrangements to fix conditions or the manner of purchase and sale of goods or services to restrict other business entities;

Other acts that are contrary to the trade competition regulations prescribed by the Trade Competition Commission.

Article 12   Cartel with foreign business persons

It is prohibited for any business entity to establish and operate a business in the Lao PDR that has business relations with a foreign business entity either by contract, share holding or other form to act to limit the opportunity of local businesses to choose to purchase from or sell goods or provide services directly to, a foreign business entity.

Article 13   Exemption

Any act stipulated in Article 8, 9,10, 11 and 12 of this Decree may be exempted for some specific sector or business for socio-economic or security reasons.

The Trade Competition Commission is assigned to consider and provide exemptions from time to time.

CHAPTER 4 Measures against offenders

Article 14   Measures against business entities who commit offences

A business entity that commits offences under this Decree shall be dealt with as follows;

Notice to change and rectify its behavior;

Temporary suspension of activity until the behavior is rectified and changed;

Close down indefinitely the activity and may be punished according to the law;

Compensate a business entity that has incurred losses as a result of the offences.

For additional analytical, business and investment opportunities information,
please contact Global Investment & Business Center, USA
at (703) 370-8082. Fax: (703) 370-8083. E-mail: ibpusa3@gmail.com
Global Business and Investment Info Databank - www.ibpus.com

Article 15   Other offences

All civil servants and authorities that commit offences under this Decree will be dealt according to the law.

CHAPTER 5 Final provisions

Article 16   Implementation

The Ministry of Commerce and the Trade Competition Commission are assigned to implement this Decree.

Article 17   Enforcement

This Decree is effective from August 1st, 2004.

All rules and regulations, which are contrary to this Decree, are superseded.

TRAVELING TO LAOS

US STATE DEPARTMENT SUGGESTIONS

COUNTRY DESCRIPTION: Laos is a developing country with a socialist government that is pursuing economic reform. Outside of Vientiane, the capital, and Luang Prabang, tourist services and facilities are relatively undeveloped.

ENTRY REQUIREMENTS: A passport and visa are required. Visas are issued upon arrival in Laos to foreign tourists and business persons, subject to certain conditions, at the following points of entry: Wattay Airport, Vientiane; Luang Prabang Airport; Friendship Bridge, Vientiane; Ban Huay Xai, Bokeo Province; and Vantao, Champasak Province. In the United States, U.S citizens may apply for visas and obtain further information about entry requirements directly from the Embassy of the Lao People's Democratic Republic, 2222 S St. N.W., Washington, D.C. 20008, tel. 202-332-6416, fax 202-332-4923, Internet home page: http://www.laoembassy.com. U.S. citizens should not attempt to enter Laos without valid travel documents or outside official ports of entry. Unscrupulous travel agents have sold U.S.-citizen travelers false Lao visas, which have resulted in those travelers being denied entry into Laos.

SAFETY AND SECURITY: The security situation in Laos can change quickly. Please refer to any Department of State Public Announcements for Laos for additional information.

Since the Spring of 2000, a number of bombings have occurred in public places frequented by foreign travelers in Vientiane, and there have been credible reports of other explosive devices found in Savannakhet and Pakse cities. While there is no evidence that this violence is directed against American citizens or institutions, American citizens should be aware that more such incidents could occur in the future. American citizens traveling to or residing anywhere in Laos are advised to exercise caution and to be alert to their surroundings.

Persons traveling overland in some areas, particularly Route 13 north between Kasi and Luang Prabang; Saisombun Special Zone; Xieng Khouang Province, including the Plain of Jars; and Route 7 east from the Route 13 junction, run the risk of ambush by insurgents or bandits. There have been violent incidents in these areas in the past year. Some groups have warned of impending insurgent attacks in these areas. Americans considering travel outside urban centers by road or river are advised to contact relevant Lao government offices and the U.S. Embassy for the most current security information.

American citizens should also avoid traveling on or across the Mekong River at night along the Thai border. In some areas, Lao militia forces have been known to shoot at boats on the river after dark.

INFORMATION ON CRIME: While Laos generally has a low rate of crime, visitors should exercise appropriate security precautions and remain aware of their surroundings. Street crime has been on the increase, particularly motorcycle drive-by theft of handbags and backpacks. The loss or theft abroad of a U.S. passport should be reported immediately to the local police and the U.S. Embassy. Useful information on safeguarding valuables and protecting personal security while traveling abroad is provided in the Department of State pamphlet, *A Safe Trip Abroad*, available from the Superintendent of Documents, U.S. Government Printing Office, Washington, D.C. 20402, via the Internet at http://www.access.gpo.gov/su_docs, on the Bureau of Consular Affairs home page at http://travel.state.gov and autofax service at 202-647-3000, or at the U.S. Embassy in Vientiane.

MEDICAL FACILITIES: Medical facilities and services are severely limited and do not meet Western standards. The blood supply is not screened for HIV or AIDS.

MEDICAL INSURANCE: U.S. medical insurance is not always valid outside the United States. U.S. Medicare and Medicaid programs do not provide payment for medical services outside the United States. Doctors and hospitals often expect immediate cash payment for health services. Uninsured travelers who require medical care overseas may face extreme difficulties.

Please check with your own insurance company to confirm whether your policy applies overseas, including provision for medical evacuation, and for adequacy of coverage. Serious medical problems requiring hospitalization and/or medical evacuation to the United States can cost tens of thousands of dollars. Please ascertain whether payment will be made to the overseas hospital or doctor or whether you will be reimbursed later for expenses that you incur. Some insurance policies also include coverage for psychiatric treatment and for disposition of remains in the event of death.

Useful information on medical emergencies abroad, including overseas insurance programs, is provided in the Department of State, Bureau of Consular Affairs brochure, *Medical Information for Americans Traveling Abroad*, available via the Bureau of Consular Affairs home page at http://travel.state.gov and autofax service at 202-647-3000.

OTHER HEALTH INFORMATION: Vaccination recommendations and prevention information for traveling abroad may be obtained through the Centers for Disease Control and Prevention's international travelers hotline from the United States at 1-877-FYI-TRIP (1-877-394-8747), via its toll-free autofax service at 1-888-CDC-FAXX (1-888-232-3299), or via their Internet site at http://www.cdc.gov.

ROAD SAFETY: While in a foreign country, U.S. citizens may encounter road conditions that differ significantly from those in the United States. The information below concerning Laos is provided for general reference only, and may not be totally accurate in a particular location or circumstance:
Safety of Public Transportation: Poor
Urban Road Conditions/Maintenance: Poor
Rural Road Conditions/Maintenance: Poor
Availability of Roadside Assistance: Poor

Roads are mostly unpaved, pot-holed and poorly maintained in most parts of the country, although there has been a successful effort to improve roads and drainage in the capital in recent years. There are no railroads. Public transportation in Vientiane is generally poor and unreliable, and it is very limited after sunset. Taxis are available. Drivers speak little or no English. Most taxis are old and poorly maintained. Traffic is increasing, and local drivers remain undisciplined. Pedestrians and drivers should exercise great caution at all times. Theoretically, traffic moves on the right, but most cars, like pedestrians and bicycles, use all parts of the street. Cyclists pay little or no heed to cars on the road, and bicycles are rarely equipped with functioning lights or reflectors. This makes driving especially dangerous at dusk and at night. Defensive driving is necessary. The U.S. Embassy in Vientiane advises its personnel to wear helmets, gloves, and sturdy shoes while operating motorcycles.

AVIATION OVERSIGHT: Serious concerns about the operation of Lao Aviation, particularly regarding its safety standards and maintenance regime, have caused the U.S. Embassy to advise its personnel to limit domestic travel on Lao Aviation to essential travel only. Americans who are required to travel by air within Laos may wish to defer their travel or consider alternate means of transportation.

Also, since there is no direct commercial air service at present, nor economic authority to operate such service between the U.S. and Laos, the U.S. Federal Aviation Administration (FAA) has not assessed Laos' Civil Aviation Authority for compliance with international aviation safety standards for oversight of Laos' air carrier operations. For further information, travelers may contact the Department of Transportation within the U.S. at tel. 1-800-322-7873, or visit the FAA Internet home page at http://www.faa.gov/avr/iasa/iasa.pdf. The U.S. Department of Defense (DOD) separately assesses some foreign air carriers for suitability as official providers of air services. For information regarding the DOD policy on specific carriers, travelers may contact the DOD at tel. 1-618-229-4801.

RELIGIOUS WORKERS: Religious proselytizing or distributing religious material is strictly prohibited. Foreigners caught distributing religious material may be arrested or deported. The Government of Laos restricts the import of religious texts and artifacts. While Lao law allows freedom of religion, the government registers and controls all associations, including religious groups. Meetings, even in private homes, must be registered, and those held outside established locations may be broken up and the participants arrested.

MARRIAGE TO A LAO CITIZEN: The Lao Government imposes requirements on foreigners intending to marry Lao citizens. U.S. citizens may obtain information about these requirements at the U.S. Embassy in Vientiane. A marriage certificate is not issued by the Lao Government unless the correct procedures are followed. Any attempt to circumvent Lao law governing the marriage of Lao citizens to foreigners may result in deportation of the foreigner and denial of permission to re-enter Laos. Similar restrictions exist prohibiting the cohabitation of Lao nationals with nationals of other countries.

PHOTOGRAPHY AND OTHER RESTRICTIONS: Police and military may arrest persons taking photographs of military installations or vehicles, bridges, airfields and government buildings, and confiscate their cameras. Confiscated cameras are seldom returned to the owners. The photographers may be arrested. Export of antiques, such as Buddha images and other old cultural artifacts, is restricted by Laotian law.

CRIMINAL PENALTIES: While in a foreign country, a U.S. citizen is subject to that country's laws and regulations, which sometimes differ significantly from those in the United States and do not afford the protections available to the individual under U.S. law. Penalties for breaking the law can be more severe than in the United States for similar offenses. Persons violating the law, even unknowingly, may be expelled, arrested or imprisoned. Penalties for possession, use or trafficking in illegal drugs in Laos are strict, and convicted offenders can expect jail sentences and fines. Local police and immigration authorities sometimes confiscate passports when outstanding business disputes and visa matters remain unsettled.

CONSULAR ACCESS: The United States and Laos are parties to the Vienna Convention on Consular Relations (VCCR). Article 36 of the VCCR provides that if an arrestee requests it, foreign authorities shall, without delay, inform the U.S. Embassy. U.S. consular officers have the right to be notified of a U.S. citizen's detention and to visit the arrestee. Lao authorities do not always notify the U.S. Embassy or grant U.S. consular officers access to incarcerated U.S. citizens in a timely manner. Nevertheless, American citizens who are arrested or detained in Laos should always request contact with the U.S. Embassy.

For additional analytical, business and investment opportunities information, please contact Global Investment & Business Center, USA at (703) 370-8082. Fax: (703) 370-8083. E-mail: ibpusa3@gmail.com Global Business and Investment Info Databank - www.ibpus.com

CUSTOMS REGULATIONS: Lao customs authorities may enforce strict regulations concerning temporary importation into or export from Laos of items such as religious materials and artifacts, and antiquities. It is advisable to contact the Embassy of the Lao People's Democratic Republic in Washington for specific information regarding customs requirements. (Please see sections on "Religious Workers" and "Photography and Other Restrictions" above.)

CHILDREN'S ISSUES: For information on international adoption of children and international parental child abduction, please refer to our Internet site at http://travel.state.gov/children's_issues.html or telephone (202) 736-7000.

REGISTRATION/EMBASSY LOCATION: U.S. citizens living in or visiting Laos are encouraged to register at the U.S. Embassy where they may obtain updated information on travel and security within the country. The U.S. Embassy is located at Rue Bartholonie (near Tat Dam), B.P. 114, in Vientiane; mail can be addressed to American Embassy Vientiane, Box V, APO AP 96546; telephone (856-21) 212-581, 212-582, 212-585; duty officer's emergency cellular telephone (856-020) 511-740; Embassy-wide fax number (856-020) 518-597; Embassy-wide fax number (856-21) 212-584; Internet home page: http://usembassy.state.gov/laos/.

BUSINESS TRAVEL

BUSINESS CUSTOMS

Business relationships in Laos are not as formal as those in other East Asian countries and are often based on personal relations developed within social circles. Since the emphasis placed on personal relationships is high, having a reliable and well-connected local agent or representative is important to the success of a foreign venture.

Events progress slowly in Laos, where the step-by-step approach reveals the cultural premium placed on caution and restraint. Representatives of US businesses seeking to enter the Lao market should plan to visit the country several times and have patience with their partners and the Lao market.

TRAVEL ADVISORY

Information on travel to and within Laos may be obtained from the consular information sheet on Laos available from the U.S. Department of State: http://travel.state.gov/travel/cis_pa_tw/cis/cis_946.html

VISA REQUIREMENTS

U.S. visitors must have both a passport and visa to enter Laos; your passport must also

have at least six months validity remaining. Visa on arrival in Laos is available for

U.S tourists who have two passport-size photographs and pay $35 at the following ports of entry: Wattay Airport, Vientiane; Pakse, Savannakhet, and Luang Prabang Airports;

Friendship Bridge, Vientiane and Savannakhet; Mittaphab Friendship Bridge I, Khammouane Province, Houyxay, Bokeo; Paksan, Bolikhamxay province; Mittaphab (Friendship) Bridge III,

Khammouane province; Mittaphab (Friendship) Bridge II, Savannakhet province; Vangtao Chongmek, Champasack; Ken Thao, Sayabury Province; Mouang Ngeun, Sayabury province

From Vietnam: Dane Savanh, Savannakhet; Nam Kan, Xieng Khouang; Na Phao, Khammouane; Nam Soy, Houaphanh province; Pang Hok, Phongsaly province; Phoukeua, Attapey; Nam Phao, Bolikhamxay.

Visa on arrival is also available at the Tha Naleng train station in Vientiane, which connects to the train station in Nongkhai, Thailand. With a visa obtained from a Lao embassy or consulate prior to your travel to Laos, travelers may also enter at the following international entry points: Napao-Chalo, Taichang-Sophoun, Pakxan-Bungkan, and Xiengkok.

Length of stay in Laos is generally for 30 days after arrival. Persons born in Laos may be admitted for 60 days or longer. 30-day tourist visas can be extended up to an additional 60 days for a fee of $2 per day through the Department of Immigration in Vientiane. Overstay of visas in Laos, is punishable by arrest and fines of $10 for each day of overstay. The Lao government calculates visa fees and fines in U.S. dollars. Thai baht and Lao kip may sometimes be accepted for the fees but at unfavorable exchange rates. Additional information is available from the Lao National Tourism Administration.

For visas in advance of travel, please contact a Lao embassy or consulate. In the United States, visa and other information about Lao entry requirements is available from the Embassy of the Lao People's Democratic Republic, 2222 S St. NW, Washington DC

20008, tel: 202-332-6416, fax: 202-332-4923. Travelers entering Laos with a visitor visa issued at a Lao embassy abroad will be allowed to stay in Laos for 60 days.

Business visas can only be arranged in advance; a company or individual "sponsor" must contact the Lao Ministry of Foreign Affairs (MFA) in Vientiane and request a visa for the traveler and offer a "guarantee." Once the Lao MFA approves the request, the approval will be sent to the Lao Embassy in Washington, DC, and business travelers may then apply for the business visa. This process usually takes one to three months.

After arrival, business visas can generally be extended for one month.

Do not attempt to enter Laos without valid travel documents or outside of official ports of entry. It is unwise to cross the border between Laos and Thailand along the Mekong River except at official immigration check crossings. Attempts to enter Laos outside of official ports of entry may result in arrest, detention, fines, and deportation. Immigration offices at some of the less-used land border crossing points are not well marked.

At Wattay Airport (Vientiane), Pakse Airport, Savannakhet Airport, and the Luang Prabang Airport, there is an international airport departure tax of US$10. This tax may be included in the price of the airline ticket, depending on the carrier. There is also a 5,000 kip (equivalent to approximately U.S. 60 cents) departure tax for domestic flights, which may be included in the price of the airline ticket, depending on the carrier. At the Friendship Bridge (Vientiane, Laos - Nong Khai, Thailand border crossing) there is an overtime fee after 4:00 pm weekdays and during weekends. Visit the Embassy of Laos web site for the most current information U.S. companies that require travel of foreign businesspersons to the United States should be advised that security evaluations are handled via an interagency process.

Visa applicants should go to the following links.

State Department Visa Website: http://travel.state.gov/visa/

U.S. Embassy Vientiane Consular Section: http://laos.usembassy.gov/visas.html

Lao Embassy to the United States: http://www.laoembassy.com/

TELECOMMUNICATIONS

The Lao telecommunications infrastructure is developing quickly. Total telephone density is currently 76/100 (these are primarily cell phones), although in towns the number is much higher.

There are five authorized enterprises providing fixed and mobile telecommunications services in Lao PDR. All of them have some share of government ownership:

Lao Telecommunication Co Ltd http://www.laotel.com/home_Eng.html

Enterprise des Telecommunications Lao http://www.etllao.com/index.php

Star Telecommunication Company http://unitel.com.la/

Beeline http://beeline.la/index.php/en/about-beeline

Sky Communications Lao Ltd

There are six public internet service providers; ETL Internet; Lao Telecom; Sky Telecom;

KPL; Planet and Beeline.

TRANSPORTATION

Laos has three international airports; Wattay International Airport in Vientiane, Luang

Prabang International Airport, and Pakse International Airport. Wattay has service to and from Thailand, Vietnam, China (Kunming), Singapore, and Cambodia.

As of 2014, state carrier Lao Airlines operates four Airbus A320 aircraft and is expanding direct service throughout the region. Several other international carriers also offer direct flights from Thailand, Vietnam, and Korea. Lao Airlines and Lao Air offer flights from Vientiane to most of the provincial capitals.

Businesspeople in Laos generally rely on their own personal vehicles or rent vehicles

with drivers. Taxis are not readily available, even in the capital, although tuk-tuk vehicles for hire are common. Rental cars are available in Vientiane.

Road conditions vary greatly throughout the country and mudslides are a concern in

For additional analytical, business and investment opportunities information,
please contact Global Investment & Business Center, USA
at (703) 370-8082. Fax: (703) 370-8083. E-mail: ibpusa3@gmail.com
Global Business and Investment Info Databank - www.ibpus.com

mountainous areas during the rainy season. However, major transportation arteries such as Route 13 running north to south and Route 9 running east to west are generally

passable. The government has made road and bridge infrastructure a priority and travel

conditions are gradually improving. There are occasional security problems along rural

roads, including Route 13. For current conditions, please check

http://travel.state.gov/travel/cis_pa_tw/cis/cis_946.html

LANGUAGE

Lao is the national language and, due to the similarity of the Lao and Thai languages,

most Lao are capable of speaking and understanding Thai as well. Some Lao residing

in Vientiane and the larger provincial capitals speak basic English, although the overall

percentage of the population that speaks English is low.

HEALTH

The quality of healthcare in Laos is extremely poor. For serious health issues, the

Embassy generally advises travelers to seek medical attention in Thailand. For

additional information regarding health issues, review the Consular Information Sheet at:

http://travel.state.gov/travel/cis_pa_tw/cis/cis_946.html

LOCAL TIME, BUSINESS HOURS, AND HOLIDAYS

Lao and U.S. Embassy Holidays
January 1 Tuesday International New Year
January 20 Monday Martin Luther King, Jr. Birthday
February 17 Monday President's Day
March 10 Friday International Women's Day
April 14 Monday Lao New Year
April 15 Tuesday Lao New Year
April 16 Wednesday Lao New Year
May 1 Thursday International Labor Day
May 26 Monday Memorial Day
July 4 Friday Independence Day
September 1 Monday Labor Day
October 9 Thursday Boat Racing Festival
October 13 Monday Columbus Day
November 6 Thursday That Luang Festival
November 11 Tuesday Veterans' Day
November 27 Thursday Thanksgiving
December 2 Tuesday Lao National Day

For additional analytical, business and investment opportunities information, please contact Global Investment & Business Center, USA at (703) 370-8082. Fax: (703) 370-8083. E-mail: ibpusa3@gmail.com Global Business and Investment Info Databank - www.ibpus.com

December 25 Thursday Chrismas Day

In addition to those listed above, numerous religious holidays are often observed informally throughout the country. The Lao government is known to change the effective dates of holidays shortly before they occur, especially around Lao New Year.

Official working hours are from 8:00 a.m. to 12:00 p.m. and from 1:00 p.m. to 4:00 p.m. from Monday to Friday. However, in factories and many private companies work hours are extended until 5:00 p.m. Lao labor law stipulates that the factory work week can be extended to six days.

TEMPORARY ENTRY OF MATERIALS AND PERSONAL BELONGINGS

Equipment imported for personal use and any goods used in exhibitions or as samples for subsequent re-export are exempt from taxes and duties. In order to obtain this exemption, visitors must declare at the port of entry that the relevant goods or equipment are being temporarily imported, and must guarantee that it will be re-exported upon the visitors' departure. Goods brought into Laos for exhibition or as samples require a license from the Ministry of Commerce or the local trade office at the port of entry.

WEB RESOURCES

U.S. Embassy Laos: http://vientiane.usembassy.gov/

Lao Embassy to the United States: http://www.laoembassy.com/

Lao Visa Information: http://travel.state.gov/visa/index.html

U.S. Visa Information: http://unitedstatesvisas.gov

U.S. State Department Travel Advisory:

http://travel.state.gov/travel/cis_pa_tw/cis/cis_946.html

CONTACTS

Lao Government:
Mr. Somvang Ninthavong,
Director General,

Lao Trade Promotion and Product Development Department,
Ministry of Industry and Commerce
104/4-5 Khounbulom Rd. P.O.Box4107, Vientiane, Lao PDR.
Tel: (856-21) 216207, MB: (856-20) 99901208 Fax: (856-21) 213623...
Email: laotpc@hotmail.com or Laotpc@yahoo.com

Mrs. Khampheng Simmasone,
Deputy Director,
Lao Trade Promotion and Product Development Department,
104/4-5 Khounbulom Rd. P.O.Box4107, Vientiane, Lao PDR.
Tel: (856-21) 216207 MB: (856-20) 55909376 Fax: (856-21) 213623
Email: laotpc@hotmail.com or Laotpc@yahoo.com

Mr. Phouvong Phommabout,
Deputy Director, Lao Trade Promotion and Product Development Department,
104/4-5 Khounbulom Rd. P.O.Box4107, Vientiane, Lao PDR. Tel: (856-21) 216207, MB:
(856-20) 55515254, Fax: (856-21) 213623.
Email: laotpc@hotmail.com or Laotpc@yahoo.com

Mr. Bounsom Phommavihanh,
Department of Foreign Trade Policy Department,
Ministry of Industry and Commerce,
Tel: (856-21) 453490-5, Fax: (856-21) 450066, 412434.
Email: bounsome5@yahoo.co.uk

Mr. Oudet Souvannvong ,
Advisor, Vice President Lao National Chamber of Commerce
Tel: (856-21) 452579, 453311-2, Fax: (856-21) 452580
Website: http://www.lncci.laotel.com ,
Email: soho@laotel.com

Mr. One-Sy Boutsyvongsakd,
Advisor, President of the Lao Textile & Garment Industry Group Vientiane,
Tel: (856-21) 214450 and 222769, Fax: (856-21) 216993,
Email: bvs@laotel.com or textilao@laotel.com

Mr. Ajong Laomao,
Director General Department of Investment Promotion
Ministry of Planning and Investment,
Tel: (856-21) 216753, Fax: (856-21) 215491,
Website: http://invest.laopdr.org

Mr. Athsaphangthong Siphanhdone,
Director General,
Customs Department Ministry of Finance, Vientiane
Tel: (856-21) 213524 Fax: (856-21) 223521

Mr. Vanhkham Volavong,
Vice President, Managing Director Banque Pour Le Commerce Exterior Lao Vientiane
Tel: (856-21) 213200/01 Fax: (856-21) 223012, 213202 or 214944.

Lachay Khanpravong
Director, Treasury and International Services Department,

For additional analytical, business and investment opportunities information,
please contact Global Investment & Business Center, USA
at (703) 370-8082. Fax: (703) 370-8083. E-mail: ibpusa3@gmail.com
Global Business and Investment Info Databank - www.ibpus.com

Banque Pour Le Commerce Exterior Lao Vientiane
Tel: (856-21) 218977. Mobile 020 5516185 Fax: (856-21) 223012, 213202
Email: lachay@bcellaos.com

Mr. Sisomboun Bounnavong,
Director of International Cooperation Department,
Ministry of Planning and Cooperation.
Tel: (856-21) 218274 Fax: (856-21) 263779

Mr.Thongphann Savanhphet,
Director General of Economic Affairs,
Ministry of Foreign Affairs.
Tel: (856-21) 414040 Fax: (856-21) 415932.
U.S. Government and Private Organizations:

Mr. Noah Geesaman
Economic/Commercial Officer
U.S. Embassy, Vientiane
Tel: (856-21) 267000 ext 7156, Fax: (856-21) 267120 or 267190
E-mail: geesamann@state.gov

Ms. Sivanphone Thoummabouth,
Econ/Commercial Assistant, U.S. Embassy, Vientiane, Unit 8165, BOX V APO AP 96546,
Tel: (856-21) 267000 ext 7198, Fax: (856-21) 267190 or 267120
Email: sivanphonetx@state.gov

Mr. Chris Manley, Group Country Manager
Lao RMA
Lao -AMCHAM Chapter President
Tel: 856-21 241108 244 408 Fax: 856-21241 109, 244 409
Email: chris.manley@rmagroup.net

Mr. Ravi Dutta,
Lao AMCHAM Chapter Coordinator
Email: amchamlaos@yahoo.com

Mr. Dean Matlack,
Commercial Attaché,
U.S. Commercial Service,
U.S. Embassy – Bangkok
GPF Witthayu Tower A, Suite 302, 93/1 Wireless Road Bangkok 10330,
Tel: [662]-205-5263 Fax: [662]-255-2915,
E-mail: dean.matlack@trade.gov

American Chamber of Commerce - Thailand,
7th Floor, GPF Witthayu A, 93/1 Wireless Road, Lumpini, Pathumwan, Bangkok 10330
Tel: +66 (0) 2254-1041, Fax: 66 (0) 2251-1605
Email: service@amchamthailand.com

Multilateral Institutions:
Ms. Keiko Miwa,
Country Manager,
The World Bank Patuxay, Neru Rd, LAO PDR,

For additional analytical, business and investment opportunities information,
please contact Global Investment & Business Center, USA
at (703) 370-8082. Fax: (703) 370-8083. E-mail: ibpusa3@gmail.com
Global Business and Investment Info Databank - www.ibpus.com

Tel: (856) 21 414209, 450010, 450003, 450011, 410012 and 450015,
Fax: (856) 21 414210

Ms. Sandra Nicoll
Country Director, Vientiane,
LAO PDR Asia Development Bank, Lao Resident Mission, corner of Lane Xang Avenue
and Samsenthai Rd Vientiane, LAO PDR P.O.BOX 9724
Tel:(856-21) 250-444, 252627, 251327, 251427, 253060
Fax:(856- 21) 250-333
Email: ghkim@adb.org

Mr. Phongsavanh Phomkong
Head of Office,
International Finance Corporation (IFC) in Vientiane. P.O. Box 9690
Tel: (856-21) 450-017 to 9
Fax: (856-21) 450-020

TRADE EVENTS

Information on upcoming trade events. http://www.export.gov/tradeevents/index.asp

For additional analytical, business and investment opportunities information,
please contact Global Investment & Business Center, USA
at (703) 370-8082. Fax: (703) 370-8083. E-mail: ibpusa3@gmail.com
Global Business and Investment Info Databank - www.ibpus.com

SUPPLEMENTS

IMPORTANT WEBSITES

Name	Internet address
ACCSQ	http://www.aseansec.org/4951.htm
ADB	www.adb.org
AFTA	http://www.aseansec.org/economic/afta/afta.htm
ASEAN	www.aseansec.org
ASEAN Protocol on Enhanced Dispute Settlement Mechanism	http://www.aseansec.org/16754.htm
Bangkok Agreement	http://www.unescap.org/tid/Bkkagr.asp
Business Law (1994)	http://www.bkklaoembassy.com/Lao laws/Business Laws.pdf
Constitution	http://www.kplnet.net/English/constitution.htm
Customs Law (1994)	http://laocustoms.laopdr.net/laws_and_regulations.htm
Decree of the Prime Minister on Trademark Registration	http://www.stea.la.wipo.net/download/decree.zip
Department of Domestic and Foreign Investment	http://invest.laopdr.org/
EU-Laos Agreement on Trade in Textile Products	http://trade-info.cec.eu.int/doclib/html/111335.htm
FAO	www.fao.org
IBRD	www.worldbank.org
ICAO	http://www.icao.org/
IDA	www.worldbank.org
IFAD	www.ifad.org
ILO	www.ilo.org
IMF	www.imf.org
ITU	www.itu.int
Labour Law (1994)	http://invest.laopdr.org/labour law.htm
Lao Customs Department	http://laocustoms.laopdr.net/index.htm
Law on the Promotion of Foreign Investment (2004)	http://invest.laopdr.org/investlaw04.pdf
MIGA	www.miga.org
MRC	http://www.mrcmekong.org/
Science, Technology and Environment Agency	http://www.stea.la.wipo.net/aboutdism/index.html
Tax Law (1995)	http://invest.laopdr.org/tax law.htm
UNCTAD	www.unctad.org
UNDP	www.undp.org
UNDP Lao	www.undplao.org
UNDP Human Development index	http://hdr.undp.org/reports/global/2004/pdf/hdr04_HDI.pdf
UNESCO	www.unescao.org
UNIDO	www.unido.org
UPU	www.upu.int
WHO	www.who.org

For additional analytical, business and investment opportunities information, please contact Global Investment & Business Center, USA at (703) 370-8082. Fax: (703) 370-8083. E-mail: ibpusa3@gmail.com
Global Business and Investment Info Databank - www.ibpus.com

WIPO	www.wipo.org
WMO	www.wmo.ch
WTO	www.wto.org

CUSTOMS OFFICE CODES

VIENTIANE	10
1. Banvang	10.1
2. Salakham	10.2
PHONGSALY	02
3. Mouangkhoa	02.1
4. Pakha	02.2
LUANGNAMTHA	03
5. Nateuay	03.1
6. Botenh	03.2
OUDOMXAY	04
BOKEO	05
7. Houaysai	05.1
8. Muongmone	05.2
LUANGPRABANG	06
HOUAPHANH	07
9. Nameo	07.1
10. Pahang	07.2
11. Xiengkheuang	07.3
SAYABOURY	08
12. Kenethao	08.1
XIENGKHOUANG	09
13. Namkan	09.1
VIENTIANE MUNICIPALITY	01
14. Thanaleng	01.1
15. Wattay Airport	01.2
16. Post	01.3
17. Fuel	01.4
18. Thadeua	01.5
19. Friendship Bridge	01.6
BOLIKHAMXAY	11
20. Khamkeuth	11.1
21. Paksan	11.2
22. Namkading	11.3
KHAMMOUANE	12
23. Thakhek	12.1
24. Paksebangfai	12.2

For additional analytical, business and investment opportunities information,
please contact Global Investment & Business Center, USA
at (703) 370-8082. Fax: (703) 370-8083. E-mail: ibpusa3@gmail.com
Global Business and Investment Info Databank - www.ibpus.com

25. Hineboune	12.3
26. Chilo	12.4
SAVANNAKHET	13
27. Denesavanh	13.1
28. Khanthaboury	13.2
29. Thapasoom	13.3
30. Kengkabao	13.4
SALAVANE	14
31. Paktaphane	14.1
SEKONG	15
CHAMPASACK	16
32. Vangtao	16.1
33. Vennekhame	16.2
ATTAPEU	17
34. Phouyang	17.1
Special Zone	18
Headquarters	99

EMBASSIES AND CONSULATES

There are a total of 20 embassies in the Lao People's Democratic Republic:

Australia Nehru Street Vat Phonsay area. Vientiane Tel.: 41-3610, 41-3805, 41-3602

http://www.laos.embassy.gov.au/laos

Brunei Darussalam

No. 333 Unit 25 Ban Phonxay Xaysettha District Lanexang Avenue Vientiane Tel.: 856 2141 6114 Fax: 856 2141 6115 E-mail: kbnbd@laonet.net

Bulgaria

Sisangvone Area Vientiane Tel.: 41-110

Cambodia

Thadeua Road; KM2 Vientiane B.P. 34 Tel.: 31-4950/52 Fax: 31-4951 E-mail: recamlao@laotel.com

China

Vat Nak Street Sisattanak Area Vientiane Tel.: (021) 315100 Fax: (021) 315104 E-mail: embassyprc@laonet.net

Cuba

Saphathong Nua Area Vientiane Tel.: 31-4902

France

Setthathirath Road Vientiane Tel.: 21-5258, 21-5259 Fax: 21-5255

http://www.ambafrance-laos.org

Germany

26 Sokpaluang Road Vientiane Tel.: 31-2111, 31-2110 E-mail: germemb@laotel.com

India

That Luang Road Vat Phonsay Area Vientiane Tel.: 41-3802 E-mail: indemblaos@laonet.net
http://www.indianembassylao.com/laopdr.html

Indonesia

Phon Kheng Road Vientiane Tel.: 41-3910, 41-3909, 41-3907, 41-3914

Japan

Sisangvone Road Vientiane Tel.: 21-2623, 41-4400-2, 41-4406 Fax: 41-4403

Malaysia

That Luang Street, Vat Phonsay Area Vientiane Tel.: 856-21-414205/06 Fax: 856-21-414201
E-mail: mwvntian@laonet.net

Myanmar

Sokpaluang Street, Sisattanak Area Vientiane Tel.: 31-2439, 31-4910

People's Democratic Republic of Korea

Vat Nak Street, Sisattanak Vientiane Tel: 31-5261, 31-5260

Poland

Thadeua Road, Km 3 Vientiane Tel.: 31-2219, 31-2085

Russian Federation

Vientiane Tel.: 31-2219, 31-222

For additional analytical, business and investment opportunities information,
please contact Global Investment & Business Center, USA
at (703) 370-8082. Fax: (703) 370-8083. E-mail: ibpusa3@gmail.com
Global Business and Investment Info Databank - www.ibpus.com

Sweden

Sokpaluang Street, Vat Nak Vientiane Tel.: 31-5018, 31-5000, 31-3772 Fax: 31-5003

Thailand

Phonkheng Road Vientiane Tel.: 21-4582-3, 21-4585

United States of America Viet Nam

That Dam That Luang Road Vientiane Vientiane Tel.: 21-2580-2, 31-2609 Tel.: 41-3400, 41-3409, 41-3403 Fax: 21-2584

http://usembassy.state.gov/laos/wwwhmain.ht ml

The Lao People's Democratic Republic has embassies and consulates general in the following countries:

Australia	Germany
1 Dalmain Crescent O'Malley Canberra ACT 2606 Tel.: (+61 6) 286-4595, 286-6933 Fax: (+61 6) 290-1910 E-mail: lao.embassy@ interact.net.au	Bismarckallee 2A 14193 Berlin Tel.: Tel: +49(0)30 890 606 47 Fax: +49(0)30 890 606 48 http://www.laosbotschaft.de E-mail: hong@laos-botschaft.de
Belgium Av. De La Brabanconne 19-21 1000 Brussels Tel.: (+32 2) 02.7400950 Fax : (+32 2) 02.7341666 http://home.tiscali.be/rambalaobx/	India E53 Panchsheel Park New Delphi-17 Tel.: (+91 11) 642-7447 Fax: (+91 11) 642-8588
Cambodia 15-17 Thanon Keomani PO BOX 19 Phnom Penh Tel.: (+855 23) 26-441, 24-781 Fax: (+855 23) 27-454	Indonesia Jalan Kintamani Raya C-15 No 33 Kuningam Timur Jakarta 12950 Tel.: (+62 21) 520-2670, 522-9602 Fax: (+91 11) 522-9601 E-mail: laoembjktof@hotmail.com
China 11 Sanlitun Dongsie Jie Beijing 100600 Tel.: (+86 1) 532-1224 Fax: (+86 1) 532-6748. Consulate General of the Lao People's	Japan 3-3-22 Nishi-Azabu Minato-Ku Tokyo 106 Tel.: (+81 3) 5411-2291, 5411-2292 Fax: (+81 3) 5411-2293.

Democratic Republic
Room 3226 Camellia Hotel
154 East Dong Feng Road
Kunming 650041
Tel.: (+86 871) 317-6623, 317-6624
Fax: (+86 871) 317-8556

Cuba
7 Ave Calle 36 A
505 Miramar
Havana
Tel.: (+53 7) 33-1056, 33-1057, 33-1058.

France
74 Ave Raymond Poincaré
75116 Paris
Tel.: (+33 1) 4553-0298, 4554-7047
Fax: (+33 1) 4727-5789
http://www.laoparis.com

Malaysia
108 Jalan Damai
Kuala Lumpur 55000
Tel.: (+60 3) 248-3895
Fax: (+60 3) 242-0344

Mongolia
Ikh Toiruu
P.O. Box 1030
Ulaanbaatar
Tel.: (+976 1) 326-440, 329-898
E-mail: laoemb@ mongol.net

Myanmar
NA1 Diplomatic Quarters
Franser Road
Yangon
Tel.: (+95 1) 22-482, 27-445
Fax: (+95 1) 27-446

Poland
UL Rejtana 15/26
02-516 Warsaw
Tel.: (+48 22) 484-786, 488-949
Fax: (+48 22) 497-122
E-mail: embaslao@warman.com.pl

Russian Federation
Moscow 121069
UI Katchalov 18
Tel.: (+7 095) 203-1454, 291-8966
Fax: (+7 095) 290-4226

Singapore
101 Thomson Road, #05-03A, United Square
Singapore 307591
Tel.: 2506044, 2506741
Fax: 2506014
E-mail: laoembsg@singnet.com.sg

Sweden
Hornsgatan 82-B1 TR 11721
Stockholm
Tel.: (+46 8) 668-5122
Fax: (+46 8) 669-2176

United States of America
2222 S. Street NW
Washington, DC 20008
Tel.: (+1 202) 332-6416, 332-6417
Fax: (+1 202) 332-4923
http://www.laoembassy.com
E-mail: laoemb@erols.com

Viet Nam
22 Rue Tran Bing Trong
Hanoi
Tel.: (+84 4) 25-4576, 29-6746
Fax: (+84 4) 22-8414.

Consulate General of the
Lao People's Democratic Republic
181 Haiba Trung
Ho Chi Minh City
Tel.: (+84 8) 29-7667, 29-9275
Fax: (+84 8) 29-9272.

Consulate General of the
Lao People's Democratic Republic
12 Tran Quy-Cap
Danang
Tel.: (+84 51) 21-208, 24-101

Thailand 520.502/1-3 Soi Ramkhamhaeng 39 Bangkapi Bangkok 10300 Tel.: (+66 2) 538-3696, 538-3735 Fax: (+66 2) 539-6678 http://www.bkklaoembassy.com E-mail: banethok@loxinfo.co.th	Fax: (+84 51) 22-628 Permanent Mission of Lao People's Democratic Republic to the United Nations 317 East 51st Street New York, NY 10022 Tel.: (+1 212) 832-2734 Fax: (+1 212) 332-4923 http://www.un.int/lao

Sources: http://www.laoembassy.com/news/embassyabroad.htm
http://www.mofa.gov.la/Addresses/AddressOfLaoDiplomatic.htm

THE DECLARATION FORM

The declaration form or single administrative document is used for all customs transactions; import, export or transit. It must be complete to be acceptable in customs.

The declaration form has three segments.

1. In the first section(Boxes No.1-23) enter general information on importer, exporter and declarant as well as transport and transaction details.

2. In the second section (Boxes No.24-42) enter details on the item declared, including amount of duties and taxes payable or exempted.

3. Summary of Payment and Responsibility of Declaration Section.

It is presented in the form of (i.) a header sheet, which is used to declare importation, exportation or in transit information for each commodity item (ii.) continuation sheets to declare other commodity items and (iii.) section sheet for official use.
Note. Declaration forms are on sale at all Regional Customs offices.
Instructions to fill each box of the form.

Box No.1   Declaration Regime

Inscribe one of the following codes to identify the type of transaction the declaration is for:

Regime Code	Description
10	Exportation of domestic Goods
14	Exportation under a drawback regime
20	Temporary Exportation
35	Re-Exportation
40	Importation of goods for Home consumption.

4A	Importation of goods for diplomatic use, returning residents, and humanitarian assistance; samples, educational materials and certain religious articles.
4B	Goods ex-warehoused to duty free shops
4C	Goods ex-warehoused for exportation out of Lao PDR
45	Home Consumption of Goods after temporary admission
47	Home Consumption of Goods entered under a warehousing regime
50	Temporary Importation
62	Re-Importation of Goods Exported temporarily
70	Warehousing of Goods
80	Transit

Office Codes.

Enter the code of the office where the declaration is presented. See Annex I for a list of all customs offices and their codes.

Manifest /Airway bill number.

Enter the cargo control number from the air waybill if the goods arrive or leave by air or from the manifest if goods arrive or leave by any other mode of transport.
Declaration Number and Date.

Customs will assign the declaration number and the date when the declaration is presented and registered with customs.

Box No.2   Exporter and Address

If you enter goods for exportation, indicate your name and address as well as the taxpayer identification number (TIN) issued by the Tax Department. If you have not yet been issued a TIN please obtain a number from the nearest tax office and use it on all subsequent customs declarations. Also include your office telephone number. For diplomatic and personal exportations, leave the number field blank.

Box No.3   Gross Mass Kg.

Indicate the gross weight in kilograms of the entire consignment of goods as declared on the manifest or air waybill.

Box No.4   Items

Indicate the total number of items as shown on the invoice.

Box No.5   Total Packages.

Indicate the total number of packages as declared on the manifest or airway bill. In case of bulk cargo, indicate BULK only.

Box No. 6   Importer and Address

If you enter goods for importation, indicate your name and address as well as the taxpayer identification number (TIN) issued by the Tax Department. If you have not been issued a TIN please obtain a number from the nearest tax office and use it on all subsequent customs declarations. Also include your office telephone number. For diplomatic and personal importations, leave the number field blank.

Box No.7   Consignee.

If you are importing goods on behalf of another person, or the other party holds title to the good at time of importation indicate the name and address of the consignee as well as the TIN issued by the Tax Department. Please contact the nearest tax office for a number and use on all subsequent declarations, or obtain the TIN number from the consignee if one has been issued to the consignee by the tax department. For diplomatic importations, leave the number field blank.

Box No.8   Declarant.

If you are a licensed agent authorized to transact business in customs, enter the TIN issued by the Tax Department. If you do not have a TIN, contact the nearest tax office.

Box No.9   Country of Consignment/Destination.

For importation, indicate the country and the code from where the goods have been consigned. For exportation, indicate the country and the code to where the goods are exported or re-exported.

See Annex II: List of Country and Currency Codes.

Box No.10   Type of License.

Indicate the type of trade or industry license held by you.

Box. No.11   Delivery Terms.

Indicate the terms of delivery of goods either CIF for importation, or FOB for exportation.

Box No.12   Total Invoice in Foreign Currency.

For importation, indicate the total amount of the invoice in foreign currency. See list of Country and Currency Codes in Annex II.

Box No.13   Total Invoice in Local Currency.

Enter here the total value of the invoice in Kip by converting the value declared in box No. 12 with the rate of exchange indicated in box No.16. If there is only one item, this value should correspond to the value declared in box no.38. If there are many items, the total value should correspond to the total of values declared in all the boxes no.38 on the Continuation sheets.

Box No.14   Total FOB (Exports)

Indicate the FOB value of the goods in foreign currency.

(if known)
Box No. 14   Total FOB (Imports)

Enter the FOB value in foreign currency. (if known)

Box No.15   Total FOB Ncy (Import/Export)

For import, leave blank.
For export, indicate the FOB value of the goods in Kip.

Box No.16   Rate of Exchange.

Indicate the rate of exchange of the foreign currency to the Kip and the code of the foreign currency. (The exchange rate shall be that which is in force at time of importation, unless otherwise advised).

Box No.17   Mode of Transport.

Indicate the mode of transport, the voyage number. Also the country code of the nationality of the aircraft, truck or ship.
(if known)

The codes for mode of transport are:

SEA	1
RAIL	2
ROAD	3
AIR	4

Box No.18   Port of Loading/Unloading.

For imports indicate the name and the code of the foreign country where goods are loaded,
For exports, indicate the name and the code of the foreign country where goods are destined.

See Annex II for a list of Country Codes.

Box No.19   Place of Shipping/ Landing.

For imports, indicate the place in Lao PDR where goods have arrived. At export, or re-export, indicate the place in Lao PDR from where the goods are exported or re-exported.

Box No.20   Entry/Exit Office.

Indicate the code of the Lao customs office where the declaration is presented for clearance.

In a transit operation, indicate the code of the customs office where the transit operation commences. Also indicate the code of the exit customs office where the transit operations is to be terminated.

Box No.21   Identification Warehouse (Leave blank until bonded warehouses are established)

Indicate the code of the bonded warehouse where goods are to be warehoused or ex-warehoused.

Box No.22   Financial and Banking Data.

Indicate the terms of payment of the transaction, as well as the name of the bank and the branch where payment for the commercial transaction is made.

Box No.23   Attached Documents.

Indicate the codes of attached documents, which support your declaration. (Documents must be originals or certified as true copies).

1		Invoice
2		Manifest
3		Airway bill
4		Packing List
5		Certificate of Origin (If required)
6		Phytosanitary Certificate (If required)
7		Import Permit from Ministry of Trade (If required)
8		Import permit from Ministry of Agriculture (If required)
9		Import Permit from Ministry of Heath (If required)
10		Authorization from Department of Transport (If required)
11		If claiming duty and tax exemptions, documents authorizing such exemptions must be presented with the declaration.

Box No.24   Marks, Numbers and Description of Goods

Indicate the marks and numbers of the packages as shown on the manifest or airway bill.

If goods arrive or leave by containers, indicate the container number as shown on the manifest.

The total number of packages should correspond to the total number of packages indicated in box No.5.

Give a detailed description of the goods. Avoid, as far as possible, trade names. Except in the case of vehicles and electronic devices, provide make and model.

Box No.25   No. of Items.

Indicate the number of items on the invoice.

Box No.26   Tariff Code

Indicate the classification code of the commodity imported. This classification code in based on the AHTN and must be eight digits.

Box No.27   Customs Procedure Codes.
 (Leave blank at this time)

Box No.28   Country of Origin/Destination

For imports, indicate the code of the country of origin of the goods imported, if the country of origin of the goods is different from the country where the goods have been consigned.

Box No.29   Zone.

It the goods originate from ASEAN member countries and are supported by a certificate of origin enter ASEAN. For other countries enter GEN. At export enter XPT.

Box No.30   Valuation Code

Indicate the code of the valuation method used to determine the customs value for duty.

There are six valuation methods and coded as follows:

	VALUATION METHOD	Code	
	Transaction Method	1	
	Identical Goods Method	2	
	Similar Goods Method	3	
	Deductive Method	4	
	Computed Method	5	
	Flexible Method	6	

Note: The transaction valuation method must be used as the primary method for valuation if possible.

Box No.31   Gross Mass.

Enter the gross weight in kilograms for the item on the first page only. The total weight of all items on the continuation sheets in the declaration should be equal to the weight declared in box no.3 of the general segment.

Box No.32   Net Mass.

Enter the net weight of the goods in kilograms for each item declared. If a continuation sheet is used a net mass must be inscribed for each item.

Box No.33   FOB Foreign Currency.

Enter the FOB value of the item in foreign currency (if known).

Box No.34   FOB Local Currency, only if transport and insurance are not prepaid by exporter. If prepaid, enter the value that includes transportation and insurance.

Enter the FOB value of the item in Kips, only if transport and insurance are not prepaid by exporter. If prepaid, enter the value that includes transportation and insurance.

Box No. 35   Freight.

Enter the amount of freight paid or payable for the item in Kip. For a shipment of various items, the freight charges are apportioned according to freight paid or payable and by weight. If freight is prepaid by exporter and included in the value, mark the box "Prepaid".

Box No.36   Insurance.

Enter the amount of insurance in Kip for the item.

For a shipment of various items, the insurance paid or payable is to be apportioned.

If the insurance is prepaid by the exporter and included in the value, mark the box "prepaid"

Box No.37   Other Costs.
Enter other costs and expenses incurred for the import of goods and paid to the exporter for the imported goods.

Box No.38   Customs Value in Local Currency.

Enter the customs value for the item, which is the total of values of boxes 33, 34, 35 and 36.

Box No. 39   Supplementary Unit/Quantity.

Some of the most common international units of quantity are as follows:

	Unit	Code	
	Cubic Metre	MTQ	
	Gigawatt-hour	GWH	
	Hundred	CEN	
	Kilogram	KGM	
	Litre	LTR	
	Metre	MTR	
	Number	NMB	
	Number of packs	NMP	
	Square Metre	MTK	
	Ten	TEN	
	Ten Pairs	TPR	
	Thousand	MIL	
	Tonne	TNE	

Enter any of the code, which describes the unit quantity of goods imported/exported. If the units of imports or exports are not included in this list, consult a customs officer for more detailed lists.

Box No.40   Duty Payable.

Enter the amount of duties and taxes payable for the item declared per category of duty, tax and excise.

For additional analytical, business and investment opportunities information,
please contact Global Investment & Business Center, USA
at (703) 370-8082. Fax: (703) 370-8083. E-mail: ibpusa3@gmail.com
Global Business and Investment Info Databank - www.ibpus.com

Enter also the taxable base for each category of duty, tax and excise. Duty rate is calculated on the Customs value. The tax is calculated on the customs value plus the duty payable. The excise tax is calculated on the customs value plus duty payable plus tax payable.

For other items of the declaration, on the continuation sheets enter the duty, tax and excise payable.

Box No.41   Permit Numbers.

Enter permit number and date of issue for the shipment, if required.

Box No.42   Previous Declaration.

If the declaration refers to a previous declaration, the registration number and date of the previous declaration is entered here.

Present a copy of the previous declaration with the declaration you have just prepared.

Responsibility of Declaration

You must enter your full name, indicate the capacity in which you are acting. And sign the declaration.

You must also indicate the mode of payment by which duty and taxes are to be paid.

After you have completed your declaration, trader can now lodge it at the designated customs office where your goods are held.

After customs review and approval of the declaration, please make the payment of all applicable duties and taxes, and present a copy of the payment receipt to the customs office where the declaration was presented.

On receipt of the customs release note, present the release note to the warehouse keeper for delivery of the imported goods and sign for receipt of the goods or have the carrier sign for receipt.

LAOS GLOSSARY

Asian Development Bank
   Established in 1967, the bank assists in economic development and promotes growth and cooperation in developing member countries. The bank is owned by its forty-seven member governments, which include both developed and developing countries in Asia and developed countries in the West.

Association of Southeast Asian Nations (ASEAN)
   Founded in 1967 primarily for economic cooperation and consisting of Brunei (since 1984), Indonesia, Malaysia, the Philippines, Singapore, and Thailand. Laos has had observer status since 1992 and applied for membership in July 1994.

ban
   Village; grouped administratively into *tasseng* (q.v.) and *muang* (q.v.).

dharma

Buddhist teaching or moral law; laws of nature, all that exists, real or imaginary.

fiscal year (FY)
October 1 to September 30.

gross domestic product (GDP)
A value measure of the flow of domestic goods and services produced by an economy over a period of time, such as a year. Only output values of goods for final consumption and intermediate production are assumed to be included in the final prices. GDP is sometimes aggregated and shown at market prices, meaning that indirect taxes and subsidies are included; when these indirect taxes and subsidies have been eliminated, the result is GDP at factor cost. The word *gross* indicates that deductions for depreciation of physical assets have not been made. Income arising from investments and possessions owned abroad is not included, only domestic production. Hence, the use of the word *domestic* to distinguish GDP from gross national product (*q.v.*).

gross national product (GNP)
The gross domestic product (GDP--*q.v.*) plus net income or loss stemming from transactions with foreign countries, including income received from abroad by residents and subtracting payments remitted abroad to nonresidents. GNP is the broadest measurement of the output of goods and services by an economy. It can be calculated at market prices, which include indirect taxes and subsidies. Because indirect taxes and subsidies are only transfer payments, GNP is often calculated at factor cost by removing indirect taxes and subsidies.

Hmong
Largest Lao Sung (*q.v.*) ethnic group of northern Laos. This tribal group dwells at higher elevations than other ethnic groups. During the period of the Royal Lao Government (RLG) (*q.v.*), the Hmong were referred to as Meo.

International Monetary Fund (IMF)
Established on July 22, 1944, the IMF began operating along with the World Bank (*q.v.*) on December 27, 1945. The IMF is a specialized agency affiliated with the United Nations that takes responsibility for stabilizing international exchange rates and payments. The IMF's main business is the provision of loans to its members when they experience balance of payments difficulties. These loans often carry conditions that require substantial internal economic adjustments by the recipients. In 1994 the IMF had 179 members.

karma
Buddhist concept of the sum of one's past actions, which affect one's current life and future reincarnations.

khoueng
Province; first order administrative division.

kip(k)
Lao currency. In June 1994, US$1=R721.

Lao Issara
Free Laos. Movement formed in 1945 to resist any attempt to return to French colonial status.

Lao Loum

Literally translated as the valley Laotian. Inclusive term for people of Tai stock living in Laos, including lowland Lao and upland Tai. Group of lowland peoples comprising the majority population of Laos; generally used to refer to ethnic Lao, the country's dominant ethnic group (approximately 66 percent of the population according to the 1985 census), and speaking Tai-Kadai languages, including Lao, Lue, Tai Dam (Black Tai), and Tai Deng (Red Tai).

Lao Patrocitic Front (LPF) (Neo Lao Hak Xat)

Sucessor to Neo Lao Issara (q.v.), the political arm of the Pathrt Liberation Army (q.v.)--formerly known as the Pathet Lao (q.v.)--is its milituary arm.

Lao People's Army

Formed in 1976 when the Lao People's Liberation Army (LPLA-- q.v.) was restructured after the establishment of the Lao People's Democratic Republic in December 1975.

Lao People's Liberation Army (LPLA)

Official title of Pathet Lao armed forces, more commonly known as the communist revolutionaries, or guerrilla forces. The LPLA originated with the Latsavong detachment, formed in January 1949 by Kaysone Phomvihan, and steadily increased in number to an estimated 8,000 guerrillas in 1960 and an estimated 48,000 troops between 1962 and 1970.

Lao People's Revolutionary Party (LPRP) (Phak Pasason Pativat Lao)

Founded secretly in 1955 as the Phak Pasason Lao (Lao People's Party--LPP); name changed in 1972. Seized full power and became the ruling (communist) party of Laos in 1975. The LPRP Central Committee formulates party policy; it is dominated by the Political Bureau (Politburo) and the Secretariat and maintains control by placing its members in key institutions throughout the government and the army.

Lao Sung

Literally translated as the Laotian of the mountain top--those who traditionally live in the high altitudes in northern Laos. In official use, term denotes a category of ethnic groups that speak Tibeto-Burmese, Miao-Yao languages; chiefly the Hmong (q.v.) (Meo) group of highland or upland minorities but also the Mien (Yao) and Akha. According to the 1985 census, these groups make up approximately 10 percent of the population.

Lao Theung

Literally, Laotian of the mountain slopes; group--including Kammu, Loven, and Lamet--that traditionally lives in medium altitudes, practices swidden, or slash-and-burn-agriculture, and speaks Mon-Khmer languages and dialects. According to the 1985 census, approximately 24 percent of the population. Regarded as original inhabitants of Laos, formally referred to by ethnic Lao as *kha*, or slave.

mandala

Indian geopolitical term referring to a variable circle of power centered on a ruler, his palace, and the religious center from which he drew his legitimization.

muang (*muong*)

Administrative district; also an independent principality; comprises several *tasseng* (q.v.), second order administrative divisions.

Lao Patriotic Front (LPF) (Neo Lao Hak Xat)

For additional analytical, business and investment opportunities information, please contact Global Investment & Business Center, USA at (703) 370-8082. Fax: (703) 370-8083. E-mail: ibpusa3@gmail.com Global Business and Investment Info Databank - www.ibpus.com

Successor to Neo Lao Issara (*q.v.*), the political arm of the Pathet Lao (*q.v.*) during the Indochina Wars (1946- 75). The Lao People's Liberation Army (*q.v.*)--formerly known as the Pathet Lao (*q.v.*)--is its military arm.

Neo Lao Issara

Free Laos Front--organization established by former Lao Issara (Free Laos) (*q.v.*) to continue anti-French resistance movement with the Viet Minh (*q.v.*); succeeded by Neo Lao Hak Xat (Lao Patriotic Front--LPF) (*q.v.*) in 1956.

net material product

Gross material output minus depreciation on capital and excluding "unproductive services." According to the World Bank (*q.v.*), net material product is "a socialist concept of national accounts."

Nonaligned Movement

Established in September 1961 with the aim of promoting political and military cooperation apart from the traditional East and West blocs. As of 1994, there were 107 members (plus the Palestine Liberation Organization), twenty-one observers, and twenty-one "guests."

Pathet Lao (Lao Nation)

Literally, land of the Lao. Until October 1965, the name for the Lao People's Liberation Army (*q.v.*), the military arm of the Lao Patriotic Front (*q.v.*).

Royal Lao Government (RLG)

The ruling authority in Laos from 1947 until the communist seizure of power in December 1975 and the proclamation of the Lao People's Democratic Republic.

Sipsong Panna

Region in southern Yunnan Province, China, from which migrated many groups that now inhabit Laos.

Southeast Asia Treaty Organization (SEATO)

Established in September 1954 as a result of the 1954 Geneva Agreements to stop the spread of communism in Southeast Asia. SEATO never had an active military role and was ultimately disbanded in June 1977 following the success of the communist movements in Cambodia, Laos, and Vietnam in 1975. Original signatories to SEATO were Australia, Britain, France, New Zealand, Pakistan, the Philippines, Thailand, and the United States.

tasseng

Administrative unit; territorial subdivision of *muang* (*q.v.*), subdistrict grouping of ten to twenty villages.

That Luang

Most sacred Buddhist stupa in Vientiane and site of annual festival on the full moon of the twelfth month.

Theravada Buddhism

Predominant branch of Buddhism practiced in Laos, Cambodia, Sri Lanka, and Thailand.

United Nations Children's Fund (UNICEF)

Acronym retained from predecessor organization, United Nations International Children's Emergency Fund, established in December 1946. Provides funds for establishing child health and welfare services.

United Nations Development Programme (UNDP)

Created by the United Nations in 1965, the UNDP is the world's largest channel for multilateral technical and preinvestment assistance to low-income countries. It functions as an overall programming, financing, and monitoring agency. The actual fieldwork is done by other UN agencies.

United Nations High Commissioner for Refugees (UNHCR)

Established by the United Nations in 1949, it did not become effective until 1951. The first world institution to aid refugees, the UNHCR seeks to ensure the humanitarian treatment of refugees and find a permanent solution to refugee problems. The agency deals with the international protection of refugees and problems arising from mass movements of people forced to seek refuge.

Viet Minh

Coalition of Vietnamese national elements formed in May 1941 and dominated by the communists in their movement calling for an uprising against the French colonial government.

World Bank

Informal name used to designate a group of four affiliated international institutions: the International Bank for Reconstruction and Development (IBRD), the International Development Association (IDA), the International Finance Corporation (IFC), and the Multilateral Investment Guarantee Agency (MIGA). The IBRD, established in 1945, has as its primary purpose the provision of loans at market-related rates of interest to developing countries at more advanced stages of development. The IDA, a legally separate loan fund but administered by the staff of the IBRD, was set up in 1960 to furnish credits to the poorest developing countries on much easier terms than those of conventional IBRD loans. The IFC, founded in 1956, supplements the activities of the IBRD through loans and assistance designed specifically to encourage the growth of productive private enterprises in the less developed countries. The MIGA, founded in 1988, insures private foreign investment in developing countries against various noncommercial risk. The president and certain senior officers of the IBRD hold the same positions in the IFC. The four institutions are owned by the governments of the countries that subscribe their capital. To participate in the World Bank group, member states must first belong to the Intentional Monetary Fund (IMF--*q.v.*).

SELECTED TOUR OPERATORS IN LAOS

The following list is issued by the National Tourism Authority of Lao PDR. This is not an exhaustive list of travel companies. You are advised to contact the travel company directly for their up-to-date itineraries and prices.

Dafi Travel Co., Ltd
093/4 Samsenthai St,
P.O. Box 5351,
Vientiane

Lao Tourism Co., Ltd
08/02 Lane Xang Ave,
P.O. Box 2511,
Vientiane

Luang Prabang Tourism Co., Ltd
P.O. Box 356,
Sisavangvong Rd,
Luang Prabang.

Phathanakhet Phoudoi Travel Co., Ltd
Phonxay Rd,
P.O. Box 5796,
Vientiane

Phathana Saysomboune Travel & Tour Co., Ltd
Km 5, 13 South Rd,
12/G Chommanytai

Xaysetha DTR,
P.O. Box 7117,
Vientiane

Chackavane Travel & Tour
92 Thongkankham Rd,
P.O. Box 590,
Vientiane

Raja Tour
03 Heng boon St,
P.O. Box 3655,
Vientiane

Sode Tour
114 Quai Fa Ngum,
P.O. Box 70,
Vientiane

LAO PDR EMBASSIES AND CONSULATES-GENERAL

Country	Address
Brunei Darussalam	Embassy of the Lao PDR Tel : 673-2-345 666 Fax : 456-888
Cambodia	Embassy of the Lao PDR 15-17 Mao Tse Tung Boulvard P.O. Box 19 Phnom Penh Tel : 855-23-982 632 Fax : 720 907
Indonesia	Embassy of the Lao PDR Jl. Patra Kuningan XIV No.1.A Kuningan Jakarta Selatan - 12950 Tel : 62-21-522 9602, 522 7862 Fax : 522 9601
Malaysia	Embassy of the Lao PDR I Lorong Damai Tiga Kuala Lumpur 55000 Tel : 60-3-248 3895, Residence: 245 6023 HP : 60-012 218 0075 Fax : 60-3- 242 0344
Myanmar	Embassy of the Lao PDR NA I Diplomatic Quarters Franser Road Yangon Tel : 95-1-222 482, 227 445 Fax : 227 446
The Philippines	Embassy of the Lao PDR N. 34 Lapu-Lapu Street Magallences Village Makati City, Manila Tel & Fax : 63-2-833 5759

Singapore	Embassy of the Lao PDR 179-B Gold Hill Centre Thomson Road Tel : 65-250 6044 Fax : 65-250 6214
Thailand	Embassy of the Lao PDR 520-502/ 1-3 Soi Ramkhamheng 39 Bangkapi Bangkok 10310 Tel : 539 6667 Fax : 66-2-539 6678 Consulate General of the Lao PDR Khonkaen Tel : 66-43-223 698, 223 473, 221 961 Fax : 223 849
Vietnam	Embassy of the Lao PDR 22 Rue Tran Bing Trong Hanoi Tel : 84-4-8- 25 4576, 29 6746 Fax : 22 8414 Consulate General of the LAO PDR 93 Larteur ST, District 1 Ho Chi Minh City Tel : 84-8-8- 29 7667, 29 9275 Fax : 29 9272 Consulate General of the LAO PDR 12 Tran Quy-Cap Danang Tel : 84-51-8- 21 208, 24 101 Fax : 22 628
Australia	Embassy of the Lao PDR I Dalman Crescent O' Malley Canberra ACT 2606 Tel : 61-2- 6286 4595, 6286 6933 Fax : 6290 1910
China	Embassy of the Lao PDR 11 Salitun Dongsie Jie Bejing 100 600 IfsTel : 86-1- 6532 1224 Fax : 6532 6748 Consulate General of the Lao PDR Room 3226 Camellia Hotel 154 East Dong Feng Road Kunming 650041 Tel : 86-871- 317 6623, 317 6624 Fax : 317 8556

For additional analytical, business and investment opportunities information,
please contact Global Investment & Business Center, USA
at (703) 370-8082. Fax: (703) 370-8083. E-mail: ibpusa3@gmail.com
Global Business and Investment Info Databank - www.ibpus.com

France	Embassy of the Lao PDR 74 Ave Raymond Poincare 75116 Paris Tel : 33-1- 4553 0298, 4553 7047 Fax : 4727 5789
Germany	Embassy of the Lao PDR Am Lessing 6 53639 Koeningswinter Tel : 49- 2223 21501 Fax : 2223 3065
India	Embassy of the Lao PDR E53 Panchsheel Park New Delhi-17 Tel : 91-11-642 7447 Fax : 642 8588
Japan	Embassy of the Lao PDR 3-3-22 Nishi-Azabu Minato-Ku Tokyo 106 Tel : 81-3-5411 2291, 5411 2292 Fax : 5411 2293
Russia	Embassy of the Lao PDR UI Katchalova 18 Moscow 121 069 Tel : 7-095-203 1454, 291 8966 Fax : 290 4246, 291 7218
Sweden	Embassy of the Lao PDR Badstrandvagen 11 11265 Stockholm Tel : 46-8-618 2010, 695 0160 Fax : 618 2001
United States of America	Embassy of the Lao PDR 2222 S Street NW Washington DC 10022 Tel : 1-202- 332 6416, 332 6417 Fax : 332 4923 Permanent Mission of the Lao PDR 317 East 51st Street New York, NY 10022 Tel : 1-212- 832 2734 Fax : 750 0039

For additional analytical, business and investment opportunities information,
please contact Global Investment & Business Center, USA
at (703) 370-8082. Fax: (703) 370-8083. E-mail: ibpusa3@gmail.com
Global Business and Investment Info Databank - www.ibpus.com

BASIC TITLE FOR LAOS

IMPORTANT!
All publications are updated annually!
Please contact IBP, Inc. at ibpusa3@gmail.com for the latest ISBNs and additional information

TITLE
Lao People's Democratic Republic Traders and Investors Handbook
Lao People's Democratic Republic Traders and Investors Handbook
Laos A "Spy" Guide - Strategic Information and Developments
Laos A Spy" Guide"
Laos Business and Investment Opportunities Yearbook
Laos Business and Investment Opportunities Yearbook
Laos Business and Investment Opportunities Yearbook Volume 1 Strategic Information and Opportunities
Laos Business Intelligence Report - Practical Information, Opportunities, Contacts
Laos Business Intelligence Report - Practical Information, Opportunities, Contacts
Laos Business Law Handbook - Strategic Information and Basic Laws
Laos Business Law Handbook - Strategic Information and Basic Laws
Laos Business Law Handbook - Strategic Information and Basic Laws
Laos Business Law Handbook - Strategic Information and Basic Laws
Laos Clothing & Textile Industry Handbook
Laos Clothing & Textile Industry Handbook
Laos Company Laws and Regulations Handbook
Laos Country Study Guide - Strategic Information and Developments
Laos Country Study Guide - Strategic Information and Developments
Laos Country Study Guide - Strategic Information and Developments Volume 1 Strategic Information and Developments
Laos Customs, Trade Regulations and Procedures Handbook
Laos Customs, Trade Regulations and Procedures Handbook
Laos Diplomatic Handbook - Strategic Information and Developments
Laos Diplomatic Handbook - Strategic Information and Developments
Laos Ecology & Nature Protection Handbook
Laos Ecology & Nature Protection Handbook
Laos Ecology & Nature Protection Laws and Regulation Handbook
Laos Economic & Development Strategy Handbook
Laos Economic & Development Strategy Handbook
Laos Education System and Policy Handbook
Laos Energy Policy, Laws and Regulation Handbook
Laos Export-Import Trade and Business Directory
Laos Export-Import Trade and Business Directory
Laos Foreign Policy and Government Guide
Laos Foreign Policy and Government Guide
Laos Industrial and Business Directory
Laos Industrial and Business Directory

TITLE
Laos Internet and E-Commerce Investment and Business Guide - Strategic and Practical Information: Regulations and Opportunities
Laos Internet and E-Commerce Investment and Business Guide - Strategic and Practical Information: Regulations and Opportunities
Laos Investment and Business Guide - Strategic and Practical Information
Laos Investment and Business Guide - Strategic and Practical Information
Laos Investment and Business Guide - Strategic and Practical Information
Laos Investment and Business Guide - Strategic and Practical Information
Laos Investment and Trade Laws and Regulations Handbook
Laos Justice System and National Police Handbook
Laos Justice System and National Police Handbook
Laos Medical & Pharmaceutical Industry Handbook
Laos Medical & Pharmaceutical Industry Handbook
Laos Mineral & Mining Sector Investment and Business Guide - Strategic and Practical Information
Laos Mineral, Mining Sector Investment and Business Guide - Strategic and Practical Information
Laos Mining Laws and Regulations Handbook
Laos Recent Economic and Political Developments Yearbook
Laos Recent Economic and Political Developments Yearbook
Laos Recent Economic and Political Developments Yearbook
Laos Research & Development Policy Handbook
Laos Research & Development Policy Handbook
Laos Research & Development Policy Handbook
Laos Starting Business (Incorporating) in....Guide
Laos Taxation Laws and Regulations Handbook
Laos Telecom Laws and Regulations Handbook
Laos Telecommunication Industry Business Opportunities Handbook
Laos Telecommunication Industry Business Opportunities Handbook
Laos Traders Manual: Export-Import, Trade, Investment
Laos Transportation Policy and Regulations Handbook
Laos: How to Invest, Start and Run Profitable Business in Laos Guide - Practical Information, Opportunities, Contacts

BASIC LAWS AND REGULATIONS AFFECTING BUSINESS[4]

COUTRY	LAW TITLE

Lao DPR	Constitution of the Lao PDR
Lao DPR	Decree on Commercial Banks
Lao DPR	Decree On Organization and Activities of the National Statistical System
Lao DPR	Decree on Procurement
Lao DPR	Decree on the Organization and Activities of the Bank Of Lao PDR
Lao DPR	Forest Law

[4] For ordering texts of specific laws in English, French, or otehr languages, please contact Global Investment Center USA at ibpusa3@gmail.com

Lao DPR	Intellectual Property Law
Lao DPR	Law governing the Management of Foreign Exchange and Precious Metals
Lao DPR	Law on Agriculture
Lao DPR	Law on Anti-Corruption
Lao DPR	Law on Bankruptcy on Enterprises
Lao DPR	Law on Civil Aviation
Lao DPR	Law on Civil Procedure
Lao DPR	Law on Commercial Banks
Lao DPR	Law on Contract
Lao DPR	Law on Court Fees
Lao DPR	Law on Criminal Procedure
Lao DPR	Law on Customs
Lao DPR	Law on Development and Protection of Women
Lao DPR	Law on Drugs and Medical Products
Lao DPR	Law on Electricity
Lao DPR	Law on Enterprise
Lao DPR	Law on Enterprise Accounting
Lao DPR	Law on Environmental Protection
Lao DPR	Law on Family
Lao DPR	Law on Family Registration
Lao DPR	Law on Food
Lao DPR	Law on Health Care
Lao DPR	Law on Heritage and Basis of Inheritance
Lao DPR	Law on Hygiene, Disease Prevention and Health Promotion
Lao DPR	Law on Industrial Processing
Lao DPR	Law on Insurance
Lao DPR	Law on Judgment Enforcement
Lao DPR	Law on Labor
Lao DPR	Law on Land
Lao DPR	Law on Land Traffic
Lao DPR	Law on Land Transport
Lao DPR	Law on Lao Nationality
Lao DPR	Law on Local Administration
Lao DPR	Law on Mining
Lao DPR	Law on National Defense Obligations
Lao DPR	Law on National Heritage
Lao DPR	Law on Notary Offices
Lao DPR	Law on Postal Services
Lao DPR	Law on Property
Lao DPR	Law on Public Roads
Lao DPR	Law on Resolution of Economic Disputes
Lao DPR	Law on Resolution of Economic Disputes
Lao DPR	Law on Secured Transactions
Lao DPR	Law on State Assets
Lao DPR	Law on State Budget
Lao DPR	Law on Tax
Lao DPR	Law on Telecommunications
Lao DPR	Law on the Bank of the Lao PDR
Lao DPR	Law on the Election of Members of the National Assembly

Lao DPR	Law on the Government of the Lao People's Democratic Republic
Lao DPR	Law on the Handling of Petitions
Lao DPR	Law on the National Assembly
Lao DPR	Law on the People's Court
Lao DPR	Law on the Promotion of Domestic Investment
Lao DPR	Law on the Promotion of Foreign Investment
Lao DPR	Law on the Promotion of Investment
Lao DPR	Law on the Protection of the Rights and Interests of Children
Lao DPR	Law on Tort
Lao DPR	Law on Tourism
Lao DPR	Law on Urban Plans
Lao DPR	Law on Value Added Tax
Lao DPR	Law on Water and Water Resources
Lao DPR	Mining Law
Lao DPR	Penal Law
Lao DPR	Wildlife and Aquatic Law

WORLD BUSINESS SUCCESS GUIDES LIBRARY

EVERYTHING YOU NEED FOR SUCCESFUL BUSINESS WORLDWIDE

World Business Information Catalog, USA: http://www.ibpus.com

Email: ibpusa@comcast.net.

Price: $99.95 Each

TITLE
Abkhazia (Republic of Abkhazia) Business Success Guide - Basic Practical Information and Contacts
Afghanistan Business Success Guide - Basic Practical Information and Contacts
Aland Business Success Guide - Basic Practical Information and Contacts
Albania Business Success Guide - Basic Practical Information and Contacts
Algeria Business Success Guide - Basic Practical Information and Contacts
Andorra Business Success Guide - Basic Practical Information and Contacts
Angola Business Success Guide - Basic Practical Information and Contacts
Anguilla Business Success Guide - Basic Practical Information and Contacts
Antigua and Barbuda Business Success Guide - Basic Practical Information and Contacts
Antilles (Netherlands) Business Success Guide - Basic Practical Information and Contacts
Argentina Business Success Guide - Basic Practical Information and Contacts
Armenia Business Success Guide - Basic Practical Information and Contacts
Aruba Business Success Guide - Basic Practical Information and Contacts
Australia Business Success Guide - Basic Practical Information and Contacts
Austria Business Success Guide - Basic Practical Information and Contacts
Azerbaijan Business Success Guide - Basic Practical Information and Contacts
Bahamas Business Success Guide - Basic Practical Information and Contacts
Bahrain Business Success Guide - Basic Practical Information and Contacts
Bangladesh Business Success Guide - Basic Practical Information and Contacts
Barbados Business Success Guide - Basic Practical Information and Contacts
Belarus Business Success Guide - Basic Practical Information and Contacts
Belgium Business Success Guide - Basic Practical Information and Contacts
Belize Business Success Guide - Basic Practical Information and Contacts
Benin Business Success Guide - Basic Practical Information and Contacts
Bermuda Business Success Guide - Basic Practical Information and Contacts
Bhutan Business Success Guide - Basic Practical Information and Contacts
Bolivia Business Success Guide - Basic Practical Information and Contacts
Bosnia and Herzegovina Business Success Guide - Basic Practical Information and Contacts
Botswana Business Success Guide - Basic Practical Information and Contacts
Brazil Business Success Guide - Basic Practical Information and Contacts
Brunei Business Success Guide - Basic Practical Information and Contacts
Bulgaria Business Success Guide - Basic Practical Information and Contacts
Burkina Faso Business Success Guide - Basic Practical Information and Contacts
Burundi Business Success Guide - Basic Practical Information and Contacts
Cambodia Business Success Guide - Basic Practical Information and Contacts
Cameroon Business Success Guide - Basic Practical Information and Contacts

For additional analytical, business and investment opportunities information,
Please contact Global Investment & Business Center, USA
at (202) 546-2103. Fax: (202) 546-3275. E-mail: ibpusa3@gmail.com

TITLE
Canada Business Success Guide - Basic Practical Information and Contacts
Cape Verde Business Success Guide - Basic Practical Information and Contacts
Cayman Islands Business Success Guide - Basic Practical Information and Contacts
Central African Republic Business Success Guide - Basic Practical Information and Contacts
Chad Business Success Guide - Basic Practical Information and Contacts
Chile Business Success Guide - Basic Practical Information and Contacts
China Business Success Guide - Basic Practical Information and Contacts
Colombia Business Success Guide - Basic Practical Information and Contacts
Comoros Business Success Guide - Basic Practical Information and Contacts
Congo Business Success Guide - Basic Practical Information and Contacts
Congo, Democratic Republic Business Success Guide - Basic Practical Information and Contacts
Cook Islands Business Success Guide - Basic Practical Information and Contacts
Costa Rica Business Success Guide - Basic Practical Information and Contacts
Cote d'Ivoire Business Success Guide - Basic Practical Information and Contacts
Croatia Business Success Guide - Basic Practical Information and Contacts
Cuba Business Success Guide - Basic Practical Information and Contacts
Cyprus Business Success Guide - Basic Practical Information and Contacts
Czech Republic Business Success Guide - Basic Practical Information and Contacts
Denmark Business Success Guide - Basic Practical Information and Contacts
Djibouti Business Success Guide - Basic Practical Information and Contacts
Dominica Business Success Guide - Basic Practical Information and Contacts
Dominican Republic Business Success Guide - Basic Practical Information and Contacts
Ecuador Business Success Guide - Basic Practical Information and Contacts
Egypt Business Success Guide - Basic Practical Information and Contacts
El Salvador Business Success Guide - Basic Practical Information and Contacts
Equatorial Guinea Business Success Guide - Basic Practical Information and Contacts
Eritrea Business Success Guide - Basic Practical Information and Contacts
Estonia Business Success Guide - Basic Practical Information and Contacts
Ethiopia Business Success Guide - Basic Practical Information and Contacts
Falkland Islands Business Success Guide - Basic Practical Information and Contacts
Faroes Islands Business Success Guide - Basic Practical Information and Contacts
Fiji Business Success Guide - Basic Practical Information and Contacts
Finland Business Success Guide - Basic Practical Information and Contacts
France Business Success Guide - Basic Practical Information and Contacts
Gabon Business Success Guide - Basic Practical Information and Contacts
Gambia Business Success Guide - Basic Practical Information and Contacts
Georgia Business Success Guide - Basic Practical Information and Contacts
Germany Business Success Guide - Basic Practical Information and Contacts
Ghana Business Success Guide - Basic Practical Information and Contacts
Gibraltar Business Success Guide - Basic Practical Information and Contacts
Greece Business Success Guide - Basic Practical Information and Contacts
Greenland Business Success Guide - Basic Practical Information and Contacts
Grenada Business Success Guide - Basic Practical Information and Contacts
Guam Business Success Guide - Basic Practical Information and Contacts
Guatemala Business Success Guide - Basic Practical Information and Contacts
Guernsey Business Success Guide - Basic Practical Information and Contacts

For additional analytical, business and investment opportunities information,
Please contact Global Investment & Business Center, USA
at (202) 546-2103. Fax: (202) 546-3275. E-mail: ibpusa3@gmail.com

TITLE
Guinea Business Success Guide - Basic Practical Information and Contacts
Guinea-Bissau Business Success Guide - Basic Practical Information and Contacts
Guyana Business Success Guide - Basic Practical Information and Contacts
Haiti Business Success Guide - Basic Practical Information and Contacts
Honduras Business Success Guide - Basic Practical Information and Contacts
Hungary Business Success Guide - Basic Practical Information and Contacts
Iceland Business Success Guide - Basic Practical Information and Contacts
India Business Success Guide - Basic Practical Information and Contacts
Indonesia Business Success Guide - Basic Practical Information and Contacts
Iran Business Success Guide - Basic Practical Information and Contacts
Iraq Business Success Guide - Basic Practical Information and Contacts
Ireland Business Success Guide - Basic Practical Information and Contacts
Israel Business Success Guide - Basic Practical Information and Contacts
Italy Business Success Guide - Basic Practical Information and Contacts
Jamaica Business Success Guide - Basic Practical Information and Contacts
Japan Business Success Guide - Basic Practical Information and Contacts
Jersey Business Success Guide - Basic Practical Information and Contacts
Jordan Business Success Guide - Basic Practical Information and Contacts
Kazakhstan Business Success Guide - Basic Practical Information and Contacts
Kenya Business Success Guide - Basic Practical Information and Contacts
Kiribati Business Success Guide - Basic Practical Information and Contacts
Korea, North Business Success Guide - Basic Practical Information and Contacts
Korea, South Business Success Guide - Basic Practical Information and Contacts
Kosovo Business Success Guide - Basic Practical Information and Contacts
Kurdistan Business Success Guide - Basic Practical Information and Contacts
Kuwait Business Success Guide - Basic Practical Information and Contacts
Kyrgyzstan Business Success Guide - Basic Practical Information and Contacts
Laos Business Success Guide - Basic Practical Information and Contacts
Latvia Business Success Guide - Basic Practical Information and Contacts
Lebanon Business Success Guide - Basic Practical Information and Contacts
Lesotho Business Success Guide - Basic Practical Information and Contacts
Liberia Business Success Guide - Basic Practical Information and Contacts
Libya Business Success Guide - Basic Practical Information and Contacts
Liechtenstein Business Success Guide - Basic Practical Information and Contacts
Lithuania Business Success Guide - Basic Practical Information and Contacts
Luxembourg Business Success Guide - Basic Practical Information and Contacts
Macao Business Success Guide - Basic Practical Information and Contacts
Macedonia Business Success Guide - Basic Practical Information and Contacts
Madagascar Business Success Guide - Basic Practical Information and Contacts
Madeira Business Success Guide - Basic Practical Information and Contacts
Malawi Business Success Guide - Basic Practical Information and Contacts
Malaysia Business Success Guide - Basic Practical Information and Contacts
Maldives Business Success Guide - Basic Practical Information and Contacts
Mali Business Success Guide - Basic Practical Information and Contacts
Malta Business Success Guide - Basic Practical Information and Contacts
Man Business Success Guide - Basic Practical Information and Contacts

For additional analytical, business and investment opportunities information,
Please contact Global Investment & Business Center, USA
at (202) 546-2103. Fax: (202) 546-3275. E-mail: ibpusa3@gmail.com

TITLE
Marshall Islands Business Success Guide - Basic Practical Information and Contacts
Mauritania Business Success Guide - Basic Practical Information and Contacts
Mauritius Business Success Guide - Basic Practical Information and Contacts
Mayotte Business Success Guide - Basic Practical Information and Contacts
Mexico Business Success Guide - Basic Practical Information and Contacts
Micronesia Business Success Guide - Basic Practical Information and Contacts
Moldova Business Success Guide - Basic Practical Information and Contacts
Monaco Business Success Guide - Basic Practical Information and Contacts
Mongolia Business Success Guide - Basic Practical Information and Contacts
Montserrat Business Success Guide - Basic Practical Information and Contacts
Montenegro Business Success Guide - Basic Practical Information and Contacts
Morocco Business Success Guide - Basic Practical Information and Contacts
Mozambique Business Success Guide - Basic Practical Information and Contacts
Myanmar Business Success Guide - Basic Practical Information and Contacts
Nagorno-Karabakh Republic Business Success Guide - Basic Practical Information and Contacts
Namibia Business Success Guide - Basic Practical Information and Contacts
Nauru Business Success Guide - Basic Practical Information and Contacts
Nepal Business Success Guide - Basic Practical Information and Contacts
Netherlands Business Success Guide - Basic Practical Information and Contacts
New Caledonia Business Success Guide - Basic Practical Information and Contacts
New Zealand Business Success Guide - Basic Practical Information and Contacts
Nicaragua Business Success Guide - Basic Practical Information and Contacts
Niger Business Success Guide - Basic Practical Information and Contacts
Nigeria Business Success Guide - Basic Practical Information and Contacts
Niue Business Success Guide - Basic Practical Information and Contacts
Northern Cyprus (Turkish Republic of Northern Cyprus) Business Success Guide - Basic Practical Information and Contacts
Northern Mariana Islands Business Success Guide - Basic Practical Information and Contacts
Norway Business Success Guide - Basic Practical Information and Contacts
Oman Business Success Guide - Basic Practical Information and Contacts
Pakistan Business Success Guide - Basic Practical Information and Contacts
Palau Business Success Guide - Basic Practical Information and Contacts
Palestine (West Bank & Gaza) Business Success Guide - Basic Practical Information and Contacts
Panama Business Success Guide - Basic Practical Information and Contacts
Papua New Guinea Business Success Guide - Basic Practical Information and Contacts
Paraguay Business Success Guide - Basic Practical Information and Contacts
Peru Business Success Guide - Basic Practical Information and Contacts
Philippines Business Success Guide - Basic Practical Information and Contacts
Pitcairn Islands Business Success Guide - Basic Practical Information and Contacts
Poland Business Success Guide - Basic Practical Information and Contacts
Polynesia French Business Success Guide - Basic Practical Information and Contacts
Portugal Business Success Guide - Basic Practical Information and Contacts
Qatar Business Success Guide - Basic Practical Information and Contacts
Romania Business Success Guide - Basic Practical Information and Contacts
Russia Business Success Guide - Basic Practical Information and Contacts
Rwanda Business Success Guide - Basic Practical Information and Contacts

For additional analytical, business and investment opportunities information,
Please contact Global Investment & Business Center, USA
at (202) 546-2103. Fax: (202) 546-3275. E-mail: ibpusa3@gmail.com

TITLE
Sahrawi Arab Democratic Republic Volume 1 Strategic Information and Developments
Saint Kitts and Nevis Business Success Guide - Basic Practical Information and Contacts
Saint Lucia Business Success Guide - Basic Practical Information and Contacts
Saint Vincent and The Grenadines Business Success Guide - Basic Practical Information and Contacts
Samoa (American) A Business Success Guide - Basic Practical Information and Contacts
Samoa (Western) Business Success Guide - Basic Practical Information and Contacts
San Marino Business Success Guide - Basic Practical Information and Contacts
Sao Tome and Principe Business Success Guide - Basic Practical Information and Contacts
Saudi Arabia Business Success Guide - Basic Practical Information and Contacts
Scotland Business Success Guide - Basic Practical Information and Contacts
Senegal Business Success Guide - Basic Practical Information and Contacts
Serbia Business Success Guide - Basic Practical Information and Contacts
Seychelles Business Success Guide - Basic Practical Information and Contacts
Sierra Leone Business Success Guide - Basic Practical Information and Contacts
Singapore Business Success Guide - Basic Practical Information and Contacts
Slovakia Business Success Guide - Basic Practical Information and Contacts
Slovenia Business Success Guide - Basic Practical Information and Contacts
Solomon Islands Business Success Guide - Basic Practical Information and Contacts
Somalia Business Success Guide - Basic Practical Information and Contacts
South Africa Business Success Guide - Basic Practical Information and Contacts
Spain Business Success Guide - Basic Practical Information and Contacts
Sri Lanka Business Success Guide - Basic Practical Information and Contacts
St. Helena Business Success Guide - Basic Practical Information and Contacts
St. Pierre & Miquelon Business Success Guide - Basic Practical Information and Contacts
Sudan (Republic of the Sudan) Business Success Guide - Basic Practical Information and Contacts
Sudan South Business Success Guide - Basic Practical Information and Contacts
Suriname Business Success Guide - Basic Practical Information and Contacts
Swaziland Business Success Guide - Basic Practical Information and Contacts
Sweden Business Success Guide - Basic Practical Information and Contacts
Switzerland Business Success Guide - Basic Practical Information and Contacts
Syria Business Success Guide - Basic Practical Information and Contacts
Taiwan Business Success Guide - Basic Practical Information and Contacts
Tajikistan Business Success Guide - Basic Practical Information and Contacts
Tanzania Business Success Guide - Basic Practical Information and Contacts
Thailand Business Success Guide - Basic Practical Information and Contacts
Timor Leste (Democratic Republic of Timor-Leste) Business Success Guide - Basic Practical Information and Contacts
Togo Business Success Guide - Basic Practical Information and Contacts
Tonga Business Success Guide - Basic Practical Information and Contacts
Trinidad and Tobago Business Success Guide - Basic Practical Information and Contacts
Tunisia Business Success Guide - Basic Practical Information and Contacts
Turkey Business Success Guide - Basic Practical Information and Contacts
Turkmenistan Business Success Guide - Basic Practical Information and Contacts
Turks & Caicos Business Success Guide - Basic Practical Information and Contacts
Tuvalu Business Success Guide - Basic Practical Information and Contacts
Uganda Business Success Guide - Basic Practical Information and Contacts

For additional analytical, business and investment opportunities information,
Please contact Global Investment & Business Center, USA
at (202) 546-2103. Fax: (202) 546-3275. E-mail: ibpusa3@gmail.com

TITLE
Ukraine Business Success Guide - Basic Practical Information and Contacts
United Arab Emirates Business Success Guide - Basic Practical Information and Contacts
United Kingdom Business Success Guide - Basic Practical Information and Contacts
United States Business Success Guide - Basic Practical Information and Contacts
Uruguay Business Success Guide - Basic Practical Information and Contacts
Uzbekistan Business Success Guide - Basic Practical Information and Contacts
Vanuatu Business Success Guide - Basic Practical Information and Contacts
Vatican City (Holy See) Business Success Guide - Basic Practical Information and Contacts
Venezuela Business Success Guide - Basic Practical Information and Contacts
Vietnam Business Success Guide - Basic Practical Information and Contacts
Virgin Islands, British Business Success Guide - Basic Practical Information and Contacts
Wake Atoll Business Success Guide - Basic Practical Information and Contacts
Wallis & Futuna Business Success Guide - Basic Practical Information and Contacts
Western Sahara Business Success Guide - Basic Practical Information and Contacts
Yemen Business Success Guide - Basic Practical Information and Contacts
Zambia Business Success Guide - Basic Practical Information and Contacts
Zimbabwe Business Success Guide - Basic Practical Information and Contacts

For additional analytical, business and investment opportunities information,
Please contact Global Investment & Business Center, USA
at (202) 546-2103. Fax: (202) 546-3275. E-mail: ibpusa3@gmail.com